Outcasts and Angels

Outcasts and Angels

The New Anthology of Deaf Characters in Literature

Edited by Edna Edith Sayers

Gallaudet University Press
Washington, DC

Gallaudet University Press
Washington, DC 20002
http://gupress.gallaudet.edu

Library of Congress Cataloging-in-Publication Data

Outcasts and angels : the new anthology of deaf characters in literature / edited by Edna Edith Sayers.

p. cm.

ISBN 978-1-56368-539-2 (hard cover: alk. paper) – ISBN 978-1-56368-540-8 (e-book)

1. Deaf in literature. 2. People with disabilities in literature. 3. Characters and characteristics in literature. I. Sayers, Edna Edith.

PN56.5.H35O98 2012

808.8'035272–dc23

2012022979

Cover photograph of the Magnolia Cemetery, Mobile, Alabama, from the George F. Landegger Collection of Alabama Photographs in Carol M. Highsmith's America, Library of Congress, Prints and Photographs Division. Photograph by Carol M. Highsmith.

Cover design by Dennis Anderson

For Will Sayers

Contents

Introduction

In the 1970s, when the academic discipline of women's studies was in its infancy, the investigation of female literary characters in novels and stories by authors of either sex was already giving way to the study of work by women writers. In Deaf studies, the focus on deaf characters in literature began to give way to the study of deaf writers in the 1990s. Disciplines devoted to the study of historically silenced groups evolve, and that is as it should be. Yet the study of literary characters still has a great deal to tell us about how such groups were seen within any given society because writers both reflect public views and contribute to shaping them. In fact, most Americans today will encounter a deaf person only in fiction, film, or television drama, not in real life.

An extremely well-read hearing friend told me he knew of only one deaf character in literature: Joel Mayes in Eudora Welty's "First Love," a 1942 story about a deaf boy who witnesses Aaron Burr making history. It is not a far-fetched guess that many teachers of literature could not even come up with that one title. Deaf characters are in fact rare, and for two very good reasons. One is that deaf people are rare in real life. In the United States, for example, about one-tenth of one percent of the population is born deaf, not much more than a quarter million souls. Even when one adds to that statistic people who became deaf as children, the numbers are small, and considering how signing deaf people tend to congregate (for example, in Rochester, New York, or Silver Spring, Maryland), even these small numbers are not to be encountered in every community today. The second reason has to do with how literature works—stories are told in dialogue between characters. With the rare exception of stories that have only one human character and must be told through the character's thoughts, a story's plot develops when characters interact with one another in language. This means that characters have to share a language, a seemingly obvious point that seems not to have occurred to some writers who have embarked on stories with a deaf character.[1] However, Wilkie Collins, creator of the deaf heroine Madonna in his novel *Hide and Seek*, understood the problem in 1854:

> I do not know that any attempt has yet been made in English fiction to draw the character of a "Deaf-Mute," simply and exactly after nature—or, in other words, to exhibit the peculiar effects produced by the loss of the senses of hearing and speaking. . . . The famous Fenella in [Walter] Scott's "Peveril of the Peak," only *assumes* deafness and dumbness; and the whole family of dumb

1

people on the stage have the remarkable faculty—so far as my
experience goes—of always being able to hear what is said to
them.[2]

We still see deaf characters with this "remarkable faculty" more than 150 years later.

Given the technical challenges of creating a deaf character who really cannot hear, why bother? Writing in 1890 of Collins's Madonna, the literary critic and folklorist Andrew Lang claimed that if this character had been hearing, "the story need not have been altered in the least" because it is her status as an orphan and as the unknown and unknowing sister of the man she loves that drives the plot. Lang faults Collins for failing to make "her deafness and dumbness" lead to anything and supposes that it merely gave Collins "a chance of studying the life of a beautiful mute."[3] Lang did not know that Madonna presented a challenge for Collins or that his research of the topic included reading *Lost Senses* by the Bible scholar John Kitto, in which Kitto details his life as a deaf man. But Lang's observation raises a question we should keep in mind as we read and study the stories in this volume: Is a deaf character exploited only to create exoticism, freakishness, or sexual titillation? Or is it integral to the story that a character be deaf? I have not reprinted any stories here that I regard as literary "freak shows," to use the phrasing of blind writer Georgina Kleege,[4] but each reader ultimately is her own judge of that.

To be clear, I agree with Lang that the plot of *Hide and Seek* would not have to be changed at all if Madonna had been hearing. To me, however, that is a good thing. If the interest of a story resides wholly in the fact that the main character is deaf (or Jewish, or gay, or what have you), then that character will fail to interest readers on any other level, and the story is less likely to be great literature that examines the human condition. Paul Robinson illustrates this point with the example of peg-legged Captain Ahab in *Moby Dick*: If Ahab's obsession with the white whale were caused by Moby Dick having killed his son instead of having taken his leg, the plot would not be changed at all. This demonstrates that *Moby Dick* is about "revenge, megalomania, and the quest for transcendence," not about life as an amputee.[5] Each work must be approached on its own terms, however. One would be wrong to say, for example, that T. C. Boyle's *Talk Talk* (2006), whose deaf heroine could well be hearing without materially altering that story, is *for this reason* a better book than Frances Itani's *Deafening* (2003), whose deaf heroine is so obsessed with being deaf that she seems to spend even her entire honeymoon discussing it with her new husband and who would, in Donna McDonald's words, "cease to exist as a character" if she were not deaf.[6] Readers of Boyle, both deaf and hearing, are apt to complain that his heroine does not act deaf enough (though hearing readers mean quite different things by this phrase than deaf readers) even though Boyle has done a tremendous job showing his heroine's typically troubled relationship with her hearing mother, her resistance to undergoing cochlear implant surgery, her marginalization among her boyfriend's hearing friends, and even her pride in her lip-reading skills, which is actually quite common among real deaf people today. Readers of Itani, in contrast, are likely to claim, as McDonald has, that *her* heroine is nothing *but* deaf. Everyone's a critic.

Writers who choose to take on the challenges of a deaf character can expect to find that critics persistently fail either to notice that a deaf character is deaf—or to notice him at all. Until the mid-1990s, the annual *MLA Bibliography of Periodical Literature*, a database that is a vital tool for literary studies, had no capacity to locate criticism having to do with deaf characters because the word *deaf* was not indexed. An egregious but not atypical example of critics' inability to process the fact that a character is deaf can be seen in academic criticism of Herman Melville's *The Confidence Man*. This Menippean satire presents a series of con men and their victims, beginning with a character who may be a con man, a mouthpiece for Melville, or something else but who is certainly deaf. Essay after essay collected in the Norton critical edition of *The Confidence Man* begins its examination of the novel with the second character to appear in the story, completely ignoring the first. Those critical essays that do discuss "the mute" generally fail to realize that he is in fact a deaf-mute or to account for how this simple fact fits or does not fit their interpretations. When critics do notice that a character is deaf, there is a strong tendency to assign this character some symbolic value. For example, Christopher Krentz points out that in Herman Melville's 1839 short story, "Fragment from a Writing Desk, #2," when the dream woman turns out to be "Dumb and Deaf!" this is understood "symbolically to comment on the loss of romance in the modern world."[7] According to the Norton critical edition, the deaf figure in *The Confidence Man* was formerly understood to be an avatar of Christ but is now seen as an avatar of Satan, yet there is no explanation, or even entertainment of the question, of why Melville would have created any "avatar" as a deaf man.

Deaf readers, in contrast, have been writing about deaf characters since at least 1893, when a certain IVJ compiled a short list of books for a Deaf community newspaper, *The Silent Worker*, that included Dickens's "Doctor Marigold," Charlotte Elizabeth's "Jack the Dumb Boy" (an excerpt from another version of this story appears in this volume), and Wilkie Collins's *Hide and Seek*. More than sixty years later, that same newspaper published a series of articles by Oscar Guire that not only listed but discussed works such as Turgenev's "Mumu" and "The Watch," Hugo's *Notre Dame de Paris*, Maupassant's "The Deaf Mute," and others. Articles by Robert F. Panara in *The Deaf American* (the successor to *The Silent Worker*) in 1972 and 1974 cover much the same ground but with greater literary insight, since they were written when he was teaching a course on deaf studies in literature at the National Technical Institute for the Deaf at the Rochester Institute of Technology (RIT). Two librarians at the Wallace Library at RIT also published annotated bibliographies: Gladys M. Taylor's 1974 article in *The Deaf American* provided the bibliography she had developed for or with Panara, and in 1992, after Panara's retirement, Jonathan Miller's article in *Library Trends* expanded that bibliography to 136 items classified according to genre (novels and short stories) and the age groups for which they were intended. Contemporaneously with Panara and Taylor, Eugene Bergman and Trenton Batson of the Gallaudet University English Department compiled *The Deaf Experience* in 1973, ultimately revised in 1985 as *Angels and Outcasts*, for their course The Deaf in Literature, which was first offered in 1972.

Angels and Outcasts is a study of characters in the literature of the nineteenth and twentieth centuries with an appended section of mostly autobiographical narratives written by deaf people. This last section was a harbinger of the present interest in the work of deaf writers, which has grown exponentially since Batson and Bergman were first active in "Deaf Lit" more than forty years ago. This section aside, the book comprises nine stories, six by canonical authors Alfred de Musset, Charles Dickens, Ivan Turgenev, Guy de Maupassant, Eudora Welty, and Bernard Malamud. The other authors are Margaret Montague, a blind and late-deafened writer for the *Atlantic Monthly*; Arnold Payne, a Church of England minister to the deaf whose father had been the deaf headmaster of a school for the deaf in Swansea, Wales, and who wrote solely to further the use of sign language; and Walter Toman, a Viennese psychologist whose piece is an allegory of some sort (as is Malamud's, actually). Batson and Bergman introduce each piece with commentary concerning the story's treatment of the deaf experience, including sign language and the dignity accorded its deaf characters, a needful endeavor in the 1980s that surely brought many readers to a better understanding of what it means to be deaf in the real world. From a twenty-first-century perspective, the anthology seems to have spread itself rather thin—a small number of long stories doing duty for two centuries—and to be fighting battles many readers will consider already won.

Brian Grant's 1987 *The Quiet Ear: Deafness in Literature* is a book from a much different perspective: unlike IVJ, Guire, Panara, and Bergman, Grant became deaf in later life and, not surprisingly, takes "deafness" to be a misfortune; for example, he writes that Harriet Martineau was "plagued by deafness."[8] His anthology is therefore heavy on the "floundering" and "bewildered" deaf figure, and his excerpts are so sharply edited as to be deprived of all meaningful context. Grant's selections, however, are exhaustive and the book can be used by interested readers to locate deaf characters in works that would bear reading in their entirety.

Each of these articles and bibliographies covers a mixed bag of characters who are hard of hearing, deafened in old age, mute from trauma, pretending to be deaf, metaphoric abstractions, and so on, as well as characters who are genuinely deaf. For the purposes of this book, I have defined *deaf* as meaning, in the words of

George Veditz, "people of the eye," characters who can engage in communication only in, or with the input of, the visual mode because speech and hearing have been inaccessible, if not from birth, for long enough that the character has settled into a visual mode of life. This definition does not limit us to deaf people who sign but includes every ordinary (sighted) deaf person from expensively educated lip readers to illiterate home-signers. It definitely excludes deafened elders, such as the title characters of Guy de Maupassant's "Old Amable" or Thomas Hardy's "Old Mrs. Chundle," as well as deafened younger adults such as Victor Hugo's Quasimodo, the "hunchback of Notre Dame," or William Faulkner's Linda Snopes, who lost her hearing fighting fascists in the Spanish Civil War before returning to her hometown in the 1959 novel *The Mansion*. The literature of late-deafened characters is exceedingly rich and would well repay study, but this is not my aim in the present book. My definition of *deaf* also excludes characters pretending to be deaf, thus eliminating the delicious 1922 story by Richmal Crompton, "Christmas Present," as well as characters like the "duke" in *Huckleberry Finn* and Holden Caulfield in *Catcher in the Rye* (who actually only thinks about pretending to be deaf). Also not considered here are literary characters who are deaf and blind. This exclusion is partly a matter of focus but mostly, I'm afraid, is due to my lack of experience with the lives of deaf-blind people, which means that I cannot pass judgment on the authenticity of fictive characterizations. John Lee Clark is preparing an anthology of writing by deaf-blind authors that will help eliminate the present gap in available literature.

A word now about my usage of the spellings *deaf* and *Deaf* here and in the closing essay, which will have drawn some readers' attention already. I have chosen to leave the word uncapitalized except when referring to Deaf studies, Deaf history, or, occasionally, Deaf people today, because the vast majority of authors whose work is collected in this volume have treated the deaf character as though she or he were an isolated individual, which, of course, most deaf people through history have been and in many parts of the world still are. In the few cases where I discuss a signing Deaf community, for example, in the stories of Joanne Greenberg and Carole Glickfeld, it would have been unhistorical to capitalize *deaf* in discussing such stories because they are set before the 1980s when capitalization was first used to denote a deaf person who was a member of such a community. In fact, even Deaf author Douglas Bullard does not capitalize the word in his 1986 novel *Islay*. In the end, the d/D distinction is just not operative, let alone useful, in this literature.

As for genre, I have excluded narratives that are primarily nonrealistic, so works like Rubén Darío's "The Deaf Satyr" or Irvine Welsh's "The House of John Deaf" were not considered. The vast science-fiction and fantasy literature with mostly notional deaf characters is therefore excluded, the one exception being Karawynn Long's 1995 "Of Silence and Slow Time," whose dystopian, futurist vision seems realistic and plausible as I write in 2012, seventeen years later. Literature written for children and adolescents was not considered, nor was crime fiction because its formulaic nature produces mostly formulaic deaf characters, although I mention a few deaf detectives, victims, and criminals where apposite in the essay. (Oddly, one of the included stories, Florence Mayberry's "The Secret," was originally published in *Ellery Queen's Mystery Magazine*, but I cannot imagine the rationale for that.) One genre that ended up very widely represented here, which I did not notice until the collection was complete, is the story in the gothic mode, both classic Southern gothic and what we might call rural gothic set in small towns or farmland in the Midwest. (Among the American stories, those set in the Ozarks, Appalachia, the Deep South, and dusty midwestern hamlets vastly outnumber those set in the urban areas of both coasts, where deaf people are far more numerous.) Whether this is a statement about the kinds of writers who undertake deaf characters would be a good question for further study. The fact that women writers, including Richard Dehan (Clothilde Inez Mary Graves), Isak Dinesen (Baroness Karen von Blixen-Finecke), and Morris Smith, constitute such a large proportion of those who create deaf characters is another issue ripe for study.

As for the word *fiction*, I use the term loosely to mean anything that is shaped as a story, no matter whether the author claims it is true or readers understand it to be. For example, Charlotte Elizabeth Browne Phelan Tonna, who signed her work "Charlotte Elizabeth," was deafened at age ten and spent much of her adult life attempting to educate deaf Irish children by means of the finger alphabet. Although her autobiography, from which our excerpt here is taken, is presented as a true story based on her diaries, she herself admits that "there is no such thing as an honest private journal" and that "to give a fair transcript of idle unprofitable thoughts and corrupt imaginings is out of the question."[9] She has therefore shaped her story to valorize her version of the Protestant ethic—by haranguing readers on the horrors of the Roman Catholic church (the "Popish delusion") and excluding anything having to do with her first husband, her brother's wife, and sex in general, which makes her deaf protégé John "Jack" Britt an oddly asexual, but properly Protestant, young man. Her autobiography is, in a word, fictionalized.

The stories collected here do not tell of deaf heroes or victims. The simple truth is that in most narratives until recent decades, few authors could imagine deaf characters at all and so deployed them as little more than furniture in the setting in which the action is played out. The relationships that the main, hearing, characters have with them frequently lack even the depth that can be found in stories about a boy and his dog. This is not to say that a story or novel with this approach is poorly written, but rather that the author has used her deaf character simply as part of the stage setting for the *agon*, or struggle, in which the (hearing) protagonist must engage, and it is our privilege and pleasure as twenty-first-century readers to rummage around these deaf supernumeraries to see what the story has to tell us about what it means to be deaf in these narrative worlds.

Morris Smith's short-story sequence *Spencer Road* provides an excellent example of a deaf character deployed this way. The presumably semi-autobiographical stories in this novel-like sequence are narrated mostly from the point of view of a little girl named Maggie. They concern her rural Southern family during the Great Depression, and they assemble themselves into a bildungsroman as little Maggie grows into adulthood and learns about poverty, alcoholism, race, and her family's role in the area's history of slavery. One of Maggie's learning experiences concerns her deaf cousin, Gwen, who is cosseted by her mother, protected from fighting her own battles in childhood games. At the beginning of the story "Stone Deaf," Maggie is jealous of Gwen's new sweater and cooks up some devilment for her cousin that turns out to be more than she intended, but by the end of a later story, "Fardels" (not included here), Maggie is mature enough to feel shame for her behavior toward Gwen. Because Smith's focus is on Maggie, readers of this volume may, on first glance, see Gwen's character as little more than a stereotype. It would be unfair, and of course unproductive, to blame an author for not doing what she never intended to do, that is, develop a fully rounded deaf character, but when we read Smith's stories with a curious mind, we see how remarkably much we have learned about Gwen and her mother.

Florence V. Mayberry's "The Secret," which presents a somewhat different example, may appear on first reading to merely caricaturize the deaf sisters Mable and Roxy, who are certainly oddballs by any standards. Mayberry, like Smith, has a little girl narrate the story, but Sary, unlike Maggie, remains naive and is never able to add up the details she narrates. Instead, Mayberry constructs the story so that readers will know, though Sary does not, why Roxy tries to kill Mable and where the baby at the end of the story has come from. The same can be said for the deaf sisters' characters: the narrator is simply too young to understand what motivates Mable and Roxy or to do more than sketch their behavior, but readers are able to put the details together and come up with a more fully fleshed pair of deaf women and the repressive society in which they live.

It should be clear to readers who have stayed with me so far that *Outcasts and Angels* departs in one significant way from *Angels and Outcasts*, where editorial comment, as Donna McDonald rightly points out, is often put to work "to advance the cause of American Sign Language," and from many other works of Deaf studies in literature today, such as those of Sharon Pajka-West and Pamela Conley, who are intent on uncovering "inappropriate perception[s] of d/Deaf people" in literary works, to use Conley's words.[10] This book, in contrast, is not intended to evaluate authors' support for the present-day interests of deaf people or otherwise question their intentions. I take the position, associated today with the critic Harold Bloom, that imaginative literature is independent of social movements and that literary criticism ought never to be reduced to a question of approval of a work's perceived social statements. Literature has no obligation, in the words of

Leslie Fiedler, "to persuade and reform us by showing us the error of our ways and moving us to right action," and when it does take on that purpose, its aesthetic value often suffers—certainly it cannot aspire to the timelessness of most of the pieces collected in this volume. In any case, until very recent decades, our authors and their readers did not know such terms as *culturally deaf, medical model,* or even *ASL* nor the concepts they denote, and their stories have very different things to say to readers. (But would you be surprised to learn that the earliest literary mention of a deaf person depicted as "not one hampered by an infirmity, but as a very original sort of little foreigner" comes from an 1868 story, "Jerry and Clarinda"?) If the story in question has any aesthetic value, it will instead tell us, again in Fiedler's words, "disquieting truths about our response to stigmatized segments of the population" such as the deaf.[11]

The stories in this volume are presented in chronological order, with only their date of first publication and their country of origin, because they are expected to stand (or fall) on their own merit. Readers will decide for themselves what to make of the stories and of the authenticity of the deaf characters, both those who sign and those who do not, and, I hope, will then go on to read the closing essay where my own responses are given. This is not to say that I am neutral on issues of Deaf values, signed languages, civil rights, and the education of the hearing. I regard myself as Deaf with a capital D, and I lived and worked in a signing Deaf community for nearly my entire career. As an adult learner of American Sign Language, I am a real pest of an evangelist for signing, most vehemently with regard to deaf children. In addition to this personal history is my professional history as a teacher of "Deaf lit" to undergraduate and continuing education students who are themselves Deaf signers or otherwise connected with the signing Deaf community. In that professional role, however, I learned a puzzling truth: not all deaf people, even those born deaf, sign or want to sign. My conscious agenda for this volume is, partly for this reason, limited to the promotion of good narrative literature and intriguing deaf fictional characters.

Although my aims as editor of this volume do not include selecting literature whose message fits my own Deaf political ideology, I nevertheless believe that literature can and does influence social understandings of deaf people. If we substitute "deaf people" for "disability" in the following statement by Michael Bérubé, as I have done, it perfectly articulates the rationale for my belief that literary depictions of deaf characters can be such a powerful force:

> The cultural representation of [deaf people] affects our understanding of what it means to be human; in more practical terms, it affects public policy, the allocation of social resources, and the

meaning of "civil rights." . . . Every representation of [a deaf person] has the potential to shape the way [being deaf] is understood in the general culture, and some of those representations can in fact do extraordinarily powerful—or harmful—cultural and political work.[12]

The aim of every anthologist is to produce a collection that is more than the sum of its parts. My hope is that the fortuitous juxtapositions and the sheer accumulated weight of inscrutable deaf character after inscrutable deaf character, each with her or his particular emotive style, from bafflement through longing, frustration, and anger to well-earned resentment, will enlighten—or at least destabilize—readers.

Acknowledgments

I thank the deaf collection librarians Diana Moore (formerly Gates) at Gallaudet University and Joan Naturale at the Wallace Library of the Rochester Institute of Technology for their assistance. Without our deaf library collections, a book such as this would scarcely be possible. Thanks to Ulf Hedberg, Gallaudet archivist, for cheerfully finding answers to my questions about possible deaf presence in the lives and times of several of the authors anthologized here. Many thanks, as well, to Gene Bergman and Trent Batson for their kind encouragement. I am grateful to John Lee Clark and Frank Bechter for their willingness over several years to discuss some of these stories with me. Both challenged me to rethink what I thought I knew. Authors who kindly entertained my questions about the genesis of their stories are Julian Barnes, Marlon Barton, Joanne Greenberg, and Karawynn Long, while Michèle LaRue went out of her way to seek answers to my questions about her late husband, Warren Kliewer, and his hometown. I also thank authors and publishers who granted permission to reprint stories, and those who helped me locate and contact the copyright holders. For reading drafts of this anthology, many thanks go to Karen Christie, Christopher Krentz, Donna McDonald, and William Sayers, all of whom made invaluable suggestions for improvement.

Notes

1. See Bragg, "Telling Silence," for discussion.
2. Collins, *Hide and Seek*, note to chapter 8.
3. Lang, "Mr. Wilkie Collins's Novels," 23.
4. Kleege, Course description for "Autobiography: Disability Memoir," 2007; quoted in McDonald, "Not Silent, Invisible," 468.
5. Robinson, "Responses to Leslie Fiedler, II," n.p.

6. McDonald, "Hearsay," 22.
7. Krentz, *Writing Deafness*, 125.
8. Grant, *The Quiet Ear*, 27.
9. Charlotte Elizabeth, "Letter Two" in *Personal Recollections*.
10. McDonald, "Hearsay," 9; Pamela Conley, "An Analysis of Two Stories with Deaf Characters," 212.
11. Fiedler, "Pity and Fear," n.p.
12. Bérubé, "On the Cultural Representation of People with Disabilities," B4–B5.

From *The Life and Adventures of Mr. Duncan Campbell*

Daniel Defoe
England, 1729

[Duncan Campbell] had, it seems, run himself into debt, and one day as he was at a coffee-house, the sign of the Three Crowns, in Great Queen-street, in rushed four bailiffs upon him, who being directed by the creditor's wife, had watched him into that house, and told him they had a warrant against him, and upon his not answering, they being unacquainted with his being deaf and dumb, offered to seize his sword. He startled at their offering of violence, and taking them for ruffians, which he had often met with, repelled the assaulters, and drawing his sword, as one man, more bold than the rest, closed in with him, he shortened his blade, and in the fall pinned the fellow through the shoulder, and himself through the leg, to the floor. After that he stood at bay with all the four officers, when the most mischievous assailant of them all, the creditor's wife, ventured to step into the fray, and very barbarously took hold of that nameless part of the man, for which, as she was a married woman, nature methinks should have taught her to have a greater tenderness, and almost squeezed and crushed those vitals to death. But at last he got free from them all, and was going away as fast as he could, not knowing what consequences might ensue. But the woman who aimed herself at committing murder, in the most savage and inhuman manner, ran out after him, crying out murder! murder! as loud as she could, and alarmed the whole street. The bailiffs following the woman, and being bloody from head to foot, by means of the wound he received, gave credit to the outcry. The late earl Rivers' footmen happening to be at the door, ran immediately to stop the supposed murderer, and they indeed did take him at last, but perceived their mistake, and discovered that instead of being assistants in taking a man whom they thought to be a murderer endeavouring to make his escape from the hands of justice, they had only been tricked in by that false cry to be adjutants to a bailiff in retaking a gentleman, who, by so gallant a defence, had rescued himself from the dangers of a prison; and when they had discovered this their mistake they were mighty sorry for what they had done. The most active and busy among the earl's footmen was a Dutchman, and the earl happening to be in a room next the street, and hearing the outcry of murder, stepped to the window, and seeing his own servants in the midst of the bustle, examined the Dutchman how the matter was, and, being told it, he chid the man for being concerned in stopping a gentleman that was getting free from such troublesome companions. But the Dutchmen excused himself, like a Dutchman, by making a very merry blunder for a reply; *Sacramente*, said he, to his lord, if I had thought they were bailiffs I would have fought for the poor dumb gentleman, but then why had he not told me they were bailiffs, my lord?

In short, Duncan Campbell was carried off as their prisoner; but the bailiff that was wounded was led back to the coffee-house, where he pretended the wound was mortal, and that he despaired of living an hour. The proverb however was of the fellow's side, and he recovered sooner than other people expected he could. As soon as all danger was over, an action for damages and smart money, as their term is, was brought against Mr. Campbell; the damages were exaggerated and the demand was so extravagant, that Duncan Campbell was neither able, just at that time, nor willing, had he been able, to pay so much, as he thought, in his own wrong, and having no bail, and being ashamed to make his case known to his better sort of friends, who were both able and willing to help him at a dead lift, he was hurried away to gaol by the bailiffs, who showed such a malignant and insolent pleasure, as commonly attends powerful revenge, when they put him into the Marshalsea. There he lay in confinement six weeks, till at last four or five of his chief friends came by mere chance to hear of it; immediately they consulted about his deliverance, and unanimously resolved to contribute for his enlargement, and they accordingly went cross the water together, and procured it out of hand.

Two of his benefactors were officers, and were just then going over to Flanders. Duncan Campbell, to whom they communicated their design, was resolved to try his fortune in a military way, out of a roving kind of humour, raised in him partly by his having taken a sort of aversion to his own profession in town, and partly by his finding that he could not live, without following a profession, as he had done, any longer. He over a bottle frankly imparted his mind to them at large; he signified to them that he hoped, since they had lately done him so great a favour in freeing him from one captivity, they would not think him too urgent if he pressed for one favour further, upon natures so generous as theirs, by whom he took as great a pleasure in being obliged, as he could receive in being capable of obliging others. He wrote to them that the favour he meant was to redeem him from another captivity, almost as irksome to him as that out of which they had lately ransomed him. This captivity, continued he, is being either forced to follow my old profession, which I have taken an entire disgust to, for a maintenance, or being forced to live in a narrower way than suits with my genius, and the better taste I have of higher life. Such a state, gentlemen, you know, is more unpalatable than half-pay; it is like either being forced to go upon the forlorn hope, or else like a man's being an entirely cashiered and broken officer, that had no younger brother's fortune, and no other support but his commission. Thus though you have set my body at liberty, my soul is still under an imprisonment, and will be till I leave England, and can find means of visiting Flanders, which I can do no otherwise than by the advantage of having you for my convoy. I have a mighty longing to experience some part of a military life, and I fancy, if you will grant me your interest, and introduce me to the valiant young lord Lorne, and be spokesmen for a dumb man, I shall meet with a favourable reception; and as for you, gentlemen, after having named that great patron and pattern of courage and conduct in the field, I can't doubt but the very name I bear, if you had not known me, would have made you taken me for a person of a military genius, and that I should do nothing but what would become a British soldier, and a gentleman; nothing, in fine, that should make you repent the recommendation.

These generous and gallant friends of his, it seems, complied with his request, and promised they would make application for him to the lord Lorne, and Duncan Campbell had nothing to do but to get his bag and baggage ready, and provide himself with a pass. His baggage was not very long a getting together, and he had it in tolerable good order, and as for his pass, a brother of the lord Forbes was so kind as to procure him one upon the first application Duncan made to him.

Accordingly, in a few days afterwards, they went on board, and having a speedy and an easy passage, arrived soon at Rotterdam. Duncan met with some of his English acquaintance in that town, and his mind being pretty much bent upon rambling, and seeing all the curiosities, customs, and humours he could, in all the foreign places he was to pass through, he went, out of a frolic, with some gentlemen, next day, in a boat to an adjacent village, to make merry over a homely Dutch entertainment, the intended repast being to consist of what the boors* there count a great delicacy, brown bread and white beer. He walked out of sight from his company, and they lost one another; and strolling about by himself at an unseasonable hour, as they call it there after the bell has tolled, Duncan Campbell, who neither knew their laws, nor if he had, was capable of being guided by the notice which their laws ordain, was taken into custody in the village, for that night, and carried away the next day to Williamstadt, where he was taken for a spy, and put into a close imprisonment for three or four days.

But some Scotch gentlemen, who had been in company with Mr. Campbell at Mr. Cloysterman's, a painter in Covent-garden, made their application to the magistrate and got him released; he knew his friends the officers, that carried him over, were gone forward to the camp, and that there was no hope of finding them at Rotterdam, if he should go thither, and so he resolved, since he had had so many days punishment in Williamstadt, to have three or four days pleasure there too, by way of amends, before he would set out on his journey after his

* farmers

From Letter VIII: The Dumb Boy, in *Personal Recollections*

Charlotte Elizabeth
England, 1841

I turned my attention to the deaf and dumb children, whose situation was deplorable indeed: I took four out of the streets to instruct them, of whom one proved irreclaimably wild and vicious; two were removed by a priest's order, lest I should infect them with heresy: the fourth was to me a crown of rejoicing, and will be so yet more at "that day.". . .

John, or Jack as we always called him, was a puny little fellow, of heavy aspect, and wholly destitute of the life and animation that generally characterize that class, who are obliged to use looks and gestures as a substitute for words. He seemed for a long while unable to comprehend my object in placing before him a dissected alphabet, and forming the letters into words significant of dog, man, hat, and other short monosyllables; and when I guided his little hard hand to trace corresponding characters on the slate, it was indeed a work of time and patience to make him draw a single stroke correctly. His unmeaning grin of good-natured acquiescence in whatever I bade him do, was more provoking than downright rebellion could have been; and I secretly agreed with my friends that the attempt would prove a complete failure, while impelled, I hardly could tell how, to persevere with re-doubled efforts. Jack's uncouth bristly hair fell in a straight mass over one of the finest foreheads ever seen, and concealed it. I happened one day to put aside this mass, for the benefit of his sight, and was so struck with the nobly expansive brow, that I exclaimed to a friend then in the act of dissuading me from the work, "No; with such a forehead as this, I can never despair of success."

❦

It was by a sudden burst that the boy's mind broke its prison and looked around on every object as though never before beheld. All seemed to appear in so new a light to him; curiosity, in which he had been strangely deficient, became an eagerly active principle, and nothing that was portable did he fail to bring to me, with an inquiring shake of the head, and the word "what?" spelled by the fingers. It was no easy matter, before we had mastered a dozen common substantives and no other parts of speech, to satisfy his inquisitiveness, which I always endeavored to do, because it is wrong to repress that indication of dawning reason in a child, and Jack at eleven years old was in the predicament of a mere infant. More especially was I puzzled when his "what?" was accompanied by a motion pointing first at the dog, then to himself, to learn wherein consisted the difference between two creatures, both of whom, as he intimated, could eat, drink, sleep, and walk about, could be merry or angry, sick or well; neither of whom could talk; and yet, that there was a very great difference, he felt. The noble nature of man, was struggling to assert its preeminence over the irrational brute, which he, nevertheless, loved and feared too; for Barrow was a splendid dog, and used to assist me very cleverly in keeping my little wild Irish crew in order. Oh what a magnificent wreck is man! I do love to watch the rapid approach of that glorious time when, the six thousand years of his degradation beneath the reign of Satan being fulfilled, he shall rise above the usurper's power, and resume his high station among the brightest works of God.

I do not remember exactly how long after his first coming to me it was that Jack began to inquire so diligently about God. He seemed full of grave but restless thought, and then approaching me, pointed towards the sun, and by a movement of the hands as if kneading something, asked me whether I made it. I shook my head. Did my mother? No. Did Mr. Roe, or Mr. Shaw—two Protestant clergymen—or the priest? He had a sign to express each of these. No. Then "What? what?" with a frown and a stamp of fretful impatience. I pointed upwards, with a look of reverential solemnity, and spelled the word "God." He seemed struck, and asked no more at that time, but next day he overwhelmed me with "whats," and seemed determined to know more about it. I told him as well as I could, that He of whom I spoke was great, powerful, and kind; and that he was always looking at us. He smiled, and informed me he did not know how the sun was made, for he could not keep his eyes on it; but the moon he thought was like a dumpling, and sent rolling over the tops of the trees, as he sent a marble across the table. As for the stars, they were cut out with a large pair of scissors, and stuck into the sky with the end of the thumb. Having thus settled his system of astronomy, he looked very happy, and patted his chest with evident self-applause.

I was amused, but of course not satisfied: my charge was necessarily an Atheist, and what I had told him was a very bare sort of Deism indeed. To communicate more, however, seemed utterly impossible, until we should have accomplished considerable things in the way of education. We had not above a dozen of the commonest words—all names of things—to which he could attach a meaning; and our signs were all of his own contriving, which I had to catch and follow as I might. So said reason, but reason is a fool. "Man shall not live by bread alone, but by every word that proceedeth out of the mouth of God." "For my ways are not your ways, neither are your thoughts my thoughts, saith the Lord." It pleased him to enlighten the mind of the boy; and instead of that work being dependent on human wisdom, all that human wisdom could do was to creep after it at a modest distance.

Next day, Jack came to me in great wrath, intimating that my tongue ought to be pulled out. This was his usual mode of accusation where a lie had been told. So I looked innocent and said, "What?" He reminded me of yesterday's conversation, telling me he had looked everywhere for God: he had been down the street, over the bridge, into the churchyard, through the fields, had peeped into the grounds of the castle, walked past the barrack-yard, and got up in the night to look out at the window. All in vain; he could not find God. *He saw nobody big enough to put up his hand and stick the stars into the sky.* I was "bad," my tongue must be pulled out; for there was "God, NO." And he repeated "God, no," so often that it went to my heart.

I considered, prayerfully. My view of the scriptures told me that without divine help none could really seek after God: and also that when he vouchsafed to give the desire, he would surely increase knowledge. Here was a poor afflicted boy getting out of his bed to look by night for one whom he had vainly sought all the day: here was Satan at work to strengthen unbelief: I was commanded to resist the devil, and surely there must be some way of resisting him. I sat silent on the opposite side of the fire, and a plan having struck me, I looked at Jack, shrugged my shoulders and seemed convicted of a deception. He shook his head at me, frowned, and appeared very much offended at my delinquency. Presently I seized a small pair of bellows, and after puffing at the fire for a while, suddenly directed a rough blast at his little red hand, which hung very near it. He snatched it back, scowled at me, and when again I repeated the operation, expressed great displeasure, shivering, and letting me know he did not like it.

I renewed the puff, saying, "What?" and looking most unconscious of having done any thing; he blew hard, and repeated that it made his hands cold; that I was very bad, and he was very angry. I puffed in all directions, looked very eagerly at the pipe of the bellows, peering on every side, and then, explaining that I could see nothing, imitated his manner, saying, "Wind? no!" shaking my head at him, and telling him his tongue must come out, mimicking his looks of rebuke and offended virtue. He opened his eyes very wide, stared at me and panted; a deep crimson suffused his whole face, and a soul, a real soul shone in his strangely altered countenance, while he triumphantly repeated, "God like wind! God like wind!" He had no word for "like;" it was signified by holding the two forefingers out, side by side, as a symbol of perfect resemblance.

Here was a step, a glorious step, out of absolute atheism into a perfect recognition of the invisible God. An idea, to call it nothing more, new, grand, and absorbing, took possession of his mind. I numbered seven years of incessant care over him from that day; and I will fearlessly assert that in his head and in his heart God reigned unrivalled. Even before he knew him as God in Christ, the Creator and

Preserver were enthroned in his bosom; and every event of the day, every object that met his view, gave rise to some touchingly simple question or remark concerning God. He made me observe that when trying to look at the sun he was forced to shut his eyes, adding, "God like sun." An analogy not very traceable, though strictly just; for the glory that dazzled his mind was not visible. He was perpetually engaged in some process of abstract reasoning on every subject, and amazed me by explaining its results; but how he carried it on without the intervention of words, was and is a puzzle to me.

Previously he had been rather teasing to the dog and other inferior creatures, and had a great desire to fish; but now he became most exquisitely tender towards every living thing, moving his hand over them in a caressing way, and saying, "God made." At first he excepted the worms from this privilege, remarking that they came up through holes from beneath earth, while God was above, over the sky; therefore they were not made by him; but I set him right, and he agreed that they might be rolled up in the world, like meat in a pudding, and bite their way out. Thenceforth, woe to the angler whom Jack detected looking for live bait!

When my first pupil from being irregular in his attendance fell off more and more, until he wholly discontinued coming, and the others were withdrawn for fear of heretical infection, I became more anxious lest this dear boy might also leave me before he had received the knowledge of Jesus Christ. I had, at his earnest entreaty, taken him into the house altogether, his home being at some distance; but I knew not how long he might be permitted to stay. The ravages of a dreadful fever among the poor, increased my solicitude to see my devout little Deist a Christian. I have, in a small memoir of this "Happy Mute," related the manner of his receiving the gospel, but I must not pass it over here. To the glory of God's rich grace it shall be recorded, as one of the most signal mercies ever vouchsafed to me. As before, the boy was led to open the way, and in the faith of the Lord's willingness to reveal himself to an inquiring soul, I followed it up.

Jack had noticed the number of funerals passing; he had occasionally seen dead bodies placed in their coffins, and one evening he alluded to it, asking me by significant gestures if they would ever open their eyes again. Considering that he had often been present at the interment of the dead, and had also witnessed the decay of animals cast out to perish, it struck me as a singular question, plainly indicating that the consciousness of immortality is natural to man, and unbelief in a future state foreign to his untaught feelings. On the present occasion, my heart being then lifted up in prayer for divine assistance on this very point. I caught at the encouragement, and instantly proceeded to improve the opportunity, I sketched on paper a crowd of persons, old and young; near them a pit with flames issuing from it, and told him all those people, among whom were we, had been "bad" and God would throw us into the fire. When his alarm was greatly excited, I introduced into the picture another individual, who I told him was God's Son; that he came out of heaven; that he had not been bad, and was not to go in the pit; but that he allowed himself to be killed; and when he died, God shut up the pit; so the people were spared. This seemed to myself too strange, vague, meagre, to convey any definite idea to the boy's mind; but how effectual does the Lord make our poorest efforts when HE wills to work! After a few moments' deep thought, Jack astonished me by an objection that proved he saw the grand doctrine of a substitute for sinners, which I was so hopeless of bringing before him. He told me the rescued people were many; he who died was one, and his earnest "What?" with the eloquent look that now peculiarly belonged to his once stupid countenance, showed his anxiety for a solution of this difficulty.

With unutterable joy in my heart, but great composure of manner, I rose, and taking from a vase a bunch of dead flowers, inadvertently left there, I cut them into small bits, laid them in a heap on the table, and beside my gold ring: then pointing to each, with the words "many- one," I asked which he would rather have? He struck his hand suddenly to his forehead, then clapped both hands, gave a jump as he sat, and with the most rapturous expression of countenance intimated that the one piece of gold was better than the room full of dead flowers. With great rapidity he applied the symbol, pointing to the picture, to the ring, to himself, to me, and finally to heaven. In the last position he stood up and paused for some time, and what a picture he would have made! A smile perfectly angelic beaming on his face, his eyes sparkling and dancing with delight, until, with a rush of tears that quite suffused them, he gazed at me, then again raised them to the ceiling, his look softened into an expression of deep awe and unbounded love, while he gently spelled on his fingers, "Good ONE, good ONE!" and ended by asking me his name.

> "How sweet the name of Jesus sounds
> In a believer's ear!"

Jack was not to hear that name with his bodily ears until the voice of the archangel and the trump of God should call him from sleeping in the dust of the earth; but he received it into his mind, and the gospel, the glorious, everlasting gospel, into his soul, and the Holy Spirit into his heart, without the intervention of that sense. In that hour it was given unto him to believe, and from that hour all things were his—the world, life, death, and a bright immortality. Never but once before had I laid my head on the pillow with such an overwhelming sense of perfect happiness. The Lord had indeed shown me his glory, by causing his goodness to pass before me.

Henceforth I had a Christian brother in my little dumb charge: his love to Jesus Christ was fervent and full; his thoughts about him most beautiful. By degrees, I gave him some knowledge of our Lord's mortal birth, his infancy, work, death, resurrection, and ascension; together with his coming to final judgment at the end of the world. . . .

Very great indeed was Jack's emotion when he discovered that the Saviour in whom he was rejoicing was the object represented by the image he had been taught to bow down before. He resented it deeply: I was quite alarmed at the sudden and violent turn his feelings took against Popery....He spurned the whole system from him, as soon as the light of the gospel fell upon its deformities.

Returning from the chapel one day, soon after this, he came up to me under great excitement: he took up a clothes-brush, set it on one end, and with a ludicrous grimace bowed down before it, joining his hands in the attitude of prayer and chattering after his fashion; then asking the brush if it could hear him, waiting in an attitude of attention for its reply, and finally knocking it over and kicking it round the room, saying, "Bad god, bad god!" I guessed pretty well what it was all about; but as he concluded by snapping his fingers exultingly and seating himself without further remark, I spoke on other subjects.

Next morning, Jack was very animated, and came to me with an evident budget of new thoughts. He told me something very small came out of the ground, pointing in opposite directions; it grew: and then two more points appeared. I found he was describing the growth of a plant, and expecting some question, was all attention; but Jack was come to teach, not to learn. He soon showed that his tree had reached a great height and size; then he made as if shouldering a hatchet, advanced to the tree and cut it down. Next came a great deal of sawing, chopping, planing, and shaping, until he made me understand he had cut out a crucifix, which he laid by, and proceeded to make a stool, a box, and other small articles; after which he gathered up the chips, flung them on the fire, and seemed to be cheering himself in the blaze. I actually trembled at the proceeding; for where had he, who could not form or understand half a sentence, where had *he* learned the Holy Spirit's testimony as recorded by Isaiah?

The sequel was what I anticipated: he feigned to set up the imaginary crucifix, and preparing to pray before it, checked himself, saying, "No;" then with animated seriousness reverted to the springing up of the little seedling, saying, "God made;" and as it grew, he described the fashioning of the trunk and branches and leaves most gracefully, still saying "God made;" he seemed to dip a pencil in color, to paint the leaves, repeating, "God made beautiful!" Then, that God made his hands too; and he came to the conclusion that the tree which God made, cut out by his hands which God made, could not be God who made them. Then he got very angry, and not satisfied with an unsubstantial object for his holy indignation to vent itself upon, he ran for the clothes-brush, and gave it a worse cuffing and kicking than before; ending with a solemn inquiry whether I worshipped crosses, etc., when I went to church.

Jerry and Clarinda

Henry William Bishop
USA, 1868

The Medfords sat at early breakfast in a tenement-house of the more respectable sort, among the battered old mansions of once fashionable Bleecker Street, New York.

A distinctly unpleasant atmosphere of temper prevailed. Some might have accounted for it by the narrow quarters or the advancing heats of the fervid July day, but there was much more than this under the surface.

"Well, give the boy something to eat, anyway," cried Thomas Medford. "You look as if you hoped every next mouthful he took might choke him."

"Maybe I do," returned the coarse woman, his companion, sullenly. "You know I didn't want him to come here. It ain't the first time you've heard me say so; nor yet it won't be the last."

The head of the household was a large, strong man of fifty, unkempt, and slouching about in his shirt-sleeves. His wife was frowzy woman of perhaps thirty-five, over-stout, and with thin, shrewish lips, yet retaining still considerable traces of good looks.

The boy they spoke of, the third member of the group, was neatly dressed, of a certain refined air, and decidedly superior in aspect to either. His expression was chronically uneasy or pained, as if trouble were no stranger to his experience, yet, curious enough, he seemed quite oblivious of the acrimonious discussion being waged in his regard.

"Look at him now," pursued Mrs. Medford, "with no more sense o' what we're talkin' about than if he was the obbylix up to Central Park."

"He's my offspring, and I'll have him well treated, or I'll know the reason why," thundered Tom Medford, pounding the table.

"Then why don't you leave him in the deef-and-dumb asylum, where he belongs? What did you put him in there for, if you'd got to keep takin' him out?"

"Jerry wants a little pleasure like anybody else. It's three years before this since he's set foot outside of it. When he kep' writin' all them letters that he was bound to come home for a part of his vacation, what could I do but bring him? And here he is, and I'll stand by him while my name's Tom Medford."

Even in the man's defiance there was a perceptible trace of skulking and surrender. His was a morally indolent and selfish nature, and thoroughly under control of his wife, whom he had married for her good looks. She was then a Mrs. Seemüller, a German bakeress of the neighborhood. She had taken him when the fortunes of the bakery ware at a low ebb, because, with the good wages he was earning at his trade as a coppersmith, he promised to be able to support her in greater comfort. She had made him put a number of other children by a former marriage into various half-orphan asylums and what not, and treated poor Jerry with great cruelty on every opportunity that offered, considering her dignity with her choice circle of acquaintance best vindicated by this means. It is safe to say that under the same sensuous influence Medford would have done, in the long run, whatever else she might demand.

From a small dark bedroom *en suite* with the parlor and the kitchen, in which the repast was being held, new came forth another boy, a son of the ex-bakeress's own, who proved himself a true chip of the old block. He wore the trim uniform of an employé in the District Messenger service, yet this could not overcome his appearance of a hulking, insolent lout.

"Dummy! dummy!" he whispered, to Jerry with malicious satisfaction, as he passed around to his own side of the table, accompanying the words with a torturing pinch and thrust of the elbow.

Medford raised his voice in reprimand. "I had to defend myself, hadn't I?" responded the cub, with an air of injured protest. "He gave me a lick, and I had to return it, hadn't I?"

"My boy's bein' the whole time set upon. I'll take my bonnet and leave the house this minute," screamed the mother, in her shrillest tones.

Medford succumbed, as was his way, before her violence. He had now, besides, to hurry away to his shop in Centre Street. When he was gone, the pair renewed persecutions of Jerry, now quite unhampered. The coarse woman, leaning one fat arm heavily on the table, mimicked the motions of his peculiar mode of speech before his very face, and laughed loudly at the excellence of the joke. Her son was an able assistant. Finally they struck the deaf boy, and then, smarting with pain, and bearing a visible mark of the blow on his cheek, he fled from them, and made his way to the place where his father was at work.

Tom Medford was but little pleased to see his unusual offspring enter his shop. Instead of being proud of the boy, who was in many ways superior, he was never any thing more than apologetic for his existence. The eyes of his shop-mates were fixed upon him with curiosity. He summoned one of the more intelligent of them, and said: "Here, talk with him a bit, will you? See what he wants."

"*Me* talk with him? Why don't you do it yourself?"

"The fact is, mate, I don't understand his lingo; he's learned the devil's own crinklum-crunklums that nobody but themselves knows anything about."

"Then how do you think I know? I never was no dummy."

"Oh, he writes it down; he can write it down for ye fast enough; but the fact is"—confidentially—"the fact is, I don't read much writin', and I wouldn't wonder if a good part o' what he's got to say goes astray at our house."

Thus urged, the other procured a soiled piece of paper, and endeavored to open communication with the youth thus so curiously cut off from intercourse even with the parent who brought him into the world. Even with so good a cause of complaint as he had, Jerry was reticent, however, before a stranger.

"As near as I can make out," summed up the interpreter, "he's been hit a pretty hard crack by some woman, and he don't like it. There's the mark of it on his face, too."

"Yes," assented Medford, "the woman o' the house don't fancy him—that's it, that's it. Well, tell him it's all right, all right," waving an arm soothingly. "I'll look after him at supper-time. Tell him he can run around town and play till then. Of course he wouldn't want to stay here."

He quite forgot to give the boy any money for lunch, but this soon proved, even to the latter, a matter of slight consequence. He had seen little of the world till now. He had a quick eye and alert movements, and was amply able to take care of himself in the crowded streets. He gazed into the shop windows, at burly policemen, and up at the tall buildings. Finally a fire-engine tore by, dropping hot coals behind it. When he followed this to its destination, and actually saw the conflagration of a dry-goods house in Worth Street, he was quite beside himself with enthusiasm, and, for the time being, at the end of all his troubles.

He was a boy much like other boys. The public institution where he had been placed for long years past was benevolent, no doubt, but it was far from his ideal of a home. Alas! since the coming of a step-mother there had been for him no home, no trace of that warm personal interest and affection that it is in the hearts of human beings to desire. His was the very old story of the heartless cruelty that so often arises from this kind of parentage, frequently so desirable in itself. He had felt that unless some change for the better arose in his friendless and desolate situation he must even run away from the school, and seek his fortune in the world. He had persuaded himself that he might have exaggerated the former repulses met with under his father's roof, or that things there, in the long interval, might have taken a favorable turn. Self-invited, he had begun this luckless visit; it had proceeded from bad to worse; its third day was now drawing to a close, and events were approaching their most embittered pass.

At the supper table the scenes of the morning were renewed, and even, if possible, in aggravated form. Medford could give no real protection, and the boy's heart sank within him. Hardly knowing whither to turn, he went alone into the stuffy little parlor, and took up one of a few cheap books lying there. The first two nights of his stay he had gone down into the street, with Mrs. Seemüller's son, to be amused, but found that this was only to be made a butt of instead by a band of companions as rough and graceless as his conductor.

The virago and her son followed him into the parlor. The latter struck the book from his hand, and the former bristled up over him in a threatening attitude. He threw out his hands in a gesture of self-defence. The messenger-boy ran to the door and summoned Medford, malevolently crying, "He's struck me mother! He's struck me mother!"

"Ah, would you? You strike a woman! That's a little too much," cried the man, seizing the cowering Jerry, and violently belaboring him. His ire had long been fuming at the idea of all this annoyance to which he found himself subjected, and, like many such natures, he now, as the easiest course, turned squarely over to the side of injustice, and vented it upon the poor victim who had already suffered so much.

Jerry escaped from his hands, blinded, stunned, and as if his heart would break—though this even less at the injuries he had received than the final dissipation of all his illusions. He found himself in the brilliantly lighted street. The electric lights, then only lately introduced there, shone vividly into the shop windows and upon the motley groups of foreigners on the sidewalks. This was no place for concealment. Even as he paused a moment to breath he saw his father coming after him.

"Hi, Jerry! come back now. I'll do ye no more harm," cried the parent. "Come back now, I say."

But the ears of the fugitive were impervious to all human sounds; thinking he was wanted only for further punishment, he sped on, fear adding wings to his feet. He plunged down a side street and through a number of dark alleys, and came out at last at the water's edge.

Medford, discomfited in the pursuit, went back to his home, swore a while, in duty bound, at the family remaining there, and then settled down in an entirely comfortable state of resignation to his loss, which was not disturbed even when he found that Jerry had not returned to school, nor was heard of from any quarter.

The great dark hulls and tangled cordage of the shipping rose mysteriously around our fugitive, and the dark waters gave their ominous chuckle at his feet. He could not return to school to-night, even if he would. The pressing question first before him was to secure a night's lodging.

While he was lost in thought, a young man of dandified pattern came by and threw a valise at his feet for him to carry. The action, though not the speech, was plainly intelligible, and Jerry, glad of the opening, shouldered the heavy bag and followed him across one of the ferries, and then a considerable distance up into the town on the other side. He received a quarter of a dollar piece in payment for his service, and with this coin in his hand found himself at ten o'clock at night in an unknown part of Jersey City—all parts of which, for that matter, were equally unknown to him.

He wandered about somewhat aimlessly, and reached the northern suburbs. There he met an ice wagon, going homeward empty after its belated rounds of the day. A high partition so cut off the rear part of it from the view of the driver—drowsing besides on the seat—that he would not be likely to see what was transacting there. Jerry took advantage of this circumstance to creep within and steal a ride. Lulled by the long-continued, monotonous motion, he at length fell fast asleep.

He was awakened next morning by a number of people—belonging to a farm attached to an ice-cutting establishment—standing over him. They scolded him at first, then manifested much curiosity about his infirmity, and gave him a good breakfast and let him go. According to Jerry's own subsequent account, his endeavor to communicate with these acquaintances was not in all respects satisfactory.

"That ice-farmer family," he wrote, "ask me how was my name, where did I go, and what did I do. I gave them a changed name, because I was not secure if they would send me back to my father. But sometimes they look to both sides of the paper, and can not know its meaning, and I had discouraged."

Among deaf-mutes there are many who learn to express themselves with perfect facility in ordinary language, but the vast majority never escape from a quaint dialect constructed upon analogy with their language of signs. They use the vernacular like the most unversed of foreigners. Jerry, with all his brightness—bearing in mind, too, that he had by no means finished his schooling—belonged to the latter class, and afforded no exception to their peculiarities.

From this first stopping-place he went on, meeting with various adventures and hardships, till he arrived at a region which must have been somewhere about the Wallkill Valley. There he worked a short time at his trade of cabinet-maker, the elements of which he acquired at the Institution, and thence set out again, this time making in the direction of the Hudson, which he finally reached at Newburgh. He was conveyed across it by a fisherman, took to catching rides on railroad trains, with the idea of getting to Canada, lost his bearings, and was at length ignominiously put off by a conductor. He found himself at the small station of Staatsburg, much south of the point where, by this time, he had expected to be.

It was there I first saw him, sitting disconsolately on the edge of the depot platform. He had fallen in already with one of our own characters of local celebrity, Barney Pringle, a strong, adult deaf-mute, of little education, employed on the railroad to move turn-tables, now here and now further up the track. He had lost both arms in an accident, but neither this nor any other of his disabilities was allowed to dampen a peculiar flow of spirits. He was a short, thick-set fellow, with a ruddy visage, and very lively ways. He could do a variety of surprising feats, the principal of which was putting on and taking off his hat with the aid of his stumps and teeth.

As I approached the pair seemed to have been conferring together, probably to no great purpose. Jerry arose and handed me a written paper, which I took and read as follows:

"Do you know a gentlemen who would be willing to let a deaf boy work how to do farming, without getting any money for several weeks?"

The hint was a modest one, and certainly much more striking than common in its form. Pringle, who stood by, and had evidently acquainted himself with the purport of the communication, waved his stumps in a cheerful way, as if conveying that the plan suggested was one that amply met his approval.

I had learned, years before, something of the method of spelling on the fingers, and now proceeded to revive it, much to Jerry's delight. It so happened that just at this time, a valuable colt on our place had been discovered to be totally deaf. He was Bulbul, son of Bullfinch, by imported Capricorn, first dam Electra, second dam Alcyone, etc., etc., a dark bay beauty with a star on his forehead and black points extending up to the knees. By his birthright he should have been one of the best of his kind, but he was likely, instead, through his unfortunate disability, to be all but wholly worthless.

A singular idea flashed across my mind; might not some affinity be developed between the boy and the colt? Perhaps some occult sympathy might arise out of their common affliction that would render Jerry a more useful guardian and educator for Bulbul than anybody else.

It was a wild and whimsical conceit, no doubt, yet it determined me to take the boy home. I had come to the station that day to meet a coppersmith who was to arrive from New York to do work on a rather elaborate fountain we were putting up in an oblong fishpond on a terrace before the house; but he disappointed me. He did not come, in fact, till a week or ten days afterwards. I therefore took Jerry up beside me, and we drove away homeward.

At a transverse road we met another wagon, containing a man and several women, coming directly across our course. All at once Jerry leaped to his feet, leaned out over the dash-board, and began to signal violently to a young girl in the other wagon, who replied to his manifestations in kind. She was a chubby little thing of fourteen or fifteen, with a comely face, and black hair tied in a twist, falling down her back. My companion seemed to ask me, in an appealing way, to stop, and when I had done so, leaping down, he ran to shake hands with his friend. Their motions, rapid as lightning, were a marvel to see. They were rather like some of the animated races of southern Europe than phlegmatic Anglo-Saxons. It seemed that they were friends or acquaintances from the same school. They met like strangers in a strange land, overjoyed at the unexpected encounter, and the recollection it brought up of the many things in common between them.

"Clarinda's my brother's child," said the man in the other vehicle, very civilly. "He left her to us when he died, and she's the pride of our house. It's a great treat to them dummies," he added, presently, "To see some o' their own sort once in a while. I'd go half a day's journey out o' my way, any time, to give the girl a treat like this."

He was a locomotive engineer, living at Tivoli, and being briefly off duty, had hired a horse and taken his family out for a drive. I told him how it was I happened to have Jerry with me.

"He's a good boy," said Clarinda, her certificate of character being passed over to me in her own handwriting, on a pad she carried for the purpose. "He can study very well. He can also play well at various many games, as such the baseball, the oar, the athletic, etc."

"You must let him come and see us," urged Clarinda's family; and the girl herself gave him such a parting salute as might some vivacious Spanish señorita.

He returned to me flushed with excitement and pleasure. The only drawback to his contentment for the time being was that his clothes were "too old-fashionable" for such an interview. Thus he described their dusty, travel-stained condition.

Our farm at Staatsburg was an attractive one. There was not much money in such an enterprise, it is true, but it was, though I say it myself, the show-place of the country round-about. I think Jerry enjoyed its charms to the full. We had from the terrace a view of the distant ranges of the Catskills, blue as a dream of fairyland. Back of the house, on a sunny slope, was a vineyard, the terraced vines of which, on their slim poles, always impressed me like rows of dismounted cavaliers on parade. A feature on which we particularly prided ourselves was our white pigeons, a flock of which were continually fluttering above the farm buildings, or sitting along the ridge crests, with a most genial, home-like effect. If by chance any of darker hue appeared among them, it was the great misfortune, if not the fault of these, for the shot-gun was at once got out, and they were picked off, to keep the flock pure white.

A certain part of the farm buildings was at no great remove from the railroad. The track, I regret to say, ran directly through our place, this being its only drawback. And yet perhaps it was not so much of a drawback after all, inasmuch as our young horses, for instance, being daily accustomed to this alarm would not be so easily frightened in after-life.

Before being introduced to the colt, Jerry was familiarized somewhat with the other stock, and set at a variety of small tasks, in all of which he acquitted himself very well. I asked him about his trade; he said he had not learned it well.

"Our boss," said he, "taught us to make only very common or old-fashionable articles, such as mostly sweeping the floor."

Meantime the coppersmith from New York arrived. He proved to be from the very shop in Center Street where Jerry's father belonged. He was, in fact, the one who had acted as interpreter in the interview described.

"His step-mother battered him round, and he ran away from 'em. I don't blame him," said he, explaining what he knew about Jerry's case.

After this we felt in but little further need of certificates to our new assistant's standing.

A letter came from Clarinda, a little overture, beginning an innocent, quaintly amusing, and original correspondence, which, first and last, extended over a long time. It was addressed to "Esq. J. Medford."

CLARINDA TO JERRY

My Friend—That is the first time I wrote to you for my improving education. I ask what is your doing now? What is your business in? Also I would like to hear of your travels. Will you tell me them? For my own person, I help my aunt, Mrs. Shackley, in house-working. Sometimes I ride with my uncle on his locomotive engine, of which its name is Ajax. My uncle says if you will come to see us here, you can ride with ourselves on Ajax, if you will have a curiosity to do so. When you come here you can find a white color house. You must turn in a eastly direction, about three blocks far, right side down. It opposites the Baptist religion's church, also white color. I am quite better in my writing now, so I close my satisfactorily letter with saying Good Morning. Your Friend,

CLARINDA SHACKLEY

The much-flattered recipient of this epistle replied to it substantially as follows:

JERRY TO CLARINDA

My Dear Friend Clarinda—My business is I work in a large farm. My employer is a fine-headed and sound man in his heart. He will give me some dollars each month or week, and will buy my fare on the railroad to go seeing you. I have to arise up at five o'clock in the morning, milking cows or animals and drive them in the woods. Also I give food to a small deaf horse name Bulbul, and have many frolic times with him. He is deaf like us; he could not hear a railroad track. When a dog, Peter, barked at him in his field he can not hear it. Bulbul leaved that dog alone till when Peter went too near his heels and he kicked his leg out backwardly. If I could be a rich farmer I would made much money by selling my fruits, corns, vegetables, poultries, and eggs. I like best country than a city life, because if we do not exercise our muscles they soon become senseless. Many city men who only play in billiard-house, rinks, etc., become weak in their bodies and pale face. I can not say now about my travels because I have not a leisure time, but another time I will tell you them. I hope you will accept my letter. I am glad to have a benevolence for you. So now I have come to an end. Your good friend,

JERRY MEDFORD

Whether it was but a mere coincidence, or that there was, in fact, an atom of truth in my theory, the colt really seemed to take to his new keeper with a peculiar kindness. Jerry was greatly interested when he heard of his condition, and set out upon his work with an evident zest. Without dwelling here at any length upon the details, it may be said that we first discovered this case of deafness by observing the conduct of the young animal at feeding-time, after the weaning period. If he chanced to be asleep at these times, he did not rouse up like the others. We at first thought it lack of appetite, but his performances at the trough, when his attention was fairly called to it, showed there was no fault on that score. Again, when the rest of the troop of rogues, in response to the call, would come galloping to the top of the slope in the pasture, and cluster there with ears erect, he would mope alone in the background. It might even be said that Bulbul was dumb as well as deaf, for he would stretch out his neck and open his mouth as if to whinny, and did not succeed even in that; there came from his mouth instead only a sort of half gurgle—amusing or pathetic, according as one chose to look at it.

Jerry bade fair to cure him of many of his eccentricities. He adopted a system of gestures and sudden gyrations to replace the use of the voice, and was soon able to control him, even from a distance, by a certain friendly sorcery, as it were, by signals with a handkerchief, and by waving arms and passes.

He found time withal to give Clarinda an account of his journey into our part of the country, as she had requested.

Jerry to Clarinda

I ran out of my father's inhabitation because it had not been in peaceful sociability with me. I had not money enough, but soon a young man of worldly pleasure gave me a quarter to brought his satchel over a Jersey ferry. I did the same. . . . Then I started, staid, and arrived in various many popular ["populous" no doubt intended] town and villages. When the sun did not shine and the weather rained I could not tell which was the east or west direction. Once I made a little house for defense from the rain, but it was all in vain. I often felt homesick, and thought if I would better go back. I met many men and boys and asked them the way by my writing, but I considered that they were mostly uneducated. . . .

When I reached to Newburgh there were many wonderful and relic things there. I would like to describe you them all. The most relic thing in Newburgh is Washington's head-quarter. I visited that head-quarter many times, both inside and outside. There was a man who was taking many fishes in a long net. I asked him would he be willing to give me a row with him across the river; he said he would do the same. There was a rough water, the waves dashed themselves and flew up in a foam, and my clothing was wetted to the skin, but I continued to smile pleasantly, because I was crossed over for nothing, and viewed many sceneries on either shores of the Hudson River. Now I tell you another thing, the last. I took much pains in walking on the track, and contrived how I could go to Canada to get work. I asked a man how I could get a ride, in the freight cars, to anywhere. He pointed the truck, under the car, for me to go there, but I informed him I would accidently be killed if I went there. When he saw I was very wet, and had no breakfast, dinner, and supper, he let me go in the caboose with him and dry on the side of a stove. Also he gave me some food, and was told I could eat as much as I choose. I spent not less than some time and had a very pleasant vacation with that man, and on parting gave him many thanks in return of his kindness, which he accepted.

The next time, I went in a passenger car, till what the conductor would say when I had no money to buy my fare. I did not care if it would go as far as California or not, but unluckily it came in a wrong direction. But I had troubled about it, and asked a passenger what would the conductor do. That passenger said he might bring some detectives to collar me to the station-house, but luckily he only put me off at a small town. Then I was sad, and my head hung down loosely. I do not say any more of it now, because I think by this time you are too busy. So I remain,

Your sincerely friend,

J. Medford

He went to visit Clarinda, and the visit appears to have been a social success. One striking feature of it was a jaunt he took in her company, on her uncle's locomotive, on the Ajax. He wrote for me, when he came back, an enthusiastic account of it, from which I extracted some sentences.

The iron horse stood in his stable till Mr. Pringle moved the turntable for his coming out on his own track. I was afraid to climb in on the leviathan Ajax, but Clarinda was not afraid. Some people made fun of ourselves by making signs at us. Mr. Shackley rolled up his coat on the sleeves. At first Ajax was lazy, and the large wheel turned slowly, but soon it turned fastly, and he seemed to ate up the railroad ground. Long smoke went off backwardly, and loud whistles blew, but alas! I could not hear them, but I could feel some of them. We back down many freight cars, and went once in a tunnel where no light larger than a needle's head could be seen.

He was installed, as his abode, in the gardener's house, but spent many evenings with us. His manners, through the influence no doubt of polished instructors, were perfectly good. We came to look upon him not as one hampered by an infirmity, but as a very original sort of little foreigner. We remarked him, when engrossed in some piece of study, unconsciously rendering the sense of it to himself with rapidly twinkling fingers, just as hearing children con over their lessons on their lips. He had been educated, too, partly by the method of visible speech, so mysterious to the unaccustomed outsider, and if we formed our words with distinctness, could often read them as we spoke.

We were interested in all this, in some novel games he had, and in the opinions on all sorts of subjects he had formed from the point of view of his isolation. Spelling on our fingers, and talking by signs, came to possess for us a sort of fascination. It was the rage. If we had any visitor with pretty hands, she was always particularly anxious to take part in it, for the purpose of showing them.

On one occasion we had Clarinda over to dine, with Jerry, and were much entertained to see them together once more. Her uncle brought her down on his locomotive—from this time on he did occasionally—and having some business further along the line, left her with us till his return.

Jerry had considerable knack in mechanical contrivances, and made her a rustic chair.

"My employer says I have some very fine faculty for it," he announced, complacently.

Clarinda acknowledged his present in these terms:

Clarinda to Jerry

I sit in the rustic chair you had made me, and show to all my hearing friends. Each one say he or she had never seen such a beautifully chair, and he or she would like to have that chair. A another my friend said she pointed once her father a rusticked one like that in a showed-case window, but he could not be able to afford the expenses of it.

Jerry desired to know if it were not true that many great men had passed through the world without a knowledge of arithmetic—in which, as may be inferred from this, he was not at first remarkably proficient. Yet, again, with a blush, he inquired if I thought he also could become a learned philosopher and celebrity by abstaining from animal food for one year, as he had heard was done by Benjamin Franklin.

I urged Jerry to return to school when the time arrived, dwelling upon the advantages of a superior education; but he said he was happy in his present situation, and he was set upon earning wages, and getting on in the world as fast as possible. I wrote to his father, and once, when in town in his vicinity, even called upon him. The interview, on the Medford side, was conducted chiefly by the ex-bakeress. Disbelieving or affecting to disbelieve that the boy could have found friends of any consideration, she said: "A good riddance to bad rubbish! If there's them that wants him, let 'em keep him, say I."

Her worthy spouse stood by, participating now and then by a monosyllable and a subdued insolent grin.

Clarinda had gone back to school, and the two still corresponded, at intervals treating of such topics as the books they had read, the studies and other occupations they were engaged in. These effusions inclined strongly to be didactic.

"I have read a Longfellow," wrote Jerry; "he is a grand poet, he poets well. Also I have read one called 'Peck, the Life of a Bad Boy,' contains many good, laughable histories."

He wrote, too, about field sports, which always had a strong interest for him. "I excite much at present," he said, for instance, "about the champion game of the New Yorks and Chicagos. I hope the New Yorks can win. I would be willing myself to play the base ball many times if the players do not quarrel so much to each other."

"The brain exercises," returned Clarinda, "in committing wisdom to memory. Arithmetic is that which avoids us from being cheated in money and other valuable mathematical articles. In history is told us much about ancient buildings, animals, huts, human beings, presidents, statesmen, and other many things. Our earth is round alike a ball; it is the centre of a polar system, which strongly attracts our earth around its heat."

The girl returned home to spend her vacations, and Jerry went to see her on these occasions. In the autumn they found some opportunity to wade among the rich-stained leaves that fall so profusely along our pleasant road-sides, and to gather nuts; and in the winter not infrequently they joined the other young people of the neighborhood in coasting down the long hills.

A considerable period now elapses, during most of which I was absent from Staatsburg, and saw little in person of what was transacting there. Jerry grew to be a mature young man, tall and strong, and a figure of no little consequence in the place. He worked a piece of land on shares, took prizes at the county fair for fruit, Queen of the Valley potatoes, and colts of his own raising, and had put money in the savings bank. Clarinda, too, had become a woman grown, and leaving school, as so many young women will, even before her education was complete, settled down as a permanent assistant to the family in which she was so kindly harbored. Examples from the epistles of the two friends, during this time, might be multiplied here at great length, but let us now pass till we find them assuming a new and much more surprising tone.

A ball and reunion of deaf-mutes was held at Tivoli to honor the birthday of some celebrity in the annals of deaf-mute education. A considerable company of mutes gathered from the country round about, or came up from the city to take part in this occasion, and to have the opportunity at the same time of enjoying the autumn scenery of the Hudson. It was shortly after my return to the farm, and I was privileged to have a brief glimpse of the proceedings.

There seemed something mysterious and almost alarming in the view of so large a hall full of people going through all the forms of animated gayety in scarcely broken silence. A parallel assemblage of hearing persons would have rent the air with their laughter and chatter. The dancing—and there was a great deal of it—was excellently done, considering all the circumstances. The drum held a position of distinguished prominence in the orchestra, its vibration being felt, I gathered, and giving the rhythm and a point of departure to the dancers.

There was no lack of genuine enjoyment. A very democratic spirit appeared to prevail. The jovial Pringle, who moved turn-tables, was there, amused the company with prodigious caperings and flourishes of his stumps. Jerry, as one of the floor managers, was resplendent with a large rosette of blue and silver. He had obtained the cherished privilege of acting as the escort of Clarinda.

"After the middle of the dancing was over," said he, in describing the affair, later on, "we formed in two by two, and marched ourselves to the supper place. Stew oysters, crackers, and richly cakes were served us on long length tables. There were only not more than about fifty couples, and we laughed and chatted merrily at each other. Clarinda was the belle of them."

He even attempted, ambitiously, to describe her toilet. There is every reason to believe that the great approaches towards a tender understanding between the pair were made at this ball, for, shortly after, the following letters of proposal and acceptance were exchanged.

Jerry to Clarinda

My Dear Friend Clarinda.—Perhaps you might miss me after our lately pleasant companionship together. I shall not soon forget how pleasantly I enjoyed myself in your company. Now I will say another important thing, which is about love and matrimony. Since greatly a long time I am thinking very much about you all day, also in night-time. When a young man become about nineteen to thirty years of age, he can not always foretell that he would be a single man. He thinks he would like a wife and a general house-keeping. Well, it is what I feel about you, my dear friend.

Since I knew you, I hold many long conversation with you, and see you in many place. I find you to be a good, honest, and beautiful young lady, very good to do general housework, so I ask you if you can be willing to marry me.

I truthfully hope your favorable answer would be, "Yes." I can give you a valuable gold ring for engagement ring. We can engage ourselves for some months or years, till when I should have money enough to support for two or more persons. Then we will wed ourselves warmly in either a public or private marriage. The pastor will speak to us about marriage while we standing opposite to him. Then the male put the finger of the female into a wedding ring, and the relatives or friends disband to their respective homes. Then we can't take our marriage trip to anywhere. Perhaps I will purchase some U. S. farming lands for nothing in Dakota, and we can have a large farm and a beautiful residence in a country. Hoping you will say a heartfully "Yes," I continue your always loving true lover,

J. Medford

Clarinda to Jerry

My Sincerely Friend Jerry,—I confess I can not say much of love and matrimony, because I do not know much of love and matrimony, and the gentleman must be more skilful to speak of those events than the lady, but I will try to tell you of them by writing. I was much interest and feel a benevolence to you for a long time. In school, I noticed first you was often bowing to me very politely with a hat. Another time in Staatsburg I meet you again, and we were often corresponding many letters. I ask many questions to your conduct, and find you to be a working-hard, industrial, kind young man, well reputed in your good name. So that makes a gentleman and lady court and soon fall in love to each other. We did not often quarrelling; it is understood that if they are often quarrelling they do not fall in love. When a gentleman meet a lady he mostly begin to woo her by helping her from being badly hurt by some one, or saving her from drowning. We have not done the same because those had not happened to us, but we often talk a short time and take a walk for pleasure, and you company to me at my house or to travel. A lady can not be wedded without the consents of her parents and guardians, who first consent the gentleman to visit her. So, you can ask my uncle Mr. Shackley when will he have a wedding. For my own person I can say I am gladly willing to love you affectionately and marry you for my husband.

Your always true-devoted and now engaged friend,

Clarinda Shackley

The engineer did not wish to lose this niece, who was both so well-appreciated and serviceable a feature in his household, but being a man of excellent heart, and having no valid objection to offer, he gracefully submitted to a contingency likely to overtake all guardians in similar circumstances. For our own part we had not thought of withholding our approval. We were not alarmists on the subject of deaf-mutes marrying among themselves. We only urged that they should not be in haste; they were both young, and could afford to wait, and happiness was more likely to be insured when they were amply prepared for the step. Our advice fell in, on the whole, with their own views, and they rested contented enough for a while in the state of engaged lovers.

When things had been in this pleasant condition for some time, Jerry was seen one day while crossing the track to hold a brief parley with a ragged tramp. Then, like Crusoe's man Friday meeting his father among the captive war party of cannibals, he fell upon his neck. The tramp, in fact, was Tom Medford. It appeared that he had been thrown out of work in consequence of taking part in an unsuccessful strike, and never recovered his place. A liking for idleness had grown with this ample taste of it, and he had taken to drink. At last, after many vicissitudes, he had to go upon the road as a vagrant. It is more likely that his meeting with his son was a pure accident than that he accurate knowledge of his whereabouts, or the supreme impudence to hunt him up.

The ex-bakeress, it further appeared, had abandoned him at the first touch of calamity. Her hopeful son had been imprisoned for some enterprising feat of thievery perpetrated under cover of his duties as a messenger boy.

I would have advised Jerry to have little or nothing to do, now, with this graceless parent who had treated him so ill, but no one could have failed to admire, and even be touched by the charming warmth of heart and ideal of filial duty, apparently still surviving, that led him to desire to confer substantial benefits upon him, even after all that had happened. He asked me, with diffident appeal, to find him at least temporary employment, and I had reason to know that he took him to his own lodgings, and clothed him from his own wardrobe.

For a while Tom Medford went about in a state of deeply-abashed humility, but by degrees began to recover his confidence, and give himself airs of importance. He let fall, among the other hands, furtive disdainful remarks on the infirmity of Jerry. He began to drink again. Of this it is not probable that Jerry, who always remained innocent on that score, was aware. When the fact of the engagement finally entered into Tom Medford's consciousness, he was extremely disagreeable about it. He forbade it, in fact, and declared that he would never receive another member into his family with such a drawback. Poor Jerry came to me in alarm and asked what he should do about it. Do? I was for turning the vaporing reprobate off the place at once; I bade him not pay the slightest attention to it.

The deaf-mute Pringle stopped one morning to leave word that Clarinda was coming down on the Ajax to pass part of the day at the farm, while her uncle was switching cars below. Pringle too had wanted to marry Clarinda, but, finding she was otherwise disposed of, and about to do better in the world, had accepted the situation with perfect acquiescence. There never was reason for Jerry's flying into a passion, as he was at first disposed to do on hearing of the presumption of this ridiculous fellow. On the contrary, Pringle was ready to run on his errands and do him any service whatever, in regard to Clarinda as in other directions.

Hardly had Pringle gone that day, when Jerry came to me, in great anguish of mind. He drew me gently by the arm past the dairy buildings to a tool-house for the storage of the lighter farm implements.

"Look within, through the hinges at the door's side," he spelled out.

I followed his injunction, and there saw his father, squalid, heavy, and inert, lying prone on some straw spread out for him. Accompanying Pringle a little way back he had found Medford wandering on the place, in a state of besotted intoxication, and brought him thither for safe-keeping. It was his first discovery of the truth, and he was overwhelmed by it.

The hour was at hand when Clarinda was to arrive, and the distant smoke of the Ajax could already be seen, approaching around the long bend that debouched at our boundaries. Jerry, with a very sad face, moved toward the usual place—a part of the bank less steep than the rest, near the southern line of the estate—where she usually landed.

All at once the colt Bulbul—now, it should be explained, fully three years old, unusually large and powerful for his age, was seen to stay upon the railroad track at some distance away. Great pains were taken ordinarily to keep him away from all that part of the estate. By some mysterious means he had broken his trammels and passed the barriers; a long rope halter with which he had been tied still trailed behind him.

Jerry was startled at the dangerous situation of the animal, and, in vivid alarm, signaled to him in his customary way, but in vain. Then, dismissing for the moment all other thoughts from his mind he ran down to try and save him.

He caught the end of the halter, but the stalwart beast, his head, as it chanced, averted from the peril, and mistakenly playful or contumacious in the extreme, resisted, and even drew his would-be rescuer upon the track after him. A conflict now ensued between horse and man like that of another Alexander with Bucephalus. The Ajax hove in sight, and gave a succession of such piercing whistles as might have waked the very dead. All of us who were in the vicinity ran out, and looked with horror at the scene. The white pigeons on the roof, as though even they felt something ominous in the air, darted and careened about like autumn leaves blown in the gale.

The whole action took less time than it does to tell. Riveted though my attention was, I was vaguely conscious that the drunken elder Medford had broken out of his place of concealment, and was approaching the immediate scene by a series of staggering lurches.

A sudden turn of his head discovered to Bulbul himself the approaching locomotive. Its thunder already shook the ground. Crazed and half-paralyzed with terror then, he leaped, plunged, and bolted furiously, yet without moving sensibly from the same spot, which seemed to hold him to it as by some fatal spell.

In his plunging the stout rope became entangled about Jerry. He was like one of the sons of Niobe in the coils of the serpent. He could no longer have saved even himself. Were we then to see our poor Jerry perish by such a fate—almost a typical one for deaf-mutes—before our very eyes? Alas! it seemed as if that swift-rushing monster could not be avoided.

Shackley leaned out in horror from one side of his engine cab. Clarinda, holding a guardrail, fluttered yet farther out from the other side. She was like some supremely anxious brooding bird, or one of those goddesses of the Homeric poem who would have snatched up her hero and saved him from harm, in the defiance of all natural laws. The Ajax had made every effort to slacken its momentum, but with only slight avail. It must needs happen that the throttle-valve, at this time of all others, would not do its work.

But at the last moment, when the jaws of destruction were opened, a new element mingled with the action. It was extraordinary, ludicrous, contemptible, but efficient. Besotted Thomas Medford stood beside the track, glowering, leering, uttering incoherent words as of interest or encouragement to the contest. Whether it was only pure, mad delight in strife, such as actuates the typical Irishman at Donnybrook Fair, or a sudden vertigo by which he was taken, or a partial sobering, a disgust with life, and vague repentance and purpose of reparation even at this late hour—all at once throwing out both arms before him, with the fists stoutly doubled, he leaped headlong into the fray, impinging violently against Jerry and the colt.

Whirling wreaths of stem, lashing coils of rope, vague forms in turmoil, and the white pigeons circling above it all like gulls in a storm.

Then the Ajax passed on. Our Jerry was found beside the track, bruised, half stunned, but practically unharmed. Tom Medford was crushed beyond recovery. The benighted colt too had tried conclusions with the mechanical force with fatal effect. Thus, though his eccentricities had been pretty well studied already, opportunity was never afforded seeing what such an exceptional animal would have become under the full-fledged responsibilities of life.

Jerry threw himself upon his father's body in a touching way, and Clarinda joined sweetly in his grief. It had always been one of the things to note that the boy—perhaps through sense of shame—had said so little about his family difficulties. He would now have liked to represent that his father had had no faults, and as to their apparent estrangement and his living away from home, it had been a plan commending itself to the judgment of both.

May I say, by way of a word in conclusion, that Jerry and Clarinda took up a quarter section of government land in Montana. They rose to a position of admitted prominence there. Jerry—and properly enough too, having the best handwriting and best average education of any one in the place—was made postmaster. He might have counted upon retaining this office indefinitely, but for charges of "offensive partisanship" laid at his door. This was unfortunate, if true, but it has the redeeming feature that a good deal of vigor of mind must have been the cause of it.

But perhaps the most interesting bit of intelligence that has come to us about them is that their first child is a hearing and speaking baby, just like any other. We often please ourselves with picturing some of the experiences likely to befall an infant to be brought up under such exceptional circumstances.

The Unknown

Auguste Villiers de L'Isle-Adam
France, 1883
Translated by Hamish Miles

To Mme. La Comtesse de Laclos

> *The swan is silent all his life, to sing well once.*
> —Old Proverb

That evening, all Paris was resplendent at the Italiens. They were giving *Norma*. It was the farewell night of Maria-Félicia Malibran.*

With the last accents of the prayer of Bellini, "*Casta diva*," the whole audience had risen to its feet and recalled the singer in a glorious uproar. Flowers were thrown, and bracelets, and wreaths. An atmosphere of immortality seemed to envelop this majestic artist, almost dying, who fled from herself in a dream of singing.

In the centre of the orchestra stalls sat young man with the marks of a proud and resolute soul written upon his features. Bursting his gloves with the violence of his applause, he was manifesting all the impassioned admiration which he was feeling.

Nobody in Parisian circles was acquainted with this spectator. He had not the air of a provincial, but rather of a foreigner. Seated there in his stall, in his somewhat new clothes, though they were of sober tint and faultless in their cut, he would have appeared almost singular, had it not been for the instinctive and mysterious elegance that emanated from his whole person. Looking at him, one would have looked around him for space and sky and solitude. It was extraordinary, but is not Paris the city of the Extraordinary?

Who was he, and whence did he come?

He was an untamed adolescent, an orphan of seigniorial rank—one of the last of this century—a melancholy squire of the North, escaped these three days from the shadows of a great mansion of Armorica.

---

* The Théâtre-Italien was an opera house in Paris in the nineteenth century. *Norma* is an opera by Vincenzo Bellini first produced in 1831; it features one of the most difficult soprano roles in opera. Malibran (1808–1836) was a celebrated soprano who left Paris for London in 1834, which is, therefore, the year in which the story is set.

His name was the Count Félicien de la Vierge, and he owned the château of Blanchelande, in Lower Brittany. Away yonder a burning thirst for existence, a curiosity as to our hell and its marvels, had suddenly seized this huntsman with its fever! He set out for his travels, and so, quite simply, there he was. His presence in Paris dated from that same morning; so his wide-open eyes still retained their splendour.

It was the first evening of his youth! He was twenty. It was his introduction to a world of flame and forgetfulness, of the commonplace, of gold and pleasures. And *by chance* he had arrived in time to hear the farewell of this woman who was quitting it.

A few minutes had been enough to accustom himself to the brilliance of the auditorium. But the first notes of Malibran had stirred his soul; the audience had vanished. The accustomed silence of the woods, the hoarse wind among the breakers, the noise of the waters on the rocks of the torrents, and the solemn fall of evening had exalted this proud youth to be a poet, and in the tone of the voice he now heard he seemed to catch the distant prayer from the soul of all these things to come back to them.

And just as he was applauding the inspired singer, in a transport of enthusiasm, his hands stopped suspended. He remained motionless.

At the balcony of a box there had just appeared a young woman of great beauty. She was watching the stage. The fine and noble lines of her lost profile were shaded in the glowing darkness of the box, like a Florentine cameo in its medallion. Pale of hue, with a gardenia in her fair hair, and quite alone, she leaned one hand upon the ledge of the balcony; its form alone was token of distinguished lineage. The corsage of her robe of black watered silk, veiled with lace, was held by a jewel of strange sickliness, a marvellous opal, in the image of her own soul, no doubt, gleaming within a circle of gold. With her solitary air, and indifferent to all the audience, she seemed to forget her own existence under the irresistible spell of this music.

Chance, however, brought her to turn her eyes straying across the throng; and at that instant, her eyes and those of the young man met, just long enough to sparkle and die down, one single second.

Had they ever known one another? No, not on this earth. But if there be any who can tell where the Past has its beginnings, let them decide where those two beings had already veritably possessed each other; for that one look had persuaded them, then and for ever, that they were older than their cradle days. The lightning, in one single flash, will illuminate the waves and the foam of the night-bound sea and, away on the horizon, the distant silvery lines of the tide; and in the same way the sensation in this young man's heart under that fleeting glance was not gradual: it was the inward and magical flash of a whole world unveiled! He lowered his eyelids, as if to hold within them the twin flames of blue which had vanished into the depths of his eyes; then he strove to resist this oppressive faintness. He raised his eyes to the unknown in her box.

Pensively she still held her gaze upon him, as if she had caught the thoughts of this untamed lover, and as if it had been the natural thing! Félicien felt himself turning pale. An impression came over him, in the twinkling of an eye, of two arms joining in exquisite languor about his neck.—All was over! The face of this woman had just cast its reflection in his soul as in a wonted mirror, had taken bodily form therein, had recognized itself therein! For ever and ever it had fixed itself there, under a spell of thoughts all but divine! He loved, and with the first, the unforgettable, love!

Meanwhile the young woman, opening her fan, with its black lace that brushed her lips, seemed thrown back into her detachment. At this moment she had the appearance of only listening to the melodies of *Norma*.

On the point of raising his glass in the direction of the box, Félicien felt that this would be unseemly.[†]

"Since I love her!" he said to himself.

Impatient for the end of the act, he recalled his wandering thoughts. How was he to speak to her? To learn her name? He knew nobody. Could he consult next day the box office list of the Italiens? And suppose it were a chance box, taken just for the sake of that evening? Time pressed, the vision was about to vanish. Well then, his carriage would follow hers, that was all. . . . It seemed to him that there were no other means. Afterwards he would reflect what should be done. Then, in all his sublime simplicity, he said: "If she loves me, she will see clearly enough and leave me some clue."

The curtain fell. Very quickly. Félicien left the theatre. Once out in the pillared gallery, he simply walked to and fro in front of the statues.

His man came up to him, and he whispered instructions to the valet, who withdrew into a recess, and remained there, closely attentive.

The mighty roar of the ovation given to the singer sank down little by little, like all the triumphant sounds of this world. People were coming down the great staircase. Félicien fixed his gaze on the top of it, between the two marble vases from between which the glittering stream of the crowd rippled down. He waited.

But of all the radiant faces, the jewels, the flowers on the brows of the young girls, the ermine capes, the dazzling flood which streamed before him he saw nothing.

And all this great gathering faded away, little by little, without the appearance of the young woman.

Had he let her slip past, then, without recognizing her? No, that was impossible!— One old servant, powdered and covered with furs, still stood in the vestibule. On the buttons of his black livery there shone the strawberry leaves of a ducal coronet.

[†] An opera glass is a small, low-powered pair of binoculars commonly used by people attending a performance in a large theater.

Suddenly, at the head of the deserted staircase, *she* came into sight! Alone! Slender under her velvet cloak, with her hair hidden by a lace mantilla, she leaned her gloved hand on the balustrade of marble. She caught sight of Félicien standing beside one of the statues, but seemed to pay no further heed to his presence.

She came down with unruffled calm. The servant approached, and she uttered a few words in a low voice. The lackey bowed, and withdrew without waiting longer. An instant later came the sound of a carriage moving off. Then she went out. Still alone, she went down the outside steps of the theatre. Félicien took just the time to fling the words to his valet:

"Go back, to the hotel by yourself."

In a moment he was out on the Place des Italiens, a few paces away from this lady. Already the crowd had dispersed into the surrounding streets. The distant echoes of the carriages were growing faint.

It was a real October night, dry and starry.

The unknown walked on, with a slow pace and as if little used to walking. —Was he to follow her? He must, he decided. The autumnal wind bore down to him the faint perfume of amber that came from her, and the trailing rich rustle of the watered-silk on the pavement.

Opposite the Rue Monsigny she paused an instant to take her bearings, then walked on, as if unconcerned, as far as the deserted and almost unlighted Rue de Grammont.

Suddenly the young man stopped. A thought darted through his mind. Perhaps she was a foreigner!

A carriage might pass by and bear her off, for ever and ever! To-morrow, he would be dashing himself against the hard stones of some city—for ever—and without ever finding her!

To be separated from her, endlessly, by the hazard of a street, by an instant that could last through all eternity! What a prospect! The thought tormented him to the point of forgetting all considerations of seemliness.

He overtook the young woman at the corner of the dark street, then turned on his steps, and became terribly pale; leaning for support against the iron pillar of a street-lamp, he greeted her. Then, very simply, and with a kind of magnetic charm radiating from all of his being, he spoke:

"Madame," he said, "you know it. I saw you this evening for the first time. I am afraid of never seeing you again; so I must say to you now" (his voice quivered) "that *I love you!*" (he ended in low tones) "and that if you pass on, I shall die without repeating these words to any soul."

She stopped, raised her veil, and looked closely and fixedly on Félicien.

"Sir," she answered, after a short silence—and in the purity of her voice the most distant inclinations of her mind were easily felt, "sir, a sentiment that would give you this pallor and this bearing must be very profound, that you should find in it the justification of your behaviour. Accordingly, I am in no way offended. Recover yourself, and count me as your friend."

Félicien was in no way surprised at this answer. It seemed to him only natural that the ideal should answer ideally.

The circumstance, indeed, was one of those where both actors had to remind themselves, if they were worthy of it, that they belonged to the race of beings who form the proprieties of conduct, and not to the race of those who merely obey them. What the generality of human beings calls, in haphazard fashion, the proprieties, is no more than an imitation, mechanical, servile, almost simian, of what has been undesignedly practised by beings of exalted natures in general circumstances.

In a transport of open-hearted tenderness, he kissed the hand which was offered him.

"Will you give me the flower that you wore in your hair all this evening?"

In silence the unknown took out the pale flower from under the lace, and offered it to Félicien.

"And now good-bye," she said, "and for ever."

"Good-bye?" he stammered. "Then you do not love me?—Ah, you are married!" he suddenly exclaimed.

"No."

"Free! In heaven's name!"

"Forget me, none the less. You must, sir."

"But in one instant you became the very beating of my heart! How can I live without you? The only air I can wish to breathe is yours! I cannot understand now the words you say: *forget you*—but how?"

"A terrible disaster has befallen me. To confide its nature to you would only throw over you a shadow of sorrow like the shadow of death: it would serve no good purpose."

"And what disaster can sever these who love?"

"This one can."

And as she uttered the words, she closed her eyes.

The street lay stretched out, absolutely deserted. A doorway opening into a small enclosure, a kind of melancholy garden, stood open beside them. It seemed to offer them the protection of its shadows.

Like an irresistible, adoring child, Félicien led her beneath the vault of darkness, encircling her yielding figure as he did so.

The intoxicating sensation of the warm and tight-stretched silk that moulded her form gave him a feverish desire to strain her to him, to bear her off, to lose himself in her embrace. He resisted. But a dizziness robbed him of the faculty of speech. He could find only the stammering and indistinct words:

"Ah, heavens! How I love you!"

Then the woman leaned her head on the breast of him who loved her, and her voice came bitter and despairing:

"I do not hear you! I am dying of shame! I do not hear you! I should not hear your name! I should not hear your last breath! I do not hear the throbs of your heart that are beating upon my brow and my eyelids! Can you not see the fearful affliction that is killing me? I am—yes—I am *deaf*."

"Deaf!" cried Félicien, thunderstruck by a chill stupor, and trembling from head to foot. "Deaf!"

"Yes, for years! Oh, all the knowledge of all mankind would not avail to draw me forth from this horrible silence. I am deaf as the sky, deaf as the tomb. It is a curse on the day, but it is the truth. So—leave me!"

"Deaf?" repeated Félicien. Under this unimaginable revelation he had remained without a thought, overwhelmed, incapable even of thinking of what he was saying. "Deaf?"

Then suddenly he exclaimed:

"But at the Italiens tonight you were applauding the music all the same!"

He stopped, thinking that she must surely not hear him. The thing was becoming abruptly so fearful that it provoked a smile.

"At the Italiens?" she answered, smiling herself. "You forget that I have had the leisure to study the semblance of many emotions. Am I alone in that? We belong to the rank which destiny allots to us, and it is part of our duty to maintain it. That noble woman who was singing fully merited some supreme tokens of sympathy, did she not? And moreover, do you think that my applause differed greatly from that of the most enthusiastic of the *dilettanti*? I was a musician myself, in my day!"

At these words Félicien looked at her, a little distractedly, and still forcing a smile.

"Oh!" he said, "can you really be playing with a heart that loves you to despair? You accuse yourself of not hearing, and yet you are answering me!"

"Alas!" she said, "you must understand . . . what you say, you think is *personal* to yourself, my friend! You speak from your heart, but your words are new only to yourself. So far as I am concerned, you are reciting a dialogue of which I have learnt every single response in advance. For years now it has always been the same for me. It is a rôle in which every phrase is dictated and necessitated with a truly frightening precision. I have it by rote so completely that if I accepted—it would be criminal to do so—to unite my distress, even for a few days, to your destiny, you would forget, with every moment, the tragic confidence wherewith I have entrusted you. Illusion—I should give you it complete, exact, *neither more nor less than another woman*. I can assure you. I should even be incomparably more real than the reality. Remember that circumstances dictate always the same words, and that with them the face always harmonizes a little! You could not believe that I do not hear you, so exactly would I read you.—But let us think no more of it, shall we?"

This time, he felt alarmed.

"Ah!" he said, "they are bitter words, but you are privileged to utter them! But if all this be true, then, I for my own part wish to share even eternal silence with you, if need be. Why would you shut me out from this ill fortune? I should have shared your happiness! And our soul can make up for all that exists!"

The young woman started; and it was with eyes brimming with light that she looked at him.

"Would you like to walk a little, and give me your arm, down this dark street?" she said. "We shall picture to ourselves that it is an alley of crowding trees, and spring, and sunlight!—I have something to tell you, something which I shall never tell again."

The two lovers, with their hearts gripped in the vice of a fateful silence, walked along, hand in hand, like exiles.

"Listen," she said, "you who are able to hear the sound of my voice. Why did I feel that you did not offend me? And why did I reply to you? Do you know?—Well, indeed, it is simple enough that I should have acquired the art of reading, on the features of a face, or in attitudes, the sentiments which determine a man's actions; but what is very different is that I can gauge the value and the quality of these sentiments, as well as their intimate harmony in the person addressing me, and gauge these things with an exactitude so profound and, as it were, so nearly infinite. When you took it upon yourself to commit, in regard to myself, the shocking indiscretion of a little while ago, I was perhaps the one and only woman who could instantly apprehend its true meaning.

"I answered you, because I seemed to see the unknown sign shining on your brow, the sign that bears witness of those whose thought, far from being obscured, overwhelmed, and gagged by their passions, sets free the element of the ideal contained in every sensation they experience. My friend, let me teach you my secret. The fatality which has stricken my bodily existence, so painful at first, has become for me a release from countless servitudes! It has delivered me from that intellectual deafness of which most women are the victims.

"It has made my mind sensitive to the vibrations of eternal things, whereof the creatures of my sex usually know nothing but a parody. To those marvellous echoes, to those glorious reverberations, their ears are sealed! And so, to the sharpness of their hearing they are indebted for nothing beyond the faculty of perceiving only the external and the instinctive in the most delicate and pure of voluptuous delights. They are as the Hesperides, guardians of the enchanted fruits, but for ever ignorant of their magic worth. Alas, I am deaf . . . but they—what do they hear? Or rather, what do they listen to in the speeches addressed to them, except the confused noise, in harmony with the play of features in whosoever speaks to them! And so they are inattentive, not to the obvious sense, but to 'the deep, revealing *quality*, to the *true* sense, in fact, of every word, and are content with distinguishing in them an intention of flattery, which amply suffices them. It is what they call, with one of their smiles, the 'practical values of life'! Oh, you'll see, if you live long enough! You will see what mysterious oceans of candour, self-sufficiency, and base frivolity are hidden only by that delicious smile!—The abyss of love, alluring, god-like, obscure, starred like night herself, love such as the beings of your nature know it—try to depict that to one of them! If your expressions do filter through to her brain, they will be deformed in it, like a pure stream flowing across a swamp. So that in reality this woman *will not have heard them.* 'Life is incapable of fulfilling these dreams,' they will say, 'and you are asking too much from it!' Ah! As if life were not made by living!"

"I am listening," murmured Félicien.

"Yes," continued the unknown, "a woman never escaped this condition of nature, a mental deafness, save perhaps by paying her ransom at an unimaginable price, as I do. You endow women with a secret, simply because they do not express themselves except through their actions. Exultant in this secret, of which they are ignorant themselves, they take a proud pleasure in conveying the impression that you can read their riddle. And every man, flattered by the thought of himself as the long-awaited solver of the riddle, squanders part of his life to marry a stone sphinx. And not one among them is capable of rising *beforehand* to the reflection that a secret, terrible though it be, is identical, if it is *never* spoken, with nothingness."

The unknown stopped short.

"I am bitter to-night," she went on. "And this is why: I no longer feel envy for what they possess, for I have seen the use they make of their possessions—and it is one which doubtless I would have made myself! But here are you! Here are you! You, whom otherwise I would have loved so greatly! I can see you! I can divine your riddle! I recognize your soul, there are your eyes—you offer it to me, *and I cannot take it from you!*"

The young woman hid her face in her hands.

"At least," answered Félicien in a whisper, with weeping eyes, "at least I can kiss yours in the breath of your lips!—Understand me! Let yourself live! You are so beautiful!—The very silence of our love will make it more ineffable, more sublime; my passion will be magnified by the sum of your griefs, of all our melancholy!—Come, dearest of women, my wedded one for all time, come, live with me; we shall live—together!"

She gazed on him, her eyes likewise bathed in tears, and laid a hand on the arm that encircled her.

"You yourself will declare that it is impossible!" she said. "Listen again. I wish, at this moment, to achieve the full revelation to you of my thought . . . for you will never hear me further . . . and I do not wish to be forgotten."

She spoke slowly, and walking with her head leaning upon the young man's shoulder.

"Live together, you say! You forget that after the first rhapsodies, life takes on a character of intimacy in which the need of expressing oneself exactly becomes inevitable. It is a sacred moment! And it is the cruel moment when those who have wedded inattentive to their words meet with irreparable punishment for the small value they have placed on the quality of the real sense, the unique sense, in fact, which these words were given by those who uttered them. 'No more illusions!' they say to themselves, thinking thus to mask beneath a trivial smile the painful contempt which in reality they feel for their kind of love—and the despair which they feel of confessing it to themselves.

"For they refuse to see that they have not possessed what they desired to possess! It is impossible for them to believe that—apart from Thought, which transfigures all things—everything on earth is only *Illusion*; and that every passion accepted and conceived in sensuality alone soon becomes more bitter than death to those who have given themselves up to it.—Look yourself at the faces of passers-by, and you will see whether I am in error!—But ourselves, to-morrow! When this moment arrives! I should have your look, but I should not have your voice! I should have your smile . . . but not your words! And I feel that your words cannot be just like other men's . . . !

"Your mind, in all its primitive simplicity, must express itself with a living directness that one could hardly reach beyond. Surely it is so? Every shade of feeling within you, then, can be betrayed only in the very music of your speech! I should feel enough that you are filled, and filled altogether, with my image. But there is a form which you give to my being in your thoughts, a manner wherein I am conceived by you, which can be made manifest only by a few chance words each day: it is a form with no precise outlines, and, aided by those same divine words, it remains nebulous and tends to cast itself into the Light, to melt into it and pass into that infinity which we hold within our hearts. And this form, this sole reality, in fact, I shall never come to know . . . ! Nay, that ineffable music which lies hid in the voice of a lover, that murmur with its unimaginable rising and falling, the music that wraps us round and casts pallor over us—all that, I should be doomed never to hear . . . ! Ah, the man who wrote on the first page of a sublime symphony the words: 'Thus does Fate knock upon the door!' had known the voices of the instruments before the day when he was stricken with the same affliction as myself!‡

"As he wrote them, he remembered! But I, how am I to remember the voice in which you have just told me for the first time that you love me?"

As he listened to these words, a gloom had fallen over the young man: and what he felt now was—terror.

"Oh!" he cried. "You are opening gulfs of woe and anger in my heart! I have one foot on the threshold of paradise, and I must needs shut upon myself the door of all

---

‡ The reference is to Beethoven and his Fifth Symphony.

joy! Are you the supreme temptress—at last? It seems as if I could see shining in your eyes a kind of pride, in having brought me thus to despair!"

"As you please! I am the woman who will never forget you!" she answered. "How is one to forget words felt and never heard?"

"Alas, alas! You slay at your pleasure all the youthful hope I had placed in you! And yet, if you are with me while my life lasts, we can vanquish the future together! Let us love with greater courage! Let yourself come."

With an unexpected feminine movement, she linked her lips with his in the darkness, gently, for several seconds. And then she went on with a kind of weariness.

"I tell you, my friend, it is impossible. There are hours of melancholy when, vexed by my infirmity, you would seek for occasions to take heed of it still more keenly! You would never be able to forget that I cannot hear . . . nor to forgive me that, I assure you! By irresistible fate, you would be driven on to the point of *no longer speaking to me*, of no longer uttering a syllable in my company! Your lips alone would say to me, 'I love you,' without one vibration of your voice troubling the silence. You would come in the end to the point of writing to me, and that would be painful. No, it is impossible! I shall not profane my life for only a moiety of Love! I am a virgin, but I am the widow of a dream, and I wish to remain unappeased. I tell you, I cannot take your soul in exchange for mine. And yet—you were the one destined to hold my being in your keeping . . . ! And for that self-same reason it is my duty to carry off my body from you. I bear it away! It is my prison! Ah, that I could be delivered from it, and soon! I do not wish to know your name . . . *I do not wish to read it* . . . ! Farewell! Farewell!"

A few paces away, at the corner of the Rue de Grammont, gleamed carriage-lamps vaguely. Félicien had recognized the lackey of the staircase of the Italians, when, at a sign from the young woman, a footman lowered the carriage step.

She left hold of Félicien's arm, shook free like a bird, and stepped into the carriage. An instant later, all had disappeared.

The Count de la Vierge set off next morning to return to his solitary château of Blanchelande—and had not been heard of again.

He could surely boast of having met, forthwith, a woman of sincerity, a woman *with the courage of her opinions.*

Chickamauga

Ambrose Bierce
USA, 1891

One sunny autumn afternoon a child strayed away from its rude home in a small field and entered a forest unobserved. It was happy in a new sense of freedom from control, happy in the opportunity of exploration and adventure; for this child's spirit, in bodies of its ancestors, had for thousands of years been trained to memorable feats of discovery and conquest—victories in battles whose critical moments were centuries, whose victors' camps were cities of hewn stone. From the cradle of its race it had conquered its way through two continents and passing a great sea had penetrated a third, there to be born to war and dominion as a heritage.

The child was a boy aged about six years, the son of a poor planter. In his younger manhood the father had been a soldier, had fought against naked savages and followed the flag of his country into the capital of a civilized race to the far South. In the peaceful life of a planter the warrior-fire survived; once kindled, it is never extinguished. The man loved military books and pictures and the boy had understood enough to make himself a wooden sword, though even the eye of his father would hardly have known it for what it was. This weapon he now bore bravely, as became the son of an heroic race, and pausing now and again in the sunny space of the forest assumed, with some exaggeration, the postures of aggression and defense that he had been taught by the engraver's art. Made reckless by the ease with which he overcame invisible foes attempting to stay his advance, he committed the common enough military error of pushing the pursuit to a dangerous extreme, until he found himself upon the margin of a wide but shallow brook, whose rapid waters barred his direct advance against the flying foe that had crossed with illogical ease. But the intrepid victor was not to be baffled; the spirit of the race which had passed the great sea burned unconquerable in that small breast and would not be denied. Finding a place where some boulders in the bed of the stream lay but a step or a leap apart, he made his way across and fell again upon the rear-guard of his imaginary foe, putting all to the sword.

Now that the battle had been won, prudence required that he withdraw to his base of operations. Alas; like many a mightier conqueror, and like one, the mightiest, he could not

> curb the lust for war,
> Nor learn that tempted Fate will leave the loftiest star.

Advancing from the bank of the creek he suddenly found himself confronted with a new and more formidable enemy: in the path that he was following, sat, bolt upright, with ears erect and paws suspended before it, a rabbit! With a startled cry the child turned and fled, he knew not in what direction, calling with inarticulate cries for his mother, weeping, stumbling, his tender skin cruelly torn by brambles, his little heart beating hard with terror—breathless, blind with tears—lost in the forest! Then, for more than an hour, he wandered with erring feet through the tangled undergrowth, till at last, overcome by fatigue, he lay down in a narrow space between two rocks, within a few yards of the stream and still grasping his toy sword, no longer a weapon but a companion, sobbed himself to sleep. The wood birds sang merrily above his head; the squirrels, whisking their bravery of tail, ran barking from tree to tree, unconscious of the pity of it, and somewhere far away was a strange, muffed thunder, as if the partridges were drumming in celebration of nature's victory over the son of her immemorial enslavers. And back at the little plantation, where white men and black were hastily searching the fields and hedges in alarm, a mother's heart was breaking for her missing child.

Hours passed, and then the little sleeper rose to his feet. The chill of the evening was in his limbs, the fear of the gloom in his heart. But he had rested, and he no longer wept. With some blind instinct which impelled to action he struggled through the undergrowth about him and came to a more open ground—on his right the brook, to the left a gentle acclivity studded with infrequent trees; over all, the gathering gloom of twilight. A thin, ghostly mist rose along the water. It frightened and repelled him; instead of recrossing, in the direction whence he had come, he turned his back upon it, and went forward toward the dark inclosing wood. Suddenly he saw before him a strange moving object which he took to be some large animal—a dog, a pig—he could not name it; perhaps it was a bear. He had seen pictures of bears, but knew of nothing to their discredit and had vaguely wished to meet one. But something in form or movement of this object—something in the awkwardness of its approach—told him that it was not a bear, and curiosity was stayed by fear. He stood still and as it came slowly on gained courage every moment, for he saw that at least it had not the long menacing ears of the rabbit. Possibly his impressionable mind was half conscious of something familiar in its shambling, awkward gait. Before it had approached near enough to resolve his doubts he saw that it was followed by another and another. To right and to left were many more; the whole open space about him was alive with them—all moving toward the brook.

They were men. They crept upon their hands and knees. They used their hands only, dragging their legs. They used their knees only, their arms hanging idle at their sides. They strove to rise to their feet, but fell prone in the attempt. They did nothing naturally, and nothing alike, save only to advance foot by foot in the same direction. Singly, in pairs and in little groups, they came on through the gloom, some halting now and again while others crept slowly past them, then resuming their movement. They came by dozens and by hundreds; as far on either hand as one could see in the deepening gloom they extended and the black wood behind them appeared to be inexhaustible. The very ground seemed in motion toward the creek. Occasionally one who had paused did not again go on, but lay motionless. He was dead. Some, pausing, made strange gestures with their hands, erected their arms and lowered them again, clasped their heads; spread their palms upward, as men are sometimes seen to do in public prayer.

Not all of this did the child note; it is what would have been noted by an elder observer; he saw little but that these were men, yet crept like babes. Being men, they were not terrible, though unfamiliarly clad. He moved among them freely, going from one to another and peering into their faces with childish curiosity. All their faces were singularly white and many were streaked and gouted* with red. Something in this—something too, perhaps, in their grotesque attitudes and movements—reminded him of the painted clown whom he had seen last summer in the circus, and he laughed as he watched them. But on and ever on they crept, these maimed and bleeding men, as heedless as he of the dramatic contrast between his laughter and their own ghastly gravity. To him it was a merry spectacle. He had seen his father's negroes creep upon their hands and knees for his amusement—had ridden them so, "making believe" they were his horses. He now approached one of these crawling figures from behind and with an agile movement mounted it astride. The man sank upon his breast, recovered, flung the small boy fiercely to the ground as an unbroken colt might have done, then turned upon him a face that lacked a lower jaw—from the upper teeth to the throat was a great red gap fringed with hanging shreds of flesh and splinters of bone. The unnatural prominence of nose, the absence of chin, the fierce eyes, gave this man the appearance of a great bird of prey crimsoned in throat and breast by the blood of its quarry. The man rose to his knees, the child to his feet. The man shook his fist at the child; the child, terrified at last, ran to a tree near by, got upon the farther side of it and took a more serious view of the situation. And so the clumsy multitude dragged itself slowly and painfully along in hideous pantomime—moved forward down the slope like a swarm of great black beetles, with never a sound of going— in silence profound, absolute.

Instead of darkening, the haunted landscape began to brighten. Through the belt of trees beyond the brook shone a strange red light, the trunks and branches of the trees making a black lacework against it. It struck the creeping figures and gave them monstrous shadows, which caricatured their movements on the lit grass. It fell upon their faces, touching their whiteness with a ruddy tinge,

---

* spotted

accentuating the stains with which so many of them were freaked and maculated. It sparkled on buttons and bits of metal in their clothing. Instinctively the child turned toward the growing splendor and moved down the slope with his horrible companions; in a few moments had passed the foremost of the throng—not much of a feat, considering his advantages. He placed himself in the lead, his wooden sword still in hand, and solemnly directed the march, conforming his pace to theirs and occasionally turning as if to see that his forces did not straggle. Surely such a leader never before had such a following.

Scattered about upon the ground now slowly narrowing by the encroachment of this awful march to water, were certain articles to which, in the leader's mind, were coupled no significant associations: an occasional blanket tightly rolled lengthwise, doubled and the ends bound together with a string; a heavy knapsack here, and there a broken rifle—such things, in short, as are found in the rear of retreating troops, the "spoor" of men flying from their hunters. Everywhere near the creek, which here had a margin of lowland, the earth was trodden into mud by the feet of men and horses. An observer of better experience in the use of his eyes would have noticed that these footprints pointed in both directions; the ground had been twice passed over—in advance and in retreat. A few hours before, these desperate, stricken men, with their more fortunate and now distant comrades, had penetrated the forest in thousands. Their successive battalions, breaking into swarms and reforming in lines, had passed the child on every side—had almost trodden on him as he slept. The rustle and murmur of their march had not awakened him. Almost within a stone's throw of where he lay they had fought a battle; but all unheard by him were the roar of the musketry, the shock of the cannon, "the thunder of the captains and the shouting." He had slept through it all, grasping his little wooden sword with perhaps a tighter clutch in unconscious sympathy with his martial environment, but as heedless of the grandeur of the struggle as the dead who had died to make the glory.

The fire beyond the belt of woods on the farther side of the creek, reflected to earth from the canopy of its own smoke, was now suffusing the whole landscape. It transformed the sinuous line of mist to the vapor of gold. The water gleamed with dashes of red, and red, too, were many of the stones protruding above the surface. But that was blood; the less desperately wounded had stained them in crossing. On them, too, the child now crossed with eager steps; he was going to the fire. As he stood upon the farther bank he turned about to look at the companions of his march. The advance was arriving at the creek. The stronger had already drawn themselves to the brink and plunged their faces into the flood. Three or four who lay without motion appeared to have no heads. At this the child's eyes expanded with wonder; even his hospitable understanding could not accept a phenomenon implying such vitality as that. After slaking their thirst these men had not had the strength to back away from the water, nor to keep their heads above it. They were drowned. In rear of these, the open spaces of the forest showed the leader as many formless figures of his grim command as at first; but not nearly so many were in motion. He waved his cap for their encouragement and smilingly pointed with his weapon in the direction of the guiding light—a pillar of fire to this strange exodus.

Confident of the fidelity of his forces, he now entered the belt of woods, passed through it easily in the red illumination, climbed a fence, ran across a field, turning now and again to coquet with his responsive shadow, and so approached the blazing ruin of a dwelling. Desolation everywhere! In all the wide glare not a living thing was visible. He cared nothing for that; the spectacle pleased, and he danced with glee in imitation of the wavering flames. He ran about, collecting fuel, but every object that he found was too heavy for him to cast in from the distance to which the heat limited his approach. In despair he flung in his sword—a surrender to the superior forces of nature. His military career was at an end.

Shifting his position, his eyes fell upon some outbuildings which had an oddly familiar appearance, as if he had dreamed of them. He stood considering them with wonder, when suddenly the entire plantation, with its inclosing forest, seemed to turn as if upon a pivot. His little world swung half around; the points of the compass were reversed. He recognized the blazing building as his own home!

For a moment he stood stupefied by the power of the revelation, then ran with stumbling feet, making a half-circuit of the ruin. There, conspicuous in the light of the conflagration, lay the dead body of a woman—the white face turned upward, the hands thrown out and clutched full of grass, the clothing deranged, the long dark hair in tangles and full of clotted blood. The greater part of the forehead was torn away, and from the jagged hole the brain protruded, overflowing the temple, a frothy mass of gray, crowned with clusters of crimson bubbles—the work of a shell.

The child moved his little hands, making wild, uncertain gestures. He uttered a series of inarticulate and indescribable cries—something between the chattering of an ape and the gobbling of a turkey—a startling, soulless, unholy sound, the language of a devil. The child was a deaf mute.

Then he stood motionless, with quivering lips, looking down upon the wreck.

Clavis

Annie Trumbull Slosson
USA, 1896

Perhaps the child's mother might have found it out sooner than I did if she had lived. I cannot tell. I know she could not have loved the little one more tenderly, watched her more closely. From the hour when I took the child into my arms, out of whose clasp the mother had just slipped away quietly and forever, the little girl was all the world to me.

There was a strange and wonderful sympathy between us two. She understood me always when no one else could, and she told me so. That this comprehension was not gained through the ear, expressed by the tongue, I did not for a long time notice. We lived so quietly, you see, far away from the busy world, in the very heart of nature, among trees and hills and streams, with birds and flowers and wild free things, and we did not talk much. When I held her close to my heart and we looked upon the shining river, up to the purple hills, into the rosy clouds, or over the dark, deep forest, there was no need of words. And when there came the rushing sound of the wind among the trees, the music of the brook whose white waters ran over the stones, the glad song of the bobolink, or the tender strain of the thrush, I looked into her deep, still eyes and felt that we were both listening, and that we both heard.

We had no neighbors, few friends, and for a long time there was no one to tell me of anything the child lacked or missed. But there came a time when it was said that my little child did not hear, that her ears were sealed to all sound, and that she would never speak to me.

I do not remember that even then it was a great grief to hear this. Even then, when she was so small, so young, I felt that, silent and deaf to others though she might be, yet she understood me well, and could tell me so. I do not know how this was; I cannot explain it. I know only that I, who had failed hitherto to make my meaning clear to those around me, found comprehension, full understanding, perfect sympathy, in my little silent child.

I had always been a shy, awkward, reticent man. A strange, sad, loveless boyhood, a youth of struggle unrewarded, privation unpitied, longing for affection unsatisfied, had made me this. And now, just when I had ceased to expect it, there came to me all I had needed, craved, despaired of so long. There had always been a strange thing in my life which no one understood or cared for. From my earliest years there had been a constant wonder in my mind, a strange, eager questioning about the meaning of things. I did not care for the answers men give to such questions—for the explanations found in learned books or the wisdom taught in schools. All my life long I had known that there was one key to all the mysteries of which this world is so full, but that no man had ever found it.

I had felt sure that if any one could learn the meaning of just one simple thing in the woods, or on the hills, or among the flowers or birds, he would understand everything; there would be no more puzzles, nothing hidden or unexplained, and from my boyhood I had striven, thirsted, to find that key. Many, many times I had seemed to almost grasp it. Some sight, some sound, some faint elusive odor, would give a hint, a suggestion, and quick, sudden as the flight of a darting bird, the truth I had sought so long would flash before me and was gone. There were so many things to wonder at even in the simple life which my little girl and I lived, and we were always wondering.

Perhaps to you there are no mysteries in the wild flowers. They are so simple, so fair, seen at a glance, passed by, or gathered and thrown aside. But to us there were such strange puzzles there. In the spring, when the little linnæa crept over the ground and lifted its pink bells on slender, hair-like stems, there came to us from it always the same fragrance, a subtle perfume we could not define. We were sure no other blossom, no other thing on earth, held that odor; and yet it brought us memories, was linked with something we could not recall; it was full of association, but with what? Where had we ever before breathed that aroma of spice, of sweetness, that it should bring us that strange feeling—half sadness, half joy, a memory so like a hope?

And the colors of the flowers—they surely held a meaning if we could but catch it. The speedwell's gentle blue, the bear-plum's pale yellow, the buttercup's polished gold, the aster's lavender and mauve and purple, the cardinal-flower's vivid red, the crimson pink of the wild rose—we knew them all, and almost understood them. One touch, one word, to help us, and the whole world of color would fall into harmony. I think my little girl understood these flower tints better than I did; perhaps because she did not hear or speak as others hear and speak her eyes saw more than most, and she would hold a brightly tinted blossom and gaze into its blue or pink or yellow with such deep content in her strange eyes that I felt she was learning much of the meaning it held.

But she did not know all. One summer she had been day after day among the cardinal-flowers by the brook. She had bent over them and touched them, drinking in the warmth and glow of their brilliant red till she seemed to comprehend all, and to know why these flowers alone held such living fire. But one hot August noon when she was among them, watching them burn to more vivid crimson under the sun's fierce heat, she found, among the others, a stalk of pure white blossoms. There were cardinal-flowers, too, but pale and cold. She led me to the place and showed me the delicate, snowy flowers, with a look on her face half sad, half frightened, and very wistful. I could not help her. How could it be? What was the meaning? It was the warmth, the glow, the depth and vividness, which made the other blossoms cardinal-flowers. But here was one which lacked all these qualities, and was like snow, not fire. Never again did my child tell me that she knew the meaning of the cardinal-flower.

And there was a certain plant which always grew in the forest, under the pines, and bore one large rose-colored blossom, just one solitary pouchlike flower upon each slender stalk, always alone, always by itself; we knew it by its oneness, its being single and solitary. One day we found among the rest a plant just the same but that its slender stalk bore two twin blossoms, and they were white, not pink.

But I think there was no puzzle among the flowers so hard to solve as that of the closed gentian. No one could help wondering over that. Why, if it is never to unfold, if no sunshine or dew or soft warm air can ever open its fast-closed petals—why should it be so fair within? For we had looked inside, gently opening the dark purple-blue, budlike blossom. It was quite finished within, tinted and veined, satin-smooth, as dainty and complete as any of its sisters who open their eyes to the light and air. We could find no secret there, no reason for the shutup, lonely life, and while I thought and queried and surmised I could see the wonder grow and deepen in my little voiceless child's tender eyes of darkest blue. But no one helped us; nothing told us the meaning of it all.

The birds made us wonder too. We could not understand their songs, though each had its meaning; we were sure of that. For she heard them too. Sealed as her ears might be, she felt the notes in some strange unexplained way, and I read them over again in her eyes. The clear, sweet, far-reaching, whistle of the white-throat sparrow, the soft, gentle whisper of the waxwing, the swamp-sparrow's trill, the plaintive cry of the wood-pewee, the glad, free strain of the bobolink, the gurgle and croon of the cuckoo—we knew them all. But why did each bring such a different thought? There was one small bird whose color was like that of the dark pine-trees where he sang, and his strain was almost like human speech, always the same—just a few appealing words, then silence. Up on the hill above the lake the winter-wren sang. There were so many different meanings in his song, bright and sad and tender. We smiled as we heard it, but the tears were very near our eyes. And in early morning and in the twilight the veery always rang his silver bells. Over and over again they rang and vibrated, till our hearts ached with the sweetness and mystery of it. Why did the bird sing that strain and never any other? And what did it mean?

And there was the hermit-thrush. I have said that there were many things which seemed at times about to give us the light we sought. But of all these the song of the hermit-thrush most often brought us such glimpses. In the evening twilight of a June day, when all nature seemed resting in quiet, the liquid, melting, lingering notes of the solitary bird would steal out upon the air and move us strangely. What was the feeling it awoke in our hearts? Was it sorrow or joy, fear or hope, memory or expectation? And while we listened, my little quiet girl and I, suddenly we would turn with quick, eager looks and read in each other's eyes the same thought. The meaning of it all—it was coming; we should know; it was trembling in the air, and in an instant it would reach us. Then it faded, it was gone, and we could not even remember what it had been.

The name of my child was Clavis. When I had first looked into her deep, earnest eyes of violet-blue there had arisen in my heart a strange hope that through this little girl I might find the meaning, the key, I had sought so long, and in that hope I gave her this name. As the years went by hope became expectation, expectation foreknowledge, and I knew that sooner or later my silent child would bring me the truth.

I do not know just how it came about, but many people learned of this strange questioning of ours. I sought no knowledge, no help, in the matter from others, even from the most learned men. For I had read their books, and I knew they themselves had never found the key. But they came to me from far and near, and each one brought his own explanation, his own theory or creed. I will own that sometimes— for they were very learned men—their words half satisfied me, and for a moment I felt that I had grasped the clue I sought. But always, always when I turned and met the quiet eyes of my child, I saw in their dark-blue depths the certainty that I had but touched the surface of things, and that far, far below lay the truth I was seeking.

There was a strange thing about these meetings. However earnest and enthusiastic the man might be who came to expound his own belief and teach us the meaning of things, I always saw a change come over him before he went away. For when he looked into my child's quiet eyes, so deep so full of hidden meaning, his own eyes were troubled, his looks confused; his voice lost its self-confident ring; his words came more slowly and with hesitation, and sometimes ceased utterly. Such a one would sometimes tell us before he went away that perhaps, after all, he had not discovered the real meaning of things: perhaps the key was yet to be sought and found.

So the months and years went by, and more and more often came to us both those faint brief glimpses of a great satisfying truth, of one single simple key which should unlock all our mysteries. There were mountains about our home, and strange things happened upon those hills. Sometimes when the summer sun lay hot and bright upon them we saw shadows upon their peaks and sides. Some were shadows of clouds which floated above them; these we saw and recognized. But there were other shadows there, strange, unfamiliar things, like nothing in the sky, like nothing on the earth, wonderful shapes and full of meaning. As I clasped my little Clavis's hand tightly and we gazed eagerly, tremblingly, upon those dark rolling shades cast there by something we could not see, of which we knew nothing, we felt the whole truth very near. There is a wonderful light that comes sometimes at evening upon those hills, creeping from base to summit, changing from pink to purple, from purple to blood-red, till all is fire and glow and glory, and every time it came it flashed a quick, fleeting hint of what we sought. And never, never did the hermit-thrush chant his silver, melting, throbbing, ringing strain without our seeming to hold for one short, vanishing instant the key to all things. If it could but sing always, we thought, or even a little longer, we should know all.

The learned men, the great scholars, thinkers, writers, came more often to us. I do not remember how it happened that at last these many great men agreed to assemble together at our home—my little girl's and mine—and listen to what we should say to them. They knew well, for we had told them so, that we had never yet found the one password, the true solution, the right key to all the strange things about us. But I think they wished to be convinced that any one key would open all, that there was but one solution to all problems, one answer to all riddles, as I believed, and as Clavis knew. And I talked to them. It was early June and in the evening twilight, and we were out-of-doors. It seems strange to me, as it doubtless does to you, that so many great men came together there to listen to one unsatis-fied, questioning man and one little, silent, expectant girl. But they came, and under the shadow of the mighty hills they gathered there, and I stood in their midst, with Clavis at my side. I cannot tell you what we said to them: because of all that came afterwards, if forget much. I know that we spoke of the strange mysteries about us even there in that quiet spot, among the dark pines and under the shadow of the mountains. Then I told them, and Clavis said it over and over again in that silent way I cannot make you comprehend, that we felt sure that there was one single clue to all these riddles, if we could but find it. The secret of the flower that never opens, like a bud, an undeveloped, immature, unfinished thing to outward seeming, but a fair, complete blossom within; the meaning of the purple light that comes upon the hills at evening; the suggestion in the perfume of the linnæa; the memories—or hopes—awakened by the thrush's song; the black shadows on the sunny mountain-side, cast there by something far above, which our eyes cannot see; the frost-white cardinal-flower springing up among its glowing sisters; the large pink blossom in the forest, whose very nature and property seems to be that it should be solitary on its slender stem, yet bearing sometimes fair twin flowers—all these things, and many more which made us wonder and question now, would lie open, plain, and simple before us could we touch the key we sought. We told them how near it some-times came to us—how a perfume, a sight, a sound, a touch, seemed so close to bringing the clue. And I saw, and my little girl's eyes shone with a glad but still light as she saw it too, that one after another remembered how such moments, such glimpses, had come to him, and how brief, how sweet, how fleeting, they had been. While I talked the breeze that always comes down at sunset from the cool moun-tains sprang up, and as it reached me it brought that strange, elusive odor of spice, of sweetness, from the pink bells of the linnæa growing thickly among the pine-trees, and for one brief, sudden instant I remembered or foresaw its meaning. Then, like the faint, evanescent perfume itself, the thought was gone, and I could not recall or tell it. I looked at Clavis. She too had read that meaning, but it had vanished; yet her deep eyes shone with a still, glad light, which said that it would surely come again, and we should keep it.

Now the wonderful light crept up the hills. It was golden at first, and turned the grass and the tree trunks yellow and russet, then it changed the leaves overhead to orange and then flushed and reddened as it crept up the hillsides, crimsoning the lower peaks, and still rising, rising, till, as it touched the top of the highest, grandest mountain, it made its rugged, rocky summit as red as blood. Suddenly all my being was flooded with a quick, glowing flame which showed me all we were seeking. For the instant I knew it; I could tell it to the people. But before my slow tongue could form the words the color upon the hilltops faded, the flush died away, and I had forgotten. I turned an almost hopeless, despairing look upon my little girl. She was very still, as always. But upon her soft cheek lingered the flush of rose which had left the sky, and in her quiet eyes there shone an almost triumphant light which spoke of victory very near. They saw it too, and clustered close together and around us, while over all came that hush which seems to throb with expectancy and thrill with anticipation.

Up in a lofty pine above our heads a little lonely bird uttered his simple strain— a few appealing, wistful notes, then silence. Then a veery rang his silver bells. Over and again they rang and vibrated, till our hearts ached with the sweetness and mystery of it.

Then from the hillside across the river a hermit-thrush began to sing. Everything besides was very still, and the air throbbed and trembled, pulsated and quivered with that wonderful strain. And I knew all: I held the key. A moment of suspense, of waiting, fearing lest it vanish as had died into silence the bird's song, then I looked into my child's eyes. Yes, she knew it too. I read it over again in the dark depths of her eyes, and the strange, sweet mysterious smile that lingered about her silent lips.

Then I spoke. For the first time in all the ages was told the secret of things. I held the key, and I showed it to them all. I cannot tell you of that hour, the wonder, the exultation, the glad surprise; no words could make you comprehend. It was my voice that spoke, but it was at Clavis that they looked, and from her stillness they gathered more than from my spoken words.

Then hands clasped hands, eyes gazed into each other, lips quivered, cheeks were wet with tears. They knew all now, and it was all so simple, learned in one brief second. How had we missed it so long, sought it so vainly? How could there have been any key but this, now ours forever? No, I say again, I cannot tell you of it. In all time there never was an hour like that. Will ever such a one come again?

Darkness came on, the breeze from the mountains grew chill, and we must separate. On the morrow we would meet again, and then decide how this great news might be told to the world. When all had gone, and my little girl and I were left alone, I took her to my heart, and we talked in our strange, silent way of what had come to us. I was full of a solemn, awed wonder, but she felt no surprise, only a still joy that what she had known was coming, should be here now. I had thought that the excitement and wonder would banish sleep from my eyes, but I slept long and dreamlessly. I awoke to dark skies, thick clouds, and a chill air. By degrees I remembered. I thought of the assembly of the night before, of the questioning looks, the earnest faces upturned to mine, of the purple light, the linnæa's fragrance, the lonesome bird in the pine-tree, then the hermit-thrush's song. I saw the glad, the solemn, exulting faces, recalled the joy, the peace, the wonder of those to whom the key was shown. But—what was that key? For an instant I had lost it as in the old days. But it would return; never could such a blessed thing as came to me that fair June evening and stayed so long—never in life could it be forgotten, lost. I was but half awake; I was yet dazed with sleep; I would go out into the morning air, look up at the hills, and remember all. But I could not grasp it; it just escaped each time I sought to seize it. Like the vanishing perfume of a flower, the fading light upon the hills, a bird's faint, dying song, it drifted from me.

But I was not afraid. So many knew it now, it could not be lost. While I stood in the raw chill air of the dark morning, one of the learned men who had been with us the night before came to me. His face was a little troubled, but brightened as he saw me, and he spoke quickly, eagerly. He told me that in his sleep the clear outlines of that wonderful truth he had held the last night had become somewhat blurred, con-fused. Would I tell him again, now in the light of day, just what had brought such joy, such peace, when he first heard it? For the moment I could not tell him, and I said so. One after another came to us those who had listened and heard and rejoiced a few hours before, and all had the same troubled confusion. Was it so with all? Had we let sleep steal away that wonderful, priceless treasure? So it seemed; for all came, and all had forgotten. For a brief instant I was seized with a terrible fear. Then I smiled, and remembered there was no cause for alarm: Clavis knew all; Clavis never forgot, never lost anything she had once held fast. I went to her. She was asleep, her fair hair like sunshine about her head, the white lids shut down over her dark eyes. As I looked at her she awoke. I need not have been afraid. One glance into her still glad eyes showed me she had not forgotten. The key was not lost: Clavis knew all. She told me in her silent way, as I took her in my arms, that all was well: she held the key; we should all have it—we need not fear; she knew all, and we should soon know all likewise. She was very weary, she said, and would like to rest a little while— only a little while, and we should come to her and know all. It was almost like the hour in which I first held out the key when I went back to the fearful, trembling men and told them that my little child remembered. Not one doubted; all believed and were at peace. By and by I went to her again. She was asleep. The white lids lay over her dark, deep eyes, and hid their meaning. But the old, mysterious, all-know-ing smile rested about the silent lips, and I was not afraid. Nor am I afraid now. No, though she never wakened. Has she not given me the secret she held?

Under the Electrics: A Show-Lady Is Eloquent

Richard Dehan
England, 1915

"Really, my dear, I think the man has gone a bit too far. Writes a play with a fast young lady in the Profession for the heroine—and where he got his model from I can't imagine—and then writes to the papers to explain, accounting for her past being a bit off colour—*twiggez-vous?*—by saying she isn't a Chorus-lady, only a Show-lady.

"Gracious! I'm short of a bit of wig-paste, my pet complexion-colour No. 2. Any lady present got half a stick to lend? I want to look my special best to-night: *somebody in the stalls*, don'tcherknow! Chuck it over!—mind that bottle of Bass! I'm aware beer is bad for the liver, but such a nourishing tonic, isn't it? When I get back to the theatre, tired after a sixty-mile ride in somebody's 20 h.p. Gohard—*twiggez?*—a tumbler with a good head to it makes my dear old self again in a twink.

"Half-hour! That new call-boy must be spoke to on the quiet, dears. Such manners, putting his nasty little head right into the show-ladies' dressing-room when he calls. I suggest, girlies, that when we're all running down for the general entrance in the First Act—and that staircase on the prompt side is the narrowest I ever struck—I suggest that when we meet that little brute—he's always coming up to give the principals the last call—I suggest that each girl bumps his head against the wall as she goes by! That'll make twenty bumps, and do him lots of good, too!

"Miss de la Regy dear, I lent you my blue pencil last night. Hand it over, there's a good old sort, when you've given the customary languish to your eyes, love. What are you saying? Stage-Manager's order that we're not to grease-black our eyelashes so much, as some people say it looks fair hideous from the front? Tell him to consume his own smoke next time he's in a beast of a cooker. Why don't he tell *her* to mind her own business?—I'm sure she's old enough! What I say is, I've always been accustomed to put lots on mine, and I don't see myself altering my usual make-up at this time o' day. Do you? Not much?—I rather thought so. What else does he say?—he'll be obliged if we'll wear the chin-strap of our Hussar busbies down instead of tucked up inside 'em? What I say is—and I'm sure you'll agree with me, girls—that it's bad enough to have to wear a fur hat with a red bag hangin' over the top, without marking a young lady's face in an unbecoming way with a chin-strap. Also he insists—what price him?—he *insists* on our leavin' our Bridgehands down in the dressing-room, and not coming on the stage with 'em stuck in the fronts of our tunics, in defiance of the Army Regulations? Rot the Regulations, and bother the Stage-Manager! How *she* must have been nagging at him, mustn't she?—because he can be quite too frightfully nice and gentlemanly when he likes. I will speak up for him that much. Not that I ever was a special favourite—I keep myself to myself too much. Different to some people not so far off. *Twiggez?* I've my pride, that's what I say, if I am a Show-girl!

"Thirty-five shillings a week, with *matinées*—you can't say it's much to look like a lady on, can you now? No, but what a girl with taste and clever fingers, and a knack of getting what she wants at a remnant sale—and the things those forward creatures in black cashmere *Princesse* robes try to shove down a lady-customer's throat are generally the things she could buy elsewhere new for less money—not but that a girl with her head screwed on the right way can turn out in first-class style for less than some people would think, and get credit in *some quarters we know of*—this is a beastly, spiteful world, my dear—for taking presents right and left.

"Now who has been and hung my wig on the electric light? If the person considers that a practical joke, it shows—that's what I say!—it shows that she's descended from the lowest circles. I won't pretend I don't suspect who has been up to her little games again, and, though I should, *as a lady*, be sorry to behave otherwise, I must caution her, unless she wishes to find her military boots full of prepared chalk one o' these nights, to quit and chuck 'em.

"Quarter of an hour! That *was* clever of you, Miss Enderville dear, to shut that imp's head in the door before he could pop it back again. Well, there! if you haven't got another diamond ring! . . . Left at the stage-door office, addressed to you, by a perfect stranger, who hasn't even enclosed a line. . . . Perhaps you'll meet him in a better land, dear; he seems a lot too shy for this one. Not that I admire the three-speeds-forward sort of fellow, but there is such a thing as being too backward in coming up to the scratch—twig?

"I ought to know something about that, considering which my life was spoiled—never you mind how long ago, because dates are a rotten nuisance—by one of those hang-backers who want the young woman—the young lady, I should say—to make all the pace for both sides. It was during the three-hundred night run of— There! I've forgotten the name of the gay old show, but Miss de la Regy was in it with me—one of the Tall Eleven, weren't you, Miss de la Regy dear? And we were Anchovian Brigands in the First Act—Sardinian Brigands, did you say? I knew it had something to do with the beginning of a dinner at the Savoy—and Marie Antoinette gentlemen in powdered wigs and long, gold-headed canes in the Second, and in the Final Tableau British tars in pink silk fleshings, pale blue socks, and black pumps, and Union Jacks. I remember how I fancied myself in that costume, and how frightfully it fetched *him*.

"Me keeping my eyes very much to myself in those days, new to the Profession as I was, I didn't tumble to the fact of having made a regular conquest till a girl older than me twigged and gave me a hint—then I saw him sitting in the stalls, dear, if you'll believe me!—dash it! I've dropped my powder-puff in the water-jug!—with his mouth wide open—not a becoming thing, but a sign of true feeling.

"He was fair and pale and slim, with large blue eyes, and lovely linen, and a diamond stud in the shirt-front, and a gardenia in the button-hole was good form then, and the white waistcoats were twill. To-day his waistcoat would be heliotrope watered silk, and his shirt-front embroidered cambric, and if he showed more than an inch of platinum watch-chain, he'd be outcast for ever from his kind. Bless you! Men think as much of being in the fashion as we do, take my word for it, dear.

"He kept his mouth open, as I've said, all through the evening, only putting the knob of his stick into it sometimes—silver knobs were all the go then—and never took his eyes off me. 'You've made a victim, Daisy,' says one of the girls as we did a step off to the chorus, two by two, 'and don't you forget to make hay while the sun shines!' I thanked her to keep her advice to herself, and moved proudly away, but my heart was doing ragtime under my corsets, and no mistake about it. When we ran downstairs after the General Entrance and the Final Tableau, I took off as much make-up as I thought necessary, and dressed in a hurry, wishing I'd come to business in a more stylish get-up. And as I came out between the swing-leaves of the stage-door, I saw *him* outside in an overcoat with a sable collar, a crush hat, and a white muffler. Dark as the light was, he knew me, and I recognised him, his mouth being ajar, same as during the show, and his eyes being fixed in the same intense gaze, which I don't blush to own gave me a sensation like what you have when the shampooing young woman at the Turkish Baths stands you up in the corner of a room lined with hot tiles and fires cold water at you from the other end of it out of a rubber hose.

"'Well, have you found his name out yet, Daisy, old girl?' was the question in the dressing-room next night. I felt red-hot with good old-crusted shame, when I found out that it was generally known he'd followed me down Wellington Street to my 'bus—not a Vanguard, but a gee-gee-er in those days—and stood on the splashy kerb to see me get in, without offering an utterance—which I dare say if he had I should have shrieked for a policeman, me being young and shy. No, I'd no idea what his name was, nor nothing more than that he looked the complete swell, and was evidently a regular goner—*twiggez?*—on the personal charms of yours truly.

"If you'll believe me, there wasn't a line or a rosebud waiting for me at the stage-door next night, though he sat in the same stall and stared in the same marked way all through the evening. Perhaps he might for ever have remained anonymous, but that the girl who dressed on my left hand—quite a rattlingly good sort, but with a passion for eating pickled gherkins out of the bottle with a fork during the stage waits and intervals such as I've never seen equalled—that girl happened to know the man—middle-aged toff, with his head through his hair and a pane in his eye—who was in the stall next my conquest the night before. She applied the pump—*twiggez?*—and learned the name and title of one I shall always remember, even though things never came to nothing definite betwixt us—twig?

"He was a Viscount—sable and not musquash—the genuine article, not dyed or made up of inferior skins; blow on the hairs and hold it to the light, you will not see the fatally regular line that bears testimony to deception. Lord Polkstone, eldest son of the Earl of— Well, there, if I haven't been and forgotten his dadda's title! Rolling in money, and an only boy. It was less usual then than now for a peer to pick a life-partner among the Show-girls, but just to keep us bright and chirpy, the thing was occasionally done—twig? And there Lord Polkstone sat night after night, *matinée* after *matinée*, in the same place in the stalls, with his mouth open and his large blue eyes nailed upon the features of yours truly. Whenever I came out after the show, there he was waiting, but it went no farther. Pitying his bashfulness, I might—I don't say I would, but I *might*—have passed a ladylike remark upon the weather, and broken the ice that way. But every girl in my room—the Tall Eleven dressed in one together—every girl's unanimous advice was, 'Let him speak first, Daisy.' Then they'd simply split with laughing and have to wipe their eyes. Me, being young and unsophis— I forget how to spell the rest of that word, but it means jolly fresh and green—never suspected them of pulling my leg. I took their crocodileish advice, and waited for Lord Polkstone to speak. My dear, I've wondered since how it was I never suspected the truth! Weeks went by, and the affair had got no farther. Young and inexperienced as I was, I could see by his eye that his was no Sunday-to-Monday affection, but a real, lasting devotion of the washable kind. Knowing that, helped me to go on waiting, though I was dying to hear his voice. But he never spoke nor wrote, though several other people did, and, my attention being otherwise taken up, I treated those fellows with more than indifference.

"I remember the Commissionaire—an obliging person when not under the influence of whisky—telling me that what he called a rum party had left several bouquets at the stage-door—no name being on them, and without saying who for—which seemed uncommonly queer. Afterwards it flashed on me—but there! never mind!

"If I had ever said a word to that dear when his imploring eyes met mine, and lingered on the kerb when I heard his faithful footsteps following me to my 'bus, the mask would have fallen, dear, and the blooming mystery been brought to light. But it shows the kind of girl I was in those days, that the 'Good-evening' ready on the tip of my tongue, I shut my mouth and didn't say it. If I had, I might have been a Countess now, sitting in a turret and sewing tapestry, or walking about a large estate in a tailor-made gown, showing happy cottagers how to do dairy-work.

"That's my romance, dear—is there a drop of Bass left in that bottle? I've a thirst on me I wouldn't sell for four 'd.' Spite and malice on the part of some I shall not condescend to accuse, helplessness on his part—poor, devoted dear!—and igno-rance on mine, nipped it in the bud; and when he vanished from the stalls—didn't turn up at the stage-door—appearing in the Royal Box, one night I shall never forget, with two young girls in white and a dowager in a diamond fender, I knew he'd given up the chase, and with it all thoughts of poor little downy Me.

"We were singing a deadly lively chorus about being 'jolly, confoundedly jolly!' and I stood and sang and sniveled with the black running off my eyes. For even to my limited capacity, and without the sneering whispers of a treacherous snake-in-the-grass, whose waist I had to keep my arm round all the time, me playing boy to her girl, first couple proscenium right, next the Royal Box, where he sat with those three women—I could see how I'd lost the prize. One glance at Lord Polkstone—prattling away on his fingers to the best-looking of those two girls, neither of 'em being over and above what I should call passable—one glance revealed the truth.

"He was deaf and dumb!—and I had been waiting a week of Sundays for him to speak out first. Hugging my happy love and my innocent hope to my heart of hearts—there's an exercise in h's for any person whose weakness lies in the letter—I'd been waiting for what couldn't never come. Why hadn't he have wrote? That question I've often asked myself, and the answer is that none of them who could have told Lord Polkstone my name could understand the deaf and dumb alphabet.

"Oh! it was a piercing shock—a freezing blow I've never got over, dear, nor never shall. He married that girl in white, that artful thing who could understand his finger language and talk back.

"Think what a blessing I lost in a husband who could never contradict or shout at me. And I feel I could have been an honour to the Peerage, and worn a coronet like one born to it. I'll stand another Bass, dear, if you'll tell the dresser to fetch it; or will you have a brandy-and-Polly? You've hit it, dear, the girls were shocking spiteful, but I was jolly well a lot too retiring and shy. I've got over the weakness since, of course, and now I positively make a point of speaking if one of 'em seems quite unusually hangbacky.

"'Who knows,' I say to myself, 'perhaps he's deaf and dumb!'"

We Were Just Saying

Viola Meynell
England, 1924

When Laura Meryon left school and began life at home, she was not so much remarkable for the erudition which might have been expected from a young lady so fresh from her studies as for her charming behaviour to everyone. Her convent-schools, first in England and then abroad, had perhaps not initiated her into the more advanced branches of learning, but had certainly imparted a whole curriculum of considerate ways and gay, gentle behaviour. She made a curiously slight and yet sweet presence in the house—slight with the self-bestowed insignificance of one who is always making others important, and gay with the gaiety of children and nuns.

She listened to many things strange to her from her mother's lips. Gossip in regard to friends, servants, grievances, triumphs, elderly admirers—or rather, admirers whose taste was mature and choice—seemed somehow not quite for her convent ears, or at any rate not in that hard and rapid flow of her mother's style. But Laura was far too admiring and enthusiastic not to identify herself with these interests. She admired everyone. She was even unable not to find charm and glamour in the deaf cousin who had been living for the last year with her mother, and who now, with the advent of Laura, felt as if she had stepped part way out of her cavern of silence, so consistently did Laura address her in a way she could hear—and with that gaiety which rarely accompanied the grudging remarks meted out to Bertha Coombe. Laura indeed so obliterated people's drawbacks in her chivalrous and enthusiastic estimate of them, that it was as if they existed not; and she could not have admitted their defects even to herself without the greatest reluctance and embarrassment. Every act and inflection of hers denied that Bertha Coombe was deaf at all. Should she be alone with Bertha, and drop the poker with a clatter on the hearth, she would not omit to utter a quick, nervous apology, though neither it nor the noisy clatter could be heard by her cousin.

Soon after Laura's return from school, Mr. William Hewett came to lunch. An arrangement was being made between himself and Mrs. Meryon for the transference of Bertha Coombe from her household to his. It was a change ardently advocated by Mrs. Meryon. Now that her daughter was back from school, and she was no longer alone, there was no vestige of benefit to be derived from Bertha's presence; it was on the contrary an intolerable burden.

As Laura accompanied Mr. Hewett to the front door upon his departure, he wished it was she that he was to take into his household, the leaven a family life that somehow had none of the charm she seemed to disseminate. Lost in the contemplation of that happy face framed in dark curls, he fumbled lengthily with his preparations at the door, his hand passing without recognition several times over the familiar handle of his stick as he groped for it in the stand.

"And how do you like leaving school?" he asked. "Not very sorry, I'll be bound."

"Oh yes, I was dreadfully sorry to leave," said Laura, "but—oh, it's so lovely to be at home!"

"Yes. So now a new chapter begins, and it'll be nothing but dances and theatres and bouquets and boxes of chocolates," said Mr. Hewett. "I don't think you're going to have a very dull time, young lady, by the look of you."

"Well, I hope not," she confessed, her eyes shining with pleasure.

"Ah! And I seem to hear the sound of wedding-bells in the near distance," said Mr. Hewett, pretending to listen.

"Oh no!" she cried bashfully, and scolding him in a way he found delightful. "You don't hear them at all!—Or if you did hear them it would be in the very farthest distance!"

"Ah, I see. You mean to break a few hearts first. Well, enjoy your young life while you can, my dear," he pressed her,—as if he would thus be relieved of some regrets on his own account. "Now's the time for pleasure, while you're young. No troubles or cares for you now—they all come later on." He found it extraordinarily pleasant to dwell on the thought of this young life without cares or disappointments, a charming gay young life, with nothing but enjoyment for its lot. "Get all you can out of it, my dear," he adjured her. "We don't have so very long to live, you know. And we'll be a long time dead."

He went out into the cold street, his heart still warmed by the air of happy service with which she had helped him on with his coat, and by the bright vision she afforded of a sorrow-free existence. And Laura went back to the drawing-room with so light a heart that she almost danced down the passage, to think that she was at a time of her life immune from care, that nothing but joy was the portion of her youth, and that she would need to be as old as Mr. Hewett before she really knew what it was to be susceptible to pain and grief.

Entering the drawing-room, she saw her mother, who rarely read, had in the few minutes since the visitor left become deeply absorbed in a book; which she held close before her face. Bertha Coombe sat on the other side of the fireplace. She looked thirty-four or five, and had at the moment an alert air of willingness to respond to any form of social overture that might be made to her, or as if at the slightest opportunity she would make one herself. Her chained *pince-nez* were very prominent in her unremarkable face, and as she was deaf and not blind one thought of them vaguely as attached rather to her hearing than to her sight.

Mrs. Meryon's intense absorption in her book was relaxed as soon as Laura came and sat between her and the deaf woman. Laura felt a strange misgiving as she saw her mother abandon her pretence of reading. It was nearly three o'clock, and Bertha Coombe habitually took a walk at three. It was somehow to be hoped most urgently that the burst of conversation which was imminent from Mrs. Meyron would be postponed till then.

Surely Bertha would not stay at home on account of the threatening weather. Most likely, she would at any rate prepare to go out, not noticing what black clouds were spreading up from the north and how they threatened hail and sleet shortly. But Bertha Coombe, as it happened, was just in a mood of almost sprightly observation of everything. She did not even have to go to the window to discover the dull inclemency of the weather; she realised it with alert vivacity from her chair by the fire, and three o'clock came and went and she did not stir.

Mrs. Meyron began to speak.

"We've really got rid of her, it seems," she said, her eyes on her book, as if she was still reading.

"Oh, Mother! Hush!"

"Why hush?" Mrs. Meyron asked, almost startled by the intensity of Laura's tone.

"Because—because she's so close," said Laura in a whisper, as she bent her head.

"Now, Laura, you know perfectly well the foolishness of what you're saying," said her mother, in a deliberately distinct voice. "Now that you're growing up why do you behave like a child? You know as well as I do that as far as hearing is concerned, it's as if Bertha was sitting not in that chair there but as far away as Timbuctoo." She stopped, but merely for one of those full little pauses that did not even suggest that she had finished. "What I mind when you say a thing like that is not so much the utter foolishness of it as the suggestion that I would be willing to inflict pain. I should have thought you would know that the last thing I am capable of is to risk hurting anyone's feelings. And considering that there's no question of that, I don't think it's very nice of you to accuse me of it."

"Oh no, mother! I know, of course, and yet—oh please, *please*, mother—."

She gave one glance at Bertha, who caught her eye with an expectant look, thinking she was about to be spoken to. But Laura could only fail her and bend her head in embarrassment. She suddenly found herself in acute misery and discomfort. Where was the immunity of youth that had sped so gaily down the passage with her but a few moments ago? Here already, without any visible change, without anything seeming to have happened, it had deserted her.

"You've had none of the trouble of Bertha," said Mrs. Meryon, "so you can afford to indulge in those fanciful ideas. No one knows how heavily the weight of making these arrangements has fallen on me, and so I think I might be allowed to be pleased at having really managed to get rid of her. It went off very well. Mr. Hewett had already said he was willing to have her, provided he liked her after a meeting. And the relationship is quite as close on his side as on ours; so as I've done my duty for a year it's time he did his."

"Oh hush! She's so close. She may not hear, but she's so close, she's touching me!" Laura implored her mother beneath her voice.

Bertha Coombe sat slightly forward in her chair, not exactly smiling, but exceedingly ready to smile. Deprived of her walk, she was prepared to take her distraction in the form of a little delightful conversation. The idlest comment— how delightful would it be to her, like good news to another! A little confidence about the housekeeping, any remark on the neighbour's affairs, any little bit of information about the visitor who had just gone, an exclamation about the weather, she was ready to hear, and would answer just exactly in the way that would best agree with the speaker's views. Surely the pleasure of being so entirely agreed with would compensate anyone for the trouble of having to speak loud. It was not unreasonable to hope that a little conversation might now take place, and be even a pleasure all round.

She could not honestly expect somehow that the desired opening would be made by Mrs. Meryon. But Laura might at any moment begin a conversation. And not only did she find little things to say on her own account, but she reported the remarks of others, a great boon, suddenly letting in light on darkness as she bent close, and not too close, and said in her clear young voice:

"We were just saying . . ." She was the chief sound that life had.

The door was opened by a maid.

"Mrs. Edwards," she announced, and the visitor came and sat among them, while Mrs. Meryon greedily welcomed her. Bertha Coombe leaned a little more forward in her chair with a look of gratified participation in the arrival of the visitor and of anything that might ensue.

"I've just been remarking," said Mrs. Meryon, after a little talk, "on the fact that we're going to be entirely relieved of the presence of a certain person sitting on your right. She's going."

"Who! Oh, I see what you mean. But—she can't hear?" Mrs. Edwards asked nervously.

"Not a word."

"You're sure?"

"Sure? Yes, I think I ought to know how deaf she is—I've had ample opportunity of knowing. My lady has seen to it, indeed, that I shouldn't make any mistake. This that I am going to tell you is only one little detail of all the trying things I've had to endure from her for a year. In my efforts to make her hear I've sometimes shouted myself ill almost, and she's drawn back as if I hurt her, and said that I didn't need to shout so loud. So I've not only not had to speak too low, if you please, but not too loud either. I've been supposed to know exactly the pitch of voice required.

You'd think that to be spoken to at all they'd take as a favour. That's only one little thing;—I do assure you that altogether it's been a martyrdom."

As they spoke, Bertha Coombe turned slightly from one to the other, with an invitation that was yet purged of all claim.

"I never realised she was so difficult," said Mrs. Edwards.

"No, no one has realised it," sighed Mrs. Meryon, "and certainly not Bertha herself. You'd think they'd be a little diffident, to make up for the trouble they give;—but no. For instance, her appetite. She eats as much as anyone making full use of their faculties. I have never grudged anyone anything in my life, but one can't help observing. Laura may think I exaggerate, but as she has only just come home she can't know very much about it. The other day, before Laura came, the cook happened to send up three pieces of chicken in the little casserole at luncheon, and when Bertha and I had each had one I offered her the last piece. She took it. I'm not complaining,—I didn't mind in the least . . ."

"Impossible! Surely she didn't know there was no more!"

"She made no attempt to know! As I say, I didn't mind, I didn't want it in the least; I'm entirely indifferent to such things. But I thought it curious."

The feeling revived in the relation of this incident made a very pronounced expression on Mrs. Meryon's face, and Mrs. Edwards showed a corresponding degree of shocked incredulity, which made Bertha Coombe watch them with pleasurable eagerness, thinking that something of such an arresting affair was bound to reach her.

"She has one great disadvantage which weights on one's mind too," continued Mrs. Meryon, encouraged by her friend's sympathy; "but it's something she knows nothing about, so one naturally doesn't expect any consideration from her on that account. It's something very painful in her history that she's never been told, something that's supposed not to be talked about in case it should ever get round to her, but it wouldn't matter your knowing."

"You don't mean it!" said Mrs. Edwards, hardly able to refrain from a long curious examination of Bertha in this new aspect—as if it were possible to look, as well as speak, with impunity. But, remembering otherwise, she managed to keep her eyes away from Bertha, and to fix them on Mrs. Meryon in expectation of the revelation she was about to hear.

"Oh, if something would stop her!—if something would stop her before she says another word! Oh mother, take care, take care!" Laura cried inwardly, pressing her hands together in a misery of apprehension.

"It's one of the most horrible stories," said Mrs. Meryon. "I was really quite afraid to have her here, in case the sight of her should perpetually remind me of it. Her mother practically killed her father."

"Killed! Do you mean it? And she doesn't know! Oh, but take care then!" whispered Mrs. Edwards, her scruples aroused once more.

"It's quite all right, she can't hear a word. I'll tell you the whole story—"

"Here? Now?" asked Mrs. Edwards, still half-uneasy.

"Why not? We're talking about the *soufflé* we had at lunch, or about my new costume, for all she knows. Or—look! I'm showing you something highly interesting in my book," she said, unable to repress a smile at her idea. She leaned over, and with great over-emphasis pretended to be showing her friend something in the book that was still in her hand.

"Well," she resumed, "Bertha was a child away at school when it happened. Her mother was deaf—as deaf as she is. She had become so gradually. Just as Bertha has done. The father was my cousin, and a most charming man. Being very good-looking and popular, you can imagine what a drag on him his wife must have become, especially as she was madly devoted to him. They lived in a tiny old-fashioned house in Chelsea. Their maid fell ill and went to hospital; and Leslie, my cousin, so as to be out of the way of the discomfort and upset, was to go and stay for a few days with some friends. On the day he was to go, his wife suddenly found him disappeared. She thought he had gone without saying good-bye, as he sometimes did after a quarrel, and she admitted there had been a scene that morning. But do you know what had happened really?"

"Mother! Stop!" implored Laura silently.

Bertha made a little hopeful movement. Such entranced glances!—surely this must be something she would be told. But however urgent and important it might seem, she must not ask—she had learnt that. People never liked it. Something was interesting them, rushing through their minds at its own pace, and they never liked it if everything had to be stopped and brought to a standstill while they communicated it to her. The only hope was to discover later, though how rarely this succeeded!—For people were generally unable to recall what they had been speaking of, even though it had looked on their faces at the time almost as if it must be a matter of life and death to them.

"What happened really," Mrs. Meryon went on, "was that just as he was ready to go, my cousin went to fetch a bottle of his special wine to take with him. It was kept in a large, dark closet that led out of the sitting-room down two or three steps. While he was there the door must have blown shut and, as it slammed, the outside bolt fell and he was fastened in.

"All that day, and the days that followed, his wife was sitting in that room, eating, reading, amusing herself, while a few yards away from her he was shouting and knocking and struggling for his life. He must have heard every movement of hers, just the other side of the door, but however much he might shout she just calmly went on with what she was doing, and let the husband she was supposed to love call and shout to her to save his life!"

"You mean she couldn't hear!" her friend broke in.

"Not a sound! Only you'd think some instinct might have told her, considering he was only two or three feet away from her. Later, when he was missed, a search was made and he was found, but he died of exhaustion as they picked him up. When his wife knew what she had done, she got into such a state that no one could do anything for her. She couldn't get over it. The thought of it must have haunted her day and night. She hardly spoke, and she never seemed more than half alive after that. I used to see her sometimes, but she died a few years later. Her closest relations decided that Bertha should never be told what had happened. She was growing deaf herself, and they thought it might prey on her mind. They may have decided rightly,—I don't know."

Bertha Coombe looked from one to the other in her docile, inevitable patience. No, she must not interrupt and ask them—it did not do. And yet could she not ask Laura? With one who was so willing and responsive it was different, it was possible. Laura had a way of seeming even pleased to be put to some little trouble. As unnoticeably as possible, Bertha spoke to her:

"What is it they are saying? Something very interesting, I know! I couldn't quite hear. What are they talking about, dear?"

"We were just saying," began Laura, bending down with her usual smiling readiness, "we were just saying . . ."

The Wife of the Deaf Man

Gianna Manzini
Italy, 1929
Translated by Corinna del Greco Lobner

The night has forgotten Giulia denying the mercy of sleep—that last refuge from shame—to her tired flesh reviled by pleasure. Fully awake by now, she lifts herself up in bed and waves her arms as if their whiteness could be sufficient to dispel the surrounding darkness. A crack in the window shutters spins a malicious innuendo on the hypocritical surface of a mirror, ready and alert.

She feels alone because Vittorio, her lover, has preceded her in sleep. Sliding again under the covers she thinks it is enough to press the eyelids with her fingers to join him, but the pupils only multiply the brightness of the mirror pierced by the street light.

She stretches next to her lover, trying to imitate the abandon that must make the members of his body as heavy as an object imbued with darkness; she even tries to synchronize her breath with the slow rhythm that makes his shoulders rise.

"Why don't we say good-bye when we fall asleep?" she asks herself thinking, for the first time, of sleep as betrayal. Actually Vittorio has his back turned as a sign of enmity, but she only senses her own solitude controlled by the mirror forgotten, like her, by the night.

Something reverberates in the pillow by her ear: a rarefied beat; then the beat becomes increasingly stifled, almost felt like a drop of water falling on the carpet. Giulia thinks it is slowly spreading gaining an opaque resonance as if marking the cadence of a step: it's him, the deaf man, the abandoned husband. Now she recognizes the direction of that step. He walks in his slippers at the foot of the bed, between the bed and the door. He stops for a moment in front of the door as if waiting.

He always stopped perplexed in front of closed doors, and, when sitting down, he was careful not to have a door behind his shoulder. In the living room, where the doors opened to three rooms, he placed the chair to view all three exits and sometimes (he always refused to say why) he purposely got up to look behind them.

The woman, her head barely above the pillow and her mouth covered by the sheet, sees him. She recognizes the eyes slightly protruding where the determination to understand and an obstinate diffidence have become frozen. Now he looks at his own slippers—it was Giulia who embroidered them in silk and silver—and raises his eyelids only in front of the door as if waiting for the handle to move. When he comes back he seems to be listening even with the nape of his neck as if his hair was concentrating on a whisper, on the air stirred by a motion: even his contracted shoulders convey a sense of anxiety.

The clock sounds the hour.

Giulia no longer hears him walk. He has stopped perhaps finding again, as he always does, the smile he has when he asks: "do you hear?" as the bells of Palazzo Vecchio sound the hour. Sometimes, the question precedes the first toll but only for a few seconds, and, if the wife perplexed and listening closely shakes her head in denial, he feels hurt and blushes . . . "Ah, why could not I nod the way he likes me to do, monitoring the sound of the hours and allowing him to repeat the gesture with approval?"

She bites the sheet not to scream, then, her head covered to the tip of the forehead, she turns brusquely to the man who is sleeping next to her and winds her arm around his neck. Close to her mouth, Vittorio continues to exhale the breath of a life held at a distance.

Now she realizes that falling asleep next to him does not mean to reach him: to sleep together only means to get lost in the same time slot.

⤚

One evening, as if sharing a mischievous confidence, her husband told her: "I hear the time." And since Giulia looked at him at a loss, the deaf man for the first time attempted an explanation: "Humanity seems cheated by clocks. It would be at peace if the day started fifteen minutes later. Looking out of the window one immediately discovers that people always run to save a few minutes. Time and I, instead, are like two friends keeping up the same step."

In seven years of marriage this had been his longest speech delivered in the monotone of someone who no longer distinguishes the sound of words spoken only to benefit others. He speaks the name of his woman as if to include himself and enunciates it as if he could savor the flavor, enjoying it with sparkling pupils.

Giulia feels she has discovered her own name now that she has tried to repeat it the way the deaf man does.

Vittorio has turned toward her. There is a moment of suspense close to the awakening when he seems to recognize her. The silence, no longer dominated by his breathing, widens in that pause of anxiety, it overflows as if it had been contained till then by that rhythm. The room seems immense. Giulia stiffens and closes her eyes as if to hide herself: she wants to escape her lover now that she understands how the deaf man must have suffered each time he has tried to say something about himself. During those tentative confidences a state of sudden inebriation made him seem almost handsome in spite of his lifeless, opaque complexion condemned to endure a bulky, lifeless flesh seemingly bloated as if it were a new manifestation of deafness. He seems constantly concerned to show an invisible listener that he is attentive and understands everything, a fiction that leads him to the comic cowardice of a perennial assent.

He was never able to close his eyes while she kissed him. Afterward he looked at her mouth for a long time seeking the trace of the word he would not hear.

Giulia discovers these things for the first time.

"Yet, I have never said anything he could not have heard," she says, seeking the shape of words with her lips and engaging all her face in an effort to imprint their meaning in the shadow, as if the shadow was the deafness of the room. "He looked at my mouth as if he wanted to extract an offense from it at any cost, she whispers with false resentment, sure as she is of having been disarmingly candid in the eye of the deaf man, year after year. She tries to escape remorse vainly trying to justify herself; her rationalization, instead, only makes her imitate her husband by motioning with the eyebrows to help the conversation along.

She wants to find him again in every moment of his day, to recognize herself near him. Here he is, in his most relaxed moments behind the newspaper, in a blessed state of wonder. He unfolds it marveling at the huge size that obliges him to stretch out his arm to keep it open. "Is it possible that so many things have happened in the world today? Just think: silence is full of adventures that newspapers never report!" The question is in the smile with which he shows his wife the pages full of news. And every little while he points out something with his finger and forces her to put down her crochet to read and comment afterward by exchanging glances.

That was their conversation of every evening.

By abandoning him she had rejected the consummate art of speaking or being silent, a skill she had mastered in seven years. Yet, it was almost an instinct of self-preservation that brought her in the arms of a lover.

One day she saw herself only as the wife of the deaf man. They had told her that her mouth was becoming arid as if drained of moisture; actually she had learned how to keep it slightly parted, attentive, in the guise of her husband. Her voice pitched to a single tonality resembled his voice; her smile, fixed and icy, seemed superimposed on her lips like the smile the deaf man adopted, anxious as he was to convey the impression that he understood everything even when no one spoke to him. Her flesh had acquired the white texture of paper, as if the color of blood was the color of joy.

Giulia thinks that her image, shaped by time during seven years of life with the deaf man, is by now reflected in every mirror, even the mirror that keeps her malignant company in the sleepy room as she endures the shade slit, like the transparent eyelid, by the luminous line.

In the lucid state of insomnia her thoughts become ratified. Silence widens its hold, even on her spirit. She listens the way the deaf man listens in front of the closed door. She only hears the breathing of her lover—the breathing of a life held at a distance.

"Vittorio" she whispers in the tone of someone starting a prayer.

He covers his ear with the pillow.

Sleep seems to Giulia a deafness without suspicion—a deafness deprived of love.

A rooster struggles to let its shrieking, tenuous call break through the fog of a very lazy dawn. Then—must be the time when the dew glistens—its voice clears and its throat suddenly swells with breath as if determined to put out the last street lights. Now it hurls four notes each distanced by a pause, as if thoroughly convinced that the sky was a solid vault where the notes were bound to bounce back and forth. But Giulia only recognizes the desperation of a late warning and jumps from bed.

The night, then, is over. She feels readmitted to the dimension of time. She feels like rising intact, untouched by remorse.

She is surprised to find all her belongings without effort; she is almost glad recalling that even when her lover was undressing her, she had been unable to close her eyes.

She crosses the threshold without looking back.

The blue sky retains the memory of the night, and Giulia, in that blessed light of awakening, feels forgiven. She even finds useless to think what she will tell her husband.

Actually she feels she never left him, sure as she is to know, minute by minute, how he spent the night. Mentally she follows him step by step. At first seeing that she is not coming home, he has surmised that she has stayed by her father, but even while waiting for her, he has sat at the table at the usual time and has eaten, becoming aware of being alone only when his glass was empty and he had to fill it himself. At the sound of the hours, he lifted his eyes and, lacking the usual nod of assent, he would pull out his watch, always on time, as if he had really heard the sound of the bells. Later he had decided to go by his in-laws and, not finding his wife there, he had said nothing. Once back in his room, he started pacing back and forth, lifting his eyes in front of the closed door.

She has arrived home.

Not even now is she able to think what she will tell her husband. It is sufficient for her to be aware that she is the only one who knows how to speak with him.

She goes into the bedroom. The room is dark. She takes off her hat and throws the gloves and the purse on the dresser. It is enough for her to approach the bed that the deaf man opens his eyes, rubs them, yawns, and searches the night stand for his cup of coffee.

Not even the newspaper is there. "Is it possible that nothing has happened in the world tonight?" He knew that nothing could have happened anywhere because the stillness was like stagnant water under a sky of *papier maché*. And it seems to him that the universe is finally reconciled with the peace of deafness.

He smiles.

Dummy

Howard T. Hofsteater
USA, 1930

Out in her backyard, Miriam Martin was hanging up two pairs of cotton stockings on a clothesline that hung perilously close to the ground. The day was young, but in the coolness of early morning life in the Cumberlands was already busily astir. It was the season of fat opossums, ripe persimmons, and black walnuts. Daily for nearly two weeks, Miriam had watched thin V-formulations of wild geese honking their way south. The robins and blue jays had departed long since, and the sparrows were now arriving in great noisy numbers.

Miriam, too, was caught up in the wild urge to migrate to new lands. Assisted by her two sisters, more excited than she herself, and their mother, Miriam had been working feverishly the past few days at last-minute tasks, critically surveying freshly-ironed gingham dresses, putting them away with proud, possessive pats in a small, camel-backed trunk.

As she propped up the sagging clothesline with a forked stick, she saw a man climbing over the rail fence that zigzagged along the ridge overlooking the house. His familiar figure, clad in faded overalls and sweat-stained shirt, brought a sudden, unlooked-for stab of regret to Miriam. She would miss him terribly. She watched him come swiftly down the steep slope in the easy mountaineer fashion, bending his knees and scuffling when the descent became too sharp and precipitate. The next moment he was beside her, running his fingers through his light brown curls.

"Hello, Dummy," she said with the bright smile she always reserved for him.

He bobbed his head and smiled. Holding up two burlap sacks, splotched with walnut stains, he pointed to the hills behind him and, with crude signs, showed that he had found a big walnut tree. He wanted her to go nutting with him as they had done every year since they could remember. That they were now grown-up people never occurred to him. His keenest pleasure was going nutting with Miriam. Of all the young girls scattered over the neighboring hills, Miriam was the kindest and certainly the most attentive to him.

They were nearly of the same age, and, living on adjacent farms as they did, they had from their earliest days been playmates. With the ready inventiveness of children, they had hit upon natural signs as the only possible means of conversation. They discovered they could understand each other to a great extent if they imitated with their hands the characteristics of the things and motions they had in mind. Whenever one of them wanted to go nutting, for instance, he or she would point to the hills back of Miriam's house where there were many hickory and walnut trees and, making a circle with the fore-finger and thumb, imitate the process of filling sacks with nuts. Their eyes would brighten up and, with their parents' permission, off they would go. When Lige, Dummy's younger brother, became big enough to toddle along, he picked up the sign language evolved by the two older children, and in the years that followed, they were often to be found together, signing vigorously, making faces at each other and amusing themselves immensely.

When Dummy found himself in the company of other young people, he often felt himself left out. They could make, at best, only vague gestures, usually of direction, and they insisted upon amplifying their signs with unintelligible spoken words. Only Miriam and Lige were able to carry on animated conversation with him, and whenever he could he spent his time in the company of either one of them.

Dummy now looked eagerly at Miriam. She shook her head, pointing to the house and making whirling motions with her hands.

His face fell. He had counted upon her going nutting with him. For a week he had worked alongside of his father, Rary Horn, and Lige from daybreak to nightfall, harvesting their corn, which they succeeded in raising in straggling patches in the most impossible places on the hillsides. For some reason or other, unexplained to him, his father had decided to take the day off, notwithstanding the excellent weather prevailing. That had left Dummy free, and he had hurried down to get Miriam. And now she was busy.

Impatiently, he made a sign of dropping everything and urgently beckoned to her to go along with him. With a wide sweep of his arms, he tried to describe the size of the tree he had discovered.

But she shook her head firmly. With a smile that burst upon Dummy like the first ray of sunrise, she held up a finger for him to wait, ran inside, and returned breathlessly with a generous slice of apple pie. He grinned and sank his teeth into the pastry. They laughed merrily as he gustily disposed of it in as few mouthfuls as possible. He wiped his lips on his shirtsleeve and looked at her in his queer way, silently.

With a sigh and a pout, she told him she had to go inside and work. He nodded slowly and, with a disappointed look on his face, turned for home. She caught at his arm, and pointed to the sun as it would be in the early afternoon, making signs for him to return then. He brightened, nodded vigorously and began to climb the hill.

When the sun came upon the huddle of weather-stained houses that was his home, from which he had never been away in all his twenty-three years longer than two days at the most, he found his father sharpening a double-handled saw and Lige grinding the axes. That meant two or three months of back-breaking labor in the timberlands, hewing logs into railroad ties, which brought them a revenue of ten to fifteen dollars a day. Of that money, Dummy received as his share only cigarette money, to obtain which he had to go to his father. When Rary was drunk, Dummy had no trouble in getting it when he asked; otherwise, it all depended upon the good humor of the thin, hatchet-faced man. For Rary Horn's word was absolute law in his household.

About an hour before dinner, Dummy went into the kitchen and found his father holding a towel against a bleeding chin. Rary scowled at him, pointed to his downy lip and scraping his own face with a crooked finger, ordered him to shave the hair off. Dummy looked at his father with amazement. This fastidiousness of Rary's was unprecedented on weekdays, shaving being associated in Dummy's mind only with churches and Sundays. It could not be Sunday for they had gone to church only the day before last. However, he cleaned the family razor and winced as he drew it against his face. When he finished, Lige came in grumbling to himself. He, too, shaved. Dummy passed away the time before dinner in idle speculation as to what Rary's pride in the personal appearance of his family presaged.

Dinner was just another mess of cornbread, sorghum, string beans, okra, and buttermilk.

Miriam would have to wash dishes, so he decided not to hurry down to her place. He was rudely startled out of his thoughts by his father's pointing to his plate and motioning him to hurry up. He noticed that his mother and his two sisters had already finished and were clearing the table. They left the plates unwashed in a pan of hot water and disappeared in their room.

When they reappeared, dressed in their Sunday clothes and white stockings, Rary and Lige put on their Sunday coats and their best hats. Rary told Dummy to do likewise. A doubt began to form in his mind. He didn't want to go anywhere with them. He was going down to Miriam's. When the women had adjusted their black straw hats, Rary beckoned to him to accompany them. He shook his head and pointed first to himself and then in the direction of Miriam's house. His father nodded and replied that they were also going in that direction.

Dummy frowned. That made it an altogether different matter. He detested those full gatherings where the women talked endlessly, rocking back and forth on the porch, and the men draped themselves over the rail fences and talked except when they were chewing. Still, there was the possibility of sneaking off with Miriam to visit that big walnut tree. He ran around to the cowshed and rolled the sacks into a compact bundle and stuffed it into his overalls pocket. Joining the others, they moved down upon Miriam's in coated and tie-less elegance.

Early as they were, they were not the first to arrive. The Packens and the Longs were already there, and in the next twenty minutes three other neighboring families made their appearance. The women hurried into the house, and through the windows they could be seen bustling about mysteriously. Miriam was nowhere to be seen, and Dummy lingered disconsolately on the fringe of men lolling about in the yard.

A heavily mustached man in a long black coat rode up on his horse. Dummy recognized him as the official who presided at all the funerals in the immediate vicinity. For a fleeting moment, he entertained the alarming thought of a death in Miriam's family, but a glance at the beaming countenance of the circuit rider dispelled all his fears and he began wondering anew.

A buggy came jolting up the rough wagon trail which branched away from the road two miles below. At the reins was a young man dressed in unmistakable store clothes, a straw hat with a colored band, and a striped shirt over which spread a glowing orange tie. Dummy began to regret keenly having come down to this family gathering. For attentive as Miriam was, she never had any time for him beyond an occasional glance and most of her smiles were reserved for the young man as he drove up.

The young man drove around to the back and presently emerged self-consciously from the house. The men gathered around him, slapped him on the back, and poked him in the ribs, guffawing at every remark he made. Dummy looked away, disgusted by Orange Tie's popularity.

Old Man Martin came out on the porch and bawled something. Hurriedly disposing of their quids, the men went inside, shoving Orange Tie before them. Dummy followed on their heels and stood in a corner, looking over the heads of the others.

The circuit rider took his stand at one end of the room, holding an open book before him. Dummy was annoyed to see Orange Tie standing near the circuit rider, looking more self-conscious than before. There was a flutter of excitement as Miriam came demurely out of her room and moved toward the circuit rider. Dummy's eyes brightened at the sight of her. She was beautiful! Her cheeks were pink and white by turns. Regretfully, he saw that, with the white dress she had on, she could not go nutting with him that day. Well, if he wasn't working the next day, they could go and shake down all the nuts their sacks could hold. He swallowed a queer lump in his throat when he saw she was looking at no one save the young man beside the circuit rider. When she reached the end of the room, Orange Tie awkwardly took her hand in his and they faced the circuit rider who began to read aloud from the book.

Dummy looked on with distaste. What was this? Possibly a new game. But Miriam's mother and her sisters were wiping away from their cheeks tears that refused to stop running down. It was strange, all very strange, that she should look so happy and they so sad. He sympathized with the latter. He didn't like this holding hands either. His wandering eye was attracted by the circuit rider's Adam's-apple, which was jumping up and down in a most diverting manner. The minutes slipped by as he amused himself watching the Adam's-apple wiggle up and down.

Orange Tie pulled from his vest pocket a gold ring and put it on Miriam's finger. Dummy's face darkened. When his father got drunk again, he would get some money to buy her a ring. He remembered, when he was in town the last time, seeing in a store with a red front, large windows, and brass lettering, a tray full of rings with shiny bits of glass. One of those would look very nice on her finger. Much prettier than that plain dull-looking ring. Yes, he'd get her one. How pleased she would be! She would smile at him, more tenderly than she was smiling at that Orange Tie beside her.

Suddenly the game of holding hands was over, and the hillsmen pressed around Miriam and the young man. Orange Tie elbowed his way through and, followed close behind by Miriam, fled outside to the buggy. The men and women ran out after them, shouting and laughing. More amused and excited than puzzled, Dummy followed and threw a leg over the porch railing.

The young man slapped his horse's flank smartly with the reins. The buggy clattered down the hill and slewed around into the wagon trail. Everybody was waving his hand, and Miriam waved back at them.

Dummy started forward suddenly. What was that in the back of the buggy behind the seat? Miriam's little trunk! She must be—. From his throat burst an inarticulate cry, so poignant was it with the fear and pain that the smiles on the faces of the startled hillsmen vanished as though snuffed out like so many candles. He waved his hand wildly. For a moment his heart stood still. Would—would she hear? She turned in her seat and saw him. With her old smile, she blew him a kiss and waved her hand. The buggy disappeared around a turn of the road. Dummy stood motionless staring at the bend.

He turned and saw beside him his brother, Lige. With a sinking heart, he asked if Miriam were returning. Lige shook his head and made a decisive gesture of her having gone away for good. Dummy repeated Lige's gesture, fighting against a growing conviction. Lige nodded and added that she was going to live fifteen miles away.

Dummy gazed at the wagon trail now empty and desolate. He did not feel Lige's pat on the shoulder. Rary Horn came up and impatiently motioned to him to go home with the family. Dummy fell in behind and trudged on along with his thoughts. He stopped by a fallen log where he and Miriam had always stopped on their way back from their nutting expeditions before separating for home. He sat down on the log. There was a big bulge in his pocket. Pulling out the burlap sacks, he gently spread them across his knees.

An hour later he got up and went home. The sacks lay on the ground behind the log.

Portrait of a Shaman

Kim Tongni
Korea, 1936
Translated by Kim Yongchŏl

The *Portrait of a Shaman* was a sort of darkish india ink picture scroll representing a scene like this: a mountain crouching in back; a dark, wide river flowing in the foreground; pale stars hanging in the sky as if to shower down on the mountain ridge, on the fields and on the dark river; it is the witching hour. On the riverside sands a huge tent has been pitched, and in its shade are village women, sitting in thick clouds, all bewitched by a sorceress' incantation. Each of their faces is touched with a pathetic excitement and a fatigue that never betrays itself until the last hours of a vigil, toward daybreak. Gasping out her suppliant chant, the sorceress now turns round and round, gently waving the skirt of her robe as if she had been transmuted into a boneless spirit.

It was in the very year of my father's wedding, they say, that this scene was painted—a time long before I was born. I am of a family of old standing. My family won fame not only by its wealth and power but also as a busy salon for learned men. It was widely known across the country, especially for its rare collections of paintings, writings, and antiques. A dilettantish taste for them was part of the family tradition that was handed down, along with the family estate, from generation to generation.

It was during my father's generation that the fortunes of the family went to ruin, but even then my grandfather could afford, as of old, to entertain roving guests in the visitors' quarters, as poets and artists were always dropping in to stay with us.

It is said that on one of those good old days—just at dusk on a spring day when the wind, mixed with sandy dust, kept blowing all day long, and the apricot blossoms burst forth in the front yard—some odd-looking wayfarers came along and knocked at the front gate. A man of small build, looking about fifty, wearing a jacket and a mourner's bamboo hat, whose top was fastened round with a silk cloth, stood there holding a donkey by the reins; mounted on the donkey was a girl of about seventeen with a terribly pale complexion. The pair seemed to be a manservant with his master's daughter.

But the next day the man said, "This lass is my daughter. They say that she is a good hand at drawing, and that is why we have paid a visit to my lord's mansion."

The girl was dressed in white, and in her face, which was whiter than the white of the dress, there was visible a touch of deep sadness.

"What is your name, young lady?"

She made no answer.

"How old are you?"

Still no answer.

The host had addressed himself to the girl, but she merely cast a glance with her big eyes and never opened her mouth.

"My daughter's name," her father at last offering to speak for her, "is Nangi. She is seventeen years old." Then he went on in a lower voice, "She inclines to hardness of hearing."

The host nodded assent. Then turning to the man, he said that he and his daughter could stay at his house as long as they wished, and that he hoped to see the girl's good hand at drawing. It is said that the father and daughter stayed at our home for more than a month; they enjoyed their stay, sometimes drawing pictures, sometimes telling stories of old times in a movingly sad tone.

On the day they left, it is said, my grandfather provided the wretched father and daughter with valuable silks and sufficient traveling expenses. The poor girl mounted on the donkey, however, kept in her face the same note of deep sadness that had been perceived since her arrival.

The girl left the picture behind—my grandfather named it the *Portrait of a Shaman*—and from him I heard a story connected with it which runs as follows.

On the outskirts of Kyŏngju, more than four miles away from the town walls, there was a small village known as Yŏmin or Chapsŏng.

In a corner of this hamlet there lived a sorceress named Mohwa—so called because she had moved in from a place of that name. She lived in an antiquated, tile-roofed house with one of its upper corners already crushed out of shape. On the roof tiles mushrooms sprouted dark green, yielding a sickening smell of decay. A thin stone wall, crumbled here and there, meandered around the household like an ancient city wall. In the spacious yard surrounded by this stone wall, the rainwater stood stagnant, as the drain was clogged; the pool of water was covered all year round with dark green moss, and above it, standing entangled, was a mass of bulrushes, goosefoots, foxtails, and many other weeds, all taller than a man of average stature. Underneath this growth long serpentine earthworms wriggled, and aged frogs, as loathsome as toads, budged once in a while, awaiting the approach of night. The house was like a haunted den, long deserted by human inhabitants—deserted perhaps over scores of years.

In this old, crumbling house lived Mohwa the sorceress and her daughter Nangi. Nangi's father peddled seafood at a street corner in a town on the east coast, about twenty-five miles away from Kyŏngju. He was so fond of Nangi, as rumor had it, that he would appear every spring and autumn to bring her delicacies such as well-dried kelp and tidily bundled seaweed. Except for Ugi, Nangi's half-brother, who made a surprise visit to this house sometime later, the only persons calling upon the two female inhabitants of this ghostly den were those who came to ask Mohwa to perform an exorcism for them, and Nangi's father, who paid a routine visit to his daughter twice a year. Indeed, mother and daughter lead a desolate life, with little contact with the outside world.

Such being the case, anyone coming to ask Mohwa for an exorcism would meet nobody even after he found himself in front of the door and had called out several times, "Hello, are you at home, Mohwa? Hello, Mohwa!" Suspecting that the house was vacant, the visitor would then take the liberty of trying to open the door. Only then would a girl take the lead in opening the door from within, and would peep out without a word. The girl, of course, was none other than Nangi. Every time this kind of thing happened, she, who was usually drawing by herself, would become terrified at the intrusion and fling down her paint brush, trembling all over, her face turning deadly pale.

Mohwa too led a strange life. Not a day did she keep house as a good wife should. At dawn every day she walked to the town wall, but never returned home till sundown. Half tipsy, she would come waltzing along with handkerchief-wrapped peaches in hand, and chant a plaintive note as she entered the edge of the village.

> Dear girl, dear girl, dear girl of the Kims,
> Flower of the Region of Water, my dear girl Nangi.
> I entered the Dragon Palace and found
> The twelve gates all locked tight.
> Open the gates, open the gates,
> Please open the twelve gates.

Often she was greeted on the way by her neighbors, who said, "You've had a wet time again today, Mohwa!"

"Yes, yes. I've been to market," she answered, twisting her shoulders as if she were shy, and making a low bow to the speaker.

Mohwa was so fond of drinking, except when she was out for an exorcism, that she spent most of her day at wineshops. On the other hand, Nangi was partial to peaches, and so her mother, however tipsy, never returned home, at least during the summer season, without bringing some. Even when she was about to enter her house, Mohwa kept up a ritualistic tone, chanting, "Dear girl, dear girl, dear girl mine!"

Then Nangi would devour her mother's peaches, just as she had, when a child, habitually dashed in and nursed at the breast of her mother who was just returning home from an outing.

According to the sorceress, Nangi was the incarnation of the dragon god's twelfth daughter, Flower, for Mohwa gave birth to Nangi seven days after she had a dream in which she met the dragon god of the Realm of Water and was treated with a peach. The dragon god had twelve daughters, Mohwa said. The oldest was Moon, the second oldest Water, the third Cloud, and so on to Flower, the twelfth. It had been agreed that the twelve of them would be wedded to the twelve sons of the mountain god—that is, Moon to Sun, Water to Tree, Cloud to Wind, and the like. As they were being matched in the order of their ages, Flower, the youngest daughter, who was impatient by nature, could not wait for her turn, and intrigued with Bird, who was to be mated with Fruit, her eleventh sister. Fruit and Butterfly, now left with no proper spouses, wept in grief, and asked aid of the dragon and the mountain gods. The dragon god became furious; as retribution for Flower's offense he not only deprived her of her hearing but expelled her from the Realm of Water. Flower, now transformed into a peach blossom, indeed blooms pink in the springtime, along the riverside or at the foot of the mountain, but the legend goes that she remains even now helplessly deaf to the earnest calling of Bird from the bough.

At the wineshop, Mohwa would often scamper suddenly away from her glass of spirits or her elated dancing with shamans, as if beside herself. If asked what caused her to act so, she would say that Nangi, daughter of the dragon god, had been entrusted to her care only for a brief time. If she did not serve the girl well enough, she feared, she might incur the wrath of the dragon god.

Mohwa conceived not only of Nangi but also of any other being she met as the incarnation of a spirit, thus calling one a tree spirit and another a stone spirit. She often asked any acquaintance of hers to pray to the Great Bear or the Dragon King.

Every time she passed a human, Mohwa twisted her shoulders as if she were shy, and made a low bow to the passerby. Even on meeting a mere child, she stood in awe of the youngster, trembling all over. Often she played the coquette with a dog or a pig.

In her eyes, she said, every creature seemed like a spirit. Not only humans, but also pigs, cats, frogs, earthworms, fish, butterflies, persimmon trees, apricot trees, pokers, jars, stone steps, straw sandals, spines on jujube trees, swallows, clouds, winds, fire, bowls of rice, kites, gourd dippers, pouches, iron pots, spoons, oil lamps . . . all these she thought of as no different from her human neighbors, with whom she could exchange glances, calls, talk, and such feelings as hatred, jealousy, and anger. So she addressed them all with the designation of "dear".

Then one day, after an absence of ten years, Ugi returned home to stay. Since he had returned, the ghostly den had taken on signs of human habitation. Nangi, who had so disliked working in the kitchen, now often cooked meals for her brother. And at night, a glimmering paper lantern hung quietly from the eaves of this crumbling house, where in former days profound darkness under the starlight had been its constant nocturnal aspect.

Ugi was illegitimate, born to Mohwa while she was still living in Mohwa hamlet, and still free from the spell of a demon. As a child, Ugi proved so bright that his neighbors called him an infant prodigy; but the fact that he was of low origin denied him a chance to receive a normal education. At nine he was sent, through the good offices of a friend of his mother's, to a Buddhist temple as a novice, and since then they had heard nothing of him until he suddenly came home. To Nangi he was a beloved brother.

When she was five or six—before she lost her hearing from an illness—Nangi was very fond of Ugi, to whom she spoke endearingly. Soon after Ugi left for the temple, Nangi fell ill with a sickness which forced her to remain in bed exactly three years. When she was at last out of bed, she could no longer hear. But no one had any idea to what degree she was deaf. Once or twice she had asked her mother, though stammeringly:

"Ugi, Ugi, where is he?"

"He's gone to a temple to study, dear."

"Where? To what temple?"

"To Chirim Temple—the great big temple."

But that was a lie, as Mohwa herself did not know to what temple Ugi had gone. She gave a random answer merely because she did not want to disclose her own ignorance.

Now, when Mohwa first caught sight of Ugi on her return home, a flash of terror suddenly crossed her pallid face. For a moment she jiggled up and down and twisted her shoulders as if to beat a hasty retreat. Then suddenly she thrust out her two long arms from her tall, thin body and rushed to hug Ugi, like a huge bird embracing her chick.

"Whoever are you? Oh, my! It's my boy!" Mohwa cried out. "My boy! My boy! You're home at last!" Though her face was drenched with tears, Mohwa was ecstatic.

"Mother! Mother!" Ugi called out, and then he too dissolved into prolonged weeping, his cheek pressed against his mother's shoulder. Like his mother, the nineteen-year-old youth was slender-waisted and slim of neck. He did not seem like a man who had lived a solitary life, wandering from one temple to another; he looked dignified and handsome.

Now even Nangi seemed to recognize the young man as none other than Ugi. At first, when this strange youth opened the door of her room and found her there alone, Nangi was stunned and startled beyond speech—speech perhaps in gesture. Then, crouching in a corner of the room, she shuddered. But when she saw her mother in tears hugging Ugi and calling out "My boy! My boy!" Nangi felt that she too was melting into tears. (After witnessing that even her mother had such feelings, Nangi was thrown into indescribable ecstasies.)

It was not many days after his return home, however, that Ugi began to seem unaccountably enigmatic to Mohwa and Nangi. For whether sitting down to table, going to bed, or arising, he never failed to make a certain incantation, with his eyes closed and his lips moving. Once in a while, from his bosom he took out a tiny book and read it. When Nangi cast a doubtful glance at the book, Ugi opened it and said with a smile on his handsome face, "You should read this book, too."

Nangi could just manage to read any work written in the vernacular, and had read over and over a book called *The Life of Sim Chŏng*. As she took a closer look at the small book handed her by Ugi, she saw clearly inscribed on the front cover in large letters, *Sin Yak Chŏn Sŏ.** It was a name she had never heard of. Again she gave a puzzled look, to which Ugi responded with another smile, saying, "Do you know who brought man into being?"

To words, of course, Nangi was deaf; what's more, the question was too difficult for her to muse on, even if she had been able to make out Ugi's words from his gestures and facial expression.

"Then do you know what becomes of a man when he dies?"

She made no answer.

"This book is full of those kinds of questions, you know." So saying, Ugi repeatedly pointed his finger at heaven, but, after all that, Nangi succeeded in making out only one word—"God."

"It is God who created mankind," said Ugi. "He created men and all the other creatures in the universe. It is before God that we are all to be brought when we die."

Several days passed with conversations like this, and the concept of "God" as inspired by Ugi roused suspicion and revulsion in the mind of Mohwa. One morning he was about to pray at breakfast, when Mohwa demanded, "Was there such a thing in the Buddhist ways?"

Believing that Ugi had been in Buddhist temples over the past years, Mohwa was apparently convinced that whatever her son did had something to do with Buddhism.

"No, mother, I am not a Buddhist."

"If you repudiate the Buddhist creed, what other creed is there to follow?"

"I came to detest the Buddhist creed while at the temple, mother, and ran away."

"Detest the Buddhist creed, you say? Buddhism is a great doctrine, I know. Are you, then, a believer in Taoism?"

"No, mother. I am a believer in the Christian creed."

"The Christian creed?"

"Up in the northern provinces they call it Christianity. It is a newly introduced religion."

"Then you must be a Tonghak adherent!"[†]

---

* *The Complete New Testament.*—Trans.

[†] The Tonghak ("Eastern learning"), as opposed to Western learning, was a popular movement, emerging at the end of the nineteenth century. A composite of Confucianism, Buddhism, Taoism, and a belief in a heavenly father, its adherents sought to remedy administrative chaos and agrarian discontent and to combat the spread of Christianity at the time. Full-scale rebellion broke out in 1894, and when the government sought Chinese help, Japan sent soldiers into Korea. The presence of the two armies eventually led to the outbreak of the Sino-Japanese War.—Trans.

"No, mother. I am not a Tonghak member. I am a Christian."

"Well, then, in that creed of Christianity or the belief of what's-its-name, are you supposed to chant a spell at every meal with your eyes close?"

"You shouldn't call it a spell, mother. It is an act of prayer before God."

"Before God?" said Mohwa, opening her eyes in wonder.

"Yes, because it was God who created mankind."

"My dear, I am afraid you are possessed by a devil!" cried Mohwa, her face at once turning pale. Then no more did she care to ask him questions.

The next day Mohwa came home from a ceremony of "rice in water" to save a neighbor-client from evil spirits.

"Where have you been, mother?" Ugi asked.

"I have been at the Pak's to exorcise the devil there."

At this Ugi seemed to give thought to something for a few moments, and then he said, "With your rites, was the devil talked into going away?"

"He surely was," said Mohwa in a tone that brushed aside such an absurd question. "The fact that the man came alive is proof enough, isn't it?"

All around Kyŏngju she had performed hundreds of exorcisms and healed thousands of people of their illnesses, yet in none of those rites had she ever doubted, or worried about, the response of her divinity. Furthermore she had regarded the driving away of someone's devil with the "rice in water" ceremony as natural and simple an act as offering a bowl of water to a thirsty man. It was not merely Mohwa herself who was convinced of this; those who asked her for exorcisms and who were possessed by devils also felt the same way. If they became ill, they would consult Mohwa first instead of going to a doctor—the exorcism by Mohwa was far more responsive, effective, and handy.

Ugi was now brooding over something, with his head bent down. Raising his head, he said, "Mother, that means you are sinning against God." He stared into her face. "Look here, mother—chapter 9, verse 32 in the Gospel of Matthew: 'As the men were leaving, some people brought to Jesus a man who could not talk because he had a demon. As soon as the demon was driven out, the man started talking.'"

By then, however, Mohwa had left her seat and sat down before the altar that was ordinarily in a corner of the room. She began:

> "Divine spirit, divine spirit—
> On the four corners, between Heaven and Earth,
> Winged creatures are on the wings,
> Crawlers are on all fours.
> Their life short as hair's breadth,
> Fleeting as the dew on the grass,
> Thin as a fine thread,
> They make their way fair and square,

They make their way fair and square,
Nestled in the bosom of divine spirit.
In the all-embracing bosom of divine spirit.
You spurn impure hands, accept decent hands,
God of the house gives us lots to live on,
God of the kitchen gives us food to live on,
God of the mountain gives us life to live with.
Seven Stars enfold us, Maitreya guards us.
Though our life is thin as a fine thread,
We make our way fair and square,
We make our way fair and square."

All this while, Mohwa's eyes sparkled like gems; her back vibrated as if she were seized with a violent fit, and she constantly rubbed her hands together. As soon as her necromancy was over, she held up the bowl of water from the altar. Sipping water from the bowl, she suddenly spouted the liquid over Ugi's face and body. Then she cried out:

"Away, demon, go away!
This is the loftiest peak, Piru of Yŏngju,
The steep and rocky cliff,
The blue water fifty fathoms deep
Never is this a place for you.
Away, evil spirit, away at once,
With a sword in the right hand,
With a firebrand in the left,
Pshaw, pshaw!"

At first Ugi gazed bewilderedly at Mohwa; after a moment, he said a short prayer, bending his head down. Then he took to his feet and went away without saying a word. Even after Ugi left the room, Mohwa kept on with her necromancy for a while, spitting water into every corner of the room and chanting a spell.

Ugi was determined to call immediately on fellow Christians in the community. He was supposed to come home early that day, but he returned neither at sunset nor at midnight. Mohwa and Nangi squatted miserably in a corner of the room, expecting him at any moment.

"Don't you have there that book of the Jesus devil?" Mohwa said to Nangi after a period of waiting.

Nangi shook her head. But then, suddenly, even Nangi could not help regretting that she had not earlier cared to keep for her brother his *New Testament*, which

Mohwa was wont to label the "book of the Jesus devil." Mohwa seemed to regard Ugi as a man possessed by some evil spirit, just as Ugi took it for granted that both Mohwa and Nangi were victims of a demon. He was convinced that an evil spirit had taken possession of both women and that Mohwa's demon had caused the girl to become deaf and dumb.

"Didn't Jesus himself cure many of the possessed dumb in the early days?" Ugi thought to himself.

He was then determined to heal his mother and sister himself or through the power of earnest prayer, as he read the appropriate words in the Bible: "And when Jesus saw that a crowd came running together, he rebuked the unclean spirit, saying to it, 'You dumb and deaf spirit, I command you, come out of him, and never enter him again.' And after crying out and convulsing him terribly, it came out, and the boy was like a corpse; so that most of them said, 'He is dead.' But Jesus took him by the hand and lifted him up, and he arose. And when he had entered the house, his disciples asked him privately, 'Why could we not cast it out?' And he said to them, 'This kind cannot be driven out by anything but prayer.'" (Mark 9:25–29)

Ugi came to the conclusion that he would be able to drive the evil spirits out of his mother and sister only if he could offer earnest prayers to God.

In the meantime, he wrote to P'yongyang, to the Reverend Hyŏn, sponsor of his education during recent years, and to Elder Lee in the same city. In his first letter he wrote:

Dear Reverend Hyŏn,

By the grace of God I have come back safe to my mother's. In this community where the gospel of our Lord has not yet reached, I find a considerable number of people possessed by devils and worshipping idols. Having seen all this, I feel that we ought to have a church built so that we may spread the Lord's gospel in this community as soon as possible.

To my great shame, I must confess to you, Reverend Hyŏn, that my mother is possessed by witchery and my sister is affected by a deaf and dumb spirit. Following the words of our Lord, Jesus Christ, in the Gospel of Mark (9:29), I offer fervent prayers to God to drive those devils away. Because there is no church available here, however, it is very difficult to find a place where I can pray in a devout mood.

Kindly pray for us to God, Reverend Hyŏn, so that we may have a new church in this community at the earliest opportunity.

The Reverend Hyŏn was an American missionary. It was entirely through his help and assistance that Ugi had been able to earn his subsistence and education.

At fifteen Ugi had been in a Buddhist temple as an altar boy. In that summer he set out for Seoul on a visit, only to wander from one place to another until he went as far as P'yongyang in the fall of the following year. In P'yongyang he came to receive the Reverend Hyŏn's assistance, with good references from Elder Lee, in the winter of that year.

When Ugi had revealed in P'yongyang his plan to pay a visit to his mother, the Reverend Hyŏn called him in and said, "Within three years I plan to go back to my own country. If you wish to come with me at that time, I would be glad to take you with me."

"Thank you, sir," said Ugi. "To go to the United States with you is my constant wish."

"Then go at once and visit your mother."

Soon after his arrival, as we have seen however, Ugi discovered that his mother's home offered a world very different from that he had enjoyed in the homes of the Reverend Hyŏn and of Elder Lee. Having seen the desolate, crumbling stone wall, the ancient tile-roofed house with dark green mushrooms sprouting above its tiles, the frogs and earthworms wriggling among the tangled weeds, and the two females living in such surroundings—one possessed by a witching charm and the other by a deaf spirit—all this in contrast to the merry voices singing hymns, the church organ sounding great melodies, the voices reciting the Bible, the brethren saying prayers, the lively faces smiling over splendid meals—Ugi now could not help wondering whether he himself was trapped in a dreadful cavern haunted by a ghost.

Since his return from recent visits to fellow Christians in the community, a strange change had come over Nangi. Always slight of build, sheet white and glassy of complexion, with big, sparkling eyes, now she confined herself all day long in the corner of her room, saying not a word, smiling not at all, and merely gazing at Ugi's movements. But then, as night fell and the grayish paper lantern hanging from the eaves was lit, she walked out to the corner of the yard where bloodthirsty mosquitos sang angrily and flitted about in swarms. There she often hurled herself onto Ugi's shoulders or chest, her hands and lips as cold as ice. Ugi started with fright every time he felt the icy, abrupt touch of her hands and lips. But each time she appeared, shaking all over as if she were about to faint, he held her frantic hands and walked with her beneath the paper lantern.

As Nangi began to show these odd changes in behavior, so Ugi's complexion grew paler and paler. A fortnight elapsed in this strange way, until Ugi again left home without telling his destination.

On the second night after Ugi left, Mohwa sat up suddenly in bed and gave a long sigh. Shaking Nangi, who lay asleep, Mohwa said in a mournful tone: "How soon did Ugi say he would return?" Then seeing that her daughter would not give an answer, she said sullenly, "How come you haven't set dinner for him as I told you to?"

As days went by, Mohwa grew more and more impatient; night after night she kept lit the perilla-oil lamp in the kitchen and offered prayers before the dinner table set for Ugi by the fireplace.

"God of the house who is ours,
God of the Seven Stars who is ours,
God of the kitchen who is ours,
I implore you, divine spirits.
Stars are in heaven, pearls are in the sea.
My heir precious as gold and silver,
Scorpion glitters as a crown jewel—
By the decree of the god of the mountain,
By the ordinance of the Three Gods of Life,
By the blessing of the Seven Stars,
By the virtue of the Dragon King.
He is given food by the god of the kitchen,
He is given gifts by the god of the house—
Stars are in heaven, pearls are in the sea.
May the Three Gods and the god of the kitchen
Never decline to answer my summons.
Jesus devil, hungry fire devil of the Western Regions,
You are burning, fire devil is burning with flames,
In the ashes sits my star Scorpion
Like gold and silver,
Now it descends to seek the Three Gods,
Now it descends to seek the god of kitchen."

Mohwa fell on her knees, rubbing her palms together in worship. As soon as she got up she danced, moving about with all the airs and graces of a madwoman. Nangi peeped through the opening in the window from her room into the kitchen; for a long time she breathlessly watched her mother's wild movements, until she suddenly felt a chill creeping over her from head to foot. Then, in spite of herself, her teeth were chattering. Frantically she sprang to her feet and took off her blouse, then her skirt. Thus, mother and daughter became a perfect pair, one in the kitchen and the other in the bedroom, both dancing as if tuned to one single rhythm and cadence.

Next day early in the morning Nangi came to herself and discovered that she was lying naked on the floor.

Before long, Ugi showed up again before his mother and sister, with a smile on his face. When he came in, Mohwa was trying on new shoes for a trip to an exorcism. Seeing Ugi, she threw her long arms, bending forward from her slender waist.

Then she started to cry, hugging her son just like a huge mother bird would brood her chick. This time she did not rave, but gave only a whimpering cry, pressing her cheek against his for a long time. Her face, though usually purplish, was now tinged with a rosy color, and, judging from her natural gestures, she did not seem like a woman possessed by an evil spirit.

"I think I will rest in the bedroom, mother," said Ugi, as he broke loose from his mother's embrace and rose to his feet. He went into the room and lay down.

Even after Ugi had gone, Mohwa kept sitting all alone on the veranda. She looked terribly forlorn, her head dropping downward. But after a moment she stood up as if something had occurred to her and walked into the room, where she began to rummage among the many pictures done by Nangi.

That night, about midnight, Ugi awoke and groped, half asleep, for the Bible he habitually kept next to his chest, only to find the book missing. At that moment he heard a voice muttering an incantation. He sat up to search more closely in his bed for the Bible, but all in vain. But then he saw that his mother, who should have been lying between Nangi and himself, was gone. A shudder ran through his body, together with an ominous feeling that something disastrous was in the offing. At that instant he heard the voice, now more distinctly, that sounded as if it were coming from a ghost weeping underground. The next moment he pressed his eyes to the opening in the window looking into the kitchen.

Dressed in white and clad in her ceremonial robe, Mohwa was making all the erotic gestures, sometimes rubbing her hands together, sometimes kneeling down, sometimes dancing hilariously. Then she was heard crying:

> "O hungry fire devil of the Western Regions,
> A firebrand in one hand and a sword in the other,
> Hither you flee only to face the god of the mountain,
> Thither you flee only to face the Dragon King,
> You run around the Seven Stars lying in ambush,
> You plod along in the cloud,
> You run about buried by the wind,
> Here the cloud waits for you,
> There the wind waits for you.
> As you reach the Dragon Palace,
> All twelve gates are locked tight.
> You knock on the first gate;
> Four Deva kings rush out
> With glaring eyes and iron hammers brandishing.
> You knock on the second gate;
> Two pairs of Fire Dogs dash out.
> The male dogs gulp down the blazing fire,

The female dogs swallow the kindling coal.
You knock on the third gate;
Two pairs of Water Dogs dash out,
The male dogs blow out the sparks,
The female dogs blow out the kindling coals . . . "

Above the kitchen fireplace the lamp of pirella oil was lit in a tidily arranged dish, and upon a tiny table, set beneath the lamp, there was only a bowl of cold water and a dish of salt. Beside the table lay the thick front cover of the *New Testament*, emitting a plume of blue smoke just after the last blaze had flickered out. The cover was now turning into a heap of pale ashes.

A wry smile came over Mohwa's lips as if she were about to bid defiance to something. She picked up some salt from its dish, and as she sprinkled it over the ashes that now turned smokeless and black, she cried:

"There goes Jesus devil of the Western Regions,
Having obtained travel money from the shrine,
Having obtained shoes from the temple,
With bells dangling from his ears,
Keeping pace with the tinkle of the bells,
Over the hills, across the waters.
He will never dare return again
Because of the sore in the foot.
He will never return in the spring;
No, because of the hunger, no."

The sounds thus uttered by Mohwa, now reeking with the scent of satanic wine, seemed to penetrate Ugi's body from head to foot. After gazing at the erotic look in her gemlike eyes and at the hand gestures she made in time with her flowing skirt, Ugi felt so depressed that his heart seemed to bleed. As if to awaken from a nightmare, he heaved a long, heavy sigh and jumped to his feet. Before he knew it he ran out of the room and into the kitchen, kicking the door open. There he tried to pick up the bowl of water from the tiny table, but before he could do so he saw a kitchen knife flashing in Mohwa's hand. She was waving the knife between Ugi and the bowl of water as she quietly danced and cried:

"Away, devil, go away at once,
Hungry mean devil of the Western Regions.
This is the highest peak, Piru of Yŏngju,
With its rocky cliff and thorny ash trees,
With its blue water fifty fathoms deep,
This is no place for you to come.
With a sword in the right hand,

With a firebrand in the left,
Away, mean devil of the Western Regions,
Go away at once!"

At this instant Mohwa made a stab at Ugi's face with the kitchen knife. As soon as he felt the blade graze his left ear, Ugi turned under her arm, picked up the bowl of water, and hurled it at his mother's face.

While this commotion went on, the lamp was pushed against the paper window which caught fire instantly. Ugi stamped on the fire to keep the blaze from spreading into the room. As the water fell about her ears, Mohwa became furious, and then she too jumped on the fire, waving the knife to and fro, and closing in on her son. Ugi dropped into the spreading blaze in a desperate effort to check it; then he felt a tingling sensation somewhere in his back. As he was about to turn over sharply, he found he was bleeding, and fell into his mother's bosom. With her white teeth set hard, Mohwa's face was now set in a grin.

Ugi was injured in his head, neck, and back; but he was ailing of something more than just these three stabs. Day after day he grew more and more haggard so that his ribs visibly stuck out and his eyes sank deeper.

Mohwa worked with all her might looking after Ugi; day and night she rushed about in search of what he needed. Once in a while she sat him up in bed to hold him in her arms. She tried everything—medication, exorcism, and incantation. Yet none of them helped to cure Ugi's illness.

Soon after she became devoted to nursing Ugi, it was apparent that Mohwa was now disenchanted with her exorcising. If someone asked her to perform one, she declined in most cases on the pretext of her son's illness. Then more and more people concluded that Mohwa's exorcising rites or incantations no longer worked as effectively as before.

About this time a small church was erected in the community, and the missionary work soon spread throughout the country like a fire in the wind. The church in Kyŏngju sent out gospel-preaching parties to every village in the country, and eventually reached Mohwa's village. The message was:

> Parents, brothers and sisters, we should give thanks to God for
> allowing us all to get together here. God created us all. He loves us
> dearly. We are all sinners. In our hearts there is nothing but wick-
> edness; but for our own sake Jesus Christ was crucified upon the
> cross. Thus by our faith in Jesus Christ shall we be saved. We shall
> praise Him with a very glad heart. We shall pray before God.

Some people said that it was more fun than watching apes to look at an American missionary with blue eyes and razor-sharp nose.

"They charge you not a penny for the watching. Let's go and see," said the villagers to one another, and gathered in crowds.

Mrs. Yang, wife of the assistant preacher, who came with the missionary and was a relative of Mr. Pang, the village elder, called upon every house in the village and said: "To believe in a sorceress or a blind soothsayer is to sin against our Father, the one and only God, who is holy. What in the world is a sorceress capable of? Behold, does not a sorceress pray and kneel down before a rotten ancient tree or a stone idol who can never see nor hear? What is a blind soothsayer capable of? Behold, with no power to see before his own steps, he walks over the ground groping with his stick; how could he possibly save men who can see? It is our Father, the one and only God, who created life. Therefore our Father said, 'Never serve another god before me . . .'"

Preaching like this was followed by numerous stories: one that Jesus, God's only son, had healed a number of possessed people who were lepers, cripples, and deaf and dumb; and another, that Jesus was resurrected and ascended to heaven on the third day after his crucifixion.

"Such worthless devils!" said Mohwa, who responded to these stories with ridicule. But it was apparent that the Christian denunciations and curses were weighing heavily on her. For she often chanted, striking the brass tambour and the gong:

"Away, devil, get along with you.
You have lived begging from old days,
How could you be unaware of this Mohwa?
If you linger on here
Your heirs will be locked and starve
In the blue water fifty fathoms deep,
In the cliff with thorny ash trees,
In the grilling iron cauldron,
In the white horse's hide.
They shall not see the light of day.
Away at once, devil get along with you.
Run away at thundering speed
To the Western Regions millions of miles away,
With sparks of fire on your tail,
With bells dangling from your ears,
Clinking, clanking, clinking, clanking."

Yet the "Jesus devils" refused to go away; on the contrary, they kept growing in number. What's more, even those who had once asked Mohwa for an exorcism or conjuration now came to be seized, one after another, with the "foul spirit" of Jesus.

In the meantime, a revivalist preacher from Seoul came to town for canvassing. Hearing that he was capable of curing the sick, the townspeople thronged around him. They said that if he offered a prayer saying, "This sinner is in great sorrow for his own sin," with his hand on the head of the sick person, in most cases a woman would be "purified" of such common disorders as menstrual irregularity or leukorrhea; or a blind man would recover his sight; or a cripple would walk again; or a deaf man would recover his hearing, or a dumb man would speak again; or even those who suffered from paralysis or epilepsy would be "purified"—as long as they were pious enough. From the pulpit it was announced daily that silver and gold rings were being contributed in growing numbers by the village women; donations poured in. Compared to these spectacles, watching an exorcism performed by Mohwa was as nothing, the villagers said.

"They're jugglers' troupes brought in by Western aliens," said Mohwa tauntingly of the Christian healers.

For it had been an extraordinary authority allowed solely to Mohwa by her divinity that she should drive evil spirits out of the human soul. And her divinity was no less than that of an ancient tree or of a stone Maitreya or of a mountain or water spirit. Yet every one of them was now despised and abhorred by the Christians.

"To believe in witchcraft and sorcery is to sin against our Father, the one and only God who is holy and holy," announced the "Christian devils" to the accompaniment of trumpets and drums. Retorting to them all alone, Mohwa struck the brass tambour and the gong as she chanted:

> "Go away, devil,
> A hundred thousand leagues to the west,
> With sparks of fire on your tail,
> With bells dangling from your ears,
> Clinking, clanking, clinking, clanking."

Autumn of that year passed. Early in the winter Ugi's illness took a sharp turn for the worse.

"My dear, my dear, what is happening to you?" Mohwa often said to her son in a trembling, mournful voice, holding him by the hand and shedding tears. "After all the trouble of coming to me from afar, what misery have you fallen into?"

"Please never mind my condition, mother" said Ugi calmly. "I shall be called before our Father in the world beyond."

Whenever Mohwa asked him if there was anything he wanted, he would quietly shake his head. But when his mother went out, leaving him at home with Nangi, Ugi often said, holding her by the hand, "I wish I had a Bible."

The next spring, just three days before he died, Ugi was visited by the Reverand Hyŏn whom the youth had missed so badly and had anxiously waited to see. When Hyŏn arrived, guided by assistant preacher Yang, he frowned at the devastated scene and the sickening smell of decay.

"Don't tell me," he said, turning to Yang, "that this miserable place is Ugi's home!"

As soon as he saw the Reverand Hyŏn walk in, Ugi, with his eyes brightening, called out "Minister! Minister!" Hyŏn came over and quietly held Ugi's wizened hands. Suddenly his face grew red all over, as if dyed, and innumerable wrinkles appeared on his brow and cheeks. He kept his eyes closed for a while, apparently trying to calm the emotion raging in him.

"It was the personal effort of this man," assistant preacher Yang said, as if to break the strained silence in the room, "that brought about the early opening of our church in Kyŏngju."

Ugi first made petition, he went on, to the Reverand Hyŏn in P'yongyang, who in turn solicited the Parish Council in Taegu for help. While the Christians in the Kyŏngju area worked together under the leadership of Ugi, they also kept in close touch with the Parish Council in Taegu. The result was, he said, that the church construction work made far more rapid progress than expected.

The Reverand Hyŏn said that he intended to make another visit, along with a physician, and as he rose to leave, Ugi said: "Would you buy me a Bible, sir?"

"You can keep this one for the time being," said Hyŏn, handing his own Bible to the youth. Ugi took the Bible and closed his eyes, holding the volume to his breast. Below his closed eyelids tears appeared.

In the garden in front of Mohwa's house weeds still grew, entangled with one another just as in previous years, and amid the rank growth there lay hidden a number of frogs and earthworms. Since her son's death, Mohwa had seldom been out to do exorcising. Instead, day after day, she kept chanting and striking the brass tambour and gong in her crumbling house, surrounded by weeds. People said that Mohwa was now completely out of her mind. From the kitchen ceiling she had hung multicolored strips of cloth and some flags made of Nangi's drawings. Being very erratic about her meals, her lips now turned a purplish black, and her eyes gradually took on a weird radiance.

Daily she repeated the same words of conjuration, accompanied by the brass tambour and gong all the while:

> "There goes Jesus devil from Western Regions,
> With sparks of fire on his tail,
> With bells dangling from his ears,
> Clinking, clanking, clinking, clanking.
> Away at once, devil, get along with you.
> Linger where you are, and your heirs
> Shall be locked to death
> In the blue water fifty fathoms deep,
> In the cliff thick with thorny ash trees,
> In the grilling iron cauldron,

In the white horse's hide.
Away at once, foul devil!"

Every once in a while her neighbors would call on her and offer wine to console her, saying, "Terribly sorry you have lost your son, Mohwa."

"It was that Jesus devil who took my son away," Mohwa would reply, sighing.

The villagers, who now took Mohwa for insane, often missed the spectacle of her incantations and said, "We wish we could once again see Mohwa's exorcising."

Then a rumor arose that Mohwa would perform an exorcism for the last time to save the departed soul of Lady Kim, the daughter-in-law of a rich man in town. Lady Kim had lately committed suicide by drowning herself in the Yegi Pond. Some said that Mohwa had been talked into performing after receiving two silk dresses as gifts. Others said that she would attempt in the forthcoming ceremony to drive the dumb spirit out of the body of Nangi so that the latter might regain her speech. Or, Mohwa was quoted as saying, "Humph! We shall see which is the more veritable being, the Jesus devil or my divinity." Thus, a lively feeling of expectancy and curiosity arose among the people of the community; they flocked to the ceremony site from beyond distant hills and rivers.

The exorcism was to be held on a tract of sand beside a stream, which took a gentle bend, flowing down from a pond that nursed in its dark blue body a deep secret and a grudge. (In the pond, deep enough to conceal a huge colorful monster, so legend goes, a man or woman is destined to drown each year.)

Onto the sands scores of people had thronged, full of commotion—taffy vendors, rice-cake vendors, wineshops, and eating houses, had all set up shop. In the midst of the tumultuous crowd there stood a huge tent, and inside it, the exorcism was in progress. There, gauze lanterns of five different colors—blue, red, green, white, and yellow—were hanging, beautiful as flowers. Beneath the lanterns were set in a row: the table for the house gods, heaped with steamed ricecakes, a jar of wine, and a whole boiled pig; the table for the Buddhist tutelary god,‡ provided with a bowl of raw rice, a coil of thread, a skewer of cured persimmons, and a cake of bean curd; the table for Maitreya, laden with fruit of three different colors, steamed snow-white ricecake, cooked vegetables, vegetable soup, salted fish, and honey candy; the table for the god of the mountain, spread with cooked mountain vegetables of twelve different kinds; the table for the god of dragons, holding seafood of twelve kinds; the table for the alley spirits, provided with plates of every kind of delicacy; the table for Mohwa, set with only a bowl of water; and many other offering tables, large and small.

---

‡ One of the tutelary gods of Buddhism who resides in the Palace of Correct Views on the summit of Mount Sumeru in the Tusita Heaven and watches over the East.—Trans.

Mohwa wore a look of unusual modesty and composure; she had been grieving over the recent loss of her son and, in addition, she had suffered the accusations and abuses of the Christian newcomers. Despite all this, however, she looked incredibly aloof and composed. Tonight she was neither ingratiating nor given to talk in public as she used to do. Nor did she seem to be content, even after looking over the sumptuous food on the offering tables. On the contrary, she pouted as if in derision.

"Scurvy bitches! How pitiable to think that a gorgeous offering is everything," she said bluntly.

Before long, some of the spectators began to whisper that a new spirit might possess Mohwa tonight.

"It's the spirit of the late Lady Kim that is with her!" cried a woman in the crowd suddenly.

"It's the Lady Kim that she is possessed by all right," other women nearby concurred. "Look at her face that appears even ominously modest and shy. And was Mohwa ever as fair as she is now? She is the very picture of Lady Kim indeed."

Then, a report sprang from villagers in one corner that tonight's exorcism might help Nangi regain her speech, while people in another corner spread a rumor that Mohwa was with child by an unknown man. The women spectators felt vaguely that all the questions raised by their common talk should be answered by the close of tonight's exorcism.

Mohwa began with a lengthy description of the deceased Lady Kim, relating the circumstances of her life from the time of her birth to her death by drowning. Her recitation over, Mohwa danced jubilantly to the tune of the flutes, pipes, and strings played by the ritual band. Her voice now sounded more plaintive than ever, and her body undulated as if it were transmuted into a fleshless, boneless spirit swinging in rhythmic cadences. The women spectators watched as if in ecstasy; their breathing rose and fell closely with the movement of Mohwa's robe. The train of her robe in turn seemed to wave after Mohwa's own breathing. And her breath seemed to have swallowed up even the stars in the sky, moving momentarily in time with the water of the mysterious, gently winding stream from Yegi Pond, as she gasped out a plaintive chant under the influence of the grieving Lady Kim's spirit.

It was now the middle of the night. People said that all their attempts to save the departed soul had been to no purpose. A group of male shamans and young sorceresses attending Mohwa had tied bowls of rice onto the ends of their "soul saver" lines, and had thrown them into the pond, one after another. Seeing no trace of the deceased woman's hair in the rice bowls raised from the water, they concluded that the late Lady Kim was apparently resisting their attempt to summon her spirit.

"It's a shame that the departed soul should be still down in the water unsaved, isn't it?" an attendant shaman whispered in Mohwa's ear with a look of agitation on her face.

Mohwa showed no sign of impatience, but walked down into the water with a soul saver rod in hand, apparently taking such delay for granted. A male shaman, who was assisting Mohwa by holding the soul saver line, shifted the rice bowl at the end to and fro in the water, following the movement of the rod.

Mohwa beat the pond water, using the soul saver rod, and summoned the departed soul in a voice choked with tears:

> "Rise, rise,
> Our Lady Kim of Wŏlsŏng, age thirty-three.
> You were born under the Scorpion,
> With offerings to the Seven Stars.
> You blossomed like a flower,
> You were reared like a gem.
> Leaving your parents still alive,
> Leaving your small child lying in bed,
> When you plunged into the dark water,
> Even the Dragon King grieved and sighed.
> Your skirt floating up,
> Did you land on the Lotus throne?
> Your locks flying about,
> Did you turn into a spirit of water?"

Step by step, Mohwa went into the deeper part of the pond, holding the soul saver rod out before her. As she walked deeper into the water, one of her skirts entwined round her body while another waved floating on the surface. Now rising as high as her waist, and now as high as her breast, the dark water kept swelling round her. Gradually her voice sounded more distant and her summons emitted greater flashes of fire:

> "Let me go, let me go,
> Sharing the white wine in dragon-shaped cups.
> Call me, my sister, call me to you.
> When peach blossoms bloom on this river bank,
> Come and hear me, my daughter Nangi, clad in white;
> Then ask the first bough of my health,
> Ask the second bough . . ."

At that instant the pond water engulfed her entire body, and her chanting ceased.

For the first few moments, the skirt of her robe was seen drifting on the surface, but even that disappeared in a short while. The soul saver rod, now out of hand, whirled round and round on the water; then it too disappeared downstream.

About ten days later, a small-statured man, who was said to peddle seafood on a street corner in a town on the east coast, came riding on a donkey to see Nangi. With sunken eyes she was still convalescing in bed.

The man soon nursed her back to health. As soon as she recognized him, Nangi called out "Father!" Her speech sounded unusually distinct and intelligible, perhaps because, as rumor had predicted, Mohwa's last exorcism took effect.

Another ten days went by.

"Get up here," said the man to his daughter, pointing to his donkey.

Without saying a word, Nangi did as her father directed.

After their departure no one ever called at Mohwa's house. Each night only mosquitos sang in swarms amidst the rank growth in the yard.

Karomenya
From *Out of Africa*

Isak Dinesen
Denmark, 1937

There was on the farm a little boy of nine named Karomenya who was deaf and dumb. He could give out a sound, a sort of short, raw roar, but it was very rare and he did not like it himself, but always stopped it at once, panting a few times. The other children were afraid of him and complained that he beat them. I first made Karomenya's acquaintance when his playfellows had knocked him on the head with the branch of a tree, so that his right cheek was thick, and festering with splinters that had to be dug out with a needle. This was not such a martyrdom to Karomenya as one would have thought; if it did hurt him, it also brought him into contact with people.

Karomenya was very dark, with fine moist black eyes and thick eyelashes; he had an earnest grave expression and hardly ever a smile on his face, and altogether much of the look of a small black Native bull-calf. He was an active, positive creature, and as he was cut off from communicating with the world by speech, fighting to him had become the manifestation of his being. He was also very good at throwing stones, and could place them where he wanted with great accuracy. At one time Karomenya had a bow and arrow, but it did not work well with him, as if an ear for the ring of the bow-string were, by necessity, part of the archer's craft. Karomenya was sturdily built and very strong for his age. He would probably not have exchanged these advantages over the other boys for their faculty of speech and hearing, for which, I felt, he had no particular admiration.

Karomenya, in spite of his fighting spirit, was no unfriendly person. If he realized that you were addressing him, his face at once lightened up, not in a smile but in a prompt resolute alacrity. Karomenya was a thief, and took sugar and cigarettes when he saw his chance, but he immediately gave away the stolen goods to the other children. I once came upon him as he was dealing out sugar to a circle of boys, himself in the centre, he did not see me, and that is the only time when I have seen him near to laughing.

I tried, for a time, to give Karomenya a job in the kitchen or in the house, but he failed in the offices, and was himself, after a while, bored with the work. What he liked, was to move heavy things about, and to drag them from one place to another. I had a row of white-washed stones along my drive, and, with his assistance, I one day moved one of them and rolled it all the way up to the house, to make the drive symmetrical. The next day, while I was out, Karomenya had taken up all the stones and had rolled them up to the house in a great heap, and I could never have believed that a person of his size would have been capable of that. It must have cost him a terrible effort. It was as if Karomenya knew his place in the world and stuck to it. He was deaf and dumb, but he was very strong.

Karomenya, most of all things in the world, wanted a knife, but I dared not give him one, for I thought that he might easily, in his striving for contact with other people, have killed one or more of the other children on the farm with it. He will have got one, though, later in life; his desire was so vehement, and God knows what use he has made of it.

The deepest impression I made on Karomenya was when I gave him a whistle. I had myself used it for some time to call in the dogs. When I showed it to him he took very little interest in it; then, as on my instruction he put it to his mouth and blew it, and the dogs, from both sides, came rushing at him, it gave him a great shock, his face darkened with surprise. He tried it once more, found the effect to be the same, and looked at me. A severe bright glance. When he got more used to the whistle, he wanted to know how it worked. He did not, to this purpose, look at the whistle itself, but when he had whistled for the dogs and they came, he scrutinized them with knit brows as if to find out where they had been hit. After this time Karomenya took a great liking to the dogs, and often, so to say, had the loan of them, taking them out for a walk. I used, when he walked off with them on a lead, to point to the place in the Western sky where the sun should be standing by the time that he must be back, and he pointed to the same place, and was always very punctual.

One day, as I was out riding, I saw Karomenya and the dogs a long way away from my house, in the Masai Reserve. He did not see me, but thought that he was all on his own and unobserved. Here he let the dogs have a run, and then whistled them in, and he repeated the performance three or four times, while I watched him from my horse. Out on the plain, where he thought that nobody knew, he gave himself up to a new idea and aspect of life.

He carried his whistle on a string round his neck, but one day he had not got it. I asked him by pantomime what had become of it, and he answered by pantomime that it was gone, —lost. He never asked me for another whistle. Either he thought that a second whistle was not to be had, or else he meant, now, to keep away altogether from something in life that was not really his affair. I am not even sure that he had not thrown away the whistle himself, unable to reconcile it with his other ideas of existence.

In five or six years, Karomenya is either to go through much suffering, or he will suddenly be lifted into heaven.

Fairer Than the Sun

Juozas Grušas
Lithuania, 1937
Translated by Kestutis Skrupskelis and Clark Mills

The fir resounded like a bell.

A tiny man in shirtsleeves, with thick, stumplike arms, lifted an axe above his head, and as he lowered it, rose from the ground. He bent over and trampled a clearing in the snow around him with his moccasined feet. The broad edge of the axe flashed in the air, and with each blow it bit out a chunk of the living wood, chaste as the snow. The fir trembled convulsively, the white wound spread like a smile.

The path was strewn with fir branches, as if for a funeral procession. The odor of fresh-cut wood mingled with that of burning yew.

Another woodsman, swinging a saw as if it were a sickle, shouted to the man with the axe, "Look—you've chopped it to the side; may your wife chop you the same way! The firs should fall here, but now it will slide into the trees."

But the tiny man continued to chop at the young tree-trunk with redoubled fury, and heavy drops of sweat fell from his face to the trampled snow.

"Adomas, you doll of dolls, your wife should fondle you like that! Listen, will you? Let's grab a saw and start sawing."

But Adomas went on, plucking chips like blossoms, until the steel edge began to sing.

The man with the saw approached, kicked at the hewer's legs and shouted for the whole forest to hear, "Deaf!"

Adomas lowered his axe, wiped his brow and smiled apologetically. "Perhaps I've already cut too deep."

"Nothing but trouble with a deaf stump! How often have I said it!"

The two of them kneeled in the snow, sawing—speechless, intense, like violinists immersed in a mysterious melody.

The fir swayed and began to lean, as slowly as a warm funeral candle. In an instant its momentum increased and the branches began to moan and thrash as if searching for something to hold on to. The tree hit the earth with a muffled sound; the trunk rebounded like a struck snake, and a smile flitted across the faces of both men.

They gazed for a while, with gentle awe, at the prostrate tree.

"Enough. We've felled them like stacks of grain. It's time. . . ." And the man with the saw indicated to the deaf man, with his lips, that it was time to eat.

The two men flung their coats over their shoulders and stalked off silently, single file, through the snow.

A fir was burning and crackling, plumes of gray smoke twisted and turned among the branches. There was an odor of bread and sap.

Around the flames sat fur-coated woodcutters with windburned cheeks. They chewed on chunks of frozen meat, and, their mouths full, laughed at each pointed word.

Adomas shyly sidled up to the fire, glanced around to be sure he was disturbing no one, and sat down on a bed of branches. He took off his cap, crossed himself, and unrolled a large linen kerchief from which he took out bread and meat. The smell of the bread tickled his throat gently, and without tasting it at all, Adomas mused on how unutterably pleasant and good it was to eat. Now he took a huge bite out of the frozen meat, on which the marks of his teeth remained. As he broke off a thick piece of bread, ice glistened in its pores. He held it to the flames until the odor of toasting bread spread through the firs and birches.

The woodcutters had already eaten. Now they warmed themselves, kicked at the burned stumps, rolled "butts" and tried to prove that their tongues were all the sharper for the lunch they had eaten. They decided to talk to the deaf man, who, alone with a crust of black bread in his hand, pondered silly thoughts in his scab-covered head.

One man sitting close to him shouted into his ear, "What is your last name, Adomas?"

Adomas answered nothing.

"As if such people had last names," another man spoke up jokingly. "There are people who aren't worth a last name. 'Adomas,' that's all; what more could he be?"

Adomas did not hear this remark. He only understood from the faces of those around him that the words were unkind. He put on his cap and prepared to go back to work.

One of the woodcutters laid his hand on Adomas's shoulder and said, sweetening each word, "Adomas, old boy, sit down next to the fire and rest. Man, why should you work so hard?"

Adomas, like a mistreated child, glowed with trust and affection because of the gentle word. He sat down on a stump and gazed smilingly at the woodcutters.

"What good are you, Adomas? You're only feeding someone else's children," another woodcutter shouted into his ear.

Adomas bent his pock-marked face toward the ground.

"Orphans . . . little ones . . .," he said in a hoarse voice. "It's hard to find work in the summer. I know how to hew out a corner, how to handle bricks. But you know, because I don't hear well, other people immediately say, 'He's a fool; he doesn't know anything.' Then nobody wants to hire me. There is no justice in the world—what can one do?"

"Why did you marry a widow? You should have chosen a young girl, and then there would have been justice."

"Why speak of it? Would anyone else have taken me? Even this one sometimes tells me that I smell of pitch. I always dream that if I could only get work during the winter. . . . You see, I need new clothes. I have only this worn-out coat. I'd really like to have beautiful clothes."

The woodcutters began to laugh; they found the conversation amusing.

"Beautiful clothes!"

"And a hat!"

"And a white collar!"

"You didn't have to get married. Couldn't you live alone? Then you would have new clothes and a hat and a white collar."

A pretty sleigh passed along the road through the silent forest. Through the trees a bay horse could be seen, stepping beautifully. The bells tinkled like a swift brook. The woodcutters followed the smartly dressed passengers with their eyes.

"Cold," said one of them when the sound of bells had faded away, and he hugged his coat more tightly around him.

"You're a fool, Adomas, the biggest fool!" shouted a young woodcutter, as if to vent his sudden anger.

"Why?"

"A fool because you got married. Now you understand!"

Adomas became thoughtful. A light wind ran through the treetops, and tiny stars of snow poured into the flames.

"On an empty plain, on the windward side, not even a tree grows. . . . I often look into the thickets of the forest and think—"

"A man isn't a tree."

"But even a man seeks shelter with someone."

"It isn't as cold in the winter, is it?" the woodcutters said, stifling their laughter.

"Not as cold," Adomas answered.

"You can feel the warmth of a body and the beating of the heart?"

"And the heart."

"And what else?" The men laughed. "But who would want to pet such a one as you?"

"Tell him he's as ugly as a toad."

"Should we talk that way about a man?"

"Tell him he's like a sodden turf."

"Listen, Adomas," one of them shouted into his ear, "they say you're as ugly as a toad!"

A shadow flitted across his pock-marked face.

"Don't worry, Adomas; never mind them."

"Why should I be sad?" asked Adomas, blinking rapidly. "I know what I am; why speak of it? But the elder girl—Steputé—told me once that I am fairer than the sun. So there! When my wife began to talk—like you now, just like you, in just the same way—Steputé cried. When her mother left she came to me and knelt down and said that I was fairer than the sun."

"But Steputé has been blind since she was little."

"Then all the more, all the more," said Adomas excitedly. "'Than the sun,' she said. One only needs to understand."

"Fairer than the sun! Fairer!"

"And the moon!"

"You understand nothing, nothing," said Adomas, blinking and turning red. "I live like a dog, I work day and night when someone hires me. Without me, they— why, those girls—. You think their mother—. You don't understand! She, Steputé, a blind girl, kissed my feet. Don't you understand?"

The woodcutters were silent. They felt ill at ease.

They all gazed at the flames.

It was quiet and lonely in the woods. The cold spread through the clearings and thickets, through the broad drifts and the blue sky, like silent, heavy breathing.

Adomas squatted by the fire, his face pale and puckered, his lips tightly clenched. With frozen gaze he peered into the blazing bonfire, and the flame became more scattered, changed into stars and glistened. He heard a silent lament that flowed on the wind, swayed with the branches.

He rose and walked away from the fire through the deep snow. And now the tears, one after another, rolled down his cheeks.

Once more the blows echoed through the forest. The axes rang, as if in a smithy. The falling firs fell with a swish, and shook the earth; their echo spread far through the forest on the green waves of the evergreens.

With each breath of the wind the forest vibrated and moaned, and in those moments the woodcutters seemed like tiny insects in a wheat-field. Throwing back their heads, they gazed at the sky-reaching firs; then they resolutely chopped at the trees' fine trunks and smiled when one of them lay stretched out at their feet.

But now some spirit, denizen of the forest, decided to play a trick on these armed insects. A fine and serious fir rebelled; as it fell, it aimed itself into the strong arms of a neighboring birch. Now it hung in the air, its branches entangled in those of its neighbor.

"You, men—over here!" shouted the woodcutters, finding themselves unable to vanquish the tree.

All laid down their axes and gathered, muttering. Adomas alone paid no attention but went on stripping a thick pine.

"You're like old women," the newcomers shouted. "Can't you see you should have felled it to this side?"

"A tree is alive, fellows; sometimes it must have its own way—it has to fall the opposite way to the one you choose. You don't understand trees. Sometimes a devil can hide in a tree, like in a man."

The woodcutters collected around the trunk and pushed it off its stump. But the fir did not consider surrendering so easily; it merely trembled, twisted and wedged itself still tighter within the thick branches of the birch.

"Devil or angel, something is hiding in those branches," muttered the woodcutters.

But there was still one way to conquer the stubborn beauty of the forest.

The men glanced at some firs that grew nearby. They counted four, any one of which might, in falling itself, dislodge its obstinate sister. They chopped into one majestic fir and then began to saw. The fir trembled and began to lean. The woodcutters ran to one side and waited, shivering and with anxious gaze, until both trees should topple to the ground in a mighty tumult.

The fir struck; as the top, like a sword-cleaved head, hit the snow, the trunk bounced up like a spring. And now both trees remained suspended in the form of a cross, between heaven and earth.

The situation was becoming more serious. The woodcutters muttered and swore. They picked another tree, still heavier, and began to cut. But this one was too close; as it fell, it touched the suspended trees before it had gained momentum. The top slid over the tangle of branches and pierced the snow. Then the trunk, now raised in the air, began to slide.

"Run!" the woodcutters shouted to one another.

Like frightened elk, the men bounded through the snow. But again the branches caught, and this honored citizen of the forest, with tragic irony, now sprawled on the battlefield with its feet in the air.

The woodcutters, furious, felled the two remaining firs, but these too caught in the web of trees.

The men no longer cursed. Their courage and self-confidence had melted, now that no tree remained to be felled without danger, in a last attempt to unravel this green wreath.

One solution alone remained: to cut the birch itself. But this was truly a really dangerous task, since a tree bearing so much weight could break at the first blow of the axe. Yet they could not leave things as they were; they would be docked a week's wages, and might even be fined because of these few trees lost.

So, stretching their necks, all the woodcutters looked up at the suspended trees and waited, like geese waiting for the clouds to descend. One after another they stalked up to the birch to assure themselves that the firs were completely wedged in. The birch's thickest branch, it seemed, had already been somewhat torn by the impact, and might break at any moment, dropping its gigantic load. One woodcutter leaped back as if he had seen a snake.

"How well does it hold?" asked those farther away.

"The branch is torn."

"If there were only one more fir; now everything would really fall."

"We can't bring up a fir."

"Then the birch must be cut; there's no other way."

"Cut it if you want; I refuse."

"I won't cut it, either."

"Don't cut, and you don't get paid. Come Saturday and your wife will scream that there is no food."

The woodcutters stamped on the snow, cursed the trees, became angry with one another, swore at whatever came in their way.

Suddenly one young woodcutter shouted, as if he had found salvation: "Adomas! He will cut the birch!"

They all looked over to where Adomas, left to himself, calmly stripped his tree. Their faces lit up. Whether he would cut it or not, at last here was someone on whom they could vent their rage.

"A stump for the birds! Here we've been laboring for an hour, while he—"

"He won't stir a feather for anyone else."

"He works day and night, but always for himself!"

"He needs new clothes—. 'Fairer than the sun—.' Snake!"

One of the woodcutters dragged Adomas up to the group. "Would you like to be crossed off the list of woodcutters?" Adomas gazed timidly at the men.

"But why?"

"Because you won't help us. Do you hear?"

"Now, as punishment, you will cut down that birch. If you refuse, don't bother to come to work tomorrow. Understand?" A giant of a man shouted at Adomas brandishing a hairy fist.

Adomas walked up to the birch, carefully studied its branches, tested the trunk with his hand, and returned to the men. "Cut it yourselves, and don't show me your fists," he said, blushing.

The woodcutters' anxiety grew. Again they cursed one another. They argued and shouted a long time. Finally they approached Adomas again. This time they adopted a different tactic.

"Be a man, Adomas, a friend—we'll repay you. On our honor! I have two suits, and one of them is still not at all bad. Believe me, I'll give it to you, if only you'll cut that birch."

"And I'll add a necktie!"

"And I, a hat and a white collar. Then you'll really be fairer than the sun."

The men spoke into Adomas's ear; they slapped him on the back, called him their best friend and comrade.

Adomas smiled; he walked over to the birch and once again examined it carefully. On his return he said, "It can't be left like this. It must be cut."

"Here is a man!" the woodcutters shouted.

Adomas still hesitated.

"Here—take an axe, prove yourself worthy of our friendship."

"The clothes, and a hat, and a white collar."

Adomas picked up his axe, walked around the birch, packed down the snow and gathered up branches that might trip him as he ran.

The men smiled and winked at one another.

"Just look at Adomas! You have to know how—with a fool. . . ."

The little man stripped off his coat, moistened his palms and raised his axe; then he lowered it again. He straightened up and shouted, "I don't want your clothes! Just manage to say a kind word to me, that will be enough."

The woodcutters looked around at one another with questioning gaze. The mirth and irony fled from their faces. They looked at him there, beneath the incredible weight, and were afraid to repeat their promise.

Adomas raised the axe and struck the first blow. The birch echoed hoarsely, like a buried bell.

The man dealt blow after blow, with as much force and determination as in mortal combat with an ancient foe. The men, a good distance away, followed his actions with feverish interest—would the firs move? They wanted to warn him, to shout loudly, so that Adomas might escape. After each blow their chests grew warmer, as if each were himself there bending down under the birch.

Adomas, beneath that suspended bridge, looked from where they stood as tiny as an ant. But he wielded the axe rhythmically and stubbornly, like an ecstatic sexton swinging the heart of a bell.

The cutter straightened, glanced up to be sure that the firs were still wedged tightly, wiped the sweat away and swung again. The axe steadily counted off the blows like a pendulum, flashing at times with a cold and eerie glitter. From a distance the wounds in the birch appeared white, like an evil smile on gnarled lips.

The firs crackled, and hardly aware of it, the men shouted in unison, "Run!"

The cutter did not hear. Like a woodpecker, he pecked at the tree, his head swinging and his whole body swaying regularly.

Color returned to their pale faces and their hearts beat more slowly. All felt grateful to the birch, which bore death upon its shoulders, and to the firs, for permitting the tiny man to play his great game.

From behind the clouds rolled the winter sun, and the snow-covered clearing glistened like white silk. The rays darted through the tangled trees and flooded the woodcutter. Suddenly he straightened up and leaped back, but still the tree did not move. Again the cutter picked up his axe.

The men wanted to speak to him—to say something, to address him as they would a real brother, to offer him friendship that might lighten his axe. They would smooth a path for him and cover it with branches, they would carry him off on their shoulders once the birch had swayed. But between them and the woodcutter yawned a gulf wider than a lifetime. There, afar, he was like a child on a battlefield playing with live grenades.

The forest, where so short a time ago had echoed the sound of falling trees, now breathed with deep calm in every branch. The rhythmical blows of the lone axe served only to deepen this endless calm that seemed to mark time. Their sound was muffled at once amidst the nearest trees, while farther away, beyond them, lay nothing but white snow, valleys, hills, fields, glades, and villages—the whole world itself.

The cutter tired; he leaned against the tree, as if on the shoulder of his best friend. He pondered awhile, his face touching the rough bark, and drops of sweat rolled like tears down the uneven birch trunk.

Everything was alive—rest and pain, each drop of sweat, the endless wait, death silently settling, and love that gathers blossoms for the goldfinch of the forest. All things were visible and heard, as the heart is audible to a deaf man, as a face fairer than the sun exists for someone who is blind.

The cutter straightened with renewed energy and struck a blow. The birch vibrated, wounded in the heart. Another blow followed, and another, like a clock striking the hour. The hands rose once more. The axe trembled and fell—together with the cutter. And at the same moment the branches whistled, the frozen earth resounded, and the men were unable even to shout, "Run!"

Between the fresh stumps lay the fallen firs, and beside them the birch—and there, covered as if with a green wreath, lay the woodcutter.

Now a clearing lay in the middle of the forest. Beyond it, near the road, scores of young firs rose along a hillside. In the whitest of garments, flooded by the rays of the sun, they stood one behind another, covering the earth with blossoms. In shining waves they rose, higher and ever higher—impalpable pure worlds reaching up to the blue heavens.

I Should Worry

Weldon Kees
USA, 1939

Arch Boyle lounged in a broken wicker chair in front of his used auto parts place. A half-smoked cigarette was pasted in one corner of his mouth, and from the other corner a broken toothpick hung. Across the street, in front of the City Mission, an old man was sweeping the sidewalk with a worn broom. A bunch of kids were rollerskating, and each time they went by, the old man had to stop sweeping, leaning on his broom until they had passed. The wheels of their skates rasped on the concrete and, whenever they rolled over divisions in the sidewalk, they made a clacking sound like a needle on a cracked Victrola record. The old man would watch them and then return to his work, raising a thin sift of dust.

Arch deftly removed the toothpick without putting his hands to his face or disturbing the cigarette, and again he thought of his sister. Now, he thought, she would be standing in front of the mirror in the room above him, the room in which his parents had killed themselves, and she would be combing her hair with one hand, her eyes wandering from her distorted image to the pictures of movie actors that she had torn from magazines and pasted on the wall. He could see her vividly, even the sling around her neck, and he wondered if she would be coming down before long.

He changed his position in the chair, trying to keep his eyes out of the sunlight without going back into the store too far. It was an open-front place: all kinds of used auto parts were scattered over shelves and boxes and tables. He got into a comfortable position, and after he was settled, he crossed his legs and began to strike himself below the kneecap with the side of his hand. He was testing his reflexes.

Satisfied that they were all right, same as they'd been yesterday, he began thinking of how much he wanted a drink of gin. He wanted a drink in the worst way, but that morning he had paid O. B. Daniels the rent on the building, and now he was flat. He didn't have a cent, and there hadn't been any business all day. It was getting close to five o'clock, and he was broke and needed a shot of gin. Better yet, two shots. He wished he had held out a little on O. B.

Next door at Womack's American Radio Repair Shop, a loudspeaker blared the final chorus of *The Love Bug Will Bite You If You Don't Watch Out*. Arch tapped his foot in time to the music, imagining a scene in which he talked O. B. into lowering the rent. *You are listening to "The World Dances," a group of recorded numbers by Howard Griffin and his Californians. We hear them next in an interrogative mood, as they ask the musical question, "Am I Wasting My Time?"* Or better yet: say he had something on O. B. Listen, O. B., I know all about this little graft you're working and maybe some other people'd like to know about it too. Huh? O. B. looked green around the gills. Well, what is it you want, Boyle? The rent on the building. That's all. O. B. not liking it but agreeing. He had to. Shaking his head, saying okay. A cinch.

Nuts.

He took a last drag from his cigarette and tossed it on the sidewalk. It rolled along, scattering sparks, then fell off the curb into the gutter. He yawned, wondering why Womack had to play that thing so loud all the time. Made so much noise you couldn't hear yourself think.

People went by: an old man in his shirtsleeves carrying a basket, a fat Negress in a violet dress who dragged along with one hand a little colored kid, a boy on a red bicycle, two young fellows in overalls carrying dinnerpails. As they passed, one of them said, They ain't going to get me over there, hell no. Two dogs trotted by, their noses to the ground. They paused a moment in front of Arch to sniff at a red popbottle cap on the sidewalk, and then went on, their tails held stiff and erect.

Arch got up and stretched. His shirtsleeves were rolled up above his elbows, and the wicker chair had left a mottled red print on his fat arms, corrugating them like a washboard. He walked over to Womack's American Radio Repair Shop and looked inside.

Womack! he yelled.

The radio was playing so loudly that his voice could scarcely be heard. The funnel-shaped loudspeaker boomed from above the doorway. Tendrils of wires escaped from its base through little holes bored in the wood.

Womack! he called again.

Finally a man came up from the cellar. He was carrying a pair of pliers. He looked up, frowning slightly, and said, What'd ya want? He stood there, the trapdoor behind him, looking first at Arch and then at the pliers in his hand.

Turn that thing down, can you? Arch said. I bet you can hear it clear over in the next block.

What's the matter? Don't you like it?

What'd you think?

That's what I'm asking you. He put the pliers down on a workbench.

Jesus, you can hear it for blocks. Why don't you turn it down?

Because maybe I want it loud, that's why.

Holy God, Arch thought. What can you do with a guy like him?

Womack came over close to him and tapped him on the chest with a pudgy forefinger. Listen, he said slowly, I play it loud on account of a good reason, see?

Music's something people like to hear. I give 'em music. Music plays. Gives me more business, get the point?

Okay, okay. Only turn it down. You don't know what a racket that thing makes. A guy has to sit out there and listen to it. You can hear it for blocks.

And maybe I like it that way.

You must, Arch said. Listen, Womack, look at it this way. It stands to reason that nobody wants their eardrums ruined. That ain't going to get you no business. Sure, give 'em music, but turn it down. Jesus, I bet you can hear it clear over on Christopher Street.

Womack scratched his head.

Hell, it just stands to reason nobody wants their eardrums ruined. That's just sense.

Maybe so, Womack said.

It's just sense, that's all.

Okay, I'll turn it down a little. I guess it won't hurt none.

A guy just can't hear himself think the way it's going now, Arch said. Say, Womack . . .

Yeh?

You couldn't loan a guy a dollar, could you. Until Monday?

No, I couldn't, said Womack.

I didn't think you could, Arch said. Okay. Forget it.

I wasn't even thinking about it none.

Okay. Okay. I just thought.

Well, think again, said Womack.

He left him regulating the volume on the radio. Arch's sister, Betty Lou, had come down from their rooms over the shop, and now she sat in the wicker chair, a green knit dress stretched tight over her body. She had broken her arm about a week before. It hung in a white sling that was tied around her neck.

Arch looked at her, wishing he were over at Freddie's picking up a couple of straight gins. He didn't say anything. She stared up at him, her jaws working at a piece of gum she had just started on. He was close enough to her to get a whiff of the wintergreen odor. She was deaf and dumb.

He wondered again just how she had broken her arm. All he knew was that some guy in a green sedan had picked her up last Thursday late in the evening, and when she had come back, alone, three or four hours later, she had a broken arm. She was whimpering, and she held her arm out to him, shaking her head and sobbing soundlessly. He had set it himself—doctors were too expensive—working carefully with the splints to make sure it would be all right.

Later, he had tried to get it out of her, tried to find out how it had happened. Time after time he had poked the piece of paper in front of her, the piece of paper on which he had written: *How did it happen? You better tell me.* He had put the pencil between her fingers, commanding her to write, but she had repeatedly thrown it on the floor, shaking her head and stamping her feet. He hadn't been able to get a thing out of her since it had happened. And now she sat there in the wicker chair, her jaws moving regularly behind the slash of scarlet on her lips that broke the paleness of her face, her green dress pulled up just a little too high, watching the cars that were going by in the five o'clock rush.

If my mother and the old man had lived, he thought. All right: break your god-damn arm, go ahead. See if I care. He put a cigarette between his lips and struck a match on his beltbuckle. Break your arm, he thought.

Womack hadn't turned down the radio so that you could notice it . . . *presenting a group of recorded selections by Howard Griffin and his Californians. Here's an old favorite for you! It's Howard Griffin's interpretation of "Ida." A recording.*

Maybe some people have lives that make sense, he thought. Maybe some of them do things that make some difference, maybe for some of them it goes some place and has some meaning. More meaning than getting up in the hot or the cold morning, it doesn't make any difference, and putting on a pair of dirty socks and clothes that you wore yesterday and eating breakfast with a sister that can't hear you or speak to you. And all of the time you're wondering what's going on in her mind. And then you go to the shop and wait on customers, if you're lucky enough to have any, and then by the time night comes around you toss a slug of gin inside of you and after you're good and drunk you fall into bed dog-tired and feel it spinning around beneath you and hear the streetcars rumbling by in the dark and your head feeling like a bomb about to explode.

He went towards the back of the shop and dug around in some rubbish to see if he could find a bottle that he might have overlooked. They were all empties, though. He stood for a moment by the dirty window. Some kids walked up the alley, kicking a tin can. You going to the movies tonight? Nah. And the can banging on the concrete. He tapped the ash from the cigarette. If I only had some dough, he thought. If I only had a little dough.

An automobile pulled up in front of the place, and without turning he knew by the sound of the motor that it was a Chevy, probably a 1934 model. When he heard the door of the car click shut, he looked around and saw a man in a gray suit walking towards him.

You got any straps for license plates? the man asked.

Arch looked him over. He was wearing a gray felt hat and a gray suit and limped slightly. He was about forty or so, Arch guessed.

Yeh. Right ever here.

Arch led him to a table and indicated the straps. But the man wasn't looking at the merchandise on the table; instead, he was standing in the aisle watching Betty Lou. She was looking at him, too, her eyes half closed and one leg crossed over the other, swinging it slowly up and down.

Here they are, Arch said.

Huh? the man said, glancing up. Oh yeh, the straps. He glanced back at the girl for a moment and then fastened his eyes on the straps. How much? I only need one. The one on the front plate just broke.

Well, here's one I'll sell you for a dime. It's used a little.

The man looked at it briefly, holding it in his hands, and said, That's all right. I'll take it. I'll take this one. He fished a dime from his pocket, and dropped it in Arch's hand. There you are, he said. Then his eyes went back to Betty Lou. His tongue kept going over his lower lip, slowly moistening it.

I've done it before, Arch thought. But never when she's had a broken arm. But I could use the dough, and she doesn't care. It's nothing to her. A thing like that.

Something else? Arch said.

The man started. No, huhuh, I guess not.

Interested in the girl?

The man laughed nervously.

Betty Lou was half turned in the wicker chair, staring at the man, smiling. Her crossed leg moved up and down regularly.

Two bucks, mister, said Arch.

The man raised an eyebrow. Two? he said, What's the matter with her arm?

It's sprained. Don't worry about that. It won't bother you none, You ain't worrying about that, are you?

The man slapped the strap softly against his leg. *For the past minutes you have been listening to a group of dance selections played by Howard Griffin and his Californians.* The man looked at Arch and then at the girl.

The wicker chair squeaked faintly as she rocked back and forth. The green dress was tight as a bathing suit.

You can go upstairs if you want to, Arch said. How about it?

Well . . .

Two bucks, said Arch. You can give the money to me. Arch stepped on the cigarette, two faint spirals of smoke escaping from his nostrils. Come on, he thought. For God's sake. Make up your mind. I'm not going to beg you.

The man smiled slightly. Make it a dollar and a half.

Two. Now, honest, ain't it worth that?

Dollar and a half. What the hell. A sprained arm . . .

Okay, Arch said slowly. Make it a dollar seventy-five. That's fair enough. He stuck his hand in his pockets, feeling the large hole in the bottom of the one on the left side.

The man glanced quickly at the girl, and said, All right. Dollar seventy-five. You get the money, you say?

That's right.

Arch took the crumpled dollar bill, holding it in his palm while the man placed the coins over the smooth engraved face of George Washington. Arch nodded to Betty Lou. He watched her get up and come to the man and smile at him, the red smear crawling up both sides of her cheeks, taking his arm and looking up into his face.

She's a dummy, Arch said.

What? the man said. I don't get it. The smile he had arranged on his face for the girl began to fade.

She's deaf and dumb, Arch said. That's all. Not that it makes any difference to you, I suppose.

The man shook his head. Deaf and dumb?

That's right, Arch said.

And then Betty Lou was pulling the man towards the door that led to the rooms above. He could hear their footsteps on the stairs. It was beginning to get dark. People were coming home from work and the streetcars went by, one after another.

He went to the front of the store and began to pull the large folding doors together, getting ready to close up for the night. One dime taken in, he thought. One dime and a dollar seventy-five. I'll put the dollar in my shoe for groceries so we'll have enough to eat on, until something turns up, and I'll get drunk on the eighty-five. I'll get drunk and come home from Freddie's with my head going around and around and then it won't make any difference. Nothing. It doesn't make any difference anyway. It made some difference a long time ago, maybe seven or eight years ago, but that was when I had a lot of different ideas than I have now. Goofy ideas. When I thought that maybe there was something to it.

I should worry about her. He took the padlock and snapped it shut over the opening between the two doors. I should worry about her, broken arm and all . . . *the weather forecast for tonight is fair and warmer in the southern part of the state. For Tuesday* . . .

The closed doors shut out all light except for the faint blue blur that hung in a square in back: the barred window. He felt his way through the store's darkness and opened the rear door. Before he closed it, he felt in his pocket to make sure that he had the keys with him.

I should worry about her. Because that's all she knows. Because it's been that way since the two of them stuffed the door of the living room with newspapers and turned on the gas and waited there, sitting in the chairs by the window, with that slow hissing sound all around them. And the smell getting stronger all the time. Because that's the way it's been ever since then with her. I tried to stop her too many times and then I gave up.

He felt for cigarettes, but there weren't any left. I'll get some when I get to Freddie's. In the alley, the telephone wires hummed above him. Some kid had drawn something on the side of one of the buildings, but he couldn't make out what it was. I gave it up a long time ago. He turned where the alley met the street and walked without haste to the corner, waiting for a moment for the lights to change from red to green before he crossed to the other side.

Miss Cudahy of Stowes Landing

George P. Elliott
USA, 1954

1

Bingham could not knock at a strange door without a sense of adventure; to greet, and win if he could, whatever smiling or screw-eyed or blank stranger the door opened onto made his heart beat a little faster, his breath come shorter. In the course of his duties with the Superior Court, he met very few new people, most of whom were lawyers or their secretaries; he liked the fact that in the manner of their official dealings lawyers still wear wigs, but he made no friends among them. He had a few acquaintances and family friends, and another friend, a woman, whom he might have married several years before but did not. Nearly every door he knocked at he had knocked at a hundred times before, except for the doors of old houses, which held his happiness.

Therefore, when one Saturday in early summer he knocked at Miss Cudahy's house in Stowes Landing and no one answered, he set about inspecting the exterior of the house with the attention it deserved. The telephone operator—in one of these small towns she is the central intelligence—had given him Miss Cudahy's name and had volunteered him the information that she was old, suffered from rheumatism, and was very much the lady. He could see from the outside of the house that the operator had been right; only a lady would befit this grandest house in town, only a lady would have maintained it so handsomely against the sea-weather of Mendocino, only a lady would have kept a marble bird-bath in the garden, a Latin sun-dial under that usually overcast sky, a bronze stark-naked well-patinaed faun in a Concord arbor.

For although he was not sure of the rose-window over the door, yet the dormer windows, the overhang, the complication of the roof, the five gables, these meant to him New England on a hostile coast. Stowes Landing had been built seventy years ago on the flats back from a 300-foot cliff, north above a logging stream; the meadows stretched freely back for a mile to the line of forest and descending hills; nothing protected the houses from the sea-breeze but a hedge for those that planted one: and yet Miss Cudahy's house stood two and a half stories tall and massive, like some determined New Englanders bunched together, suspicious and prepared, resisting whatever the Indians, Spaniards, Mexicans, Russians, Southerners, Middle

Westerners, Chinese, Filipinos, Japanese, Africans, Italians, Armenians, of this dangerous land might have settled among themselves heathenishly to do. That was all right, what one expected, for 1880; but to find it so purely preserved, still yellow with green shutters, in these provinces of light stucco or stained wood, to be able to walk up to it behind its hedge in a legitimate because pure curiosity, that affected Bingham as strongly as some people are affected by shaking the hand that shook the hand of Lincoln. He was more excited, as he began his tour, than was altogether reasonable.

On the southern side of the house, the side where the hedge was only twenty feet tall, he found a grizzled little man leaning on the handle of a shovel. His stance and dull stare bespoke one who has worked hard and learned how to rest like a horse standing up; but there was no new-turned bed, no deep hole, only a small cleared space where he was probably going to plant a fuchsia, there being already sixty or seventy fuchsias about the garden.

"Hello," said Bingham. The man did not respond; people frequently didn't. "The lady of the house is not home."

"Happen Phoebe's out buying," he said in a British dialect so heavy Bingham could hardly understand him.

"I see. I hope you don't mind my looking around till she returns."

He had always made it a point not to start small talk in a situation like this; but that unresponsive gaze said to him, Birth marriage death may be sizable enough to talk about mister but they are none too large; the man rubbed his chin on the end of the handle.

"I'm only interested in the house," Bingham went on, embarrassed to be introducing a subject so fugitive. "Miss Cudahy—could you tell me . . . "

But he heard, for the second time, he realized, a sharp sound behind and above him, a sound as of a gem rapped against glass; when he felt the hairs stand up on the back of his hand, he knew that he was being watched from behind the curtains by the eyes of one who had heard but had not answered his knock at the door. He left his sentence to dangle as it would and went on with his inspection; the man began to dig.

In the rear, there was a pile of wood, far more orderly than most of the garden, a vegetable patch, and a clothesline. And in the corner beyond the clothesline half hidden by an arc of delphiniums, there was a garden to itself, earth scratched and leveled, scarcely a dead petal on the blossoms, no rows but a wandering intermixed variety of plants and shrubs, steppingstones for paths; there were single roses and single geraniums, three tulips, Indian paintbrush and succulents from the sea-cliffs, most of them with small bright flowers, for June is spring in Mendocino, and a rolling fringe of yellow oxalis. He stood in a sort of wonder at the sweetness of that garden, at how dainty and feminine and itself it seemed down between the still too vigorous old huge house and the hedge which here was more than thirty feet in height. He wondered who Phoebe was.

That hedge; there were a number of such hedges along that part of the coast, but Miss Cudahy's was as dense and perfectly trimmed as any he had seen and was much the highest. These hedges were dark green and thick and not very noisy even in the wind, very dark green; they were kept trimmed smooth as moss, with rounded edges, and this one had ascents and dips in it for no reason that he could make out, at one point rose taller than the house; dark, impermeable cypress green, for though it kept out the wind it kept out everything else as well. He could not imagine how Chin-on-Shovel did the job of trimming, and he did not even want to imagine what it was like to live out a life with a prospect of grey skies, unkept fuchsias, and the dark of the green.

One at the front and the other at the rear, arches ran through the hedge like the mouse-runs that pierced the vast walls of Muscovite palaces. Through the rear gate, as he was standing there, entered a young woman with a basket of groceries in one hand, a bonnet on her head—more than a hat—and a spring to her step. "Hello," he said, but she did not look at him. He stepped forward between two delphiniums and called again. She stopped, her lips a little open with surprise, and looked at him with a directness, a lack of demure withdrawal, which rather surprised him. "Could you tell me, please," he began, but she turned from him and ran, quite ran, up the stairs and into the house. He could think of no better course than to wait for a few discreet minutes and go knock at the front door. This he did, though not without trepidation.

She answered, with lowered eyes. He apologized for having startled her, and handed her his card. Without a word she walked back into the house. She appeared, at closer sight, a plain young woman, her hair drawn severely back to a bun, her face devoid of make-up yet not sallow, her clothes undistinguished for their color or grace; yet there was a certain tone to her body that quite set her off from an ordinary maid or housekeeper, a vigor to her step and a flirt, a fillip perhaps, to her skirts when she turned, that charmed him. She returned and opened the door wide to him; he thanked her and stepped into the hall; she smiled, not just politely but as though she were suppressing some private amusement, and ushered him into the parlor.

There lay, swathed in pastel chiffons, a large old woman on a chaise-longue.

"Mr. Bingham!" she called forth like a captain of one brig to the captain of another. "Come in, sir. Sit down." And she made what seemed to be some sort of complicated hailing motions with her hands.

"Thank you. Miss Cudahy," he said, and sat in a pale-oak horse-hair chair near her. When he looked around, the girl had disappeared. "I'm afraid I rather startled Phoebe out in the garden a few minutes ago."

"Did you?" she cried. "She did not inform me of that. And how do you know her name?"

"Your gardener, I gathered it from him."

"Ah yes, of course." And he saw how, with a loll of her great head and a flick of her left hand, heavy with rings, she peered out between the curtains invisibly.

Then she, with a suddenness that surprised him, tuned back and said to him sharply. "You're from the FBI."

He had seen witnesses caught off-balance, and had pitied them for their slowness and dullness, but here he was thrown by an old woman's judo.

"Who, me?" he said. "Oh no, gracious no. I'm only . . ."

"Very well," she waved his stuttering aside. "One of the other investigators. Which?"

"No, I assure you, I am interested in old houses. I enjoy them very much, and I . . ."

"I see." She paused, the sort of pause that did not permit him to speak. He sat watching her fill a curved pipe with tobacco, tamp it expertly, and light up. "You may smoke," she said, and docilely he lit a cigarette. "You traced me through the California Historical Society."

"No," he said, "I am merely traveling, alone, along the Mendocino coast, looking for houses of the New England captains that settled here. And I found yours simply by driving down the street looking for it."

"How did you discover me behind this hedge?"

"By getting out of my automobile and looking through the gate."

"I see." She stared with a concentration as great as Phoebe's; it had an altogether different effect on him. "Well, you've seen the outside and you're in the parlor. What do you think?"

He began to exclaim over it, and rising asked her permission to investigate the parlor more closely.

"In good time," she said. "Sit down, Mr. Bingham. We will have tea."

She pulled a tasseled cord behind her head, and Phoebe appeared. She waved her hands at Phoebe with a mixture of fluttering and grace and indolence, and threw her head back onto the pillows. "Pardon me," she murmured; her mouth fell a little ajar. "One has to rest a good deal. More than one would have chosen."

He could look at her closely now. It was a heavy, pale, sensual face with dark pouches under the deep eyes; she was not so old as he had originally thought, not over sixty. Her arms were bare and fleshy; day was, he imagined, when those white arms had excited at least the admiration of men. He could see that one of her legs, extended on the chaise-longue, was bound in some sort of rubber legging reaching halfway down the calf; the other, foot on the floor, would have served well on a duke in the days of knee breeches. She breathed heavily, nearly wheezing. "Asthma," she muttered, "damned nuisance." He sat straight in his slick, hard chair.

At the sound of Phoebe with the tea-tray at the door, he turned in pleased expectation. "Don't bother to speak to her," said Miss Cudahy scarcely moving her grey lips; he realized that she must have been watching him from under her lids. "Phoebe is deaf and dumb." He blushed, and did not know where to look.

2

He did not see them again for a month and would not have gone back at all, even to see the rest of the house, had it not been for the newel, which he had only glanced at as he had been leaving the house; there was not another in California to compare to it. The month was workaday and legal, marked only by his failure to persuade an owner in North Oakland not to redecorate a Victorian specimen with mourning veil eaves, and by a rather curious invitation to speak. He received a telephone call and then a visit from a cultivated, charming, shrewd little woman named Pickman-Ellsworth who wanted him to speak to the Alameda Fuchsia Society about the use of fuchsias in New England. He had to explain to her that he knew little about the subject and nothing at first hand. She received his refusal without protest, yet she continued talking, about one thing and another; she said that she had read some of his articles in the magazine *Golden West*; she kept throwing him subjects, visibly trying to "draw him out." He did not quite understand her purpose. She had black, quick eyes and sat very erect in her chair. She spoke to her chauffeur, as she left, with precisely that combination of dryness, condescension, and politeness with which she had addressed Bingham.

The newel at the foot of the stairs drew him back, that exquisitely carved, white newel with its promise of fine interiors on the second floor; the fluted newel, and, he had to confess it to himself, a curiosity about Miss Cudahy's household stronger than his repugnance for her herself.

He opened the gate, went through the hedge tunnel and walked up the stairs to the porch without seeing the Englishman gardener. He knocked the grand knocker—Miss Cudahy had no doorbell, indeed he felt that the electric lights in the old gas fixtures had furthered progress enough for her—and he stood waiting for Phoebe to open to him. He had calculated to himself what expression and gesture would best let Phoebe know the friendliness and pity he felt for her, what smile would blend recognition and warmth and yet least intrude upon her intimacy: the deference of the superior to the afflicted seemed to Bingham one of the few courtesies surviving from that high and better-mannered world lost to us to our diminution. This he had calculated—or, rather, had hoped to achieve—but he reckoned without Phoebe. How could he have known her? A glimpse of her, brown-dressed in the garden scurrying like a quail for cover; as maid in the hall, eyes downcast, smiling; a tea through which she had sat like a little girl, knees tightly pressed together, watching with a twinkle in her eye everything they did. How could he have known that the moment she opened the door now and saw him her eyes would light up, her cheeks would flush rosy red, her poor voice would crack a little, her hands would open out to him? Open so warmly and impetuously that he, smiling, would clasp them warmly in his, to the distress of all courtesy but to his most grateful pleasure. He did not touch people with casual affection, but rather shrank from it; he preferred words of congratulation to a slap on the back, the smile of privacy to a cocktail-party kiss; fastidiousness entails its dangers: he accepted them knowingly. But Phoebe's hands, rough-skinned and strong with work yet smaller than his, feminine in his, did not presume any intimacy or force any warmth of response: they extended him her words of greeting, inflection of her pleasure, her affection even, yet with hand's immediacy, touch's conviction. He smiled at her, foolish with sudden pleasure; his condescension snapped in her hands like a twig. He did not even feel embarrassed. It was as though he had known her a long time.

She took his hat and coat—it was a windy afternoon—and when she returned from hanging them up and found him admiring the newel, she pointed out to him something he had not yet noticed, the baseboard running along below the banisters, fretted beautifully and out of pure exuberance, uselessly, obscurely. She clasped her hands in pleasure at his pleasure. He started to his feet at Miss Cudahy's large voice: "Mr. Bingham, is that you?" He pointed, and Phoebe led him by the hand to the parlor door; as she opened the door she let go his hand; after he had gone in she withdrew from them like a maid.

"Mr. Bingham," said Miss Cudahy, frowning as he advanced, "what delayed you in the hall?"

"The newel," he said. "And Phoebe drew my attention to the fretted baseboard on the staircase."

"Did she?" said Miss Cudahy. "I hope you are well." And she took his hand.

"Very well," he answered, and it was all he could do to outsqueeze the grey-faced, lame old woman. "I hope in turn that your health has improved."

"How could it?" she said; she lolled back and pulled the rope. "At my age, in a climate like this, with no one to talk to?"

"It is hard," he said; he could scarcely have said less.

"Do you know how hard?" she replied scornfully. Phoebe appeared and Miss Cudahy waved some message to her. "Mr. Bingham, are you intending to buy my house? What do you want of me?"

"Believe me, I am interested only in the beauty of your house. I study old houses as an avocation."

"Beauty comes high on the market these days," she said fixing him with her eye. "Some kinds of beauty. Does this kind?"

"No," he answered rather flatly. "It does not."

"Are you just here for the day again, Mr. Bingham?"

"No, I am spending part of my vacation exploring these parts."

"How much of it, do you think?"

"That depends on many considerations."

"One of which is me, I take it?"

"Indeed," he said in the manner of a gallant, "how could it be otherwise?"

"The *Golden West* said you were a lawyer."

"Not exactly a lawyer. I am in legal work."

"Not a lawyer but in legal work," she repeated. "Slippery."

"Miss Cudahy," he said, arising, with all the dignity he could muster, "I would very much appreciate your permission to explore the rest of this house. I will take no photographs of it, and write nothing about it for publication, without your signed permission." This was more than she had let him get out during his entire first visit, only his anger had broken him through her complex defense so that he could now confront her simply with what he wanted.

"Ho," she shouted, "I've offended you, have I? I offend people. It usually takes longer with others. You are different. Sit down, young man, you've seen only this room and the hall, there's more here worth the seeing, you may be sure."

He sat down, gritting his teeth behind his smile. "The newel, Miss Cudahy, is worthy of McIntire himself."

"Yes," she said quizzically, "worthy of him. In the master bedroom"—she knew how to play her mouse—"on the second floor, Mr. Bingham, where I have not been for three years . . . My damned joints," she said banging the knee of her left leg. "In the master bedroom, when you get to it, you will notice the mantel. McIntire, is it? I must tell you about that some day."

"Why not tell me now?" he said with the last of his anger.

Phoebe came in bearing the tea things; neither of them turned towards her.

"Because, Mr. Bingham, it is not my pleasure."

They had tea.

3

For the twentieth time he looked at the note she had slipped into his hand: "Meet me outside the rear gate at 4:30." Already he had waited a quarter of an hour; a cold wind was blowing in from the sea; every fantasy of waiting afflicted him, wrong time, wrong place, accident, change of heart; he shivered back into his car. He did not happen to be looking when she came through the hedge and ran around the back of his car. Suddenly there she was, opening the door and slipping in beside him smiling. The ruefulness, the trace of anxiety, vanished from her face when she saw how gladly he forgave her, her forehead smoothed, she squeezed his arm. What could he do but take her hands in his? The good humor and affection of her smile became a sort of radiance which warmed him as he would not have believed possible three hours before.

What did she want? He started to draw out a pencil and paper, but she gently restrained his hands. With perfect good humor and seriousness, in a few quick gestures, she suggested driving somewhere, getting out, and walking. He started the car; she directed. On the cliff above a turbulent, rocky surf, she stopped them and led him down a path. He heard a bell buoy offshore busy in its melancholy; he had never stood close to rough weather on the sea before. Phoebe sprang up onto a rock beside him and leaned her hand on his shoulder; her hair glistened with blown spray, there were tiny drops on her eyelashes; she kept looking from the surf back at his face expectantly; he did not disappoint her for she clapped her hands and occasionally her voice emitted some of its pathetic, ugly symptoms of excitement. She led him to a sort of overhang where they could squat protected from the wind; he noticed that Phoebe's free hand pressed feelingly against the rock, and he imagined her delicate excitement from the waves' crashing on the outside of the rocks of their cave. He knew that later he would worry about the propriety of his behavior with Phoebe, wonder what he should have done instead, speculate on what she was thinking, what his actions meant to her; but for the time they huddled together there, his affection for her, pure and unamorous as though she were a child, dissolved all questions of motive, propriety, consequence, and left only a residue of unalloyed content. Squatting in a cold cave, with a view of lashing breakers under a heavy sky, damp, feet cold, holding hands with a deaf-mute girl he had met only once before, truly he thought himself seven sorts of fool, but he grinned at the thought.

She peered out of the cave at the sky, looked at him ruefully, and made some sign gestures; then, remembering he could not understand them, she put her hands gently on his arms, with a look of apology. Phoebe's gestures, the movements of her features, expressed, with the economy and delicacy of a trout swimming in a clear pool, a range of ideas and emotions as great as many a person can manage with words. Yet physically she was not delicate but rather blunt and unsymmetrical, not pretty but, as Bingham thought, one of the beautiful opposites of pretty. She taught him then and there in the cave a dozen ordinary words in sign language: I, you, car, home, day, like, go, sea, be together, mama, not, must. They laughed a great deal as his fingers blundered some sentences together: I you together like go sea. When he asked her how to say happy she showed him, and house, and door; but when he wrote love on the sand with a twig, she shook her head. She made the gestures of liking and being together, but pointed at love and looked him reprovingly. He saw that she had more tact than he, and very likely more honesty. She told him then she had to go home to mama. Mama? he asked her, and she nodded. Who? he said with his lips. Miss Cudahy, she wrote on the sand, sprang up and ran off towards the path. For a few moments he watched her, incredulous and frustrated; he felt very fond of her. He watched her climb the path, not thinking, but only looking at the slight figure quick and graceful in its brown, practical, shapeless clothes, not feeling even, only wishing he knew her well. And just before he got up to follow her he remembered Miss Cudahy's hard look when Phoebe had spilled some tea on the table, and he shuddered to feel cold little feet creeping about his back as they would when, lying in bed on the way to sleep, he chanced to think about the latest advances in bomb-making.

Next morning, arriving just after the postman, he carried Miss Cudahy's mail up to the front door with him. He saw one from Mrs. Pickman-Ellsworth. He was feeling grim when Phoebe let him into the parlor.

"Oh ho," cried Miss Cudahy after the civilities; she waved an envelope at him. "Let's see what Nell has to say about you. Just step into the dining room till I call you, Mr. Bingham, if you don't mind. You'll find Phoebe polishing the silver."

He fumbled among his unsorted emotions, unable to find the one that would suit his response; what he did was simply to thank her and do what she said—after all, he reflected, he had not yet seen the dining room.

Phoebe did not stop polishing, but whenever, in his inspection of the room, he passed near her she would rub against him a little like a cat. Miss Cudahy shouted him back.

"She says you're respectable," she said, and puffed on her pipe a few times gazing at him. "Good reputation, good family. I want you to stay with me, Mr. Bingham, for as long as you're going to be in this vicinity. I like you. You may have the master bedroom: I'll tell you who it was made for, some day. Phoebe needs the society of a cultivated man. Poor creature. Do you like her?"

"Very much." But he did not want to talk about her to Miss Cudahy. "Thank you for the invitation. I do not want to intrude . . . "

"Nonsense, that's my concern, not yours. There are not many literate people hereabouts. Mrs. Townson in Mendocino City, the Chiverses in Fort Bragg, who else? You ask me why I continue to live in Stowes Landing. My answer to you is, I don't. I live in this house."

"You have good taste in houses."

"Because it is your taste? Well, I like to be flattered, Mr. Bingham, but don't try to flatter me about my knowledge of New England houses. Between us we could write a good book on the old houses of this county." She puffed reflectively, gazing at him. "Mine's the best of course. Think it over. You could live here while we were at it, of course. I want to look at my mail now. Would you be so good as to step into the garden and tell Japheth to spray the roses?"

He looked at the appointments of the parlor and hall with a new eye as he walked out: they were his to use, and she would tell him all she knew. On the front step he imagined a roseate fantasy—a month, even six weeks of solid research and photographing, then one of the major contributions to the history of California architecture would be his. He even looked with a benevolent eye at Japheth, whom he found standing with some cuttings in one hand and clippers in the other, staring at a rose. He delivered his message with positive friendliness; Japheth winked at him, touched his cap with the clippers, and then, leering, pulled off a rose-branch so that it half split the cane. "It wasn't so in the old country," he whispered. Bingham left unhurriedly. Walking away, he rummaged about in his mind for his fantasy, but he could not find it again.

Half from plan and half because it was the nearest entrance, he ran up the back stairs and into the kitchen.

Glistening copper pots and pans hung on the walls; the old wood stove took up far more room than it needed to by the standards of modern efficiency; there was a hatchet in the box with the kindling; three comfortable, mended kitchen chairs, envy of snobs, sat about the stove; the worn linoleum, black and white checkered, was as clean with scrubbing as a boy's ears; it smelled good in the kitchen, of apples and coffee. Some sort of odd combination of flag-arms, as in a railroad signal, was attached to the wall over the pantry door; even as he was wondering what it was for, one of the flags, the white one, fell out at right angles; obviously a signal for Phoebe. It jiggled up and down; he stepped through the pantry into the dining room, and went with Phoebe into the parlor again.

"Do you approve of my kitchen, Mr. Bingham?"

"I do. Phoebe keeps it in admirable order."

"It's a pleasant place to spend the supper hours in the winter, let me tell you. You must visit us in the winter."

"I should be delighted." He felt constrained to say something more. "Your garden must have been a prize at one time."

"It was."

"A great pity it has fallen into neglect."

"Do you have any ideas for it, Mr. Bingham?" She was full of animation.

"Only the obvious ideas for the circumstances."

"The very thing!" she cried. "It would give you some exercise as we worked on our book. I can see by your figure you don't get enough exercise. Splendid, sir, a splendid addition."

He smiled painfully. "I don't enjoy gardening."

"Nonsense. You need it." She saw that she had gone too far. "Of course, of course," she went on heavily, "there would be no necessity. Japheth keeps the fuchsias from dying out. Phoebe would work with you in the garden. She likes it. She likes being with you."

Phoebe, having lip-read the gist of the conversation, smiled up at Bingham so sweetly that he, in relief from the old woman, half reached out his hand to her in response; propriety halted him. Phoebe, seeing his broken gesture, stepped beside him and took his hand; all three laughed at his blush.

"Well," said Miss Cudahy, shifting her bulk about, "everything is working out handsomely. Phoebe must show you your room. You must fetch your things and install yourself. We shall take an outing one day soon, Mr. Bingham. Zenobia Dobbs has a house in Greenwood you should see the inside of before you leave here, and I doubt if you went alone that she would be so hospitable to you as I have been."

He did not thank her for her hospitality, as she apparently wanted him to do, because he did not think she had been moved by hospitality to do what she was doing. He said he should like to see the house in Greenwood.

"But where is this town?" he asked. "I don't recognize the name."

"They took to calling it Elk a few years ago," she said. "There are not many like you, Mr. Bingham, who cherish the old things. The world rots and we rot with it."

She tossed some keys to Phoebe, fluttered her hand, and shifted herself back on her chair. Among her pale violet clothes, in that light that cast no shadow, her face seemed nearly ethereal, yet her body was huge.

Upstairs, Phoebe showed him the master bedroom; she kept looking from his face to the mantel or the bedstead or the moulding, pleased yet puzzled by the great impression the room was making on him, trying to see it with his eyes. She showed him the bathroom, Japheth's room, which was a dark cupboard, and her own room facing west, austere this side of barrenness, feminine only in the lace curtains. Then, with sparkling eyes, dancing a little in excitement, taking both his hands in one of hers, she opened the door to the last bedroom. His impression was one of darkness, scent, frills, musty old letters. She threw open the shutters; they were in a boudoir, among a luxury which had made feminine and intimate the stern woodwork, the right-angled room. There was a satin quilt on the low bed; at the sight of it he made a mock-gesture of indolence, and in an instant Phoebe was lying there. She took some pins out of her hair and shook it free; it was brown, fine hair. She laid her head at a certain angle on the pillows, curved one arm up over her head and the other onto her stomach, and turned her body in the fashion of all experience and luxuriation. It was only a moment until she bounced up smiling and clasping his hand, simple and young again.

He heard a clicking in the hall, and Miss Cudahy shouting that she wanted Phoebe. He told her; she put up her hair in a second; on their way down, she flipped the hall flag back up into place. On the landing of the stairs, yielding to what impulse he did not know, he stopped Phoebe just to look at her intently. Her face was cheery and flushed; when she saw his expression, she pressed herself against him, her head bowed onto his shoulder; he held her tightly a moment and kissed the top of her head. Miss Cudahy called again and they went on down.

She looked thunderous.

"Mr. Bingham," she said. "I heard the springs squeak."

He was very angry. "I dare say you did. I pressed the mattress to see what it was like, and Phoebe sat on the bed in the south room."

"Sat on it!" cried Miss Cudahy and motioned to Phoebe to go stand beside her. "Sat on it indeed! She jumped on it."

"Yes, and lay on it," he said, thin-lipped. "It is more luxury than she is used to."

"That was my room, and my mother's before me. I have restored it. I intended that you should look at the architecture and not the décor. I am displeased."

"Indeed. As though the one were not a part of the other."

"Well," she said, and suddenly she smiled and put her arm around Phoebe's legs, stroking her thigh. "One cannot be too careful. What is your opinion of what you saw upstairs?"

"It all but equals the newel in excellence."

"Quite so. Now then, Mr. Bingham," she said affably, "I think we can manage a way of working together. There are problems of course, not insuperable ones, I trust. How soon will you be able to come?"

"Why . . . I am not sure. I would have to arrange for a leave of absence beyond my usual vacation allowance."

"Rather. It will take us months at least, by my plan."

"Oh, I don't . . . "

"You have no sentimental ties in Oakland?—No, and Phoebe will be with us. You will be kind to Phoebe, Mr. Bingham? She has suffered from the lack of suitable male acquaintance."

"Why," he stammered, not knowing how to avoid indelicacy, "to be sure, I am fond of Phoebe, I will be kind, there is no problem."

"She means much to me, sir. Perhaps I try, as they say, to relive my youth through her. What does it matter? I mean her to be happy." She pressed her cheek against Phoebe's hip. "Did you ever see finer legs, sir?" Phoebe smoothed, indulgently, the iron-grey hair, smiling at Bingham. "We must handle Phoebe with care, must we not?"

4

On his fourth morning at Miss Cudahy's, he left at dawn to drive up the coast as far as Fort Bragg; the rugged coastline, the sombre landscape illuminated by spring flowers, the old barns patched with moss, the sheep, the small towns, all pleased him greatly, but he found no architectural points of interest to him, nothing he had not seen the like of before. He was not concentrating well, to be sure; he rubbered along, the amateur tourist; he said to himself that he had exhausted the district, but in truth he had left this thoughts disassembled behind. He returned to Stowes Landing not long after lunch, having intended to stay away until dark.

He knocked at the door, which was kept always locked; he had not been entrusted with a key. Finally the old woman herself answered.

"Ho," she said, and pounded her cane on the floor in her pleasure. "I was wanting you. It's too fine a day to waste in old houses. We're going for an outing down to Greenwood. Good. Good. Give me ten minutes in my room and I'll be ready."

"Fifteen," he said. "I want to clean up before going out again."

"Very well," she answered and stalked down the hall towards her room. "That's a fine sun they've got out there. Damn the hedge on a day like this."

There was not a sound upstairs as he washed and changed. There seldom was. He wished he knew whether Phoebe was in her room.

Miss Cudahy clumped back into the hall again and called him down. She was in front of the hall mirror arranging on her head a wide-brimmed, violet hat with a fringe of tiny tassels.

"We're off!" she cried. "Zenobia Dobbs, you must see her house. I haven't been in it for years. So you like my newel, Mr. Bingham." He exclaimed again that he did. "It's never been photographed." He said what she wanted him to say. "Well, help me down the stairs."

"I did not realize you could go down steps, Miss Cudahy."

"Down I can make it. It's up that breaks my back. You'll have to get Japheth to help you get me up."

She leaned heavily on his shoulder, taking the steps one at a time, and at the bottom she paused to snort like a horse.

"Where is Phoebe?" he asked.

"In the kitchen, I suppose. Where she belongs at any rate."

"She is coming with us?" he asked, just barely polite.

"I had not planned that she should."

"She would enjoy it," he said. "I will fetch her."

"Zenobia and she do not hit it off."

"Then I shall take Phoebe for a walk while you have tea with Mrs. Dobbs."

She did not answer him but started off toward the south side of the house.

Phoebe was not in the kitchen, not anywhere downstairs. He had to open the door to her room to see if she was in it. She was lying crosswise on her bed like a child, her head and bare arms bright in the sunshine that poured through her window. She had taken off her shoes and stockings; her legs were stretched up the side of the wall, one foot rubbing the other. He shook his head to clear it, and told her—he had learned more of her sign-language—to put on her bathing suit and come for a trip. She clapped her hands with joy, leaped up, and pushed him out of her room playfully.

They found Miss Cudahy waving her cane at glowering Japheth and threatening to beat him. Bingham led her to the car.

"Hmph," she snorted as they drove away. "They said he was hopeless but I knew I could handle him. The fools, they decided he needed love and kindness, but he took it for weakness. I've had him for years, and I give him unbuttered bread and a whip. And liquor on Saturday night."

"Miss Cudahy," he said, "have you ever considered having Phoebe taught to speak? I believe there are people who . . . "

"I have considered it, Mr. Bingham, but I shall not have it done. She is happy. At Mrs. Dobbs', you will return for me at five o'clock, and she will show you the house. You might leave Phoebe in the car."

"I would hate to leave Phoebe in the car," he said, and he told himself that only if the house were very attractive would he do it.

Phoebe, having seen their angry heads, leaned forward from the back seat and laid a restraining hand on each of them.

"In the eyes of God, Mr. Bingham, she may be worth ten of us. Meanwhile she does what I tell her to do, and I'd thank you to remember it." He just managed to swallow his anger; as it were in payment she said, "My grandfather, of whom I was telling you yesterday, brought the newel and the two mantels around the Horn on his own ship. They cost him a fortune."

He touched Phoebe's hand with his, and so did Miss Cudahy. They smiled at her and fell silent. There was brilliant sunlight all the way to Elk.

They spent two hours on the beach alone. There was a tunnel through a tall rock island a few yards offshore, through which the ocean drove frothing and soughing; once, the tide coming in, a great wave made a whistling noise in the tunnel. A northbound ship near the horizon spent the two hours going out of sight. They found some crabs in a pool and scared them back into their ledge, and laughed at their anger and clicking. The water was too cold for swimming but they waded in it a little; most of the time they lay on the sand. Bingham thought her legs to be in the lovely hinterland between trim and heavy, and the way she took off her skirt, from the way she displayed them and drew his head once down into her lap, he knew she wanted him to admire them, to touch them with his fingers. There was scarcely a moment when they were not touching.

He asked her if she wanted to learn to speak. She smiled rather wistfully, and nodded; but she told him she was happy anyway. He told her it was a shame that Miss Cudahy would not do it. She shook her head and put a finger on his lips. He told her there was a school in Oakland where she could learn to speak. She closed her eyes, smiling, till he promised not to continue with the subject, and she kissed the tip of his nose. They were half an hour late for Miss Cudahy. He did not think the Dobbs house worth enough to abandon Phoebe in the car just to see it.

Miss Cudahy did not seem to mind their being late; she seemed mellow. Several times on the way home she motioned for Phoebe's hand, pressed it against her cheek, nipped at her finger with her lips. "You are keeping our bargain, Mr. Bingham," she said. "I have never known Phoebe to be happier. Tomorrow may be a good day for you to commence your photography."

Japheth and he together got her up the front steps; the problem was now to transport her in such a way as to let her think they were only helping her. Japheth did not even try, and she was furious with him. Once she beat Bingham on the neck. "I'm so sorry," she trumpeted. "Mistake, mistake." And she beat Japheth the harder for her error. He spat on the steps as he went back to work in the garden.

At dinner Bingham found it just possible to be civil. Miss Cudahy was wheezing a good deal and did not make much demand upon him; he was able to brood inward upon his own thoughts. They were not even thoughts, just two strong sensations, about which his mind prowled and peered with no result: Miss Cudahy's mistaken blow on his neck and, quite as vivid as that though smaller and softer, the warm light kiss Phoebe had put there as soon as she could, to make up for the blow.

He had not been struck in anger since he was a child, nor kissed since then so tenderly. He did not know what to make of such strong experience. He felt neither anger nor gratitude, felt nothing that deserved so differentiated a name as resentment, say, or affection; indeed, so far as he knew he felt nothing except, on the skin and down into the muscles of his neck, the two touches of the two women. Yet, when at the end of the meal, staring at a crumb like a yogi, he did not hear Miss Cudahy ask him a question and she rapped on her tumbler with her ring, barking out "Mr. Bingham," he started from his chair and glared at her wildly a moment, leaned on the edge of the table and whispered intently "No! No!" "No coffee?" she said, a little taken aback. He subsided under Phoebe's restraining hand. "Sorry," he mumbled; "I was thinking of something else. Yes, coffee, please." He had been feeling more than touches on the neck, and with that feudal rap on the glass some of it began turmoiling up and out.

He did not even assist Miss Cudahy from her chair, but bolted into the kitchen where, for the first time, he wiped dishes for Phoebe as she washed. She kept her eyes downcast on her business; even when he patted her arm for attention or physically turned her head about, she did not look at his eyes, but only at his lips, or at his hands stumbling and tripping in their rush like lips stuttering from anger; once, she caught the frustrated things and kissed each palm gently, then turned back to her suds. He stood beside her, the kisses warm in his hands, just staring at her; feeling his chin nearly begin to quiver he bustled back to his job; but his anger was gone, and all he felt now was that Phoebe was altogether delicate and alive and pitiable and needing to be saved. He understood now, without hatred, how Miss Cudahy would want to hold her; but Phoebe must be saved; and more, she must want to be saved.

As she was hanging up the dishcloth, finished, he held her waist with a gentleness she immediately recognized, she looked back over her shoulder up into his eyes; he kissed her; scarcely moving, she yielded against him. There were tears in their eyes when they drew apart, and at that instant Bingham felt that he might have fetched her coat and hat and driven her off to Oakland without an objection from her. But she must freely desire to leave Miss Cudahy; she must not be swayed from that old woman's will only to become subject to his, though better, will. He sat her by the oven, poured a cup of coffee for each of them, sat in front of her so that their knees touched, and asked her, "Will you come to Oakland with me?" It would have been coy of her, gazing against his earnest gaze, to treat his question playfully, to pretend she didn't take him seriously: the leap of eagerness that brightened her eyes and pressed her hands together meant to him only that she wanted to come to Oakland; yet she did not sign the answer in return. "I can take you with me when I go. I have friends you can stay with till we find a permanent arrangement for you. Don't worry, I will make it a point to see you often." It would have been weak of her, under his insistence, to have begun crying in order to avoid meeting his challenge: yet he saw tears come to her eyes after his last pressing; he would have relented—must she not choose freely?—but that she answered him then: I owe Miss Cudahy so much. "Of course," he answered, "and you can return to her if you want, but you owe it to yourself to go to the school." She needs me, Phoebe pleaded; what would she do without me? And with that he pounded the table; but not too loud, for fear Miss Cudahy would hear him. It would be like a betrayal, Phoebe told him. "You must leave her sooner or later," he responded (No, her head shook), "you owe it to yourself to go now." She buried her face in her hands, but in a heat of compelling he pulled them away and, clutching her wrists hard, said with his lips, "You must come with me." She wilted then, as though he had uttered a magic formula— composed of common words perhaps, but nonetheless magic. She would come if he would get Miss Cudahy's permission. "But no, but no! You must come of your own free will." Shaking her head, miserable, she sat on his lap and hid her face against his neck, so that all he could do, imagining how that old woman would greet such a proposal, was to hold Phoebe as though she were crying, in need of comforting; yet he was conscious of her warm breathing, of her lips half kissing the soft joining of his shoulder and neck; of her woman's body which his hands were embarrassed how to hold. Old Japheth came in for coffee and at the sight of them muttered "Bitch! Bitch!" In a sort of desperation of confusion, Bingham pushed Phoebe off his lap and, flapping his hands, went up to his room.

But there was no peace for him there at all. To rescue her became, as he writhed on the bed in that handsome, alien room, his obsession and immediate need. His pain was purer and stronger than it could have been had he suspected for a second that there was more causing it than the desire to liberate an oppressed, afflicted person he knew. But as it was, that pain was so great that he had to creep back downstairs again hoping to find Phoebe in the kitchen alone where he could bring matters to a head; for he did not know what he would do if she did not assert herself tonight. The afterwards would work itself out, and if Miss Cudahy should suffer, then she should suffer.

As he reached, silently, the bottom step, he saw through the half-open door to the parlor Phoebe sitting beside Miss Cudahy, who was lolling back in the chaise-longue looking at her from under her eyelids and fondling her arm. For a long time he froze on that step; all he felt for that painful time was the gracefully curving, worn, smooth old wood of the rail in his hand. Quivering with emotions he did not understand and no longer cared about controlling, he went into the room. As he spoke, but not until then, he realized from the suspicion of quiver in his voice that he would not be able to stand up to the old woman.

"Miss Cudahy," he said, as evenly as he could manage, "I thank you for your hospitality, but I am leaving."

"What?" she cried, altogether surprised. "You are just becoming one of us."

"I am not. I am leaving immediately."

"You have not taken your photograph yet."

"No," he said; he had thought he would be adamant. "I am obliged to leave suddenly." He would make no excuse, only get out. But his eye was drawn by the exquisite proportions of the frame around the window behind the two women. "Perhaps when I come back up later this summer I shall be able to complete my study."

"*Our* book, Mr. Bingham?"

"Of course, of course, complete our study."

"Perhaps. We shall see." She thrust unhappy Phoebe from the chair. "I shall get to the bottom of this."

He had packed in five minutes. Phoebe was waiting for him in the hall, tears in her eyes. He wrote down the name of the motel where he was going to stay the night and told her to come there first thing in the morning. She nodded, and looked at him in bewilderment, longingly.

At the front door he was touching her hands goodbye and telling her she must come as soon as she could, when Miss Cudahy shouted, "Send Phoebe to me at once!" He kissed her quickly on the cheek, and left.

5

He could not remain alone and waking in that alien, ugly motel, but neither did he want to go near the surge of the sea. He walked towards the hills through a pleasant pasture, and as he was walking he heard on the other side of a fence bleating sheep; he went to the fence to watch them in the light of the high moon. They stared at him for a moment like citizens in a bus, and when he rattled the top rail of the fence they stared at him again and shied away; he played with them off and on for an hour or more, an hour of relief: their stares were simple and sufficient, they left him alone.

He lay in bed feeling as though he were floating. He put his hands under his head and gazed at the moon, not thinking so much as watching thoughts dance through his mind. The moon had wheeled into the western sky by the time he had fallen asleep.

A rattle at the door awoke him. The moon had set. He sat up and called, "Who is it?" There was another rattle and a low, amorphous cry. He opened the door to Phoebe. She grasped both his hands in hers hard, and threw herself face down on the bed crying, turned away from him. He closed the windows and built a fire in the stove, and then for fifteen minutes or so sat on the bed beside her stroking her hair and arms, shuddering a little with alarm, ready to weep himself that he could say nothing to her.

At last she turned her face towards him, and gradually her crying subsided. Her mouth, now that he came to watch her face so closely, lost the contours of grief and reassumed its usual expression; hers was somehow softer than most mouths, less revealing of character, more innocent. She ceased to make those hard, inchoate cries that disturbed him. She became Phoebe again. He was astonished in a new way at how tenderly he felt toward her, thinking of what she must be suffering now, partly for his sake.

"Did she scold you?" he asked, and her answer was only the most rueful smile in the world. "What is this?" he cried suddenly and bent down to look at three fresh bruises on the back of Phoebe's leg, just above the knee. "Did she hurt you?" he said to her. She shrugged: what difference did it make? "Pinch?" She shrugged: yes, but it was the least of my pain. "Vicious," he muttered to himself pounding the fist of one hand into the palm of the other, "damned, cruel, vicious old bitch."

Phoebe made him sit beside her and asked him if he would ever come back to the house; he told her no. Her lip quivered; she threw her arms around him as though to hold him forever, and pulled him down beside her. When he could, he freed himself and told her she must go with him. When are you leaving? Tomorrow, he answered, and she turned from him again to cry. He was trembling with anger so hard that Phoebe finally turned over and smiled as best she could. He gave her his handkerchief to use for her tears.

He lay down facing her and put his arm over her waist; their legs were touching. They lay looking at each other peacefully, touching gently. But it seemed to him after a time that something was required of him; the simplest, easiest thing to do would be to kiss her, but just because it was so easy he distrusted it, and besides it would be taking advantage of her as he had sworn to himself not to do; perhaps he should renew his offer to take her to the school in Oakland, assuring her again that he had meant it. But when she saw what he was starting to tell her she stopped him, tenderly, but certainly. Her hand, still and yet alive, lay curled against his throat, warm and other and loving, and seemed to him to reproach him for some lack. It was all he could do to support her unflinching gaze; in no way did she actually reproach him, yet he could not respond to that gaze with a smile or in fact with any expression at all; it was not a response her gaze sought, but somehow him himself; and unpitying, devouring, utterly unmalicious gaze; it did not demand, it took. As the uneasy night wore on, lying half embraced on his left side awkwardly, he gradually suffocated with the knowledge that Phoebe had the unopposable rights of one who, in a way he was appalled to imagine, loved.

At the first evidences of dawn he leaped up and dressed, telling her that for the sake of her reputation she must leave the motel immediately. She lay watching his bustle with her steady, innocent, direct gaze. He stood before her urging her to rise. Is this the last time I shall ever see you? He could not bear her directness. "No, no, of course not, it's all settled. How could you say such a thing? You are going with me to Oakland, today, now, as soon as you've packed your bags. We're going to Miss Cudahy's now." He was frenetic and pressed too hard. "I'll be waiting for you in the car outside the hedge at nine o'clock. It's all settled?" She smiled into tears, into the tears, he thought, of joy, and nodded. She pulled him down on top of her and held him so hard and kissed him so ardently that he was alarmed. They left the motel. For a moment, parking outside the hedge, kissing her again, he had the wild notion of driving off with Phoebe then and there, however it might look; but before he had time either to act on the impulse or to reject it, with a cry that startled him she had opened the door of the car and run in.

At nine o'clock she had not emerged from that tunnel in the hedge, nor at quarter past. At nine-thirty he got out of the car and went in the front gate.

At the window of her room on the second floor, Phoebe was standing, wearing her bathrobe, evidently crying. She kept shaking her head. She made a gesture, from her heart to her lips to him, that could have meant only one thing. His heart throbbing in his throat with the pity and the loss, he made the signs "Together, we must go together." If there had been any way for him to get her free from that house he would have used it at that moment; he blamed himself for having let her come back at all; he could scarcely bear to think of her life locked in as it would be and had been. She buried her face in her hands and turned slowly from the window.

He ran to the front door and pounded the knocker; there was no response. He knocked till the great door reverberated; he would have shouted had he not been afraid of alarming the neighbors. Finally there was the sound of a cane and of coughing at the end of the hallway. He trembled; his lips were tense with the recriminations with which he would greet Miss Cudahy. She opened the door, wide, and stood staring at him. "Yes?" Instantly he became aware of his disheveled appearance. "As you know, my work, it is . . . " "Go get your Kodak, Mr. Bingham," she said, guttural with scorn. She pointed with her cane, holding her arm out full length, the garments trailing. "You may photograph my newel if you're quick about it." His mouth opened, but he did not say anything. "Mind you don't go upstairs," said Miss Cudahy and returned down the hall. He turned, went down the steps, and ran to his car. On his way back in, burdened with his camera and lighting equipment, he glanced furtively up, and was grateful to see that Phoebe had drawn the curtains to her room. He had run out again for his tripod, because he could not hold the camera steady. There was not another sound in the house as he worked. In fifteen minutes he had finished and left.

The Life You Save May Be Your Own

Flannery O'Connor
USA, 1955

The old woman and her daughter were sitting on their porch when Mr. Shiftlet came up their road for the first time. The old woman slid to the edge of her chair and leaned forward, shading her eyes from the piercing sunset with her hand. The daughter could not see far in front of her and continued to play with her fingers. Although the old woman lived in this desolate spot with only her daughter and she had never seen Mr. Shiftlet before, she could tell, even from a distance, that he was a tramp and no one to be afraid of. His left coat sleeve was folded up to show there was only half an arm in it and his gaunt figure listed slightly to the side as if the breeze were pushing him. He had on a black town suit and a brown felt hat that was turned up in the front and down in the back and he carried a tin tool box by a handle. He came on, at an amble, up her road, his face turned toward the sun which appeared to be balancing itself on the peak of a small mountain.

The old woman didn't change her position until he was almost into her yard; then she rose with one hand fisted on her hip. The daughter, a large girl in a short blue organdy dress, saw him all at once and jumped up and began to stamp and point and make excited speechless sounds.

Mr. Shiftlet stopped just inside the yard and set his box on the ground and tipped his hat at her as if she were not in the least afflicted; then he turned toward the old woman and swung the hat all the way off. He had long black slick hair that hung flat from a part in the middle to beyond the tips of his ears on either side. His face descended in forehead for more than half its length and ended suddenly with his features just balanced over a jutting steel-trap jaw. He seemed to be a young man but he had a look of composed dissatisfaction as if he understood life thoroughly.

"Good evening," the old woman said. She was about the size of a cedar fence post and she had a man's gray hat pulled down low over her head.

The tramp stood looking at her and didn't answer. He turned his back and faced the sunset. He swung both his whole and his short arm up slowly so that they indicated an expanse of sky and his figure formed a crooked cross. The old woman watched him with her arms folded across her chest as if she were the owner of the sun, and the daughter watched, her head thrust forward and her fat helpless hands hanging at the wrists. She had long pink-gold hair and eyes as blue as a peacock's neck.

He held the pose for almost fifty seconds and then he picked up his box and came on to the porch and dropped down on the bottom step. "Lady," he said in a firm nasal voice, "I'd give a fortune to live where I could see me a sun do that every evening."

"Does it every evening," the old woman said and sat back down. The daughter sat down too and watched him with a cautious sly look as if he were a bird that had come up very close. He leaned to one side, rooting in his pants pocket, and in a second he brought out a package of chewing gum and offered her a piece. She took it and unpeeled it and began to chew without taking her eyes off him. He offered the old woman a piece but she only raised her upper lip to indicate she had no teeth.

Mr. Shiftlet's pale sharp glance had already passed over everything in the yard—the pump near the corner of the house and the big fig tree that three or four chickens were preparing to roost in —and had moved to a shed where he saw the square rusted back of an automobile. "You ladies drive?" he asked.

"That car ain't run in fifteen year," the old woman said. "The day my husband died, it quit running."

"Nothing is like it used to be, lady," he said. "The world is almost rotten."

"That's right," the old woman said. "You from around here?"

"Name Tom T. Shiftlet," he murmured, looking at the tires.

"I'm pleased to meet you," the old woman said. "Name Lucynell Crater and daughter Lucynell Crater. What you doing around here, Mr. Shiftlet?"

He judged the car to be about a 1928 or '29 Ford. "Lady," he said, and turned and gave her his full attention, "lemme tell you something. There's one of these doctors in Atlanta that's taken a knife and cut the human heart—the human heart," he repeated, leaning forward, "out of a man's chest and held it in his hand," and he held his hand out, palm up, as if it were slightly weighted with the human heart, "and studied it like it was a day-old chicken, and lady," he said, allowing a long significant pause in which his head slid forward and his clay-colored eyes brightened, "he don't know no more about it than you or me."

"That's right," the old woman said.

"Why, if he was to take that knife and cut into every corner of it, he still wouldn't know no more than you or me. What you want to bet?"

"Nothing," the old woman said wisely. "Where you come from, Mr. Shiftlet?"

He didn't answer. He reached into his pocket and brought out a sack of tobacco and a package of cigarette papers and rolled himself a cigarette, expertly with one hand, and attached it in a hanging position to his upper lip. Then he took a box of wooden matches from his pocket and struck one on his shoe. He held the burning match as if he were studying the mystery of flame while it traveled dangerously toward his skin. The daughter began to make loud noises and to point to his hand

and shake her finger at him, but when the flame was just before touching him, he leaned down with his hand cupped over it as if he were going to set fire to his nose and lit the cigarette.

He flipped away the dead match and blew a stream of gray into the evening. A sly look came over his face. "Lady," he said, "nowadays, people'll do anything anyways. I can tell you my name is Tom T. Shiftlet and I come from Tarwater, Tennessee, but you never have seen me before: how you know I ain't lying? How you know my name ain't Aaron Sparks, lady, and I come from Singleberry, Georgia, or how you know it's not George Speeds and I come from Lucy, Alabama, or how you know I ain't Thompson Bright from Toolafalls, Mississippi?"

"I don't know nothing about you," the old woman muttered, irked.

"Lady," he said, "people don't care how they lie. Maybe the best I can tell you is, I'm a man; but listen lady," he said and paused and made his tone more ominous still, "what is a man?"

The old woman began to gum a seed. "What you carry in that tin box, Mr. Shiftlet?" she asked.

"Tools," he said, put back. "I'm a carpenter."

"Well, if you come out here to work, I'll be able to feed you and give you a place to sleep but I can't pay. I'll tell you that before you begin," she said.

There was no answer at once and no particular expression on his face. He leaned back against the two-by-four that helped support the porch roof. "Lady," he said slowly, "there's some men that some things mean more to them than money." The old woman rocked without comment and the daughter watched the trigger that moved up and down in his neck. He told the old woman then that all most people were interested in was money, but he asked what a man was made for. He asked her if a man was made for money, or what. He asked her what she thought she was made for but she didn't answer, she only sat rocking and wondered if a one-armed man could put a new roof on her garden house. He asked a lot of questions that she didn't answer. He told her that he was twenty-eight years old and had lived a varied life. He had been a gospel singer, a foreman on the railroad, an assistant in an undertaking parlor, and he come over the radio for three months with Uncle Roy and his Red Creek Wranglers. He said he had fought and bled in the Arm Service of his country and visited every foreign land and that everywhere he had seen people that didn't care if they did a thing one way or another. He said he hadn't been raised thataway.

A fat yellow moon appeared in the branches of the fig tree as if it were going to roost there with the chickens. He said that a man had to escape to the country to see the world whole and that he wished he lived in a desolate place like this where he could see the sun go down every evening like God made it to do.

"Are you married or are you single?" the old woman asked.

There was a long silence. "Lady," he asked finally, "where would you find you an innocent woman today? I wouldn't have any of this trash I could just pick up."

The daughter was leaning very far down, hanging her head almost between her knees watching him through a triangular door she had made in her overturned hair; and she suddenly fell in a heap on the floor and began to whimper. Mr. Shiftlet straightened her out and helped her get back in the chair.

"Is she your baby girl?" he asked.

"My only," the old woman said "and she's the sweetest girl in the world. I would give her up for nothing on earth. She's smart too. She can sweep the floor, cook, wash, feed the chickens, and hoe. I wouldn't give her up for a casket of jewels."

"No," he said kindly, "don't ever let any man take her away from you."

"Any man come after her," the old woman said, " 'll have to stay around the place."

Mr. Shiftlet's eye in the darkness was focused on a part of the automobile bumper that glittered in the distance. "Lady," he said, jerking his short arm up as if he could point with it to her house and yard and pump, "there ain't a broken thing on this plantation that I couldn't fix for you, one-arm jackleg or not. I'm a man," he said with a sullen dignity, "even if I ain't a whole one. I got," he said, tapping his knuckles on the floor to emphasize the immensity of what he was going to say, "a moral intelligence!" and his face pierced out of the darkness into a shaft of door-light and he stared at her as if he were astonished himself at this impossible truth.

The old woman was not impressed with the phrase. "I told you you could hang around and work for food," she said, "if you don't mind sleeping in that car yonder."

"Why listen, lady," he said with a grin of delight, "the monks of old slept in their coffins!"

"They wasn't as advanced as we are," the old woman said.

The next morning he began on the roof of the garden house while Lucynell, the daughter, sat on a rock and watched him work.

He had not been around a week before the change he had made in the place was apparent. He had patched the front and back steps, built a new hog pen, restored a fence, and taught Lucynell, who was completely deaf and had never said a word in her life, to say the word "bird." The big rosy-faced girl followed him everywhere, saying "Burrttddt ddbirrrttddt," and clapping her hands. The old woman watched from a distance, secretly pleased. She was ravenous for a son-in-law.

Mr. Shiftlet slept on the hard narrow back seat of the car with his feet out the side window. He had his razor and a can of water on a crate that served him as a bedside table and he put up a piece of mirror against the back glass and kept his coat neatly on a hanger that he hung over one of the windows.

In the evenings he sat on the steps and talked while the old woman and Lucynell rocked violently in their chairs on either side of him. The old woman's three mountains were black against the dark blue sky and were visited off and on by various planets and by the moon after it had left the chickens. Mr. Shiftlet pointed out that the reason he had improved this plantation was because he had taken a personal interest in it. He said he was even going to make the automobile run.

He had raised the hood and studied the mechanism and he said he could tell that the car had been built in the days when cars were really built. You take now, he said, one man puts in one bolt and another man puts in another bolt and another man puts in another bolt so that it's a man for a bolt. That's why you have to pay so much for a car: you're paying all those men. Now if you didn't have to pay but one man, you could get you a cheaper car and one that had had a personal interest taken in it, and it would be a better car. The old woman agreed with him that this was so.

Mr. Shiftlet said that the trouble with the world was that nobody cared, or stopped and took any trouble. He said he never would have been able to teach Lucynell to say a word if he hadn't cared and stopped long enough.

"Teach her to say something else," the old woman said.

"What you want her to say next?" Mr. Shiftlet asked.

The old woman's smile was broad and toothless and suggestive. "Teach her to say 'sugarpie,'" she said.

Mr. Shiftlet already knew what was on her mind.

The next day he began to tinker with the automobile and that evening he told her that if she would buy a fan belt, he would be able to make the car run.

The old woman said she would give him the money. "You see that girl yonder?" she asked, pointing to Lucynell who was sitting on the floor a foot away, watching him, her eyes blue even in the dark. "If it was ever a man wanted to take her away, I would say, 'No man on earth is going to take that sweet girl of mine away from me!' but if he was to say, 'Lady, I don't want to take her away, I want her right here,' I would say, 'Mister, I don't blame you none. I wouldn't pass up a chance to live in a permanent place and get the sweetest girl in the world myself. You ain't no fool,' I would say."

"How old is she?" Mr. Shiftlet asked casually.

"Fifteen, sixteen," the old woman said. The girl was nearly thirty but because of her innocence it was impossible to guess.

"It would be a good idea to paint it too," Mr. Shiftlet remarked. "You don't want it to rust out."

"We'll see about that later," the old woman said.

The next day he walked into town and returned with the parts he needed and a can of gasoline. Late in the afternoon, terrible noises issued from the shed and the old woman rushed out of the house, thinking Lucynell was somewhere having a fit. Lucynell was sitting on a chicken crate, stamping her feet and screaming, "Burrddttt! Bddurrddtttt!" but her fuss was drowned out by the car. With a volley of blasts it emerged from the shed, moving in a fierce and stately way. Mr. Shiftlet was in the driver's seat, sitting very erect. He had an expression of serious modesty on his face as if he had just raised the dead.

That night, rocking on the porch, the old woman began her business, at once. "You want you an innocent woman, don't you?" she asked sympathetically. "You don't want none of this trash."

"No'm, I don't," Mr. Shiftlet said.

"One that can't talk," she continued, "can't sass you back or use foul language. That's the kind for you to have. Right there," and she pointed to Lucynell sitting cross-legged in her chair, holding both feet in her hands.

"That's right," he admitted. "She wouldn't give me any trouble."

"Saturday," the old woman said, "you and her and me can drive into town and get married."

Mr. Shiftlet eased his position on the steps.

"I can't get married right now," he said. "Everything you want to do takes money and I ain't got any."

"What you need with money?" she asked.

"It takes money," he said. "Some people'll do anything anyhow these days, but the way I think, I wouldn't marry no woman that I couldn't take on a trip like she was somebody. I mean take her to a hotel and treat her. I wouldn't marry the Duchesser Windsor," he said firmly, "unless I could take her to a hotel and giver something good to eat.

"I was raised thataway and there ain't a thing I can do about it. My old mother taught me how to do."

"Lucynell don't even know what a hotel is," the old woman muttered. "Listen here, Mr. Shiftlet," she said, sliding forward in her chair, "you'd be getting a permanent house and a deep well and the most innocent girl in the world. You don't need no money. Lemme tell you something: there ain't any place in the world for a poor disabled friendless drifting man."

The ugly words settled in Mr. Shiftlet's head like a group of buzzards in the top of a tree. He didn't answer at once. He rolled himself a cigarette and lit it and then he said in an even voice, "Lady, a man is divided into two parts, body and spirit."

The old woman clamped her gums together.

"A body and a spirit," he repeated. "The body, lady, is like a house: it don't go anywhere; but the spirit, lady, is like a automobile: always on the move, always . . . "

"Listen, Mr. Shiftlet," she said, "my well never goes dry and my house is always warm in the winter and there's no mortgage on a thing about this place. You can go to the courthouse and see for yourself. And yonder under that shed is a fine automobile." She laid the bait carefully. "You can have it painted by Saturday. I'll pay for the paint."

In the darkness, Mr. Shiftlet's smile stretched like a weary snake waking up by a fire. After a second he recalled himself and said, "I'm only saying a man's spirit means more to him than anything else. I would have to take my wife off for the weekend without no regards at all for cost. I got to follow where my spirit says to go."

"I'll give you fifteen dollars for a weekend trip," the old woman said in a crabbed voice. "That's the best I can do."

"That wouldn't hardly pay for more than the gas and the hotel," he said. "It wouldn't feed her."

"Seventeen-fifty," the old woman said. "That's all I got so it isn't any use you trying to milk me. You can take a lunch."

Mr. Shiftlet was deeply hurt by the word "milk." He didn't doubt that she had more money sewed up in her mattress but he had already told her he was not interested in her money. "I'll make that do," he said and rose and walked off without treating with her further.

On Saturday the three of them drove into town in the car that the paint had barely dried on and Mr. Shiftlet and Lucynell were married in the Ordinary's office while the old woman witnessed. As they came out of the courthouse, Mr. Shiftlet began twisting his neck in his collar. He looked morose and bitter as if he had been insulted while someone held him. "That didn't satisfy me none," he said. "That was just something a woman in an office did, nothing but paper work and blood tests. What do they know about my blood? If they was to take my heart and cut it out," he said, "they wouldn't know a thing about me. It didn't satisfy me at all."

"It satisfied the law," the old woman said sharply.

"The law," Mr. Shiftlet said and spit. "It's the law that don't satisfy me."

He had painted the car dark green with a yellow band around it just under the windows. The three of them climbed in the front seat and the old woman said, "Don't Lucynell look pretty? Looks like a baby doll." Lucynell was dressed up in a white dress that her mother had uprooted from a trunk and there was a Panama hat on her head with a bunch of red wooden cherries on the brim. Every now and then her placid expression was changed by a sly isolated little thought like a shoot of green in the desert. "You got a prize!" the old woman said.

Mr. Shiftlet didn't even look at her.

They drove back to the house to let the old woman off and pick up the lunch. When they were ready to leave, she stood staring in the window of the car, with her fingers clenched around the glass. Tears began to seep sideways out of her eyes and run along the dirty creases in her face. "I ain't ever been parted with her for two days before," she said.

Mr. Shiftlet started the motor.

"And I wouldn't let no man have her but you because I seen you would do right. Good-by, Sugarbaby," she said, clutching at the sleeve of the white dress. Lucynell looked straight at her and didn't seem to see her there at all. Mr. Shiftlet eased the car forward so that she had to move her hands.

The early afternoon was clear and open and surrounded by pale blue sky. Although the car would go only thirty miles an hour, Mr. Shiftlet imagined a terrific climb and dip and swerve that went entirely to his head so that he forgot his morning bitterness. He had always wanted an automobile but he had never been able to afford one before. He drove very fast because he wanted to make Mobile by nightfall.

Occasionally he stopped his thoughts long enough to look at Lucynell in the seat beside him. She had eaten the lunch as soon as they were out of the yard and now she was pulling the cherries off the hat one by one and throwing them out the window. He became depressed in spite of the car. He had driven about a hundred miles when he decided that she must be hungry again and at the next small town they came to, he stopped in front of an aluminum-painted eating place called The Hot Spot and took her in and ordered her a plate of ham and grits. The ride had made her sleepy and as soon as she got up on the stool, she rested her head on the counter and shut her eyes. There was no one in The Hot Spot but Mr. Shiftlet and the boy behind the counter, a pale youth with a greasy rag hung over his shoulder. Before he could dish up the food, she was snoring gently.

"Give it to her when she wakes up," Mr. Shiftlet said. "I'll pay for it now."

The boy bent over her and stared at the long pink-gold hair and the half-shut sleeping eyes. Then he looked up and stared at Mr. Shiftlet. "She looks like an angel of Gawd," he murmured.

"Hitchhiker," Mr. Shiftlet explained. "I can't wait. I got to make Tuscaloosa."

The boy bent over again and very carefully touched his finger to a strand of the golden hair and Mr. Shiftlet left.

He was more depressed than ever as he drove on by himself. The late afternoon had grown hot and sultry and the country had flattened out. Deep in the sky a storm was preparing very slowly and without thunder as if it meant to drain every drop of air from the earth before it broke. There were times when Mr. Shiftlet preferred not to be alone. He felt too that a man with a car had a responsibility to others and he kept his eye out for a hitchhiker. Occasionally he saw a sign that warned: "Drive carefully. The life you save may be your own."

The narrow road dropped off on either side into dry fields and here and there a shack or a filling station stood in a clearing. The sun began to set directly in front of the automobile. It was a reddening ball that through his windshield was slightly flat on the bottom and top. He saw a boy in overalls and a gray hat standing on the edge of the road and he slowed the car down and stopped in front of him. The boy didn't have his hand raised to thumb the ride, he was only standing there, but he had small cardboard suitcase and his hat was set on his head in a way to indicate that he had left somewhere for good. "Son," Mr. Shiftlet said, "I see you want a ride."

The boy didn't say he did or he didn't but he opened the door of the car and got in, and Mr. Shiftlet started driving again. The child held the suitcase on his lap and folded his arms on top of it. He turned his head and looked out the window away from Mr. Shiftlet. Mr. Shiftlet felt oppressed. "Son," he said after a minute, "I got the best old mother in the world so I reckon you only got the second best."

The boy gave him a quick dark glance and then turned his face back out the window.

"It's nothing so sweet," Mr. Shiftlet continued, "as a boy's mother. She taught him his first prayers at her knee, she give him love when no other would, she told him what was right and what wasn't, and she seen that he done the right thing. Son," he said, "I never rued a day in my life like the one I rued when I left that old mother of mine."

The boy shifted in his seat but he didn't look at Mr. Shiftlet. He unfolded his arms and put one hand on the door handle.

"My mother was a angel of Gawd," Mr. Shiftlet said in a very strained voice. "He took her from heaven and giver to me and I left her." His eyes were instantly clouded over with a mist of tears. The car was barely moving.

The boy turned angrily in the seat. "You go to the devil!" he cried. "My old woman is a flea bag and yours is a stinking pole cat!" and with that he flung the door open and jumped out with his suitcase into the ditch.

Mr. Shiftlet was so shocked that for about a hundred feet he drove along slowly with the door still open. A cloud, the exact color of the boy's hat and shaped like a turnip, had descended over the sun, and another, worse looking, crouched behind the car. Mr. Shiftlet felt that the rottenness of the world was about to engulf him. He raised his arm and let it fall again to his breast. "Oh Lord!" he prayed. "Break forth and wash the slime from this earth!"

The turnip continued slowly to descend. After a few minutes there was a guffawing peal of thunder from behind and fantastic raindrops, like tin-can tops, crashed over the rear of Mr. Shiftlet's car. Very quickly he stepped on the gas and with his stump sticking out the window he raced the galloping shower into Mobile.

The Edge of Sound

Gordon Woodward
Canada, 1955

Ronnie watched the car turn the corner, hard bright windshield smashing against the warm September sunlight, soundless little wheels sucking up spumes of fine yellow dust; and then he turned and went past his brother Gregory who was reading a book and he walked into the hall and put both his arms around the bitter-smelling post on top of the banister and looked down at the bottom of stairs. He wondered how long it took to get to be eleven years old, always waiting for someone to rip off that last calendar-page month; then he thought that maybe it only seemed a long time to him because he couldn't hear anything or speak to anyone. How did you mouth-speak anyway?

The hall below was like a shade-green vault. There were crooked brown stains in one corner of the wall mirror, like rust-worms crawling somewhere behind the glass. And the old lady was standing by the open door; she was waiting for the doctor. He knew she was crying because her daughter had already been dead when they brought her in from the street only an hour ago after the car had hit her. Still the old lady's back stayed; like an old striped laundry bag stuffed with straw.

But the sandal was there. It had fallen from Abbie's foot when they had carried her in from the street, now it was lying beside the hatrack with the toe pointed out as it wanted to walk somewhere. Anywhere. Perhaps even out over the whole town of Cobalt, British Columbia, Canada, North America, World, in which she had lived for fifteen years and then had been run over by a car. He was sure that if he spread his arms and jumped from the landing he could swoop down and pick up the sandal. His arms ached to fly, his legs to jump.

The sunlight slipped past the old lady and made a bright path across the linoleum; and it touched against the sandal. Laceholes glittering like chips of silver. Then suddenly the old lady moved her foot. She moved again. Then she stepped outside and closed the door and the sunlight disappeared and so did the sandal. And then he started to cry again. He leaned his cheek against the cool varnished banister; the damp wood gave off a sharp bitter odor of dark stain. He wept. Tears moving slowly down like trickles of hot wax.

The old lady came back in followed by the doctor and for a moment the whole hallway was alive with sharp brittle sunshine; then she closed the door and there was only the dim orange bulb hanging on a twisted cord from the ceiling, like a viscid fruit.

He was sure the bulb would be warm and sticky if he touched it with his hand.

The two of them were standing beneath the light in the hall and the old lady's lips were moving but he couldn't tell what she was saying; she hated him. It had been different with Abbie; she had huge dark eyes and a warm soft mouth. He even knew what Abbie's voice had sounded like although he never heard it. Like being on the edge of sound. But Abbie was dead; she couldn't speak anymore. She was going to be buried in the ground. Small black carts for dead children.

He rubbed his eyes and when he looked up again the hall was empty. Walls like dull green moss. He went slowly down the stairs and kept sliding one hand along the banister; then when he reached the bottom he made a sudden dash across the hall and snatched up the sandal and raced back upstairs. At the top he looked back over his shoulder. Dim bulb reflected in the wall mirror like a hot orange.

He stuffed the sandal in his shirt and slid it around so that his bulge was hidden beneath his arm and then went down the hall to the rooms where his family lived.

II

His mother was sewing when he went in, and he knew that his father had been shouting at her because her eyes were red-rimmed. He couldn't seem to remember her any other way: sewing and crying. Her hands fluttered like plump naked little birds. He didn't like the feel of his mother's hands; they were like softy putty. He started across the room and though he wasn't looking her way, she reached out and touched his arm. "My poor baby," her lips said. "It has been a terrible shock, hasn't it? But you mustn't cry, poor child." She picked up her sewing again and kept folding and folding it with her soft white hands. "I don't know who will take you out now that dear little Abbie is gone. Your father won't, and Gregory never seems to think about his little brother." Tears in her eyes, like drops of hot rain. "You poor little boy," her lips said. She lowered her head. He went into the bedroom and stuffed the sandal under the mattress on his bed.

He was looking out of the window. Clouds like drawn-out white smoke. Bright-colored children's sweaters bobbing up and down in the distance like sharp chips of joy. A car moved down the street, dust-sucking, noiseless: a huge black beetle.

His father came in and tapped him on the shoulder and then jerked his thumb towards the other room. His father seldom spoke to him; he pointed to things. His father was always calling him half-witted because he cried and wet his pants and dropped things; he was always saying they should have put him away somewhere because he was deaf and dumb. Ronnie followed him, wondering if they put crazy people in prisons.

His mother smiled to him from the stove. Gregory was sitting in his place reading a book. Gregory was always reading. The table steamed from blue-and-white dishes. He sat down in his place across from Gregory and his mother came around and tucked a napkin in the collar of his shirt. Her fingers were warm and dry, like soft fudge.

He looked across the table at Gregory's thin pimply face peering at a book. Gregory was sixteen. His father was reading the paper, and the upper part of his face showed above the page, his eyes blue, like hard pale marbles. Ronnie was afraid of his father; he often tried to remember a time when he hadn't been afraid of those fixed staring eyes and the thick brown mustache, but he couldn't. He slumped in his chair. His father was reading and Gregory was reading and his mother was waiting with her hands smoothing the tablecloth which was already smooth. The steam rose slowly.

Finally his father folded the paper and put it on the table beside him and kept looking at it for a minute. Then he reached over and touched Gregory on the elbow. "Come on, son," his lips said. "Dinner." Gregory mumbled something and started to put the book down but kept on reading. He wondered why Gregory wanted to keep reading when the words were going away from him. Gregory's long yellow hair hung down over one eye, but he kept following the going-away words with the other, like a one-eyed giant. When his mother put a plate in front of him, he picked up his fork and put some potatoes in his mouth and started to chew; the potatoes looked like damp white sawdust.

Then Gregory put his book down and sat up in his chair and poured himself some milk. Ronnie reached out one hand and made a short moaning sound to attract attention. Gregory stopped moving and glanced quickly at his father; there was a sudden flutter of his mother's white hands and then they all sat quite still and their eyes kept staring and staring. Ronnie drew his arm slowly back across the table until it dropped into his lap; then he looked up cautiously.

His father was looking at him. His eyes weren't blinking or moving, but just staring, like eyes coming out of a picture. Then the eyes left him and traveled on down the table until they came to his mother. "I wonder if you would mind asking this animal-son of yours to be quiet?" the mouth said. "He *is* your son, isn't he? He's a half-wit, you'll agree, but he is your baby, isn't he?" His father's fist hit the table. The dishes jumped and slopped over still steaming. His mother was crying all over, like bleeding tears.

Then his father reached over and very carefully picked up the jug of milk and put it down beside his plate. "Since you can't wait until people are through speaking," his lips said. "If you must act like an animal, then you must be fed. Take some!"

Ronnie tried to slide out of the chair, but his father put out one hand and left it there like a barrier and then his lips moved again. "Take some," he said. "You wanted it: now take some!"

Ronnie didn't move. His father was waiting, and the dishes were still steaming, but he kept looking at the silvery flowers sewn right into the tablecloth like the frost-patterns on the window in winter time.

"Take some!" the mouth said.

Ronnie reached for the jug. His mother and Gregory were watching, his father leaning forward with his mouth open and his fingers tapping and tapping. The glass jug was cool and heavy, like ice with a handle. He held the spout over the drinking glass and the milk came out trickling and splashing; then all at once he dropped the jug and shattered the thin glass to splinters and the milk gushed across the table in small white waves. He dropped his head and choked with tears.

The table gave a lurch and his father got up quickly while his mother sat all huddled up in her chair, like a soft bag of tears. Ronnie thought he saw Abbie crawling underneath the table on her hands and knees looking for her sandal.

III

That night he slept with the sandal in his hand, and when he opened his eyes the next morning there were flaming sparks of sunlight dancing on Gregory's gold brush-and-comb set. He got up and put on his clothes and went into the kitchen. His mother was ironing. She looked up and smiled and then went on working. The iron was a steel boat sliding on a flat steaming ocean. He sat down at the table. His mother came over and gave him some cereal and then went back to the ironing board. He filled his mouth with the wet crunchy flakes and watched her. He wondered if irons made any noise when they slid.

His mother was taking the wrinkled clothes and ironing them and folding them up and hanging them on a line above the stove. He wondered why she smoothed his father's clothes when all he did was shout at her until she cried. His father worked in a factory and didn't like his mother; he only liked Gregory. *He loved Gregory.* Ronnie didn't see how his father and mother could sleep in the same bed without touching each other's skin. He slept alone; he didn't sleep with Gregory because he sometimes wet the bed at night.

He watched her fold one of Gregory's shirts. Then she came over and sat down beside him, putting her warm hand over his. Her lips started to move. "Will you promise to behave yourself if I let you go out in the yard for a while?" He nodded. She just sat and sat and he saw the grey in her hair, like thin streaks of white paint. "You remember the fuss Mrs. Finch made the last time you picked her flowers?" He nodded again. She got up and started to move away and then she turned suddenly and came back and slid into a chair and rested both her elbows on the table and her fist hit. And hit, and hit. "Oh, what does he expect?" her lips said. "How can I keep the child shut up in this house? There's no one to look after him and I can't . . . I can't . . ." He saw lips and eyes all over his mother's head, all moving. And then her fist hit again, and hit. He escaped into the hall. There was a bright shaft of sunlight slanting through the window at the end of the hall and he put his hand in it to see what would happen; it stayed.

IV

Ronnie walked to the head of the stairs and put one hand on the banister. Then he saw Mrs. Bregani coming up, soft bulges of fat on her front moving the tight black dress as she climbed, like big round puddings. She was carrying two large paper bags and had her head down. She put each foot down carefully and kept on coming up, puffing and stepping. Then she took the last step and stopped on the landing and she looked at him but her arms kept clutching the bags and she went on sucking and blowing out air, like a soft black bellows. "My God!" her lips finally said. "My God! I swear that old battleaxe makes those stairs higher every day!"

She stood still and went on puffing all by herself. Then she turned and handed him one of the bags and smiled, her teeth like chips of white enamel. "How's my bambino?" her lips said. Ronnie smiled. It always made him feel good when she called him "my bambino" because Mrs. Bregani didn't have any children and he often wondered if they all died, like Abbie. Then Mrs. Bregani turned and trundled off down the hall like a big black silk balloon; and she was holding his hand and her lips were moving, but he could only tell what the words were when she turned her head and looked at him: " . . . my old man's lazy sonofabitch . . . someday I kick him out . . . Mama, he say, you fat enough for the whole world to love . . ." Mrs. Bregani's hand like warm loving. "You comin', Bambino?" Her lips were close to him. He nodded. He wondered if Mrs. Bregani ever cried like his mother did.

When they came to her door, she took the bag from him and went in and put them both on the table and then she went over to the cupboard. Kitchen smelling like warm spice. Old sun coming through the window and dabbing things with hot amber. Mrs. Bregani came over and gave him some thick square cookies and then she put her hand on his head and smiled. "You best lookin' bambino I know," her lips said. "I tell my old man I'm gonna run off with you."

She turned towards the stove and then all at once she came back fast and stood in front of him and raised her eyes, like looking through the ceiling. "Why in hell ain't you outside in the sun, bambino?" Then her glance skidded up over his head and she was standing there staring at nothing and she kept slapping one fist in her other hand. "It's the old lady," her lips said. "She's been to your Mama again. Her blasted flowers!" She brought her fist down hard and it smacked into her hand and this time it stayed, as though it was stuck. "Someday I go down and strangle that old bitch!"

Then she bent down and took both his hands in her own and she was smiling but her eyes looked sad. "You go out and play in the sun, bambino," her mouth said. "You don't listen to nobody. You come tell Mama Bregani if they stop you." She straightened up slowly and kept on smiling with her white teeth and then gave him a slap on the behind. He went along the hall and started down the stairs. He wondered if his father called Mrs. Bregani a dago because she was fat and used swear words.

V

The front yard was full of neat-colored little flower beds and strips of grass and white cement walks; and the front steps smelled of warm grey paint. Bright sunlight shimmering, like amber-tinted sparks. There was a tall iron-picket fence across the front of the yard. He sat down on the bottom step and put out his hand and gently stroked the smooth wood beside him. A cat squeezed out under the front gate, like grey wool rolling under a table.

He went and sat on the grass. Then he flopped on his stomach and quickly rolled over on his back and squirmed and crawled and twisted while he made little growling sounds in his throat. Grass like thick green fur. Air smelling sweet and sharp. He lay perfectly still, shielding his eyes from the bright sun. O Abbie, Abbie! He got up suddenly and went down to the gate and took hold of the black iron bars and stood looking out.

VI

Three boys came down the street. One of them wore a bright red cap and each of them had a towel draped around his neck. They came on down the sidewalk laughing and pushing and then breaking away fast to scuffle over a tin can and tangle their feet and then move back on to the sidewalk and keep coming. The boy in the red cap stopped and picked up a stone and took out a slingshot and then smacked the stone against a tree. The others smacked stones. He smacked. Then they all smacked stones as fast as they could find them and load them in the sling-shots. Smack! Smack! Smack! Chips flying. Naked tree-flesh where the stones tore the bark. They came on down.

When they were even with the gate, the boy in the red cap hung back a step and looked at Ronnie and then he stopped and his lips moved. "What's your name, kid?"

Ronnie smiled.

The boy hesitated and turned to go, and then the other two came slouching on back, mouths calling out, limp arms draped over one another's shoulders. The boy in the red cap said something with his head turned the other way and one of the boys who had freckles and a button-nose doubled over with laughter and his one hand kept slapping and slapping while he stamped the pavement with his foot. Slappety-stamp. Slappety-stamp. His swinging towel-ends danced with joy.

Sure they were going to play games with him, Ronnie stood up on his toes, eager and excited.

Then the boy in the red cap walked over and offered him the slingshot with the handle pointing out. When Ronnie reached for it, he snatched it back and stood grinning. The others grinned.

Ronnie stood still for a moment and then he, too, grinned. The handle of the slingshot had thin rings carved in the bark like white bands on a green snake.

The boy in the red cap held the handle out again and this time his mouth said, "What'd you say your name was, kid? It wouldn't be ninny, would it? Ninny?" He was moving the handle back and forth just out of reach. "Ninny?" Ronnie started to put out his hand and then changed his mind and the smile slowly faded from his face. He had a sudden feeling that they were making fun of him and that they would just go on poking and poking and hoping he would get mad.

The boy in the red cap turned and said something to the others and then suddenly he turned and came back real close and pointed the handle at Ronnie's chest; and poked and poked and poked. "Here! Take it!" his mouth said. Ronnie reached and the handle was snatched away. Button-nose started to laugh; he slapped and stamped in delighted little circles all over the sidewalk and on to the grass and then he screwed up his face and squirmed against a tree.

The boy poked again. Ronnie made a sudden wild grab and felt his fingers close on the handle and he snatched it through the gate and held it behind his back. The game had been to catch the handle. He wondered how hard you had to smack a stone before it would go through a cloud.

Button-nose came down off the tree fast and the three boys crowded in front of the gate and all their mouths were going and going, like goldfish looking out of a bowl. Then the boy in the red cap shook his fist and the other two started shaking their fists and all the time their mouths were going and going. Small pink mouths and freckles like sprinkles of warm cinnamon. Ronnie couldn't tell what they were saying; he stood with one hand grasping the gate, head tilted, prodding everything before him with feeling eyes. Then all at once one of them stepped forward and grabbed his arm and the other two grabbed and they all pulled and twisted and shouted threats. Ronnie threw back his head and wailed.

VII

Then all at once he felt the hands release him and when he looked up Gregory was running across the street with his feet splaying out and his long yellow hair flying. The boys ran down the sidewalk and then they stopped in a small indignant cluster and when Gregory made a sudden dash towards them they ran like frightened animals, but when he stopped then they stopped, like being tied together. Finally Gregory went over to the gate and put his hand on Ronnie's shoulder and shook his fist at the boys. "You stop teasin' the kid!" his mouth said.

The boy in the red cap stepped forward and his eyes looked like huge brown and white marbles and he kept stabbing the air in front of him with one finger. "Yeah? Well, he stole my slingshot!"

Gregory looked all around him and then he saw the slingshot lying on the ground inside the yard; he walked over and picked it up and then took it out and threw it to the boys. Elastic sides writhing in air like flying snakes. "Now beat it!" his lips said. The boy picked up the slingshot and they went on down the street; they went on fingering their noses at Gregory and making faces and going on down out of sight.

Ronnie still clung to the gate. Gregory went over and put a big fumbling hand on his shoulder and tried to lead him away, but he kept gripping the black iron bars and looking out into the street. A car swooshed by, green and silver flashing in a sucking swirl of dust. Ronnie turned suddenly and started down the sidewalk to the house with his head down and Gregory walking beside him. He hated Gregory for giving away his slingshot. He wondered if all big boys had face-pimples and hair on their stomach before they put their clothes on in the morning. Gregory did. He quickened his pace to rid himself of Gregory's touch; then he went on with his head bowed.

VIII

The old lady was standing on the top step. She must have heard the noise and come out on to the porch. Now she was just standing, her eyes puffed and swollen. She didn't do anything or say anything or even move, but just kept standing, like a dead stone statue alive with hair and clothing. As he went to pass her, she reached out her hand and patted him gently on the head and her lips moved; he was so terrified that he fled through the door without stopping.

His mother had once told him that every child had once been a part of its mother; he wondered what part of the old lady Abbie had been.

His mother was there waiting, and he could tell that she knew what had happened. Her white hands did a little dance of misery. He slipped past her and walked over and sat down in a chair by the window with the breeze tickling his neck like soft feathers. Room smelling of hot damp ironing. Small china elephants and dogs and cats everywhere, like a frozen zoo. He decided he wanted to run away.

His mother went and sat in a chair, her hand flapping against the arm, and then when she heard Gregory close the door she looked up and her mouth started to move. "What happened this time?" she asked. "I thought I asked you to watch him. You know what he's like and I've asked you time and again . . ."

"I was only across the street and I came over as soon as I heard him holler," Gregory's mouth always opened wide and gulping, like a fish; his lips stumbled all over the words. "A-w, Ma! You know what he's like. He's always grabbin' something that don't belong to him and then he starts crying and makin' a fuss." Gregory swallowed and the lump in his throat moved over. "I can't watch him every minute, can I?" He walked over and put his hand on the door knob and shook the hair out of his eyes; it kept falling down almost to his mouth which went on gulping. "And you know what Dad says, Ma. In a few years he's gonna start chasing little girls and you know what'll happen then." He went out and closed the door and it sprang open again so he came back and pulled it shut and this time it stayed closed. Tired old door full of scuffed banging.

There was Gregory taking his big feet down the stairs and into the hot bright sun and telling everyone that his brother cried and wet his pants and chased little girls. Gregory didn't chase girls; he giggled at them. Ronnie imagined that he was chasing some little girls across a huge green field and Gregory was running after him with his big feet going flap, flap, flap; and his hands were as big as pillows and all covered with warts. Then all at once the little girls vanished and when he looked around Gregory was gone, too. He was all alone and there was no one to play games with and he lay down flat on his stomach and took small furious bites out of the earth. He hated Gregory.

They didn't want him. Sometimes he would wake in the night and the room seemed to be full of mouths, and he knew they were all his father's because he could see the thick brown moustache, saying, and saying, "What good is he? What good? Answer me that! What good will he ever be? Thank God we have Gregory . . . We have Gregory . . . Gregory . . . *Gregory!*"

He wanted to hurt something. He looked out of the window where the cars went by churning up bright soundless dust. Bright red geranium on the window sill, like a hot splash of paint in dull shadow. He reached out very carefully and snapped the bloom from its stock and held it in the palm of his hand looking at it; then he closed his hand and squeezed hard until the bright juice trickled slowly out between his fingers and ran down across his knuckles. Wet and cool, like damp morning grass. He opened his fist and stared for a moment at the sodden bloody pulp in his hand, and then he dropped his head and wept silently. O Abbie!

His mother came up out of the chair and she didn't seem to notice him, but she kept staring straight ahead as though she was looking through the walls. She started to walk away and then changed her mind and backed up and sat down again, resting her arms on the chair and her hand moved one way and then moved back. Face like worn-out memories. Then suddenly she got up again without looking at him and went into the bedroom and partly closed the door; and her tears went on drying and drying without making a sound.

He went into the bedroom and dug the blue sandal out from under the mattress and stuffed it inside his shirt and then sat down on the end of the bed. Sun coming through the window like warm gold air. Grey pigeons perched in a row on the porch roof, like fat sleepy children sitting on a bench. Tears drying quietly in the next room. His mother and father and Gregory all went walking around in the hot sun and kept him shut up in the house because they didn't want people to see him. He wondered if it would be better to fly away, instead of running. He had often stood on the landing in the hall and knew that if he just spread his arms and leaned forward he would float down over the banister and out through the door without touching anything, just like a bird. And he sometimes had dreams where he was falling down, down, down, into a black pit.

He got down from the bed and went through the kitchen where the headless plant was oozing sticky white fluid from a broken stem; then he went into the hall and walked down to the end and opened the window as far as it would go. Air smelling sweet, like fresh-cut grass. Grey pigeons edging and nudging and taking noiseless swallows with smooth fat throats. Eyes watching him, like moist pink beads. He stepped through the window on to the roof. The birds rose in a flapping grey swarm, dropping bits of down and feathers on him. He was alone. To be a bird.

IX

He crawled away from the window until he was straddling the peak of the roof at the fat end and looking down on the front steps, like a neat pile of flat grey slats. Cement sidewalk far below like thick white tape laid across the grass. He thought the old lady might be still standing on the porch and he leaned over as far as he could and gave a short screech of defiance. There was no movement and no one went down the grey-slat steps so he sat back and looked around. Red-stained shingles sloping steeply down the roof, overlapping like square flat scales. He thought that someday he would like to get up as high as the sun. The pigeons watched him from the roof of the next house like a silent jury.

A man came down the street; he was an old man with wrinkles and dead-grey hair fastened on and feet that kept moving and moving him so he wouldn't die. Like a dried-up bag of tears. He glanced up at him perched on the roof and went on moving and then all at once he stopped and turned around and his lips moved a little. He hesitated a moment and then slowly retraced his steps and turned in at the gate and walked up the sidewalk. He climbed the grey-slat steps as though they were wet and slippery.

Then all at once the old lady came out of the house and ran down the front steps with her feet going fast and when she reached the sidewalk she turned around and looked up and her mouth said, "Oh!" Then she ran back up the steps and disappeared in the house. The old man was standing on the bottom step looking up, lips moving, and then he turned and shuffled along the sidewalk to the gate with his head shaking from side to side as though scolding himself.

He watched the old man going down the street. People were coming out of the house: flap, flap, flap down the grey-slat steps. Faces in the yard looking up at him, like balloons drifting around on the grass with eyes and mouths painted on them. Mrs. Bregani was standing to one side with a tiny white apron tied around her wide black middle. The man who looked after the garden walked over and stood directly beneath him and his mouth opened slowly as though he was chewing sticky taffy. "Stay there!" his lips said. "Don't move!" Then he walked across the grass and disappeared along the side of the house.

Ronnie stood up. He knew then that they were going to take him down from the roof, and it made him angry. Maybe he would start to cry again, but it wouldn't do any good because they would leave him in a corner to stamp his feet and scratch his own face.

He decided he would run away from them. He no longer wanted to glide from the roof because they had spoiled it with their stupid faces that turned up at him, just staring and staring. Old sun like a hot bright coin. He saw the man come around the corner with a long ladder and the faces all floated out of the way and then as soon as he passed they all floated back in place again. Like sunflowers in a strong gust of wind. Ronnie was sure that if he climbed back in the window and ran quickly downstairs he could get out the side door before they caught him. He felt for Abbie's sandal and turned to crawl along the roof. Then he saw them and he stopped.

They were crowding in the window: Gregory and his mother and the old lady. His mother was standing behind the others, her face bobbing and dancing around like a fat white balloon on a stick. Mouth wide open. The she disappeared and he thought maybe she had fainted. Old lady smiling; it was funny to see the old lady smiling because she looked a little bit like Abbie. And Gregory was coming through the window with his long hair and big feet and mouth hanging open like a hound-dog. "C'mon, Ronnie! You're gonna hurt yourself out here." Gregory clung to the top of the roof and shook the hair out of his eyes and put out his hand. "C'mon kid."

Ronnie backed up a little. Gregory's eyes opened, wider, and he dropped his hand and didn't move but just sat there with his mouth hanging open loosely, like a wet pouch of glistening lips. He decided that if Gregory touched him he would bite him hard. He gave a short, sobbing screech in Gregory's face. The end of the ladder bumped against the roof and then a man's head came into view and Ronnie looked at him and then back at Gregory and then he sat down.

He wondered if they put all the crazy people in the world in dark stone dungeons and chained them to the walls without any clothes on and then beat them with whips.

He got up without warning and ran down the shingled incline with his eyes fixed on the roof of the next house. Startled pigeons beating frantic wings against the air, like ragged grey fans. The narrow strip of shadow between the roofs kept widening and widening until suddenly it had become a black yawning void. Ronnie made a wild clawing leap; he raked at the warm unmoving air with frenzied fingers and then jolted on to the roof and hung there scratching and clawing at the smooth dry shingles. Eaves trough cutting into his chest, like a sharp heavy blade.

Then all at once he stopped struggling and his fingers felt numb and he was just hanging there, like a rag draped over a fence. He was looking over his shoulder at the people below and the faces all went floating around and looking up. The mouths weren't saying anything but the heads went on swirling and bobbing around, like pale balloons in a tank of black water.

Mrs. Bregani had her fat arms stretched upwards, like praying, and her lips were twisting and moving. "Oh, Jesus! Oh, Jesus!" She rubbed at her eyes with a white hanky and put it in her pocket and then took it out quick and rubbed again. "The poor . . . Oh, Jesus!" her lips said.

Then all at once something let go and he slipped and dropped head-first into deep silent shadows. There was a long piercing vibration searing through his skull, shriek-like; then he felt a sudden jolt which numbed him and swept him into an endless void of blackness.

Charmed Lives

Nadine Gordimer
Republic of South Africa, 1956

There were two men in the town—a deaf man and a drunkard.

The one was a watchmaker and the other a doctor, and they never met except when the watchmaker consulted the doctor about his stomach ulcer, or the doctor's watch needed cleaning, but they belonged together in the mind of twenty-year-old Kate Shand. Extraordinary to think in what unimaginable partnerships one may exist in the minds of others, with what faces one's own may be bracketed forever, through some categorical connection, of which one will never know, in the memory of a third person.

The association between the watchmaker and the doctor in Kate Shand's mind began when she and her brothers were children. For the Shand children there were two kinds of people. There were people their mother had a lot of time for, and people she had no time for. The definitions were not only expressive but literal. The people she had a lot of time for she would allow to delay her endlessly, talking to them on street corners when she met them out shopping, visiting them when they were ill, stretching telephone conversations far beyond her normal brusque limits; the people she had no time for took up no more than the duration of a curt nod, or a half sentence of dismissal should their names come up in conversation.

Both the watchmaker and the doctor were in Mrs. Shand's favored category. The deaf watchmaker, Simon Datnow, was employed by Kate's father in his jeweler's shop. "I've got a lot of time for Simon," Mrs. Shand would say consideredly, with a "mind you," a sage reservation in her voice. That was because, on the whole, she did not care for relatives, and this man was, in fact, one of the procession of Lithuanian and Russian relatives whom Marcus Shand had "brought out" to South Africa, before Kate was born, in the early Twenties and whom, ever after, he regarded with a surly indifference quite out of character with his gentle nature—a churlishness created by the conflict in him between family feeling for them and a resentment against them for being the kind of people he would not have expected his wife to like. For though he winced under his wife's scorn of his relatives, there was a perverse pride in him that he should have succeeded in marrying a wife who *would* scorn them. They were used to sleeping, these foreigners (Mrs. Shand said), on top of the stove. They did not bathe more than once a week. They ate disgusting food—salted fish and soup made of beetroot. At that time the Shand kitchen still had a coal range; the children pictured these strange aunts and cousins huddled together on the sooty surface after the fire had been raked out in the evening, greasy-fingered, like Eskimos. It would not have surprised Kate, William and Dykie to hear that the aunts chewed their husbands' boots to soften them.

Simon Datnow was not actually a blood relation of Marcus Shand, but merely the brother of one of Mr. Shand's sisters' husbands. The husband was dead and Simon had "come out" with his sister-in-law as a kind of substitute protector. Perhaps it was because there was no blood tie to rein his resentment with guilt that, if Mrs. Shand liked Simon most, Mr. Shand liked him least of the immigrant relations. It seemed to annoy Marcus Shand that, after the first year, the deaf watchmaker really owed him nothing; had, unlike the others, nothing in particular for which to be grateful to him. Simon Datnow had paid back the passage money which Mr. Shand had advanced, and he was a skilled watchmaker whose equal Mr. Shand could not have hoped to find in South Africa. Kate, whenever she entered her father's shop, always remembered the watchmaker as she used to see him from the door—sitting in his little three-sided glass cage with the inscription WATCH REPAIR DEPARTMENT showing in gold leaf like a banner across his bent head. As Kate grew up, the gold leaf began to peel, and behind the faint loop of the first P you could see his left ear more and more clearly. In that ear, from time to time, a new hearing aid, flesh-colored, black or pearly, would appear, but usually, when he was working, he did not wear one. He would put it on only when you approached to speak to him, and in the moment before you did speak, the moment when the device dropped into contact with his ear, you would see him wince as the roar of the world, from which he had been sealed off like a man dropped in a diving bell to the floor of the ocean, burst in upon him.

A curved bite had been sawed out of the work table at which he sat, and the edge of the wood had long since been worn smooth by the rub of his body as he leaned forward over his work, and it seemed to Kate that he fitted into the table as the table fitted into its glass walls. Before him were tiny, shallow receptacles and metal work platforms a few inches square on which the delicate tweezers and probelike instruments with which he worked stalked like timid, long-legged insects among specks of red jewel and minute wheels, and springs that looked like a baby's hair you had run through thumb and fingernail. Tiny glass bells protected the innards of watches on which he was not working. She felt she dared not breathe too near the exposed ones, lest they took off on the current and sailed into some crack in the scored and worn table top. Yet the instruments that worried at them delicately, that picked them up and dipped them into a dewdrop of oil or spirit and finally fitted them together, were controlled by a pair of blunt, curled hands with broken nails like plates of horn imbedded in, rather than growing from, chapped fingers. The skin of these hands was permanently tarnished from contact with oil and metal, and, in winter, was swollen and fissured with dreadful chilblains. The WATCH REPAIR DEPARTMENT was in the draftiest corner of the shop, and it was then that the watchmaker, blue-nosed and pale above his gray muffler, reminded Kate of one of those zoo animals which, denied the lair of its natural habitat, shudders out the cold months in a corner of its cage.

In the summer the watchmaker worked in his shirt sleeves, with shiny expanding armbands to pull the cuffs up out of the way, and a constant trickle of sweat making his short, graying hair spring out slowly into curl from its confinement of pomade. Summer and winter, most days he looked up only when Marcus Shand came stumping over to shove at him a watch for diagnosis, bellowing, "Loses twenty-five minutes in twenty-four hours" or "Oiling and cleaning. See if it's in working order." "What?" the deaf man would say in his half-inaudible voice, frowning vacantly and fumbling for his "machine"—as he always called his hearing aid—while he held back from the force of his employer in nervous distaste. Shand would shout in impatient repetition, so that half of what he said would not be heard by the watchmaker, and the other half would thunder in upon him as his aid was switched on. The force of this half-sentence would strike the watchmaker like a blow, so that for a moment he was bewildered and unable to understand anything. Then Shand would become more impatient than ever and shout twice as loud. Because of this communication at cross purposes, Marcus Shand tended to phrase everything he had to say to his watchmaker as shortly as possible, and to dispense with all graces of politeness, and so almost all that came to Simon Datnow of the outside world for eight hours a day was an assault of surly questions and demands.

Because his watchmaker and relation by marriage was sensitive to the tick of a watch but not an undertone of the human voice, Marcus Shand got into the habit of abusing Simon Datnow in mumbled asides, before his very face. It was a great comfort to Shand to be able to abuse someone with impunity. Yet although it was true that he was able to say abusive things without being heard, it was, of course, not possible for these not to show on his face while he said them; and so it was that Simon Datnow felt the revilement more cuttingly than if it had come to him in words, and a wall of thick, inarticulate hostility, far more impenetrable than that of deafness, came to exist between the two men.

It infuriated Mrs. Shand that the only person whom her husband should have the courage to abuse should be someone only half of this world, and, as a result, too uncertain of his ground to take a stand upon it. She herself had tried, and, in fact, went on trying all her life, to get her husband to stand up to *her*. But no; the only person before whom Marcus would dare raise the timid flag of his spirit was a man who couldn't trust himself to interpret the challenge clearly. Mrs. Shand retaliated by championing Simon Datnow. Datnow, she gave her children to understand, was a natural gentleman, a kind of freak incidence among the immigrant relations. His drudgery became an ideal of conscientious service; his enforced remoteness from the world, an ideal of contemplation. The bewildered, impotent rage that showed in his eyes—the repressed daze of savagery in the eyes of the bull who cannot see where the darts have lodged in the nerves of his shoulders—before the rudeness of her husband which he could not hear, she interpreted as the self-control of a superior being. The meek aspect which his deafness imposed upon him as he went about the town during his lunch hour seemed to her the quality that should inherit the earth. Even the stomach ulcer from which he suffered as a result of the tension of his work and the fragmentary intensity of his communication with the world came, through their mother, to be associated in the minds of the Shand children with a quality of exceptional sensitivity.

When Kate was small she would sometimes stand for a long time with her face close to the glass cage, smiling respectfully at the watchmaker when he smiled his slow, saliva-gleaming smile back at her, and nodding her interest when he held up some part of a watch, a piece of metal confetti, for her to see. At the approach of her father she would go still—taking cover from the crude and puzzling aspect of him which showed when he spoke to Simon Datnow. This gruff man with the thick strings of vein rising against his collar had nothing to do with the father who would put his cheek to hers and ask, humbly, for a kiss.

One day, a week before Christmas in the year when Kate was nine years old, she was hanging about her father's shop. In the burning midsummer December of South Africa, the gold-mining town was seedily festive with borax snow in the shop windows, red and blue lights strung round the Town Hall, and the beery voices of miners in sports blazers slapping one another on the back outside the bars. The jeweler's shop was very busy. Kate ran errands for her father and the young Afrikaans sales girl, and drank lukewarm lemon squash in the room behind the shop where cardboard boxes and straw and sheets of tissue packing were kept, and the mice were so impudent that anything edible disappeared while you turned your back.

At this time of year the watchmaker was constantly interrupted at his work by requests to fit gleaming new watch straps to customers' watches, or to make minor adjustments to necklaces that were too long, or to mend silver bracelets with faulty catches. In order to get his watch repairing done, he came to work early in the morning, before the shop was open, and stayed behind long after it was closed. And all day, while the bustle of customers and the rustle of parcels and the ring of the cash register filled the shop around him, he was bent over his table, trying to do several things at once, often under the harassing, impatient eye of Marcus Shand or the salesgirl. His lunch sandwiches remained uneaten. Once, a mouse from the back room ventured into the shop to gnaw at them. His morning and afternoon tea turned pale and scummy in the cup. On the crowded table before him, the tiny viscera of his watches got mislaid beneath the metal straps, the necklaces, the bracelets. He looked like a worried mouse himself, gray-backed, rustling furtively over his jumble of work.

On this particular day he was so busy that the face of the little girl, who had wandered over to watch him through the glass, did not penetrate his concentration. She watched him a minute or two, nevertheless. He fitted a tiny spring into the intricacy of a watch's belly; over it went a wheel; into some pin-sized holes, three chips of ruby. Then he put out his long tweezers to peck from its spirit bath something that proved not to be there. He felt about with the tweezers, looked in another dish; at last he lifted his eyebrow so that the jeweler's loop in his left eye socket fell out into his hand. He stood up from his stool and looked carefully and methodically under every glass bell, in every dish. He rummaged systematically through the cardboard box lid where he kept the filings, little twirls of yellow and silver metal like punctuation marks, from the watchstraps, the necklaces, the bracelets. He paused a moment, as if deliberating where he should look next. And then, the light of a solution, a calm relief relaxed his face. Slowly, he stood back, creaking his stool away behind him over the cement floor. Then he grasped his work table firmly, palms up under its top, and brought it over, crashing and slithering all its conglomeration of contents on top of himself.

He stood there amid the wreckage with his hands hanging at his sides. His eyes glittered and his mouth was clenched, so that the skin in which the growing beard showed like fine blue shot was white above and below his stiffened lips. He was breathing so loudly that it could be heard right across the sudden silence of the shop full of people.

Before the shock of that silence broke, Kate ran. Her running broke the silence; she heard, as she pulled the heavy back door of the shop closed behind her, babble and movement spill out. She went trembling across the dirty yard which the shop shared with several other contiguous with it, and sat on a rotting packing case against the wall of the lavatory. It was dank there, with the solitude of dank places. She stayed a long time, playing with some old letterheads puffy with rain.

When she went back into the shop again, there was a cheerful delegation from a mine, in the part of the shop known as the jewelry department, choosing a canteen of cutlery for presentation to a retiring official. Behind the WATCH REPAIR DEPARTMENT the watchmaker was putting the last of his tiny containers back at the angle at which it had always stood; only the glass bells were missing, and they must have been swept away by Albert, the African cleaner. The face of the watchmaker, behind the gold-leaf letters, was pale and calm.

Presently, he looked up and beckoned to her across the shop, and, hesitantly, she went to him. He gave her one of the three-cornered buns filled with poppyseed that he had brought for his tea and that he knew she loved. Holding it between finger and thumb, she took the bun into the back room and hid it in a corner, for the mice.

Mrs. Shand had even more time for the doctor than she had for the watch-maker. When Kate, or William, or Dykie were ill, and Mrs. Shand was expecting Dr. Connor on his morning round of calls, she would have a plate of fresh scones baked ready for tea from before ten o'clock. And if he happened to come earlier, while the Shand house was still in the uproar of cleaning which not even consideration for the patient was allowed to interrupt, Amos and Fat Katie, the servants, and their shining vacuum cleaner and buzzing floor polisher were banished at his approach, trailing the cords of their machines behind them. Mrs. Shand would stand smiling, with her hands on her hips, while the doctor did his examination of the patient. Even if she had been voicing the gravest misgivings about the nature of the child's malady to her sister or mother over the telephone ten minutes before, Mrs. Shand always seemed to be transformed into a mood of levelheaded confidence the moment the doctor appeared. Her attitude became jocular and skittish: "Show Doctor the old tum-tum, darling. Really, Dykie, must you wear these pajamas? Why do they take fancies to the most unsuitable things, sometimes? Children, oh, children! . . ."

Then, the moment the examination was completed, Mrs. Shand and the doctor would disappear into the living room, talking in an intimate undertone, and the child, fevered with self-importance and the desire to know if the pain really might be appendicitis, would lie cross and rigid, straining to separate the murmuring voices into words. If the other children were at home, they would hang about the passage outside the living room, and now and then the door would open suddenly and their mother's face would appear, requesting more hot water or another jug of milk. There would be a glimpse of the living room, blue with cigarette smoke, fragrant with tea, the doctor sitting in the big armchair—and then the door would shut firmly again. When Dr. Connor rose to leave, Mrs. Shand would accompany him all the way down the garden path and then stand talking over the gate, or at the window of his car.

She would come slowly back up the path to the house after he had driven off, holding carefully in her hand the prescription he had written. Slowly through the house and into the bedroom where her child lay. The child seemed almost a surprise to her. "Well, there you are, darling," she would say absently. "No school for you for a few days. Now I must go down to the chemist and get this made up. And you're to stay in your bed and not jump about, do you hear? Dr. Connor says . . ." Then she would go to the telephone and speak to her mother and her sister again. "Well, he's been. That's what I like about him—when you need him, he's there at once. And, of course, it's just as I thought—a real chill on the stomach, that's all, and he recognized it at once. Good old Robert Eldridge. I'd trust him with my life any day, in spite of his faults."

Their mother always talked about Dr. Connor by the two imposing Christian names which she had seen on his degree diplomas in his consulting rooms—Robert

Eldridge. For years Kate thought of this form of address vaguely as some sort of designation; it was like speaking of the Major, or the General Manager, or the Editor. The "faults" in spite of which Mrs. Shand—and, indeed, half the town—trusted Robert Eldridge were, of course, his drunkenness. He was not merely addicted to drink; he was dejectedly chained to it, as the great sheepish dog whom he resembled might be chained to a kennel. He did not drink at parties or with friends, but only in his own company, in solitary, irregular and frequent bouts—sometimes every week, sometimes at intervals of several months, sometimes every day for a month. Once he was sober for more than a year; once he was scarcely sober at all for a year. Unless he had had a particularly long bout and was in very bad shape indeed, he did not drink at home, but drove out into the veld with his African garden boy and a case of South African brandy—the cheapest brand; he did not care what he drank. There he would stay for two or three days. The brandy ensured oblivion, and the African, who asked no questions and offered neither protest nor sympathy nor arguments for reformation, ensured survival. For the odd thing was that this wretched man—who crept away to drink himself not into euphoria but into stupor and delirium, shamefully, like a sick animal following the instinct to hide its sickness from the sight of others of its kind—wanted to survive. The desire was so strong in him that it seemed to protect him from harm. He drove his car when he was drunk and did not kill himself, and he operated on his patients when he was drunk and did not kill them. So it was that he came to bear, for the people of the town, the legend of a charmed life, and they were not afraid to entrust themselves to him.

He lived alone with his old mother in a large, neglected house that had the stunned, withdrawn atmosphere of walls, furniture, possessions which have absorbed the unhappy stare of silent inmates. Here, in the living room with the empty vases, he had sat in morose penitence with his unreproachful mother. Here, in the consulting room where he examined his patients beneath a pale photograph of his first wife in a Suzanne Lenglen tennis outfit (his wives had come and gone without any sympathy from anyone), he had, in desperate times, concealed brandy in the bottles bearing the labels of medicaments. And here, in the hall, where years of dust had turned the black shaggy curls of a mounted wildebeest head into a powdered wig, he had lain at the foot of the stairs whole nights, unable to get up to his room.

The house was silent, yet spoke of all this. Kate, when she was thirteen, heard it. She was going to Dr. Connor's house every day at the time to have a course of penicillin injections for an outbreak of adolescent boils. She was filled with a bewildering self-disgust because of the boils (her body was punishing her, or being punished; she was guilty, that she knew, though she did not know of what), and there was something in this house of Dr. Connor's that recognized instantly, found common cause with, self-disgust. The wildebeest head, the vases, the pale dead girl in the bandeau claimed kinship with her. You are not alone, they said; there is a whole side of life along with which your feeling belongs. The claim filled her with dismay and a sense of struggle against some knowledge being forced upon her that she did not want. For the first time, the bony, prematurely white head of Dr. Connor, bent over his big, clean hands as they snapped the top off an ampule and plunged into it the needle of a syringe, did not seem to her the image of succor and skill and reassurance that it had been all those other times, the times of measles, of tonsillectomy, of the broken arm. He was a mouth-breather with a loose, wet, kindly lower lip; but today there was no comfort in that audible intake and outlet of breath. Today the uninhabited blue eyes—she had not noticed before that there was no one there—filled her with an indignant, frightened questioning. Where was he gone, and why did everyone go on pretending he was still there? Why, why, why? He had been someone to revere, someone for whom her mother had had a lot of time, "in spite of." Yet why must there always be excuses for grownups? Why couldn't they be strong, beautiful, happy? Lying down on the white-covered couch and baring her behind for the needle, she felt her young heart fill with cold cruelty toward the mild-voiced, broken man bending over her.

As Kate Shand grew up, she went less and less often into her father's shop. She was away from the town, of course, first at a boarding school and then at a university. When she did come home, it was always with something of a shock that she saw the shop exactly as it had always been, the watchmaker still at his work in the booth behind the gold-leaf lettering. At seventeen, eighteen she felt the world revolving with her; how could it be that *these* remained static, were found as you had left them, like the castle where the princess pricked her finger and put everything to sleep for a hundred years? She smiled at the watchmaker across the shop, but she did not cross to speak to him, as if to do so would be to fill with substance again the shadow of the little girl who used to stand there, on the other side of the lettering, watching. The little girl who had seen, one hot Christmas time, the work table turn over shuddering to the ground, as if some beast that slept beneath industry and submissiveness stirred in impotent protest.

Once the childish ills were behind her (the Shand children had run through the whole alphabet of them, from croup to whooping cough, under Dr. Connor) Kate did not need a doctor again for many years, but her mother often did; and, home from the university one vacation, Kate was irritated to hear that Mrs. Shand had "just been over to see Robert Eldridge." "Good God, Mother! Why can't you go to a *doctor*?"

"That's all right. I'd rather have him than any of these fancy young men."

Dr. Connor still drove about in the car that people gave way to as if it were a sacred cow wandering about the streets, was still accepted without comment, back under the photograph in the consulting room in the old house, after his periodical disappearances.

In books, worms turned, drunkards ended violently in the gutter, the world moved; in the small town, Kate felt, everything held back tolerantly to the pace of—well, for example, those two men for whom her mother had such a lot of time, two men who apprehended the world from a remove, the one looking through glass into an aquarium where silent, mouthing fish swam up to him incomprehensibly and swam away, the other through the glassiness of his own eyes, through which he saw even his own hands, as if he had escaped from them, going on mechanically stitching flesh and feeling pulses.

When Kate graduated and her mother, with her usual capability, announced that she had used her influence with the school board (there were people on it who had a lot of time for *her*) and that a post awaited Kate in a local school, all the reasons the girl gave why she would not, could not, ever live in the town again were the logical, rational ones which children have always used in the process of severing themselves from their parents. But, oddly, for Kate, even as she argued them, pleaded them, they were not true. She was not thinking about the greater academic opportunities, the wider social choice, the cultural stimulation of the city to which she would go; and even if she had dropped the clichés and bluntly substituted for them more money, more men, more pleasure, she would have been no nearer the real reason why she had to go. This reason—and it was a kind of panic in her—had taken shape for her, slowly, out of all her childhood, in the persons of those two men whom she had known, really so slightly—the deaf man and the drunkard. Why them? Two harmless and handicapped people who, as her mother often said, had never done a scrap of harm; whom, as a child, Kate had automatically respected because they belonged to the people for whom her mother had a lot of time.

And yet, at twenty, it was because of *them* that Kate knew she could not come back to live in the town. They belonged together in her mind, and from them, from the shards of their images there, she must turn away, to live.

The Sibyl

Warren Kliewer
USA, 1964

The gusts of the northwest wind, grown stronger, now rattled the windows in the old, wooden church and sent small drifts of snow through the sash to pile up on the sill and on the floor.

Mrs. Becker looked up from the dogeared hymn book she was thumbing through and moved a little nearer to the small potbellied wood stove near the center of the church. She was short, less than five feet tall, and her shoulders were stooped. Her long black dress reached down to her ankles. Mrs. Becker's thin cheeks and wrinkled forehead were covered with a black kerchief.

Maria, her nineteen-year-old daughter, sat huddled in the corner of the pew behind Mrs. Becker. The girl was no taller than her mother, and when she hunched down in her coat, her head barely reached the top of the pew. The girl's pale face was now wrinkled into a frown. Often when she was waiting for something or had nothing to do, she would pull scraps of paper out of her coat pocket and with the stub of a chewed pencil scribble small pictures from one corner of the paper to the other.

"What you drawing now?" Mrs. Becker asked.

Maria simply shrugged her shoulders and ran her hand over her tight braids of black hair.

The girl had drawn a picture of a woman in a black kerchief, and she held up the paper to look at it for a moment before placing it in her lap again. Then she added a sketch of herself looking at the woman.

The minister, Reverend Schultz, stood with his arms crossed before his potbelly, warming his hands at the stove. His red face wore a perpetual smile. "She still does not talk?" he said to Mrs. Becker.

"No," the woman said, "Two years now. Can't hear either. Ever since he went away."

"Yes, yes," the minister smiled. "Even from them that have not, the Lord has taken away."

"But now," the woman added, "she will talk again. And hear."

"Yes. Yes."

Maria glanced up as if she were aware that they were talking about her, but immediately bent down to her paper again.

"She cried the whole day Johnny was getting ready to go," Mrs. Becker said. "And then he went to Winnipeg and she can't talk any more and don't hear nothing. And John wouldn't come back, and I wrote him letter after letter. Wouldn't come back even if his own sister is deaf and dumb for his going away."

"Yes," the minister said. "The city is full of wickedness." He nodded for emphasis.

Another gust of the wind blasted the side of the church. The woman's hands were wringing when she glanced up at the rattling windows.

"Maria don't know he's coming back. She don't even read his letters. Maria was such a good little girl and then she can't talk and hear when Johnny goes away."

"The Lord is merciful. Yes." Reverend Schultz smiled.

"Johnny said he likes his work in the warehouse in Winnipeg, but he's just a farmer. Don't you think he's just a farmer?"

"Yes."

"He should be on the farm."

The wind blew the door open and Reverend Schultz moved from the stove to push the door back again. But a young man, the stranger who had moved down from Winnipeg three weeks ago (no one knew why) stepped inside the door, shook the snow from his collar and wiped out his sunken, dark shadowed eyes. If his shoulders had not stooped, the young man would have been taller than Reverend Schultz. But now the stranger looked much shorter than his six feet. He walked with a limp.

Maria glanced up but immediately resumed drawing the sketch of herself. Neither Reverend Schultz nor Mrs. Becker spoke, but rather they stared at the young man.

Finally the young man muttered, "They told me on the street corner that the depot burned down."

"What'd you say?" Reverend Schultz said, smiling.

"I said, they told me the depot burned down and I have to wait for the train here."

"Yes," the minister said. "The Lord gives and the Lord hath taken away."

"Why do they have to wait for the train here?" the stranger said.

"There's no other place," the minister said, "except the grain elevator and that's cold. No stove in it."

"Where's the depot agent? He stay here too when the train's coming?"

The minister smiled. "I'm the depot agent now. He passed away in the fire. God called him to His Heavenly Home."

The young stranger stood awkwardly in the aisle for a few minutes, gazing at the rafters stained dark brown with smoke and at the dimly lit black pulpit scarcely visible though it was only thirty feet away.

"I never been in a church before," the stranger said.

"Never?" Reverend Schultz said. "God called down the fire so you could come to church."

Mrs. Becker shuddered and spoke for the first time. "Don't you go to church in Winnipeg?"

"Naw."

"Don't anybody go to church?"

"Naw. There aren't any churches in Winnipeg. Not a single one."

Mrs. Becker shook her head.

Maria had finished the drawing of herself and had now begun sketching the face of a fat man who looked very much like Reverend Schultz.

"Hey," the stranger said. "What're you drawing?"

Reverend Schultz began to wave his hands slightly, as if to quiet the impudence of the stranger's question.

"Hey, you. Why don't you say something?"

"She doesn't hear you. She can't talk." The minister smiled. "The handmaiden of the Lord has been afflicted."

The stranger grunted. "What's she drawing?"

"Drawing pictures."

"Why's she drawing pictures?"

"It's the gift of the Lord. To some are given ten talents and to some only one."

The stranger grunted again and backed away from the girl to the other side of the stove.

Mrs. Becker mumbled, "No churches in Winnipeg. Wickedness." She continued to wring her hands. "How I'll get home in this snowstorm with a deef and dumb girl I don't know. Two miles in the snow."

The minister said, "The Lord will provide."

"If Johnny comes," she said, "he can take us home. If my Johnny comes."

"The Lord will bring your son home from the husks of the ungodly."

"The letter said he would come home. He'll come if the letter said so, won't he?"

"Yes," the minister said. He nodded.

The young stranger took off his sheepskin coat, and it made a loud metallic clank when he dropped it on the pew. Maria glanced up at him.

"She can hear," the stranger said.

"No, she can't hear anything," Mrs. Becker said.

The stranger continued to stare at the girl.

Maria had finished the drawing of Reverend Schultz and she began another of herself, this time looking at the round nose of Reverend Schultz. In the second drawing her tight braids were hanging loosely over her shoulders.

"How much time more?" Mrs. Becker said.

The minister glanced at his big pocket watch. "It ought to be here in fifteen minutes."

"Fifteen minutes?" the stranger said. "Is it always on time?"

"No," the minister said. "Usually not."

The stranger surreptitiously slipped his hand into the bulging pocket of his sheepskin. "How much longer do I have to wait?"

"Don't know." The minister nodded his red face. "You waiting for someone on the train?"

"Yea. I'm waiting for someone." The stranger pulled his hand out of the coat pocket.

Maria had finished the second drawing of herself and she began a new sketch, a picture of Johnny with his eyes drawn together into a frown and his hair slicked straight back from his forehead. And then without glancing up, Maria hastily drew a sketch of the young stranger in the opposite corner of the small scrap of paper.

The minister turned and with his back toward the stove he nodded at the stranger and folded his hands across his fat belly. "Are you saved, young man?"

The young stranger scratched his head under the long, uncombed hair growing down across his ears. "Are you like them Salvation Army guys who won't leave you alone until you say you're saved?"

"The Salvation Army is the instrument of the Lord."

The stranger shrugged. "Yeah. Then I'm saved." He pulled a cigarette out of his pocket.

"Mustn't smoke in the church," Reverend Schultz said. Then he smiled as he again turned his back on the stranger. "Blessed be the name of the Lord."

The stranger lit the cigarette. "It's getting dark. Why don't you turn on a light in here?" The minister smiled but did not move. "All right. Don't turn it on." He shrugged again.

It was almost dark now, and the small drifts of gray snow radiating from the cracks in the door and the windows were growing longer. Maria was still drawing. Between the portraits of Johnny and the stranger, she had drawn a cluster of small circles and rectangles. She now added a few lines and the cluster became a pistol pointing at Johnny.

Mrs. Becker was wringing her hands. "Oh wickedness in Winnipeg," she muttered. Then she asked Reverend Schultz, "How much more time?"

He pulled out his watch and snapped open the cover. "Five more minutes, if it's on time."

The stranger stood up and looked carefully around the church. Then without a word he drew the pistol out of his coat pocket. "I'm going to wait for him…" the stranger said, limping down the aisle toward the front of the church. He climbed up the platform and stood behind the pulpit. "Up here," he continued, and then he crouched down out of sight behind the black pulpit. "Don't move, any one of you."

The minister's smile had suddenly vanished. His hands were now wringing like Mrs. Becker's when he said to her, "Did you see what he's doing? He came here to kill someone when he gets off the train. Go talk to him. Go. Maybe if you talk to him he won't do it."

But Mrs. Becker was unaware of what was happening, for Maria had begun grunting and waving her hand. "Go turn on the light," Mrs. Becker said. "Maria wants to draw and it's too dark for her."

Reverend Schultz got a lamp from the table near the door, but his hands were shaking so much that three matches burned out before the wick finally caught flame. Then Maria smiled and finished her last sketch, a drawing of a small passenger train. Mrs. Becker sat back in the pew and folded her hands. "Johnny," she said. "My boy coming home to his mama." Reverend Schultz stood in the aisle again, his back toward the stove and toward the pulpit. "Oh God. Oh God. Help me. Help me." His jaws shook as he whispered. The minister again drew out his watch, but he dropped it when he tried to open the cover, and the works of the watch fell out. "Oh God. Help me."

"Hey, you," the stranger whispered from behind the pulpit. "Come here." The minister shuffled down the aisle. "What time is it?" the stranger said.

"I don't know. I dropped my watch. Don't hurt us. You aren't going to hurt us, are you?"

"Go back to your stove."

Another half hour they waited. Maria completed the train, and then there was no more room on the paper. She put the pencil back into her pocket, turned down the kerosene lamp, and folded her hands. Mrs. Becker was sometimes wringing her hands and muttering, "Wickedness," or sometimes smiling as she said, "Johnny coming back." But the pastor stood facing the door, his back to the pulpit, while he prayed, "God help me. God help me." And after a few minutes his face became red again and he smiled. "The Lord will provide. Yes. A sacrifice for us all. Aaron and the goat. Yes. The Lord will provide."

In spite of the northwest wind blasting the side of the church and rattling the windows, the whistle of the train seemed to split the storm and the walls of the church. The stranger moved slightly but made no noise in the darkness behind the pulpit. Maria straightened up in the pew, as if she had heard the whistle, and Mrs. Becker stood and walked to the door. The pastor mumbled, "The Lord is good."

They listened to the pounding of the train's driving wheel and the intermittent shrieks of the whistle, and they felt the church tremble and shake and then rock as the train rushed over the trestle and through the town without stopping.

The stranger limped down the aisle again and quickly put on his sheepskin coat. Mrs. Becker hobbled back to her pew and groaned as she sat down. "Wickedness in those big cities," she mumbled. The minister, with his back to the stove, folded and unfolded his hands. He smiled at Maria. "You want to draw another picture? I'll get you some more paper."

And Sarah Laughed

Joanne Greenberg
USA, 1967

She went to the window every fifteen minutes to see if they were coming. They would be taking the new highway cutoff; it would bring them past the south side of the farm; past the unused, dilapidated outbuildings instead of the orchards and fields that were now full and green. It would look like a poor place to the new bride. Her first impression of their farm would be of age and bleached-out, dried-out buildings on which the doors hung open like a row of gaping mouths that said nothing.

All day, Sarah had gone about her work clumsy with eagerness and hesitant with dread, picking up utensils to forget them in holding, finding them two minutes later a surprise in her hand. She had been planning and working ever since Abel wrote to them from Chicago that he was coming home with a wife. Everything should have been clean and orderly. She wanted the bride to know as soon as she walked inside what kind of woman Abel's mother was—to feel, without a word having to be said, the house's dignity, honesty, simplicity, and love. But the spring cleaning had been late, and Alma Yoder had gotten sick—Sarah had had to go over to the Yoders and help out.

Now she looked around and saw that it was no use trying to have everything ready in time. Abel and his bride would be coming any minute. If she didn't want to get caught shedding tears of frustration, she'd better get herself under control. She stepped over the pile of clothes still unsorted for the laundry and went out on the back porch.

The sky was blue and silent but as she watched, a bird passed over the fields crying. The garden spread out before her, displaying its varying greens. Beyond it, along the creek, there was a row of poplars. It always calmed her to look at them. She looked today. She and Matthew had planted those trees. They stood thirty feet high now, stately as figures in a procession. Once—only once and many years ago—she had tried to describe in words the sounds that the wind made as it combed those trees on its way west. The little boy to whom she had spoken was a grown man now, and he was bringing home a wife. *Married* . . .

Ever since he had written to tell them he was coming with his bride, Sarah had been going back in her mind to the days when she and Matthew were bride and groom and then mother and father. Until now, it hadn't seemed so long ago. Her life had flowed on past her, blurring the early days with Matthew when this farm was strange and new to her and when the silence of it was sharp and bitter like pain, not dulled and familiar like an echo of old age.

Matthew hadn't changed much. He was a tall, lean man, but had had a boy's sparseness then. She remembered how his smile came, wavered and went uncertainly, but how his eyes had never left her. He followed everything with his eyes. Matthew had always been a silent man; his face was expressionless and his body stiff with reticence, but his eyes had sought her out eagerly and held her and she had been warm in his look.

Sarah and Matthew had always known each other—their families had been neighbors. Sarah was a plain girl, a serious "decent" girl. Not many of the young men asked her out, and when Matthew did and did again, her parents had been pleased. Her father told her that Matthew was a good man, as steady as any woman could want. He came from honest, hard-working people and he would prosper any farm he had. Her mother spoke shyly of how his eyes woke when Sarah came into the room, and how they followed her. If she married him, her life would be full of the things she knew and loved, an easy, familiar world with her parents' farm not two miles down the road. But no one wanted to mention the one thing that worried Sarah: the fact that Matthew was deaf. It was what stopped her from saying yes right away; she loved him, but she was worried about his deafness. The things she feared about it were the practical things: a fall or a fire when he wouldn't hear her cry for help. Only long after she had put those fears aside and moved the scant two miles into his different world, did she realize that the things she had feared were the wrong things.

Now they had been married for twenty-five years. It was a good marriage—good enough. Matthew was generous, strong, and loving. The farm prospered. His silence made him seem more patient, and because she became more silent also, their neighbors saw in them the dignity and strength of two people who do not rail against misfortune, who were beyond trivial talk and gossip; whose lives needed no words. Over the years of help given and meetings attended, people noticed how little they needed to say. Only Sarah's friend Luita knew that in the beginning, when they were first married, they had written yearning notes to each other. But Luita didn't know that the notes also were mute. Sarah had never shown them to anyone, although she kept them all, and sometimes she would go up and get the box out of her closet and read them over. She had saved every scrap, from questions about the eggs to the tattered note he had left beside his plate on their first anniversary. He had written it when she was busy at the stove and then he'd gone out and she hadn't seen it until she cleared the table.

The note said: "I love you derest wife I pray you have happy day all day your life."

When she wanted to tell him something, she spoke to him slowly, facing him, and he took the words as they formed on her lips. His speaking voice was thick and hard to understand and he perceived that it was unpleasant. He didn't like to use it. When he had to say something, he used his odd, grunting tone, and she came to understand what he said. If she ever hungered for laughter from him or the little meaningless talk that confirms existence and affection, she told herself angrily that Matthew talked through his work. Words die in the air; they can be turned one way or another, but Matthew's work prayed and laughed for him. He took good care of her and the boys, and they idolized him. Surely that counted more than all the words—words that meant and didn't mean—behind which people could hide.

Over the years she seldom noticed her own increasing silence, and there were times when his tenderness, which was always given without words, seemed to her to make his silence beautiful.

She thought of the morning she had come downstairs feeling heavy and off balance with her first pregnancy—with Abel. She had gone to the kitchen to begin the day, taking the coffeepot down and beginning to fill it when her eye caught something on the kitchen table. For a minute she looked around in confusion. They had already laid away what the baby would need: diapers, little shirts and bedding, all folded away in the drawer upstairs, but here on the table was a bounty of cloth, all planned and scrimped for and bought from careful, careful study of the catalogue—yards of patterned flannel and plissé, coat wool and bright red corduroy. Sixteen yards of yellow ribbon for bindings. Under the coat wool was cloth Matthew had chosen for her; blue with a little gray figure. It was silk, and there was a card on which was rolled precisely enough lace edging for her collar and sleeves. All the long studying and careful planning, all in silence.

She had run upstairs and thanked him and hugged him, but it was no use showing delight with words, making plans, matching cloth and figuring which pieces would be for the jacket and which for sleepers. Most wives used such fussing to tell their husbands how much they thought of their gifts. But Matthew's silence was her silence too.

When he had left to go to the orchard after breakfast that morning, she had gone to their room and stuffed her ears with cotton, trying to understand the world as it must be to him, with no sound. The cotton dulled the outside noises at little, but it only magnified all the noises in her head. Scratching her cheek caused a roar like a downpour of rain; her own voice was like thunder. She knew Matthew could not hear his own voice in his head. She could not be deaf as he was deaf. She could not know such silence ever.

So she found herself talking to the baby inside her, telling it the things she would have told Matthew, the idle daily things: Didn't Margaret Amson look peaked in town? Wasn't it a shame the drugstore had stopped stocking lump alum—her pickles wouldn't be the same.

Abel was a good baby. He had Matthew's great eyes and gentle ways. She chattered to him all day, looking forward to his growing up, when there would be confidences between them. She looked to the time when he would have his own picture of the world, and with that keen hunger and hope she had a kind of late blooming into a beauty that made people in turn to look at her when she passed in the street holding the baby in the fine clothes she had made for him. She took Abel everywhere, and came to know a pride that was very new to her, a plain girl from a modest family who had married a neighbor boy. When they went to town, they always stopped over to see Matthew's parents and her mother.

Mama had moved to town after Pa died. Of course they had offered to have Mama come and live with them, but Sarah was glad she had gone to a little place in town, living where there were people she knew and things happening right outside her door. Sarah remembered them visiting on a certain spring day, all sitting in Mama's new front room. They sat uncomfortably in the genteel chairs, and Abel crawled around on the floor as the women talked, looking up every now and then for his father's nod of approval. After a while he went to catch the sunlight that was glancing off a crystal nut dish and scattering rainbow bands on the floor. Sarah smiled down at him. She too had a radiance, and, for the first time in her life, she knew it. She was wearing the dress she had made from Matthew's cloth—it became her and she knew that too, so she gave her joy freely as she traded news with Mama.

Suddenly they heard the fire bell ringing up on the hill. She caught Matthew's eye and mouthed, "Fire engines," pointing uphill to the firehouse. He nodded.

In the next minutes there was the strident, off-key blare as every single one of Arcadia's volunteer firemen—his car horn plugged with a matchstick and his duty before him—drove hell-bent for the firehouse in an ecstasy of bell and siren. In a minute the ding-ding-ding-ding careened in deafening, happy privilege through every red light in town.

"Big bunch of boys!" Mama laughed. "You can count two Saturdays in good weather when they don't have a fire, and during the hunting season!"

They laughed. Then Sarah looked down at Abel, who was still trying to catch the wonderful colors. A madhouse of bells, horns, screaming sirens had gone right past them and he hadn't cried, he hadn't looked, he hadn't turned. Sarah twisted her head sharply away and screamed to the china cats on the whatnot shelf as loud as she could, but Abel's eyes only flickered to the movement and then went back to the sun and its colors.

Mama whispered, "Oh, my dear God!"

Sarah began to cry bitterly, uncontrollably, while her husband and son looked on, confused, embarrassed, unknowing.

The silence drew itself over the seasons and the seasons layered into years. Abel was a good boy; Matthew was a good man.

Later, Rutherford, Lindsay, and Franklin Delano came. They too were silent. Hereditary nerve deafness was rare, the doctors all said. The boys might marry and produce deaf children, but it was not likely. When they started to school, the administrators and teachers told her that the boys would be taught specially to read lips and to speak. They would not be "abnormal," she was told. Nothing would show their handicap, and with training no one need know that they were deaf. But the boys seldom used their lifeless voices to call to their friends; they seldom joined games unless they were forced to join. No one but their mother understood their speech. No teacher could stop all the jumping, turning, gum-chewing schoolboys, or remember herself to face front from the blackboard to the sound-closed boys. The lip-reading exercises never seemed to make plain differences—"man," "pan," "began."

But the boys had work and pride in the farm. The seasons varied their silence with colors—crows flocked in the snowy fields in winter, and tones of golden wheat darkened across acres of summer wind. If the boys couldn't hear the bedsheets flapping on the washline, they could see and feel the autumn day. There were chores and holidays and the wheel of birth and planting, hunting, fishing, and harvest. The boys were familiar in town; nobody ever laughed at them, and when Sarah met neighbors at the store, they praised her sons with exaggerated praise, well meant, saying that no one could tell, no one could really tell unless they knew, about the boys not hearing.

Sarah wanted to cry to these kindly women that the simple orders the boys obeyed by reading her lips were not a miracle. If she could ever hear in their long-practiced robot voices a question that had to do with feelings and not facts, and answer it in words that rose beyond the daily, tangible things done or not done, *that* would be a miracle.

Her neighbors didn't know that they themselves confided to one another from a universe of hopes, a world they wanted half lost in the world that was; how often they spoke pitting inflection against meaning to soften it, harden it, make a joke of it, curse by it, bless by it. They didn't realize how they wrapped the bare words of love in gentle humor or wild insults that the loved ones knew were ways of keeping the secret of love between the speaker and the hearer. Mothers lovingly called their children crow-bait, mouse-meat, devils. They predicted dark ends for them, and the children heard the secrets beneath the words, heard them and smiled and knew, and let the love said-unsaid caress their souls. With her own bitter knowledge Sarah could only thank them for well-meaning and return to silence.

Standing on the back porch now, Sarah heard the wind in the poplars and she sighed. It was getting on to noon. Warm air was beginning to ripple the fields. Matthew would be ready for lunch soon, but she wished she could stand out under the warm sky forever and listen to birds stitching sounds into the endless silence.

She found herself thinking about Abel again, and the bride. She wondered what Janice would be like. Abel had gone all the way to Chicago to be trained in drafting. He had met her there, in the school. Sarah was afraid of a girl like that. They had been married quickly, without family or friends or toasts or gifts or questions. It hinted at some kind of secret shame. It frightened her. That kind of girl was independent and she might be scornful of a dowdy mother-in-law. And the house was still a mess.

From down the road, dust was rising. Matthew must have seen it too. He came over the rise and toward the house walking faster than usual. He'd want to slick his hair down and wash up to meet the stranger his son had become. She ran inside and bundled up the unsorted laundry, ran upstairs and pulled a comb through her hair, put on a crooked dab of lipstick, banged her shin, took off her apron and saw a spot on her dress, put the apron on again and shouted a curse to all the disorder she suddenly saw around her.

Now the car was crunching up the thin gravel of the driveway. She heard Matthew downstairs washing up, not realizing that the bride and groom were already at the house. Protect your own, she thought, and ran down to tell him. Together they went to the door and opened it, hoping that at least Abel's familiar face would comfort them.

They didn't recognize him at first, and he didn't see them. He and the tiny bride might have been alone in the world. He was walking around to open the door for her, helping her out, bringing her up the path to the house, and all the time their fingers and hands moved and spun meanings at which they smiled and laughed; they were talking somehow, painting thoughts in the air so fast with their fingers that Sarah couldn't see where one began and the other ended. She stared. The school people had always told her that such finger-talk set the deaf apart. It was abnormal; it made freaks of them. . . . How soon Abel had accepted someone else's strangeness and bad ways. She felt so dizzy she thought she was going to fall, and she was more bitterly jealous than she had ever been before.

The little bride stopped before them appealingly and in her dead, deaf-rote voice, said, "Ah-am pliizd to meet 'ou." Sarah put out her hand dumbly and it was taken and the girl's eyes shone. Matthew smiled, and this time the girl spoke and waved her hands in time to her words, and then gave Matthew her hand. So Abel had told that girl about Matthew's deafness. It had never been a secret, but Sarah felt somehow betrayed.

They had lunch, saw the farm, the other boys came home from their summer school and met Janice. Sarah put out cake and tea and showed Abel and Janice up to the room she had made ready for them, and all the time the two of them went on with love-talk in their fingers; the jokes and secrets knitted silently between them, fears told and calmed, hopes spoken and echoed in the silence of a kitchen where twenty-five years of silence had imprisoned her. Always they would stop and pull themselves back to their good manners, speaking or writing polite questions and answers for the family; but in a moment or two, the talk would flag, the urgent hunger would overcome them and they would fight it, resolutely turning their eyes to Sarah's mouth. Then the signs would creep into their fingers, and the joy of talk into their faces, and they would fall before the conquering need of their communion.

Sarah's friend Luita came the next day, in the afternoon. They sat over tea with the kitchen window open for the cool breeze and Sarah was relieved and grateful to hold to a familiar thing now that her life had suddenly become so strange to her. Luita hadn't changed at all, thank God—not the hand that waved her tea cool or the high giggle that broke into generous laughter.

"She's darling!" Luita said after Janice had been introduced, and, thankfully, had left them. Sarah didn't want to talk about her, so she agreed without enthusiasm.

Luita only smiled back. "Sarah, you'll never pass for pleased with a face like that."

"It's just—just her ways," Sarah said. "She never even wrote to us before the wedding, and now she comes in and—and changes everything. I'll be honest, Luita, I didn't want Abel to marry someone who was deaf. What did we train him for, all those special classes? . . . *not* to marry another deaf person. And she hangs on him like a wood tick all day . . . " She didn't mention the signs. She couldn't.

Luita said, "It's just somebody new in the house, that's all. She's important to you, but a stranger. Addie Purkhard felt the same and you know what a lovely girl Velma turned out to be. It just took time. . . . She's going to have a baby, did she tell you?"

"Baby? Who?" Sarah cried, feeling cold and terrified.

"Why *Velma*. A baby due about a month after my Dolores."

It had never occurred to Sarah that Janice and Abel could have a baby. She wanted to stop thinking about it and she looked back at Luita whose eyes were glowing with something joyful that had to be said. Luita hadn't been able to see beyond it to the anguish of her friend.

Luita said, "You know, Sarah, things haven't been so good between Sam and me. . . . " She cleared her throat. "You know how stubborn he is. The last few weeks, it's been like a whole new start for us. I came over to tell you about it because I'm so happy, and I had to share it with you."

She looked away shyly, and Sarah pulled herself together and leaned forward, putting her hand on her friend's arm. "I'm so happy for you. What happened?"

"It started about three weeks ago—a night that neither of us could get to sleep. We hadn't been arguing; there was just that awful coldness, as if we'd both been frozen stiff. One of us started talking—just lying there in the dark. I don't even know who started, but pretty soon we were telling each other the most secret things—things we never could have said in the light. He finally told me that Dolores having a baby makes him feel old and scared. He's afraid of it, Sarah, and I never knew it, and it explains why he hates to go over and see them, and why he argues with Ken all the time. Right there beside me he told me so many things I'd forgotten or misunderstood. In the dark it's like thinking out loud—like being alone and yet together at the same time. I love him so and I came so close to forgetting it. . . . "

Sarah lay in bed and thought about Luita and Sam sharing their secrets in the dark. Maybe even now they were talking in their flower-papered upstairs room, moving against the engulfing seas of silence as if in little boats, finding each other and touching and then looking out in awe at the vastness all around them where they might have rowed alone and mute forever. She wondered if Janice and Abel fingered those signs in the dark on each other's body. She began to cry. There was that freedom, at least; other wives had to strangle their weeping.

When she was cried out, she lay in bed and counted all the good things she had: children, possessions, acres of land, respect of neighbors, the years of certainty and success. Then she conjured the little bride, and saw her standing in front of Abel's old car as she had at first—with nothing; all her virtues still unproven, all her fears still forming, and her bed in another woman's house. Against the new gold ring on the bride's finger, Sarah threw all the substance of her years to weigh for her. The balance went with the bride. It wasn't fair! The balance went with the bride because she had put that communion in the scales as well, and all the thoughts that must have been given and taken between them. It outweighed Sarah's twenty-five years of muteness; outweighed the house and barn and well-tended land, and the sleeping family keeping their silent thoughts.

The days went by. Sarah tortured herself with elaborate courtesy to Janice and politeness to the accomplice son, but she couldn't guard her own envy from herself and she found fault wherever she looked. Now the silence of her house was throbbing with her anger. Every morning Janice would come and ask to help, but Sarah was too restless to teach her, so Janice would sit for a while waiting and then get up and go outside to look for Abel. Then Sarah would decide to make coleslaw and sit with the chopping bowl in her lap, smashing the chopper against the wood with a vindictive joy that she alone could hear the sounds she was making, that she alone knew how savage they were and how satisfying.

At church she would see the younger boys all clean and handsome, Matthew greeting friends, Janice demure and fragile, and Abel proud and loving, and she would feel a terrible guilt for her unreasonable anger; but back from town afterwards, and after Sunday dinner, she noticed as never before how disheveled the boys looked, how ugly their hollow voices sounded. Had Matthew always been so patient and unruffled? He was like one of his own stock, an animal, a dumb animal.

Janice kept asking to help and Sarah kept saying there wasn't time to teach her. She was amazed when Matthew, who was very fussy about his fruit, suggested to her that Janice might be able to take care of the grapes and, later, work in the orchard.

"I haven't time to teach her!"

"Ah owill teeech Ja-nuss," Abel said and they left right after dinner in too much of a hurry.

Matthew stopped Sarah when she was clearing the table and asked why she didn't like Janice. Now it was Sarah's turn to be silent, and when Matthew insisted, Sarah finally turned on him. "You don't understand," she shouted. "You don't understand a thing!" And she saw on his face the same look of confusion she had seen that day in Mama's fussy front room when she had suddenly begun to cry and could not stop. She turned away with the plates, but suddenly his hand shot out and he struck them to the floor, and the voice he couldn't hear or control rose to an awful cry, "Ah ahm dehf! Ah ahm dehf!" Then he went out, slamming the door without the satisfaction of its sound.

If a leaf fell or a stalk sprouted in the grape arbor, Janice told it over like a set of prayers. One night at supper, Sarah saw the younger boys framing those dumb-signs of hers, and she took them outside and slapped their hands. "*We* don't do that!" she shouted at them, and to Janice later she said, "Those . . . signs you make—I know they must have taught you to do that, but out here . . . well, it isn't our way."

Janice looked back at her in a confusion for which there were no words.

It was no use raging at Janice. Before she had come there had never been any-thing for Sarah to be angry about. . . . What did they all expect of her? Wasn't it enough that she was left out of a world that heard and laughed without being humiliated by the love-madness they made with their hands? It was like watching them undressing.

The wind cannot be caught. Poplars may sift it, a rising bird can breast it, but it will pass by and no one can stop it. She saw the boys coming home at a dead run now, and they couldn't keep their hands from taking letters, words, and pictures from the fingers of the lovers. If they saw an eagle, caught a fish, or got scolded, they ran to their brother or his wife, and Sarah had to stand in the background and demand to be told.

One day Matthew came up to her and smiled and said, "Look." He put out his two index fingers and hooked the right down on the left, then down gently on the right. "Fwren," he said, "Ja-nuss say, fwren."

To Sarah there was something obscene about all those gestures, and she said, "I don't like people waving their hands around like monkeys in a zoo!" She said it very clearly so that he couldn't mistake it.

He shook his head violently and gestured as he spoke. "Mouth eat; mouth kiss, mouth tawk! Fin-ger wohk; fin-ger tawk. E-ah" (and he grabbed his ear, violently), "e-ah dehf. *Mihn*," (and he rapped his head, violently, as if turning a terrible impatience against himself so as to spare her) "*mihn not* dehf!"

Later she went to the barn after something and she ran into Lindsay and Franklin Delano standing guiltily, and when she caught them in her eye as she turned, she saw their hands framing signs. They didn't come into the house until it was nearly dark. Was their hunger for those signs so great that only darkness could bring them home? They weren't bad boys, the kind who would do a thing just because you told them not to. Did their days have a hunger too, or was it only the spell of the lovers, honey-honeying to shut out a world of moving mouths and silence?

At supper she looked around the table and was reassured. It could have been any family sitting there, respectable and quiet. A glance from the father was all that was needed to keep order or summon another helping. Their eyes were lowered, their faces composed. The hands were quiet. She smiled and went to the kitchen to fix the shortcake she had made as a surprise.

When she came back, they did not notice her immediately. They were all busy talking. Janice was telling them something and they all had their mouths ridiculously pursed with the word. Janice smiled in assent and each one showed her his sign and she smiled at each one and nodded, and the signers turned to one another in their joy, accepting and begging acceptance. Then they saw Sarah standing there; the hands came down, the faces faded.

She took the dinner plates away and brought in the dessert things, and when she went back to the kitchen for the cake, she began to cry. It was beyond envy now; it was too late for measuring or weighing. She had lost. In the country of the blind, Mama used to say, the one-eyed man is king. Having been a citizen of such a country, she knew better. In the country of the deaf, the hearing man is lonely. Into that country a girl had come who, with a wave of her hand, had given the deaf ears for one another, and had made Sarah the deaf one.

Sarah stood, staring at her cake and feeling for that moment the profundity of the silence which she had once tried to match by stuffing cotton in her ears. Everyone she loved was in the other room, talking, sharing, standing before the awful, impersonal heaven and the unhearing earth with pictures of his thoughts, and she was the deaf one now. It wasn't "any farm family," silent in its strength. It was a yearning family, silent in its hunger, and a demure little bride had shown them all how deep the hunger was. She had shown Sarah that her youth had been sold into silence. She was too old to change now.

An anger rose in her as she stared at the cake. Why should they be free to move and gesture and look different while she was kept in bondage to their silence? Then she remembered Matthew's mute notes, his pride in Abel's training, his face when he had cried, "I am deaf!" over and over. She had actually fought that terrible yearning, that hunger they all must have had for their own words. If they could all speak somehow, what would the boys tell her?

She knew what she wanted to tell them. That the wind sounds through the poplar trees, and people have a hard time speaking to one another even if they aren't deaf. Luita and Sam had to have a night to hide their faces while they spoke. It suddenly occurred to her that if Matthew made one of those signs with his hands in the darkness, and read the meaning—that if she learned those signs she could hear him. . . .

She dried her eyes hurriedly and took in the cake. They saw her and the hands stopped, drooping lifelessly again; the faces waited mutely. Silence. It was a silence she could no longer bear. She looked from face to face. What was behind those eyes she loved? Didn't everyone's world go deeper than chores and bread and sleep?

"I want to talk to you," she said. "I want to talk, to know what you think." She put her hands out before her, offering them.

Six pairs of eyes watched her.

Janice said, "Mo-ther."

Eyes snapped away to Janice; thumb was under lip: the Sign.

Sarah followed them. "Wife," she said, showing her ring.

"Wife," Janice echoed, thumb under lip to the clasp of hands.

Sarah said, "I love. . . . "

Janice showed her and she followed hesitantly and then turned to Matthew to give and to be received in that sign.

The Sexton's Deaf Son

Rasheed A. Gbadamosi
Nigeria, 1969

Joshua Keino's parents had no objection to his bringing the boy home to Sunday lunch. But Auntie Roda's indignation was ill-concealed. She shrugged indifferently everytime Mrs. Keino offered her the next course. She spoke very little. She took it out on the electric fan. "The awful thing doesn't work efficiently," she said. Perhaps it was in the wrong angle. She got up a few times to fix the fan. She really would like to tell her stories now, her exaggerated rumours about various individuals at the church. But all the attention was taken up by the guest and Mr. Keino was probably relieved he would not have to endure Auntie Roda's blabbing.

Mr. Keino ate voraciously. Mrs. Keino made signs to the deaf and dumb boy to check if he had enough to eat. Joshua was exhilarated. He had now acquired a new playmate. He had met the boy earlier in the day at the junior church service. They had roamed in the huge park together after the service. The boy made incomprehensible sounds by way of speaking. Joshua felt attracted in a curious way to the chubby, unspeaking boy. They had climbed the guava tree together and, finding no fruit, they had sat on the branches looking at the lake and the coastline beyond. It was cool in the shade of the leaves and now and again the breeze rustled the leaves permitting the sun to pierce through. On the lake, two paddling boats were racing towards a tiny island on which there stood two coconut trees. A fishing net was fastened to the trunks of the trees. The fishermen soon loosened the cords and they rolled up the dry net and shoved it into one boat. Then they anchored the other boat and paddled off in the one with the net.

It was time to go home and Joshua indicated to the boy he had to go home. The boy's face tightened in disappointment. Joshua beckoned to him to come. The boy uttered something indiscernible. Joshua climbed down the tree and gesticulated to the boy to come on. And so they came home.

After lunch, Auntie Roda went to her room for what she called "her health rest."

"Now Joshua," Mr. Keino said, "where did you meet your friend?"

"At the church. He is the new sexton's son."

"What is his name?"

"I don't know. He couldn't tell me."

"I see. I suppose you'll take him back soon. His parents must be looking for him now."

"Can I show him how to ride my new bike?"

"If you wish. Don't go out into the street. Stay in the garden."

"All right, dad."

But they sneaked out into the street. Joshua's intention, really, was to show off his new friend to the other boys in the neighbourhood. Presently they came to a group of three boys who were leaping over bamboo make-shift high jumps. The idea was to progress from a low height, and taking turns, everyone had to make a clean jump. Anyone who fell the cross bar was flogged by the others and you dropped out after three unsuccessful tries.

Joshua was dubious about involving his new friend in the competition. But it was a problem of communication. Perhaps his friend wanted to join in.

The game started. Joshua went first and he sailed over the bar. So did the others. The deaf and dumb boy did not take part. The height went up about three inches.

Then to the astonishment of others, the deaf and dumb boy took off his shirt, took a few paces backward and then ran forward and leapt up and across the bar, hitting the ground on the other side with great glee. They all cheered him except for the biggest boy.

The height was increased. The smallest of the three boys fell the jump three times. He dropped out. Each time he was whipped by others according to the rules of the game. But the deaf and dumb boy did not join in any flogging. Neither Joshua could make that height in three attempts. Then another of the three boys dropped out. The biggest boy took the next turn. He succeeded in the third attempt, taking only two beatings. The deaf and dumb boy did not flog him.

Now came Joshua's friend's turn. He stood beneath the crossbar and then counted a few paces forward. The biggest boy flexed his bamboo cane. Now the deaf boy stopped, turned around and came running, his checks slightly puffed, faster now and up and, crash! The cross bar fell. The biggest boy rushed forward and assailed the deaf boy.

"Stop it!" Joshua shouted. "He did not cane you, why should you cane him. Leave him alone."

"It is the rule of the game," the biggest boy defiantly said.

He lashed his cane on the deaf boy again. The other boys stepped in and hit the boy who was now uttering a torrent of incomprehensible words. Joshua pushed them off.

The biggest boy again hit the deaf boy across his chest and bruised him. "Nobody invited you," he said. "Why did you barge in with that deaf boy. Nobody invited you."

Joshua promptly punched the big boy in the face. The deaf boy started to cry. He was sitting in the sand. A melee ensued. Joshua did not have a chance against the three of them. Somehow he bruised the smallest boy on the eyelid. The smallest boy and the dumb boy were both crying. Presently, a man showed up and broke up the fight. Joshua's lower lip was cut and he was licking it all the way back to the church. There, he waved good bye to his friend and strolled on home.

Auntie Roda was knitting in the living room.

"Joshua, what happened?" she asked.

"We had a fight."

"Who cut your lip? Where is the dumb boy?"

"I don't know. I lost him."

"That serves you right. Of all the boys in the neighbourhood you can't choose a playmate but a deaf boy. Do you know deaf boys are animals? They don't talk and they can't hear; just like animals. They have strength like wild animals. Don't get mixed up with him again. You hear me?"

Joshua did not say anything. He got up to leave the room.

"Where are you going? Wait, I'll treat your wound."

"My bike is parked down the street."

But Joshua went back to the park and he climbed up the guava tree. Now he could see the fishermen were back on the island of two palm trees. The sun was tracing the horizon down and the surface of the lake reflected the aging sunlight. Auntie Roda; she's just like those brutes, just because he doesn't talk; he's not an animal; he can't be an animal; he's too likeable to be an animal; those boys were animals, my friend can't be an animal. Maybe he should talk, Joshua was thinking. Pity, he can't. Why was he created deaf? Yes, who made him dumb?

Like a Native

Joanne Greenberg
USA, 1985

Rose's parents had come from a place called Eagle Spring. When they talked about it, their eyes turned long-lonesome and little smiles came on their faces. Playing between the houses with Freckles, Tee, and Mary, she had once heard her father talking at the open window. His voice and words sounded different from the people here, people he called "city-born." "Day like this I'd head for Chilion's Grove," he said. "Fishin'd be good, a day like this." She was listening, smiling, and Freckles, annoyed, hit her hand because she had it up, saying something-nothing, caught in listening to what he could not hear.

They were "Deafies," her friends, Freckles, Tee, and Mary. Their parents were *Deafandum*. Daddy said it was a mistake to let her stay so long with people like that, parents and kids all Deafandum, but then, he sighed and said, "*Poor* means you got no choice." They had moved here to work in the defense plant, to make the electricity that was in airplanes. At first Rose thought they must have been chosen for this work because they were from Eagle Spring, a place connected with flight. When she talked about Eagle Spring to Freckles, she would use the Sign for springtime so that the name carried her parents' sense of its beauty, a springtime of eagles.

Rose's people had quiet voices that didn't move up and down. Their hands and bodies did not move when they talked and they showed no feeling by obvious looks. To read them, you had to look for the twitch of a muscle in Daddy's face when he was angry, or around his eyes, tired. Mama primped when she felt good and let her hair go lank when she was cross or tired. And there were two lines up near the top of her nose that said, "Get gone."

Her friends, the Allmons, spoke with their whole bodies. Each one claimed a space around himself and filled it. They pointed people in the air, "you," "he," "them," and gave them parts to say with body habits that defined them. Their language was all finger, hand, face. Rose sometimes went with them to Deaf church. She had learned their language easily, without thinking how.

When the war was over, the plant changed and began to make television sets. Everyone was happy. Daddy had his job there, Mama was home and kept house.

Rose was ten then, and the Allmon children, one after the other, had gone away to Deaf school. When they came back summers, they were full of secret school talk and wit and new Signs and private jokes. They had Sign nicknames and their conversation was about boys and girls Rose didn't know. In her own school she was shy and quiet in her speech and most of the time was forgotten on the sidelines.

She had learned long ago not to use any of the Allmons' language at home or school, not even the simplest movements, the slip of "who cares" down from the nose, or pointing to herself—"I think." The Allmons and their language made people nervous, but Rose loved the long green and golden summers when she and the kids spent days together down near the river or on past the outskirts of town. They played games long after the Hearing kids had given them up, running games or stick games. Their talk was witty and funny and in it they imitated people they knew.

But Rose began to notice as she was thirteen and fourteen and fifteen that their world was slower to widen than the world of the Hearing kids at her school. They seemed to know less, about ordinary things. They didn't read books or newspapers. Their television was childish.

In ways she couldn't explain, Rose began to feel separated from Tee and Freckles. She began to try harder to be where the Hearing kids gathered, to follow their talk and learn their tastes. It wasn't easy to translate the immediate impressions of a thing from an air-drawn image, spontaneous joy or sorrow—to stop the hand before it rose.

The summer she was sixteen, she worked at the five-and-dime. All day, humid, hungering, moose-faced boy-men hung around the jukebox playing records. She learned the lyrics and the boys' "lines," but she had to be careful not to look straight at them the way she had always looked straight into the faces of the Allmons and their friends. There had been trouble in the beginning because of it.

One day Daddy came home and said, "That's all." Only that. The factory had closed. He and then Mama tried to get other work, but there was nothing to be had. For three weeks in late August, Rose's income was the only money coming in. They lived on biscuits and beans. In December the car gave out. At Christmas Daddy said, "We're going back to Eagle Spring."

The voice that spoke the beautiful name said it dead flat. Rose wanted suddenly to Sign to him: *You* didn't fail; things failed *you*. It would have been quick flip—subject out, object in, and the negative definite as a stubbed toe.

They were unhappy, which puzzled Rose. Where was the soft stream of memory now? "Winter we'd get around the fire," Daddy had said every winter, "and tell

stories and roast chestnuts—you know, nothing's nicer than a hickory wood fire—"
She remembered clearly the yearning in the words, fragile as Signs in the air, gone
now, unprovable.

Going back, the miraculous land unrolled itself before her. Mountains and
rivers. Even with the trees bare and black in the winter silence, the places had a rolling grandeur, a distant-vista sense of space, and a dignity that made Rose catch her
breath. And the names: Fourways, Hidden Creek—names Mama had used as
lullabye words—Rest Easy and Sayward. At Bethany they got off the bus. It was a
two-mile walk to Eagle Spring and another two to Grandpa's where they would stay.
"We'll be with Granny and Grandpa," Mama said, "but I got money saved to get
you gone from this place. Now, you go in when we get there, and you take off
them clothes and save 'em for leavin'—all your clothes, you hear?" The tone was
winter-bitter.

They started up the dirt road, walking slowly but never stopping. "That's the
hill way, you'll learn," Daddy said. "No, she won't!" Mama snapped.

They stayed with Mama's folks, "on The Branch." Rose learned to skin and hang
meat, to smoke-dry fish, to can venison. Outside the odorous, bare-floored house,
the mountains spread away in fog-sea mornings; winter closed them in. She learned
hard and slow day by day. She lost eggs and broke lamp chimneys and made them go
black. She spooked the chickens and ruined the cheese, but the strangeness was in
more than surface things. It was in the language, the words she spoke, the way she
spoke them. When spring came they all went down to Eagle Spring to shop and go to
church and Rose knew that an indefinable difference held her from the people of The
Branch and the people of Eagle Spring and kept her at arms' length, forever apart.

Mama was proud. "You keep on talkin' nice, like you do. You ain't to get comfortable and stay here!" But the young men and girls from Mountain Meadows and
Chilion's Grove looked at her and were curious. Among themselves they laughed
and talked and teased, but when she talked, they went quiet and the boys backed
away a little, politely, and the girls lost their lightness in her presence. Rose made
them feel countrified. When she tried, carefully, to use their words, the boys went
shy and the girls turned aside, and went away to be together without her.

⌒

She began going to school again as Mama insisted. Her city schooling impressed
the teachers, and they allowed her to slip ahead and be a senior. When she was
accepted at nurses' training, Mama gave her all the quilt money and all the egg
money and all her savings and a suitcase with the city clothes, now a size too small.
They saw her away down the mountain and then from Eagle Spring to the bus, and
she was away into what they called The World.

Learning the language. She had to be more serious than most of the other students. She had to drill night after night on the difficult medical words, the secret language of doctors and disease, and slowly she learned to hear the words and then to speak them until it was easy for her to say them. She was less lonely in nursing school than she had ever been except for her years with the Allmons, but there was something missing still, a place she had not found.

As time went by, Rose began to have a special identity around the hospital. "Is the hillbilly around?" "Ask the hillbilly to come, too." She listened for scorn, but there was none. It was interest and even some affection. Her accent seemed part of the charm of her strangeness, "authentic," one intern said, "natural." She couldn't begin to explain how wrong they were, so she said nothing.

Because she had never been natural or authentic in Eagle Spring, and with every visit she was moving further from Mama and Daddy. The words she used, even their arrangement, were changing. Her language was a new way of seeing the world. "You think of things I never even heered of," Mama said. Less and less was possible to express, to share with the people on the high, silent arms of the mountains where Grandpa and Granny's cabin was.

Sometimes in dreams she would venture back to the first people of all, to the primal language, the language that remembered perpetual summer, the language of first intensities and first memories—the Sign. Many of the people in her dreams were not Deaf but Signed anyway, because it was, in the dream, the natural language of mankind.

The psychiatry affiliation came during Rose's senior year. It was three months' service at the state hospital. On the third day, Rose and her partner, a girl named Ellie Metcalf, stood frozen at their posts in the day room on a male ward, "observing" as they had been told to do. After lunch, she found herself, without knowing why, moving toward an empty-faced, shaved-skull man who had been standing alone, one of a line of such men in a denim shirt and soft cotton pants. Her hands came up naturally, her body readied itself for the questioning posture—her Sign quick and colloquial. "You like lunch?" standing so as to ready the space between them for conversation. She might have slapped him, kissed him, given him the electric shock they used here. His head came up, his eyes focused, going wide. "Who?" he Signed, his posture question-and-amazement. He moved away from the wall. "Who are you?"

"Rose," spelling it and pointing to her student's name tag.

It was the pure tongue long dormant in both of them and for both, spoken without thought to the words. "She—Lettie " He put "Lettie's" place beside him and established it there so as to speak of her the Deaf way. "Did she send you— oh, God, did she send you to end—" He drew the loneliness Sign in long ellipses, large and slow, so that Rose was made to see each day the loneliness, all day the loneliness, day after day the loneliness, to the end of endurance and beyond.

"How long?" she asked. "How long here?"

"I don't know." One single Sign down from a face that showed he had no way of asking, knowing, or measuring. They stood hung together stock-still. They wanted to fall into each other's arms, but such a thing would be misinterpreted before the Hearies. "Once," he said, "on a walk I saw—there's another here, a Deaf—we talked a minute. I looked for him again, but—could you find—will you find—"

"Oh, yes, if I can."

"Did Lettie send you?"

"No, this is part of my training—to be a nurse."

"So it has an end."

"Not now, not now. We'll talk about that later."

He stood, the Deaf way, and wept. They became aware at the same time of people around them, of the head nurse. He went stiff—"Will you be hurt by this?"

"We'll see, soon enough."

He laughed.

The nurses and attendants were amazed. "Saunders hasn't moved so much in all the years he's been here!" "How did you know?" "How did you learn…"

She got permission to walk the wards with Saunders. No one had known he was deaf, or how many others there were. To the Deaf, they were irresistible. Here, there, living statues broke from the walls, their fingers erupting in the cry, eyes widened, faces collapsed. Some ran to them, Telling The Story for the first time, Sign coming crude or elegant, angry or fearful; many had the patched and ugly home-Sign of Deaf who had never been taught to Sign and had not had contact with anyone but Hearing families now dead or scattered. Male wards and female wards, chronic and acute, custodial and treatment, they bore their own along, talking to themselves and each other, a passionate, swelling mob, twenty, thirty, whose eyes were now set on one another for the first time. "You here?" "How long?" "I live on—" "My name is—"

And Rose told them about Freckles and Tee and Mary, and Mr. and Mrs. Allmon. She spoke as she had known them when she was five, ten, and fifteen. She couldn't believe how good it felt, how happy, to fill a soundless world with meaning, speaking the true word out of the heart of life.

Rose was allowed run of the wards during her three months' affiliation. She found other, shyer deaf people. Some she found were profoundly ill, their Signs disordered and irrational, but many seemed ordinary to her, and she often spent her days off socializing with them, easy and happy in their company. She spoke to the doctors on behalf of some, and a few times interpreted in staffings. She was not allowed more. When the rotation was over and she was to leave, old Mrs. Sprinkles pulled at her sweater and said, "Come back and work here—you're as good as Deaf. It's for *you*. We Deaf see how your eyes shine, how your face shines when you are with us. Don't go into Hearie life. They have enough people already. See how they waste them? Stay Deaf—we are the honest people. We put our feelings on our faces and don't mouth, mouth and say nothing." Rose said she would think about it.

But a ward head nurse said, "This place isn't for you. The pay is low, no city in miles, and in the town nobody your own age to meet. My husband is sickly; we live here because it's cheap—that's what this is for, for people in retreat." She was right. So was Mrs. Sprinkles.

When Rose went back to her school hospital, news of her "gift" went with her. She was sometimes called on to interpret where there were deaf people. They usually turned out to be hearing people deafened in old age, who did not Sign and were horrified by her "gestures."

On the weekend before graduation, Rose took a bus north, to the city and the friends she had left at sixteen. It was a long trip, and the old neighborhood had altered. Like the face of a dying friend, it was familiar in the bone, but not in the flesh. Bad luck, like a disease, had set in. The neighborhood was riddled with it. Trees had been cut down or died, the yards overgrown and uncared for.

She came to the block on which she had lived. There were many black people there now. Brightly dressed but ragged children were going up and down on skates as she had done once. She passed her own house. A brown woman sat on the steps playing with a baby. Rose went to the next house, the Allmons' house, and knocked. The Allmons had had a dog who used to get their attention when someone was at the door. Rose waited, then knocked again. The door opened and half a face became visible on the other side. "Whut you wan?"

Rose explained. It took a long time; when she finished, the woman said, "They ain't no dead people here!" Rose explained again. The woman opened a little wider to listen.

"Their name was Allmon; there was a man and wife and three children —"

"Girl, this house done change owner so many time I can't keep up with it, but there's a old woman live up the street, Mrs. Thompson, three houses up. Blue roof. You go see her."

Mrs. Thompson remembered the Allmons but not where they had gone. She turned watering, confused eyes on Rose and said, "Yes, I remember them. They and those crackers who lived next to them, they started all this. It used to be a nice neighborhood—poor, yes, but decent, until the odd ones started coming." She had not remembered Rose's name or introduction. It had taken a moment for Rose to realize that "the crackers" had been her own family.

Rose stood in the sunny street. She tried to think of the names of the Allmons' friends, of the place at which Mr. Allmon had worked. The church was the only other place she could try.

It was still there, five blocks away past vacant lots and vacant factories. She went to the parish house and knocked. "Oh, yes," the minister said, "we still have the deaf people who come to morning service on Sundays. They meet in the basement for social hour. There's an interpreter. The former pastor Signed himself but he retired." The man seemed sympathetic, and she thought she heard in his speech the barest echo of Eagle Spring but she was afraid to ask.

She spent the night at the bus station. On Sunday, she stood near the church door looking at people as they came in. Except for a faintly familiar face, they were strangers to her. She had grown into unrecognizability and one after another—this couple was not the Allmons, nor this, nor this. People began to fill the church.

The Deaf all walked to the left and took the pews up front. Rose followed them there and sat down, looking hard at them, hoping she would at last recognize some of the friends, remember some of the names. The service began.

The interpreter was an earnest man, serious, accurate, and totally without Shine. The words were Signed large as the minister's voice went up, smaller as it went down, but there was no poetry, no play, no finger-dance or look of the face that commented on the words of the hands. People watched respectfully but now and then as the service went on, they began to communicate: air-quick wit or greetings to new people coming. In their eagerness at seeing one another, one or two people talked through the sermon as though the church were empty.

Rose began to watch these people, relishing their language, their play. At every pause in the prayers the hands would go up, a forest of hands a silent babble of voices, nothing at all to do with the prayers or the minister or the sermon, any more than television shows have to do with the commercials that bracket and interrupt them. Amen at last and up to go.

The Hearing left with great decorum, nodding serenely at the Deaf. The Deaf rose into their talk, which had it been sound would have blown the four walls down. In two's, three's, they drifted downstairs to the basement.

As they lined up for the coffee and cookies, Rose caught the momentary upward-eye-downward-hand-glide of end-thought of a woman and broke in. "Please excuse me—I'm from Morgantown and I'm looking for a family, the

Allmons, Mr. and Mrs. Allmon, we used to live on Sanford Street. Three children, Freckles, Tee, Mary—"

"Sorry, no, how long ago?"

"Five years."

"I don't know them, but this is Mrs. Oliver—they've been here longer—"

And again, "Sorry, no, we changed to this church four years ago, when St. James stopped its Deaf Mission."

"Who?"

"Allmon. Three children, Freckles…"

"Yes, I've heard of them, but I don't know where they went—"

By now there was a small, interested following walking with her, from group to group. "Allmon? Where did he work?"

"The foundry. There were other Deaf there…"

"That closed, that foundry, or it moved."

"Jenny, wasn't there a woman who used to—yes, oh, yes, three children—"

So it happened naturally that Rose began to be the center of the group remembering or trying to remember the Allmons and where they had gone. Until one woman said, "Where do *you* live? Where is *your* group?"

"I'm a nurse," Rose answered for the first time. "I've just graduated, and…"

There was a silence not of voices, but of the molecules in the room. Hands no longer stirred them. The hands had stopped. "You're not Deaf," one woman said. The Sign tone was not incredulous or wondering, but accusatory. She turned to her friend. "She's not Deaf," she said, with a finger toward Rose.

"Oh, no" Rose said, "I'm not Deaf."

"Then why do you act like you are?"

"Many Hearing use Sign," Rose said. "The interpreter at services today was Hearing."

"Yes, but he Signs like a Hearie. You Sign like a Deaf. You act Deaf. Hearies use our *Signs*," the woman said, and she began to speak. The Signs were the same, but the grammar, the structure was changed in a way Rose felt but could not frame.

"It's not my fault," Rose said. "I grew up with Mr. and Mrs. Allmon and with their kids. We all played together—"

"See, see, that's a school Sign, residential school. She's making out like she went to residential school—"

"I'm not tricking," Rose said. "I need to find my old friends. I need to know where they went."

A man stepped forward from the group that was now gathered around Rose. "Excuse us, please," he said, "you surprised us. The foundry closed five years ago. I remember John Allmon, but I don't know where they went. I don't think they stayed around here because if they did they would be at the social club or some Deaf clubs or churches here that we would know."

"She shouldn't try to act Deaf." The woman beside him put disapproval on her upper lip.

The woman who had begun to ask the other people for Rose touched her on the shoulder. "We were surprised, that's all. Fanny there doesn't like surprises. We should say we're sorry."

And so they did, but guardedly, stiffly, their Signs formal and stilted and more like English. Later, as she was leaving, Rose said, "I talked to all the deaf people at the state hospital. They knew I was Hearing, and they—" But by then she realized that such isolated and lonely souls cut their expectations to a much more modest shape in the air. And she knew, too, as she left the church, that if she ever met Freckles or Tee or even the Allmons again, they would address her in the formal, Anglicized Sign they used for outsiders, the Sign that defined her as Hearing and assigned her and them to the worlds in which they did, in fact, belong.

From Chapter 3 of *Islay*

Douglas Bullard
USA, 1986

[Lyson has just checked into a hotel.]

Fortunately he had to pause to turn on the light before entering the bathroom because only then did he notice that the tiled floor was one step higher than the room proper. The bathtub on four leonine paws was huge and old-fashioned and stood apart from the walls. The toilet matched the general decor, with its tank hung high on the wall with an ivory handle dangling on a brass chain attached to the flushing lever. How quaint! Beside the toilet was a contrivance strange to Lyson but familiar to world travelers: a bidet. Must be an old fashioned urinal, he decided as he acted to get his money's worth out of this extra piece of plumbing.

Now how to flush this thing? A pair of enamel faucets at the rear of the bidet seemed the answer. Why two? Probably a convenience for left-handed customers, guessed Lyson as he leaned over and turned one on. A jet of water shot up in his face.

I've got to learn the ways of high class, he cried to himself as he dried his face, glaring at the bidet. The front of his clothes were soaked and a pool of water on the floor squished under his socks. A disheveled self grumped back at him from the mirror: So you thought you knew your way around. The Great Cosmopolitan Lyson C. Sulla of Washington, D.C., Center of the World!

A satisfying bath requires adequate prior strategy so after starting the water running in the tub, Lyson went to his suitcase for the whiskey. He filled a glass and, for want of a flat surface on the rim of the tub, set it in the soap dish recessed into the wall. Cheating a bit, he realized but nevertheless deciding that the circumstances justified it, he took a long swig from the bottle before tucking it away for the night. A capful of bath bubbles dashed into the rising water soon frothed into an airy white foam. But he hadn't noticed that while he was leaning over the tub, some more, quite a bit more, of the bubble liquid spilled from the bottle into the tub. He propped up *The Wall Street Journal* within easy reach on the floor by the bath mat.

He remembered the shampoo and went to the small suitcase. He opened it and found the teletypewriter. It glared back in the mocking way only a machine can muster. Forgot to call Mary! Lyson slapped his head, lifted the teletypewriter out quickly, and rushed into the bedroom, searching frantically for the telephone. The telephone was also a period piece, similar to the one downstairs in the office.

He set the teletypewriter carefully on the table, and after a bit of searching found the outlet and plugged in. Then he recognized a problem: the teletypewriter was designed for the modern cradle telephone. He tried fitting the pedestal telephone on it and was relieved that it could be done though he would have to hold the speaker on the sending part of the machine while typing with his free hand. The earpiece of the phone could balance itself just fine on the teletypewriter receiver.

The teletypewriter is a marvelous machine, he thought to himself, that makes it possible for the deaf to use the telephone, though only if there also is a teletypewriter on the other end. Lyson's model had an additional feature: a small lamp originally designed to signal only sounds coming over the telephone but further developed to catch any sound reaching it such as knocks on the door, the crying of a wet baby, the sound of a smoke alarm and other supposedly useful signals. The only complication was that it also signaled the noises of passing traffic, airplanes, coughing, and other superfluous noises.

When Lyson turned on the teletypewriter, the light immediately flickered, announcing the presence of sound in the room though he had yet to dial the telephone. The big problem with this feature, he thought, was that it is sometimes too helpful in catching any and all sounds, making it difficult to interpret the signals over the telephone: perhaps a busy signal, a ringing, or people answering by voice. Maybe someone was at the door, he thought, and went to check. But there was no one, and the hallway stood empty throughout its entire length. Inside his room the light was still flickering irregularly. Ah! It's the traffic outside, he reasoned. He shut the windows and drew the curtains close. But the machine still blinked. He removed the ear piece from the receiver on the machine. The light winked, almost wickedly, maniacally mocking him. Lyson looked around the room, vexed.

A scent of soap bubbles brought a slap to his forehead and a rush for the bathroom. Soap bubbles frothing out of the bathroom floor into the dressing hallway covered the step; he tripped over it and disappeared into the bubbles. He slid on his stomach beneath the bubbles over a pool of water and slid to a stop against the tub. His glasses slipped off into the foam. His eyes burning from the bubbles, he groped along the rim and found the faucets, shutting them off. For a long moment he remained kneeling in the bubbles, his head on hands still gripping the faucets, sobbing and giggling. Because his sense of balance was as nonexistent as his hearing, he kept a firm grip on the tub rim as he struggled to his feet on the slippery floor, his eyes shut tightly, his head swathed in bubbles. He tried to remember exactly where the lavatory was but could only remember the bidet. Don't step on the glasses! he reminded himself. He gingerly moved his toes along the floor, groping for the glasses, one hand steady on the tub, the other thrashing in the bubbles for the bidet. Ah! He grasped the bidet firmly and kneeled over, bracing his face, and turned the faucet. The water was cool, refreshing, wonderful as he turned and twisted his head in the geyser, wallowing in the same luxury the French enjoy while using bidets the French way.

Drying his eyes, he noticed that the bubble foam was thigh high, higher over the tub. How to get rid of them? The problem irked him as he felt for his glasses in the bubbles. He just simply couldn't find them and had to content himself with the hope that at least they weren't where he could step on them. He clothes were soaking wet and he struggled out of their wet grasp, thanking Mary for having insisted on drip-dry material. He wanted to call her but decided to get the bath over and done with before something else happened and he ended up in the soap all night. He lowered himself into the tub, unmindful of the water pouring over the rim onto the floor. The hot, caressing water soothed his battered ego as he played with the floating foam, blowing grooves in it, carving his name and drawing pictures. He remembered the glass of whiskey. It seared away the soapy taste from his mouth and gave a satisfying palatable aroma as he exhaled through his nose. He held the glass up to the light, admiring the ethereal amber color of the liquor and then in one swoop drained it, wincing deliciously, shivering, baring his teeth, reveling in the sensation of a flaming fireball sizzling, sinking down his throat. He lay in a happy stupor in the tub, senseless but quite luxuriant in the weightless comfort of the warm water and the tingling of the whiskey through his bloodstream.

As the whiskey reached his nose and toes, setting them atingling, he opened his eyes and remembered Mary. The water was cooling, losing its zest so he reluctantly heaved his sluggish body out of the tub. Having already soaked the two bath towels, he was dismayed to find only the washcloths and face towel still on the rack still dry. He dried himself the best he could with these tiny pieces of cloth and threaded his way through the condensing, sticky foam to the dressing room. The carpet was wet there too but fortunately not in the room proper. He moved his luggage beside the bed and slipped into pajamas, robe, and slippers. Now I'm ready to call Mary, he decided.

He sat down on the chair and prepared to dial the telephone. But he could barely make out the numbers without his glasses. Squinting and looking closer, he could just make out their forms, so he went ahead and dialed the number. The lamp flickered with just one ring before Mary started typing. Lyson never failed to marvel at the green letters streaming across the display board of the typewriter.*

MARY HERE GA.

HI. LYSON HERE ISLAY HOTEL ROOM 628. HOW ARE YOU Q GA.

LYSON WHY YOU LATE CALL ME Q GA

---

* Because the tty (as it was more commonly known) could carry only one party's message at a time, callers could not interrupt one another and, therefore, needed a set of signals to indicate turn-taking. GA = "go ahead"; SK = "stop keying"; SKSK = "I'm hanging up."

The development of the videophone, which allows deaf callers to communicate in ASL instead of typed English and permits the two parties to sign to each other at the same time, spelled the end of this jargon, which few hearing people ever mastered.

STOP MAD AT ME PLEASE—

I'M SORRY CANT HELP IT WORRY AND WAIT AND WAIT FOR FOUR HOURS GA.

FORGIVE ME BUT CANT HELP VERY BUSY DAY. VISITED THE GOVERNORANDTHENHADIMPORTANTDINNERANDTHENCRAZYBATH—

Mary interrupted again:

CRAZY BATH WHERE Q GA.

MY HOTEL ROOM. HAD A LONG BATH. THOUGHT ABOUT YOU ALL DAY GA.

The teletypewriter was silent for an unconscionably long time before Mary typed:

STILL CANT UNDERSTAND WHAT YOU MEAN, CRAZY BATH. GA.

WILL EXPLAIN WHEN I GET HOME—

YOUR FAMOUS ALWAYS EXPLAIN EXPLAIN. AND WHY NOT YOU CALL BEFORE DINNER Q GA.

I DID TRY TO CALL BEFORE DINNER BUT GOT LOST—

WHAT YOU MEAN—

Lyson cut in:

WILL TELL YOU WHEN I GET HOME GA.

OK SURPRISED YOU FOUND HOTEL OK. AND SURPRISED YOU ALREADY VISIT GOVERNOR. GOOD Q OR BAD Q GA.

REALLY JUST HAPPENED. ACCIDENT. HARD TO SAY IF IT WAS GOOD BUT DON'T THINK ANYTHING BAD HAPPENED –

LYSON YOUR WAY FAMOUS ALWAYS ACCIDENT. WATCH YOURSELF GA.

I KNOW, CANT HELP—

WHY CANT YOU KNOW—

SORRY—

he butted in, exasperated at the inquisitive way of women.

MAYBE I SHOULD GO UP AND TAKE CARE OF YOU BEFORE SOMETHING HAPPENS GA.

SWEET OF YOU. I WOULD LIKE THAT BUT I AM OK AND LETS WAIT A FEW DAYS UNTIL—

Lyson paused, trying to think of a good stall.

YOU DONT WANT ME WITH YOU, IS THAT WHAT YOU MEAN Q GA.

NO NO NO I MEAN UNTIL I FIND OUT IF THIS STATE IS A GOOD IDEA. ABOUT TWO DAYS THEN DECIDE IF I GO HOME OR IF YOU COME HERE. MISS YOU GA.

OK BUT PLEASE BE CAREFUL, THINK TWICE. MISS YOU TOO GA.

YOU LOVE GA OR SK

LOVE YOU, BE GOOD, SK.
SKSK.

He hung up, and an awful shame came over him how he handled the call with his wife. Poor Mary. To shunt aside the shame, he assigned himself the task, before turning off the teletypewriter, of studying its little lamp. It flickered very dimly, barely perceptible. Must be the people next door. Could be, he shrugged as he crawled into bed and found the whiskey under the pillow. He couldn't remember ever putting it there but decided to seize this fine opportunity to take a long, lingering sip. Almost immediately he dropped off into the deep sweet sleep of the innocent, hugging the bottle.

Speech

Richard Umans
USA, 1986

Danny Murray and I were best friends for years, through elementary school all the way into junior high. We never had to ask if we'd be spending Saturday together, just what we'd be doing. Weather permitting, we'd usually ride bikes. Danny and I were great bikers.

Our Saturday afternoon expeditions took us not over country roads but into city streets, far from the calm predictability of our boring suburb. We explored much of the city on our bicycles, sailing freely through unfamiliar neighborhoods, walking our bikes past the exotic window displays downtown. We imagined ourselves tough city kids, looking for a gang to join. In fact, without knowing it, we were practicing for times to come, when this city or its like would provide the setting for our high school dating, our college adventures, our adult careers.

We were not without safe havens, even downtown. My uncle had a shoe store on Clarendon Street. He would sometimes take us for sandwiches or at least treat us to ice cream. But the real excitement lay all the way in the downtown shopping center, on Washington Street, where Danny's father's store stood. My uncle's little shoe shop paled by comparison.

I. J. Murray occupied its own six-story building. The first three floors were retail space, selling women's clothing, especially furs. Danny and I, unlike mere customers, were allowed to ride the service elevator to the top three floors, where the furs were stored, cut, and stitched into coats. We would visit Danny's father's grand fourth-floor office and be treated to lunch. And we had the run of the place.

The most absorbing area was the fifth-floor cutting rooms. Here the furs would be laid out, backed, and cut to shape by skilled craftsmen. The process remained forever magical to me, and two factors gave it special meaning. First, a single mistake could cost hundreds, even thousands, of dollars. Second, one of the cutters was Danny's Uncle Leo.

Leo Murray was dashingly handsome. Even in a long grey work apron, his fine slacks and pure white shirt set him worlds apart from the other cutters. His hair gleamed with sleek blackness, one curl sometimes tumbling Gene Vincent-like over the crest of his forehead. His large black eyes gazed with sensitive alertness, and his jaw stood square and firm, framing thick, straight lips. Altogether, he reminded me of Superman, barely disguised as Clark Kent.

When Danny and I entered the cutting room, Uncle Leo stopped whatever he was doing. He gave Danny a long, powerful hug, his face brilliant with delight, and they would talk. Uncle Leo's voice would soar and whoop, and Danny's mouth would silently form big, emphatic words. I never learned to understand more than a little of Uncle Leo's strange speech, and Danny told me that most people had the same problem. But Danny, his deaf uncle's favorite, had grown up hearing that speech and understood it with ease.

Danny's sharing of a secret language with this intriguing adult, who would drop everything to hurry over and chat, seemed to me the height of special friendship. In my school, some of the girls had trained themselves to speak a variation of Pig Latin, at lightning speed, in order to confound the boys and undermine the teachers. Since I'd long ago learned to decipher my parents' use of spelled words when they wished to disguise their meaning from me, nothing had so excluded me as the girls' annoying gobbledygook. Miffed, I'd taught myself through lonely practice to understand it, though speaking it in public was beneath masculine dignity.

Danny's conversations with Uncle Leo remained impenetrable to me, however. Far more than schoolgirls' nonsense talk, the excited exchanges of my best friend and his dazzling uncle thrilled me with a sense of witnessing a rare intimacy, a bond between man and boy that crossed social boundaries. It was the kind of buddyhood common on television, where heroes often had a young sidekick—the Range Rider and Dick West, The Rifleman and Mark, even Tarzan and Boy. But real life held few openings for sidekicks. My friends and I all had harried, overworked fathers, well-meaning but locked within their own worlds. Other male grownups—gym teachers, camp counselors—managed us where necessary, but always from the unbridgeable distance of their adulthood.

Only Danny Murray, of all the boys I knew, seemed able to enter the private world of an adult male—not only adult, but moviestar glamorous, and appealingly set off from the rest of the world by his mysterious speech. Danny had a rare and precious access, and I watched enviously as Danny communicated with his uncle with far greater ease than even Mr. Murray, Danny's father, who was Uncle Leo's brother and boss.

Only Ernie, Uncle Leo's elderly co-worker, seemed able to understand him as well as Danny did. Ernie, Danny said, had trained Leo Murray as a fur-cutter when the youth had come out of a prestigious school for the deaf with few skills in lip-reading or speech and little academic training of any kind. Uncle Leo had always been a rebel, Danny confided. He'd been thrown out of school several times, and only his father's wealth and position had gotten him back in. Crusty old I. J. Murray had intended for young Leo to "overcome" his deafness and become an executive like his older brother. Instead, Leo had taken avidly to the craftsmanship of cutting fur, married a deaf woman from school, fathered three hearing children, and moved into a lesser neighborhood of the same suburb where Danny and I lived.

Sometimes Uncle Leo would pull Danny and me over to his work table to show us what he was working on or lead us to the storage vaults to show us a new shipment of gleaming pelts. His voice would swoop like a crazed sparrow, his hands and face signaling most of his intent. I would smile and nod along, imagining I understood. Then Danny and his uncle, and sometimes old Ernie as well, would explode into laughter at a remark of Leo's, a remark I could no more distinguish from the cascade of his vocalizing than a particular quart of water from a gushing torrent. Danny would translate for me, and I would laugh energetically, glad to be part of the interchange once more, even if emptily, and too late.

One summer afternoon, on a trip home in my late twenties, I chanced to visit a small country club in a suburb near the one in which I'd grown up. The country club had no golf course, only a pool and clubhouse, and it failed to hold its own against clubs that offered golf and tennis. Some gay entrepreneurs had bought it, and now it was prospering as a gay pool club.

The poolside atmosphere was pleasant and low-pressure, with people who had moved to the suburbs for many of the same reasons as my parents. The men lounged and chatted, and the women horsed around. A few show-offs practiced diving or swam self-conscious laps in the pool. Here and there sat pairs of recent lovers, with eyes for no one but each other.

A tall, handsome man in his early forties strode past. Shocked, I determined to listen for the voice, but the black, sympathetic eyes were the giveaway. At once I fell to smoothing my hair and sucking in my stomach. Then I realized that I had with any luck changed far too much in fifteen years for Leo Murray to recognize me now.

He still looked fine. His body was thicker, but not fat, and his hair was wavy and dark, graying slightly at the temples. I watched him cross to his lounge chair and sit beside a tall, skinny blond, with whom he began to talk comfortably. His eyes still flashed with lively humor.

Screwing up my courage, I approached Leo Murray and his companion and introduced myself as Danny Murray's boyhood chum. Leo's face enlivened instantly, just the way I remembered, though his friend's held some residual suspicion. As I asked for details of Danny's recent years, however, Carl had to repeat most of Leo's answers for me, and he began to warm to his role as go-between.

I quickly satisfied myself regarding Danny's progress and pressed on about Leo himself. He obliged me with the information that he was divorced, his kids grown, and he still worked for I. J. Murray, though the firm was much reduced by declines in the fur market. He lived, he said, with his sister. Carl, though obviously close, was apparently not Leo's lover.

I listened greedily. Leo Murray's voice still darted wildly up and down, detached from the meaning of his words. But reading the constant flicker of emotion across his face, I felt the remembered impression of comprehending his message without actually making out his words. It was as pleasing a sensation now as then, a kind of private, prelingual communication, full of intimacy even in blazing sunlight beside a crowded pool. I sat talking long after there was anything left to say.

Returning to my own friends at their lounges, I found myself making disparaging remarks—not about Leo, whom I simply described as an acquaintance from childhood, but about Carl. Cattily I described his skinny body, his pockmarked face, his lisping, pretentious speech. Slowly it dawned on me that I was jealous. Once again I had had to speak to Leo Murray through an intermediary. Once again he had chosen another to be his intimate. Why not me? Why was I again, unfairly, too late?

Several years later, on another pass through town, I was left with two hours to kill before my train left. It was an awkward space of time, not enough to call friends, too much to spend comfortably in a train station. I rented a locker for my suitcase and went for a walk.

The train station stood alongside the financial district, and at early evening the sidewalks were already nearly empty. There was only one movie theater in this end of town, and my timing would be unlikely to permit me a full feature. At this theater, however, it mattered little at what point you walked in. I paid the high admission fee and went in to watch the grainy, scratched film with its mismatched soundtrack.

When I entered, all eyes turned to survey the new arrival. The audience was all male, as I knew it would be. Men were seated at odd intervals throughout the small theater, occasionally in pairs. There was a cluster standing behind the back row of seats. A steady stream of individuals trooped back and forth from the lounges located at the very front of the theater, behind the screen.

I watched the film for a few minutes, and the crowd. Then I took a walk through the lounge area. It was dimly lit. There were men standing within and outside both bathrooms. Some of the stall doors stood ajar. No one spoke. The shadowy figures passed in and out in silence, sometimes lingering, blending into deeper shadows. Back in the theater, the flickering light of the movie made the spectators' faces superficially alive.

On my second pass through the lounge area, I spotted Leo Murray. He was cruising the same way I was, moving slowly through the hallway, which was lined with slouched figures. He looked me full in the face, but I couldn't tell whether he recognized me or not. His eyes were already wide, engorged with perception, before he caught sight of me.

I carefully passed him two or three more times, doing everything possible within the conventions of this place to alert him to my presence. Reluctantly I refrained from planting myself in front of him, tapping him on the shoulder, or signaling him directly. I slowed to a crawl each time he approached; I eyed him sullenly. He simply moved past like a figure in a dream, at ease in this silent world, his black eyes glinting, bottomless. We each glided along like the others, stopping sometimes to cling to a wall, floating past each other in the purgatory murk. Different stall doors stood ajar.

At length I drifted back out to the theater. I took a seat as far as possible from everyone else and applied myself to the unwatchable movie. Some minutes later a figure joined me in my row. It was Leo Murray, watching the screen with a gentle, beatific smile illuminating his face. I moved over two seats and sat beside him. Like a spotlight on a pivot, he turned and flooded me with his smile. His eyes glowed, black and wet.

I placed a daring hand on his knee. The fabric of the slacks was thick, luxurious, elegant. His own hand danced across my thigh, and he turned toward me further. Then he spoke to me, only to me, and I dropped my head back and listened.

My Father's Darling

Carole Glickfeld
USA, 1989

Before Labor Day, Melva asked my father for some money to buy some clothes for school. I was sitting with the cards on the floor in the living room, playing war with myself, and I saw her follow him into the bedroom to ask. I didn't expect him to reach into his pocket and give her the money right away, but he did. So what did Melva do? She told him ten dollars wasn't enough.

"Think me rich?" my father signed.

"You cheapskate," she signed right back, maybe because she couldn't help herself.

In two seconds flat he had her up against the wall and was twisting her arm behind her. She was screaming as I ran to get my mother from the kitchen. "Afraid break arm," my mother said before she rushed to the bedroom.

When we got there, Melva was holding her arms crossed in front of her face. My father was smacking the side of her head. He sounded like he had a terrible sore throat, yelling, "Honorfatherhonorfatherhonorfather."

My sister sank down to the floor when my father waved my mother away. "Misermisermiser," Melva said, but not in sign language, hardly moving her lips. Like one of those ventriloquists on Ed Sullivan.

My mother tried to stick her arms between my father and Melva, making noises like she was crying. When he turned around, I looked away because I knew what was coming. He pushed my mother so hard she fell down.

Melva didn't get to keep the ten dollars. "He'll get his," she told me. "Everyone gets what's coming to them." She told me it had to be true because she read it in the Old Testament. And then she cried.

After lunch my father said he was going for a walk. Melva was supposed to do the dishes but she said, "I'm getting out of this hell house." That meant she was going to see her best friend, Toni. So I said I'd do the drying. For some reason, Melva gave me a look like she could kill.

My mother filled up the deep sink with suds and put the dishes in. She rinsed them off in the little sink and handed them to me, one by one, until she stopped to talk to me. "Fine, fine, present necklace M-r-s K-l-e-p-p," she signed, shaking her head. She said all the deaf people were gossiping about it. I guess that's how she found out. "Not think first o-w-n daughter," she said.

"Daddy present M-r-s K-l-e-p-p?" I asked. "Why?"

She scrunched up her face like she was going to cry. "Clever, try make like. Understand?" She said my father was probably going to see her on his walk.

I nodded. I didn't really understand why my father was trying to get Mrs. Klepp to like him. She was deaf and lived over on the next block from us.

My mother put her hands in the soapy water. When she took them out to sign again, she sprayed me. "Sorry," she said, taking the dish towel to brush off some suds from my hair. "Think high c-l-a-s-s. Real t-r-a-m-p."

A tramp was what Melva called the girls in her high school who smoked in the bathroom. I knew Mrs. Klepp was always smoking, but I don't think that's what my mother meant.

"D-o-n-t tell M-e-l-v-a, S-i-d-n-e-y," she said.

Even though Melva and Sidney were much older than me, my mother talked to me like I knew better than they did.

"Shhhh," I told her, hearing the key in the outside door.

My father stuck his head in the kitchen but didn't say anything. I heard him go into the living room where he always took his afternoon nap.

My mother smiled a funny smile. "B-e-t no one home," she said, about Mrs. Klepp.

The next Sunday, when we were all having dinner in the kitchen, my brother asked my father for money to get a catcher's mitt so he could play on the Sluggers. That was the team that was sponsored by O'Hanlon's Tavern on Nagle Avenue.

My father dropped his fork and knife down on his plate on purpose. "N-o play b-u-m-s Catholic," he signed.

"Not b-u-m-s," my brother signed back. "J-u-s-t play baseball."

"Catholic, no good," my father said, getting a very angry look on his face.

Melva did her ventriloquist act again. Without moving her lips, she said, "Sidney, take it easy."

But by that time my brother was real angry. "I-f Catholic no good, why you friend M-r-s K-l-e-p-p?"

Right away my mother tried to tell my father that Sidney didn't mean what he said. My father told her not to butt in. He told Sidney to go to the bathroom. That meant he was going to get a strapping. For a few seconds we all sat there like stone.

"Go!" my father yelled in his hoarse voice. As he got up he banged his fist down on the table, hard enough to make the plates jump. My mother stood up in front of him but he pushed her down in the chair. He grabbed Sidney by the arm and pushed him toward the door. A few seconds later my mother went running out of the kitchen after them.

"Why did Sidney say that?" I asked Melva.

"He saw them go into a movie together. Downtown. But don't tell Mama. It would hurt her feelings."

"Why does Daddy like Mrs. Klepp?"

"She's a tramp," Melva said.

When we heard Sidney screaming, we went in the living room. We could even hear the belt every time my father hit him. My mother was crying outside the bathroom door.

"I could murder him," Melva said. "He doesn't deserve to live."

I went back into the kitchen and put my hands over my ears.

That night I heard my father come home from the U.L., which is short for Union League of the Deaf, where he went to play cards on Saturdays and some afternoons before going to work at the post office. I would wake up sometimes when he came home and listen to him go through his routine. I could hear him hang up his jacket in the hallway closet and open and close the frigidaire before he sat down in the kitchen to read the *Daily News* with a snack, probably pumpernickel with prune butter, which was his favorite. I saw him once through the hallway mirror, but he didn't see me watching him, and he couldn't hear me, of course.

After he got done in the kitchen, I heard him praying outside the room I shared with Melva, beneath the mezuzah. He made smacking sounds. I knew he was kissing his palm and then the shiny gold case that my sister explained has the parchment with writings from the Bible. I could even hear him mumbling in Hebrew. He made more smacking sounds before he went into the bathroom. Like always, I heard the toilet flush and the sink water running for a long, long time (which I could never figure out), then his footsteps back past our room and into the bedroom where my mother was already sleeping.

"Do you think he was sorry?" I asked my pretend-friend Mary, who was lying next to me. Mary said if he was really sorry he would stop making everyone so miserable.

"I hate him," I told her.

Mary said that was terrible, especially after how nice he was to me. I was the only one who didn't get into trouble with him. I told her that when she was bigger she would understand, and then she fell asleep. I tried to think of something to do that would make my family happier but I fell asleep before I thought of anything.

On Saturday morning I went roller-skating. Robin Reinstein and Tommy Shanahan came around the corner with me, so we could skate in the street without anyone seeing, but at the last minute Robin got chicken and stayed on the sidewalk, so it was just Tommy and me, out in the middle of Sherman Avenue. The street is a lot smoother than the scratchy sidewalk and doesn't have all those cracks, so it's a lot more fun to skate.

I was coming down real fast toward Arden when I heard my brother's booming voice calling, "Ruthie!" I stopped so fast I fell, and before I could get up I heard a car screeching on its brakes just a few inches from where I was. The next thing I knew, my brother lifted me right up and put me down on the sidewalk where Melva was. They were both dressed up because they had just come from Temple.

"What the hell are you doing in the street?" Sidney yelled, so that everyone could hear, including Tommy Shanahan. When Tommy saw me looking at him, he disappeared around the corner of Arden Street. Robin was gone by then.

"Daddy would kill you if he saw," Sidney said.

"Her? He wouldn't lay a finger on her," Melva said. "She's her father's darling. Aren't you!" she said, smiling real sarcastic like.

"I don't ask for trouble," I said. "That's why I'm around the corner."

"Well if I ever see you skate in the street again . . . " Sidney threatened, but he didn't finish because when I looked down at my knee and saw it was all bloody I started to cry. "Go upstairs and put iodine on it," he said.

I skated ahead of them, took off my skates, and ran upstairs. My father woke up from his nap and came in the kitchen while my mother was putting Mercurochrome on, since iodine hurts so much. I told him I fell skating, but not where.

"You not watch right," he said to my mother, practically standing over her.

"Can't know what d-o-i-n-g every minute," she said to him. She put the Band-Aid on my knee.

"Not f-i-t mother," he told her.

"Why me, me? You never watch," she said. "A-l-l t-i-m-e m-e."

I got out of there and went to tell Mary what happened. She said it wasn't my fault, and then my father came in.

"Want go U-L with me?" he asked.

"Now?"

He hadn't taken me to his club for a long time. I always liked going, especially because of the subway ride downtown. I said okay.

"First change dress," he said, because he liked me to look nice when I went with him.

He dressed up, too, in his brown suit. I saw him brushing his hair with the brush my Aunt Lois gave him for his birthday. It had a real silver back. He combed his mustache with the matching comb. His hair in both places was strawberry blonde, like in the song my brother liked to sing about this man Casey waltzing.

When we got to the U.L., which is in the basement of a hotel on 72nd Street, my father acted very different. He waved hello to everyone, real friendly, with a big smile. He was very handsome when he smiled, my mother said. The room was smoky on account of the cigarettes and cigars from the men who sat at the folding tables playing cards, waving their arms as they signed and making grunting noises. There were only a few women. They looked up when my father took me around. The deaf people always asked the same questions. This time it was Mr. Fiorini who asked, "Can sign?" meaning me.

"A-s-k," my father said, meaning he should ask me, so he did.

"I can sign," I told him.

"Wonderful!" Mr. Fiorini said.

I never knew why they thought it was such a big deal that I could sign, just because I could hear. My father looked awfully happy.

We went over to a table where Mr. Weisbaum, Max Cohen, and Mrs. Klepp were sitting right under a fluorescent light, the kind with long tubes. Mr. Weisbaum was wearing his yarmulke, of course. He and my father made jokes in Hebrew, which I didn't understand. They said the Hebrew out loud (I don't know if you can even sign in Hebrew), reading each other's lips. Both of them were bar mitzvahed, which my Uncle Sol said was really something, because they were deaf.

Max Cohen and my father went to the horse races together sometimes. Max Cohen bet a lot, my mother said, and was always in trouble with his wife, Mrs. Cohen. One year he didn't go to the U.L. because he was in Florida, hiding from the bookies.

Mrs. Klepp was one of the few women who went to the U.L. She got in because her husband was a member, but Mr. Klepp wasn't there. "How g-a-m-e?" she asked my father, meaning baseball.

"Not hear," my father said, meaning no one had told him the score. When Sidney was home, he listened to the game on the radio and told my father what was happening.

As Mrs. Klepp signed, smoke came up from the cigarette hanging out the side of her mouth. When the cigarette was between her fingers, smoke came all around us, because she waved her arms a lot.

"You millionaire," my father teased her, about the money she spent on cigarettes.

"Me win poker, can a-f-f-o-r-d smoke all day," she said, and then they both laughed.

I never saw my father laugh at home. He sat down at the table and I sat on a chair next to him and watched Max Cohen deal the cards. I knew a little about poker but not enough to play. I looked over Mrs. Klepp's clothes. She had on a beige cardigan and a black straight skirt, like a high school girl. My mother wore dresses with flowers on them, unless they were pastels. She said Mrs. Klepp was a show-off, but I couldn't figure out what she meant, unless it was the high heels.

After a while I got up and went to the buffet table to get a slice of American cheese, which I ate real fast. My father didn't like me to eat it without bread, for some reason. Mrs. Jacobs got some paper and pens for me to draw with from the office. I wasn't very good at drawing, so I wrote a story about a boy and his dog. The dog runs away, so his father hits him and says it's the boy's fault, but later the father buys him another dog. I knew my father wouldn't ask me to show it to him.

At four-thirty my father had to leave to go to the post office. He wanted Mrs. Klepp to walk him to the subway but she wanted to play more poker, so she stayed. I had to stay, too, since she was taking me home.

They got a sub for my father in the game, Mr. Fiorini. He teased me about being a great poker player like my father. "A-l-b-e-r-t b-e-s-t," he said. "Me g-l-a-d he leave."

I saw my Father take all the coins off the table, so I knew he'd won.

When they were done playing, Mrs. Klepp lit up a cigarette. She asked me, "How brother?" and when I said fine, "How sister?" Then she wanted to know what my mother was doing that afternoon. I shrugged.

I thought we were going to leave when she got up, but she had me walk her over to another table, where Mrs. Gertzner was. She was a friend of my mother's although we didn't see her very often. She lived in Brooklyn, near the Steeplechase, with a blind and deaf husband. He could read the sign language by feeling your hand when you signed. My mother said Mrs. Gertzner went to the U.L. to get away from her worries.

Mrs. Gertzner asked me how my mother was. "Home?"

"Fine," I told her. "Ironing."

Mrs. Klepp said, "R-u-t-h my daughter. See, same dimples. Me her mother."

Mrs. Gertzner said, "You wish."

"You fresh?" Mrs. Klepp asked.

"You hungry A-l-b-e-r-t," Mrs. Gertzner said, meaning my father.

Then Mrs. Klepp said, "I smack your face."

"D-a-r-e," Mrs. Gertzner spelled out slowly. "You d-a-r-e."

And Mrs. Klepp did. Mrs. Gertzner smacked her back. Then they started pulling each other's hair and clothes, until the men stopped them. Then Mrs. Klepp took me home.

On the subway ride to Dyckman Street, Mrs. Klepp told me how fresh Anna Gertzner was. "You see yourself. Fresh. Say me hungry A-l-b-e-r-t."

"Maybe true," I signed, suddenly feeling like I couldn't breathe. My heart was pounding so fast I could hear it over the roar of the train.

"You fresh," she said. "I tell your father."

"I tell my mother," I said, looking right into her eyes, which were like blue marbles.

We went the rest of the way without signing.

When I got home, I wanted to tell Melva, but I decided not to, so I told Mary. She said I should apologize to God for being fresh, and I did. I said that if He didn't let Mrs. Klepp tell my father about it, I'd do good things for people when I grew up, like become a nurse.

The next Saturday my father said he couldn't take me to the U.L. because Mrs. Klepp had a dentist appointment, so there wouldn't be anyone to take me home. I nodded, trying not to show him how happy I was, but I felt like bursting. He looked at me real funny. For a second I wondered if he could read my mind, like he was God.

Behind his back I shouted, "Mrs. Klepp is ugly and stupid!" My father turned around very suddenly. That really scared me, but he didn't say anything. I started to skip out of the room. "She's ugly and stupid!" I shouted again.

"Ruth!" he roared, real loud. He only yelled that loud when he was very angry. When I turned, I saw him waving at me to come back. I crossed my toes and walked slowly toward him. He reached into his pants pocket and took out a quarter and gave it to me. A nickel was what he usually gave me on Saturdays.

"You love father?" he asked.

I nodded.

"Show me."

I threw my arms around him and hugged him. He gave me a kiss that made a big smacking sound on my cheek. "You good girl," he said.

I took the quarter and put it under my blouses in the dresser drawer, then got my skates. Tommy Shanahan was already on the stoop when I got there. He dared me to skate Nagle.

"You're crazy," I told him. "You can get killed on Nagle from all the trucks."

So we went around the corner and skated Sherman Avenue until eleven-thirty, which is when Sidney and Melva got out of Temple.

On Monday, when I was coming home from school, I saw a police car in front of the stoop. When I got almost to the fourth landing, there was a policeman standing in our doorway. Next to him I saw my Father and then another policeman in the foyer, and my mother holding a bloody handkerchief over her nose. The cops seemed very glad I was there to interpret.

"Ask your mother if she wants to press charges," one cop said.

I made the sign for "press" like in "iron" and "charges" like in "price." I knew that made no sense, but I didn't know what "press charges" meant.

My mother stopped crying. She signed, "Go jail."

"I think my mother wants him to go to jail," I said, not looking at my father and trying not to move my mouth very much, so he couldn't lip-read me.

He looked pretty sick when they made signs like he had to come with them. I grabbed onto his leg. "I'm sorry," the policeman said to me when he took my hands off.

When they left, my mother told me how my father had pushed her down on the kitchen floor and beaten her up. She thought our neighbor, Mrs. Cafferty, must of called the police.

"Who s-u-p-p-o-r-t me and children?" she kept saying. Then she answered her own question. "S-t-a-r-v-e," she said, meaning we'd all starve with my father in jail. I couldn't help crying. I was afraid I'd never see him anymore.

When my brother came home from working in the cleaners, my mother told him to go to the police station and get my father. "Change mind," she said to tell the police.

"Sonofabitch," Sidney said. "That's one thing when he picks on me, but using his fists on a woman . . ."

While he was gone, Melva came home from baby-sitting. "Oh, God!" she said when she saw my mother's swollen face and the bruises on her arm. "Stay jail," she told my mother. "He should rot there," she said to me. "He deserves to die for every rotten thing he's done."

My brother came back alone. He told my mother that after my father got out of jail he decided to go to the U.L.

"Funny, not work," my mother said.

Then Sidney called the post office to tell them Mr. Zimmer had a toothache and to charge it to sick leave.

We all sat around the kitchen table after that. My mother was knitting a sweater for me. Sidney had the *Daily Mirror* open in front of him on the table but he wasn't really reading it. Melva was saying terrible things about my father and sometimes she'd start to cry, which made me cry.

"Sonofabitch," my brother said again. "I could kill him. Just pick up a knife and let him have it while he's asleep. He'd never hear me coming."

"Sidney!" Melva said. "You better ask God to forgive you."

When my mother asked what we were talking about, all Melva said was "Daddy." Melva told Sidney and me she should be the one to kill him, though, because they weren't so tough on girls. "They might put me in reform school for a while," she said, "but you'd have to go to jail." She meant Sidney.

That's when I got the idea. They would never suspect me if I did it. For one thing, I wasn't a grown-up. For another, I was my father's darling.

That night I woke up when I heard the double locks open on the outside door. Mary and I lay in the dark, listening, while my father went through his whole routine, kissing the mezuzah on the door, leaving the sink water running, and then going to bed. I told Mary not to worry, and then I got up real carefully, so as not to wake Melva, who's a real light sleeper. I didn't have to worry about waking up Sidney. I could hear him snoring as I went past his hide-a-bed in the living room on the way to the kitchen.

My mother came in while I was looking through the kitchen drawer for the big knife. I forgot that the light always wakes her up. It shines into the hallway mirror and into her bedroom.

"What d-o-i-n-g?" she asked me.

"Hungry," I said. "Make sandwich."

"Big girl," she said, but she made the sandwich for me, shmeering some peanut butter on rye bread.

After I ate it, we both went back to bed. I thought a lot about what to do next time. It got light out before I fell asleep.

The next day was Rosh Hashanah. My mother made a big dinner, with chicken soup and matzo balls and potato pancakes. She and my father weren't speaking, though. Her eye was still swollen and there was a little scar under her nose. After dinner my father didn't go to work because of the holiday. He and my Uncle Sol went to the Orthodox synagogue. Sidney and Melva went to the Reform. My mother and I hung out the window. When she went to the bathroom, I ran and got the knife from the kitchen and put it under my pillow.

As soon as she came back to the window, she asked, "What wrong?"

"Nothing," I told her.

"Devil?" she said.

"No," I said, but she looked like she didn't believe me.

It was hard staying awake after everyone went to bed. I told Mary a lot of stories I remembered from the books I read from the 207th Street Library. When I heard my sister breathing like she was asleep, I took the knife out from under the pillow a while, until I could see in the dark, then I went over to the bed.

My heart was pounding so loud that I thought I might have a heart attack and die. I told myself to hurry and get it over with. I jabbed the knife in my father's back, over his pajama top. Nothing happened, except he made some funny sounds before he started his regular snore. I tried harder. This time my father jerked and his arm slapped my mother, who woke up. She saw me right away. I dropped the knife on the floor and kicked it under the bed before she came around to where I was. "Sick?" she asked me.

"Headache," I told her, but she couldn't see what I said, so we went over to the window where there was moonlight. I signed, "Headache," again.

We went to the bathroom and got a Bayer's. In the kitchen she looked in the drawer for the big knife to cut it in half. "Funny, gone," she said. She used another one and gave me half to take. "Go bed," she said. "Me stay read. Can't sleep, think too much A-l-b-e-r-t."

On my way back I remembered that my mother dusted with the mop every morning under her bed, so I couldn't leave the knife there. I went to get it, but I couldn't see where it was in the dark. While I was down on my knees feeling around, my father got up. I rolled all the way under the bed, practically dying. When he went to the bathroom, I grabbed the knife and ran back to the bedroom. I could hardly breathe I was so scared.

After he flushed the toilet, I heard him go through the living room. I put the knife under my pillow and went to the hallway just outside the kitchen and peeked in the mirror.

My father was kissing my mother. Real kissing. On the lips, which I'd never seen him do. He was bending her slightly back over the kitchen table. Their arms were around each other, like in the movies. For a second I thought he might be trying to smother her, but then they stood up straight.

"Bed?" my father asked her.

My mother nodded.

He started walking out of the kitchen. Just before she pulled the light cord, I saw her stick her tongue out at his back.

I ran for dear life through the living room and almost squashed Mary when I jumped into bed. In a little while I heard funny noises coming from the other bedroom. I was scared my father was beating my mother again, but I didn't hear her crying or anything. I put the pillow over my head and Mary's and we fell asleep.

In the morning my mother was in the kitchen, so I couldn't put the knife back. I hid it in the dresser drawer where I kept the quarter my father had given me. When I came home from school, my mother was ironing my father's shirts.

"Make u-p," she said, meaning she made up with my father. She was smiling kind of funny.

I wondered how come. "Daddy pray sorry?" I asked her.

She shrugged. "Brother uncle advise," she said, meaning my Uncle Sol had told my father to do it. "Not believe pray."

"Not believe G-o-d?" I asked her, to make sure.

"Good teach children, that a-l-l."

"S-i-n not believe," I told her, which is what Melva had told me.

"Shh," she said, placing a finger over her lips. "N-o tell Daddy."

I put a finger over my lips.

She gave me a shirt of my father's to hang up. Carefully, I buttoned the top button, like she taught me once. "You very d-a-r-l-i-n-g. A-l-b-e-r-t l-u-c-k-y," she said.

I burst out crying but I wouldn't tell her why.

"You sorry see me hurt," she said, pointing to the large reddish purple mark on her upper arm. "D-o-n-t worry, will better," she said, telling me that she and my father were going to the movies later and my sister would baby-sit me. Then she squeezed me against her soft round belly and big bust.

Later I got the knife back into the kitchen drawer, but I couldn't figure out what to do with the quarter. Mary said I should give it back because I didn't deserve it.

On Yom Kippur, when everyone was in Temple except my mother, who was hanging out the window to see what people were wearing, I did something I'd never done before. I kissed the mezuzah. It wasn't easy, because it was way up high on the doorjamb. I had to jump up a couple times to reach it and I didn't know the right prayer. I told God I was sorry and that if He could forgive my father, maybe He could forgive my mother, too, because she didn't mean Him any harm. I was going to promise not to skate in the street anymore, but at the last minute I thought of something better. I told God I would bury the quarter in the garden. If it was still there on my next birthday, that would mean I was supposed to have it.

"Hungry o-r f-a-s-t?" my mother asked when I went to the window.

"F-a-s-t," I said. "You?"

She nodded.

"Why? You not believe."

"You devil, t-o-o many nosey," she said, but I could tell she wasn't angry or anything.

After I got dressed I went down to the stoop and climbed over the wrought-iron on top of the little brick wall around the garden. I buried the quarter in the ground where we fed the sparrows sometimes, between the middle two bushes, four steps from the building.

As I was climbing, my father came up the stoop. "Why there?" he asked.

"Play," I said.

"Not play today. Religious holiday," he said.

Behind him, Melva and Sidney were walking up the first level. Sidney was in his good suit and Melva was wearing a coat she got secondhand from our Cousin Rona in New Jersey. But she had on her new shoes, with high heels and straps across, like Mrs. Klepp's.

"What me say?" my father signed to me, real gruff.

"Uh oh, she's gonna get hers," Melva said, loud so I could hear.

"Not play," I said. "Sorry," I told him.

When my father started coming toward me, Sidney rushed up. I guess he thought my father was going to hit me, but all he did was kiss me on the forehead. Melva gave me this look, like she was real disgusted.

My father turned and saw them. His face got all cranky. "Not think sister, bring Temple," he said to them, meaning they should of taken me with them to synagogue. I could see Sidney getting angry back. "Jesus Christ!" he said out loud.

"Be careful," I told them, without moving my lips.

"Shut up!" Melva said to me, without moving hers. "We know what side you're on."

By this time my father was yelling so that everyone on the stoop could hear him. I kept my eyes on the ground, even though I could feel Melva looking daggers at me. Later she would do an imitation of us talking like ventriloquists and Sidney would imitate my father yelling and we'd all get hysterical, but right then I stood there with my face burning, wishing myself dead.

Miracles in America

Sheila Kohler
USA/Republic of South Africa, 1990

It was not something you could actually see, not something you would ever want to see, so they didn't notice it for the longest time. They were very young, too—neither the boy nor the girl had turned twenty-one—and probably they were not used to noticing much.

As a matter of fact, they were not the ones who finally noticed it, when it was finally noticed. It was the grandmother who noticed first, and not only noticed but told everyone about it; it was the grandmother who, you might say, opened up the box and let the devils loose. Not that, even then, they recognized the devils as such that summer in Italy down by the sea.

It took the years to do that.

It was a hot, breathless summer on the Italian Riviera. The wind was dead calm, the Mediterranean like a lifeless lake. Only small lazy ripples broke on the shore with what sounded like a sigh of exhaustion. The glare of the white sky blended with the glitter of the steel-gray sea. Even the tips of the stunted pine by the window were still. The only sounds the grandmother heard in the villa in the early mornings were the faint clucking of the chickens and the sound of the child's high-pitched cries.

Every morning they rose early, before the heat was too great, and sat on the terrace, eating white crumbly bread and drinking bitter coffee, before they traipsed down the daisy-studded stone steps that led like a chain from the terrace to the void of the sea.

The children—the grandmother thought of her son and her daughter-in-law as children—strolled indolently ahead. The boy had the long, slender, shapely legs of a tall girl. He carried the yellow deck chairs under one arm and the newspaper and books under the other. The girl carried the child casually on one hip holding her with one arm, absentmindedly, her other hand on the boy's shoulder before her.

The maid, Speranza, who had come with the villa the grandmother had rented, followed, clutching the large straw picnic basket with the midday meal against her breast, stopping from time to time to catch her breath and to listen. She was, apparently, listening to the only sound to be heard, the clucking of the chickens.

The grandmother thought the maid was probably trying to tell, from the sound of the clucking, if the chickens had laid any eggs.

The grandmother, a thin woman with piercing blue eyes, brought up the rear, walking even slower and not carrying anything, only holding her hat on her head, the shadow of the leghorn trembling on her face.

All the time the family was walking down the steps, the chickens were clucking and Speranza was listening with what seemed to the grandmother to be hope. Speranza visited the chickens each morning and evening, looking for any possible eggs, but the chickens that summer, under the searing beams of the relentless sun, laid poorly, out of sight, halfway down the hill, sufficiently far away that the noise and the odor would not disturb the guests in the rented villa or on the beach.

Still, sometimes, when the grandmother lay restlessly on her bed in the night, disturbed by dreams or the sounds of the child's cry, she thought she could smell the stench from the chickens' cage, which rose in the heat of the night.

The small pebble-stone beach lay at the foot of the hill between rocks. The family stretched out, lined up in a row in the yellow deck chairs. Only Speranza and the baby sat on the stones. Speranza apparently preferred to sit on a towel on the stones with her short legs spread out before her under her full gray skirt.

The grandmother, draped importantly across the deck chair, her hands lying in her lap, watched her daughter-in-law rise and sit on the boy's lap, laying one white limp arm around his neck, playing with the blond curls at the nape of his neck. With their dark-blond heads side by side, close together, their ivory-white skin with its almost blue tinge around the forehead and the eyes, their pale, insouciant gray eyes, the grandmother thought the couple might have been brother and sister. Even their bodies, long-limbed and narrow, their backs arching exaggeratedly, and the veins in the white hands visible, seemed strangely similar. Perhaps, the grandmother thought, they had, somewhere, a common ancestor.

Only the curve of the girl's abdomen showed the faint lines where the skin had stretched, as though her body had been too narrow to carry the weight of the child.

There was about both of them a vague natural carelessness, an unawareness of danger that the grandmother found touching but slightly irritating. The grandmother found the couple's youthfulness, their vulnerability, a little frightening, and at the same time rather boring. The couple made her feel, at fifty, very old. She considered that this sort of amorous display—the girl was now kissing the boy behind one ear—could just as well take place in the privacy of their own bedroom.

She had to admit that she actually preferred her grandchild's or even the maid's company. She really rather preferred the long afternoons in the cool of the kitchen to the sultriness of the mornings, trapped between the rocks, without shade, on the narrow beach. She liked it when the couple rose from the luncheon table, their hands linked, and went to lie down—they seemed to spend an inordinate amount of time lying down under the mosquito net on the mahogany four-poster bed, half-naked, with their books and their newspapers.

Once, the grandmother had inadvertently entered the couple's room. She walked in, raised her eyes to the ceiling, turned and left the room, but not before she had glimpsed the couple, entwined, half-naked, reading their books.

Sometimes the grandmother wondered if that was all they actually did under the mosquito net. She wondered how the baby had come into being at all. The children themselves seemed to share this sentiment, as her daughter-in-law had once said to her, laughing, "All he had to do was to look me in the eye, and I was pregnant."

When the grandmother passed the couple's open window, she often heard the sound of their rather high-pitched voices. They seemed to be talking and laughing, and sometimes, she thought, a little surprised, the girl was singing to the boy.

Whatever it was they did under the mosquito net seemed to take them a great deal of time. They spent most of the afternoon there and retired to bed early at night. After lunch, when they ate in the villa, the children usually left the table before the coffee. The girl would sometimes say something cryptic like, "Got to get back to Septimus," apparently referring to some book, or the boy might say, "Got to find out what's going on in the world," and laugh.

The grandmother would reply, "Oh, go on with you," and wave them away with a lift of her hand, really rather glad to see them go. She found their conversation at table well-meaning but dull. They seemed to her very earnest. They talked about books that she had never read and had no intention of reading. They spoke of Virginia Woolf and Robbe-Grillet. They had even wanted to call the child Virginia, until the grandmother pointed out that Virginia sounded rather like another word, something she had always called her "heart of hearts." In the way of reading, the grandmother herself liked something meaty, something she could get her teeth into, something with a good strong plot and plenty of sex.

But the children spoke with great seriousness of books without plots and of current events, which they followed carefully, exclaiming in horror over certain happenings that shocked them. A lot of things seemed to shock them; they seemed to find a lot of things "beyond the pale"—riots, rapes, thievery and perjury, kidnappings and hijackings. Nothing much, she had to admit, shocked the grandmother anymore; in fact, she had the rather uneasy feeling, at times, that she had done things that would have shocked the children much more, had they known about them, than the events that shocked them.

There was the night she had spent in a hotel with a stranger, a perfect stranger, a man she had met on a train. She had noticed him eyeing her legs—her legs she always felt were her best point—and before she could have said Jack Robinson, there the man was—he was really rather handsome, dark and a little thickset—beside her, with his hand on her heart of hearts. Well, she couldn't help wondering what her son and her daughter-in-law would have thought about that! And she couldn't even say that she regretted it. No, if she was absolutely honest with herself, she didn't really regret anything much in her life, except, perhaps, a few lost opportunities, and there hadn't been many of those.

If the children weren't exclaiming over shocking events (kidnappings or hijackings, thievery and perjury, riots or rapes), they were complimenting each other playfully and calling on the grandmother for her approval, so that the grandmother had the impression she was being called upon to compliment them both.

"She's got the most beautiful eyes, now, doesn't she, Mother? Did you ever see such beautiful gray eyes?" her boy would say, staring at the girl and laughing.

"Of course she does," the grandmother would say, looking from the girl's eyes to the boy's eyes.

Finally, the couple would rise, and the grandmother would sip her black coffee alone and then get up and go out onto the terrace for a while to smoke a cigarette and join Speranza. She would sit in the shadows of the thick walls in the stone-floored kitchen with the child and the maid, sipping iced tea with lemons from the tree in the garden and nibbling the sugary pastries Speranza baked.

The child would often wake early from her nap—for some reason she didn't sleep well that summer—and Speranza would take her to her grandmother. The little girl would sit happily on her grandmother's lap in nothing but an undershirt and pants, glad to have escaped her cot, tugging wordlessly at her grandmother's pearls, until the grandmother, who understood what she wanted, pulled the child's pink toes, one by one, for each of the little piggies and, when the last little piggy ran all the way home, let her hand run up the child's fat leg all the way across the little undershirt to the child's smooth, warm underarm.

If the child was silent, Speranza was never at a loss for words. She talked mainly about food, but sometimes about her past. Like everybody else Speranza had had her love story, or so she told the grandmother over the tea in the kitchen. She told the grandmother of her husband, a man of culture, she said, a musician, a violinist, with what she called a magnificent mustache, who had quite unaccountably gone off, actually jilted her, run away with her hard-earned cash, leaving her to face life alone with her embonpoint and her squint.

As Speranza talked, the child would watch her face as though she could see something interesting happening there. At the time the grandmother thought it was Speranza's squint the child was noticing.

Speranza, sitting now on the beach, knitting, probably dreamed of returning to America with the family and opening a pizza parlor, the grandmother thought. Speranza knitted fast, and sang bits and pieces of a song that sounded, to the grandmother, who sat beside her, something like "*Vado da Lodi a Milano per cercà la mia ginga ging.*"

The grandmother watched as the couple rose, picked their way lightly, walking hand in hand across the pebbles, going to the edge of the water, sinking down gently into the sea, reaching out with long languid strokes, swimming until she could hardly see them anymore, turning on their backs, kicking up a rainbow spray in the air.

As they swam back to the shore, the girl called out suddenly from the water to her child, as though she had just remembered her presence. She called over and over again, "Isabelle, belle, Isabelle, IIIsaaaabelllle," until the child's name, with its long-drawn vowel sounds, seemed to fill the beach with a cadence that was both sad and wild. The child, however, ignored her mother's call completely, crouching down in her light blue romper on her little, fat legs, placing the smooth gray stones very carefully one by one into her green bucket.

It was, perhaps, at that moment that the grandmother began to realize the truth, though afterward she found it hard to say exactly when it had come to her. Perhaps, she thought, she had somehow known what would happen from the start.

The grandmother had been against the marriage, though she had not actually said anything to stop the couple from marrying or at any rate, had not said as much as her ex-husband had said. Her ex-husband had said a great deal. He had been dead set against the match, particularly as the ex-husband himself had been married four times. He told his son he was too young. He had not even finished college. He told him that, with all the alimony he was paying already, he couldn't afford to support yet another woman, and certainly not his son's wife.

The grandmother had been against the match, but she had thought it inevitable. After all, there was the child on the way, and the girl had money of her own, and the couple had, apparently, always been in love.

As long as the grandmother could remember, the girl had been there, like an omen, she thought sometimes. The couple had known each other since birth, or almost since birth, had always been together, or so it seemed to the grandmother. Whenever she turned around to look for her son, that girl was there, with those slender white arms around his neck, like a weed, she had thought sometimes, or even a leech. The girl was at every one of her son's birthday parties, sitting in the flickering light, watching Charlie Chaplin, one arm flung around the boy's neck; she went to the same school he did, she followed him to camp.

There was something about the girl, something delicate, something hopeless, the grandmother had always thought. She wasn't sure what it was. Perhaps it was the very white, almost blue teeth, or the way the girl forgot things, was unable to remember her keys or even the dog, which she left once, for a whole day, howling, tied up at the baker's.

The grandmother had hoped for something better for her boy. But he didn't seem to notice his loss. He had never known anything else.

He was an only child. She should have given him a real sister, perhaps, she thought, not this look-alike, this white shadow, but she had not had the time to make a second child before her husband left her. And perhaps, she thought, it wouldn't have made any difference if she had.

The heat on the beach at noon hung over them ominously. The sky was a glaring void. A vendor came by, bending against the weight of the box on his back, his bare toes splayed on the stones. "*Candit . . . chi vuole?*" he called. No one moved. The girl lay stretched out on the pebbles, resting after her swim, wrapped in a white towel, which she wore drawn up underneath her shoulder, so that her head was cradled on her arm.

Even as the grandmother dozed, her eyes shut on the glare, she was conscious of her daughter-in-law before her and somehow unaccountably perturbed by her still presence.

"I think the treasure is hungry," Speranza said, referring to the child, who was tottering across the pebbles in the general direction of the sea. The maid staggered after the little girl, waving a chicken bone at her.

"Come eat, come eat." Speranza yelled the only two words of English she had learned at the child's back. The child continued, going toward the edge of the water, carrying her green bucket over one arm, gazing out toward the horizon, as though bent on a voyage of discovery.

"Come eat, come eat." Speranza's loud, accented voice filled the beach like a rallying cry.

The grandmother stared at the child and the maid, at the boy and the girl, and it came to the grandmother, then, that what she had suspected all along was perfectly obvious, was there for the whole world to perceive. For a moment, she almost gasped with amazement, not at what she had discovered, but that no one had discovered it before her. What was amazing to her was that no one else had noticed, had been able to notice something so evident. For all these months, the boy and the girl and the child had lived together, day after day and night after night, and never noticed what had become perfectly obvious to the grandmother in the space of a few moments.

The grandmother watched with astonishment as her daughter-in-law rose languidly, with a laugh, and walked on her tiptoes across the stones to pick up the child at the edge of the sea. The mother swung her child around in the air playfully. The girl was actually swinging her child over the water and throwing her head back and laughing, the child's little bare feet rising and falling, rising and falling, rising and falling, skimming the surface of the sea.

The grandmother looked at her son. Her boy was sitting in his deck chair with his straight nose tilted toward the sun, with his perfect profile at the exact angle to obtain the maximum amount of the sun's rays, with his eyes shut and his book spread open on his lap. As for Speranza, she stood with her chicken bone still raised in her hand, probably contemplating the quality of the aspic, the grandmother thought.

The sea and the sky and the pebble-stone beach all looked suddenly gray to the grandmother, as gray as the girl's gray eyes. The sky seemed low and cloudy, and even the smell of the sea, thick and bitter.

As she watched the child fly through the air, she thought that the world would never look quite the same again.

The grandmother had a sudden desire to shout out something obscene; she wanted to say something that would wake everyone up. Instead, she said, "I think it's going to rain," and thought, I'll tell them after lunch.

She waited until dinner. At dinner her son was discussing *The Brothers Karamazov*, or it might have been *War and Peace*. The grandmother was not really listening. Whatever it was, it was long and serious, and not the sort of thing one could easily interrupt. When her son finally paused, and the grandmother was about to broach the subject on her mind, Speranza came in with a huge dish of spaghetti, balanced on the palm of her hand, and launched into a long and detailed description of how to make *ragu*. As Speranza talked, the grandmother thought she had better put the thing off. After all, it was just possible that she might be wrong about the causes, if not the effect. These things were obviously difficult to measure exactly. Perhaps it would be wiser to have a professional opinion, a medical opinion. Perhaps she ought to get a doctor. That was it. Obviously that would be the thing to do. She decided, while Speranza explained the part about letting the red wine simmer, that she would call the doctor the next day, without saying anything to anyone, and have him confirm what she already knew.

The doctor arrived at two the next day, while the couple were napping. He was a slightly stout man with a florid face and wore a dark suit with a linen waistcoat. He mopped his brow, sweating, after his climb up the hill. The grandmother noticed the slight bulge under his waistcoat and his gold watch. She had a penchant for chubby men, and she liked the way the thick gold watch dangled over the swell of his stomach. She stood talking to him for a moment on the terrace and even offered him a cup of coffee. He drank the coffee while admiring the view.

The doctor knew the people who lived next door to the villa.

"She's a Dufour, you know," he said, raising his eyebrows appreciatively.

"Oh really," the grandmother said, as though she did know, pleased anyway to find herself in such good company.

"And the house on the left belongs to a German, a big industrialist, you know," the doctor went on, nodding with approval at the view.

The grandmother would have liked to prolong the conversation; she even considered, for one mad moment, putting the whole thing off and throwing an elegant dinner party for her neighbors and the doctor. She saw herself in her best blue dress, coming out onto the candlelit terrace, followed by Speranza with a silver dish of canapés.

Instead, she ushered the doctor through the French doors that led from the terrace into the child's room.

The child's room was dimly lit, the curtains closed on the heat of the afternoon. There was a faint odor of urine in the air. The little girl was standing up in nothing but her diaper, in her crib. She was bouncing, rocking herself back and forth against the bars of the crib, so that it had moved halfway across the floor.

When the child saw the grandmother, she lifted her arms to her. The grandmother picked up the child and put her down by the window, giving her her box of blocks and drawing back the curtains to let the light into the room.

While the child piled the blocks into a neat tower, the doctor clapped his hands loudly behind her back.

The child went on making her tower.

The doctor moved a little closer and clapped again.

The child carefully balanced the last tiny block on the top of the tower.

The grandmother looked at the doctor inquiringly.

"Of course these things are difficult to assess with a young child," the doctor said, and mopped his brow. He cleared his throat and added, "They can do wonderful things these days. You would be amazed at what they can do. They can practically build you a new ear these days. And in America, I'm sure, they can do miracles. In America they're always coming up with something new. Why, who knows what they might be inventing even at this very moment. Of course, now, if it should be . . ."

At that point the couple came into the doorway. They stood on the threshold of the small room, the boy leaning against the jamb, the girl leaning against the boy, one arm around his waist. The boy wore his shorts cut off at the knee and an undershirt, and the girl, a sleeveless cotton dress. You could see her pink knees. Neither of the children had brushed their hair, and their faces were creased with sleep. For a moment they stood there in silence.

In the garden halfway down the hill, the chickens clucked in the heat, and the cicada shrilled.

"What's going on?" the boy said eventually, shaking his head, looking from the doctor to the child, who sat on the floor with the tower of brightly colored blocks before her.

The girl went over to pick up the child, sweeping her from the floor fast, as though she were in danger of some sort. As she swept the child up, she inadvertently knocked over the tower of blocks. The child began to wail. The girl clutched her child to her chest.

The grandmother looked at the doctor, who wiped his face with his handkerchief.

"I don't think that child can hear," the grandmother said in a clear voice over Isabelle's screams.

The girl looked at the grandmother as though she had insulted her personally. She drew herself up. "What are you talking about? What is the doctor doing here? Why did you call the doctor without telling us? How could you call the doctor without even asking our opinion? Isabelle is not ill," the girl said, hugging the child to her breast protectively, jiggling the screaming child up and down fast.

The doctor looked embarrassed. He glanced at the grandmother and then at the couple, and murmured something vague: "*Una bella bambina*, a beautiful child, not so? Perhaps, eventually, a checkup, when you get her back home, just to make sure all is perfectly well. Just a routine checkup to make sure everything's in order. Very difficult to say anything at such a young age." Then he looked at the gold watch on his chest and added, "I have an appointment. I'm afraid I'll have to be going," and he hurried out of the room through the French doors onto the terrace.

Everyone followed the doctor out onto the terrace. Even Speranza, in her best lace cap, had made an appearance by then, drawn by the sounds of drama. The doctor shook hands hastily all around, bowed and murmured something no one could catch through the child's cries.

As the doctor walked down the stone steps to the road, he called out over his shoulder, waving his plump hand in the air. "They can do wonderful things these days, you know. In America they can do wonderful things; they can do miracles in America," he called as he descended the daisy-studded stone steps that led like a chain through the garden.

The grandmother hurried after the doctor, calling to him, suddenly remembering that she had not paid the man. At first he told her the visit had cost nothing, nothing at all, bowing and mopping his forehead at the same time. The grandmother insisted, pulling the large Italian bills out of her handbag. As she pulled the lire from her purse, a slight breeze blew up the hill, and the stench of the chickens in their cage came to her. She shook the doctor's damp hand again and thanked him and walked slowly back up the steep steps. Really, she thought, with what they charged for a month in the villa, they could have removed their chickens.

She heard Speranza say, "What does everybody want for dinner tonight?"

"Spaghetti," both children called out at once, joyfully. "We want spaghetti," they said, and laughed.

A Quarrelsome Man

Pauline Melville
England/Guyana, 1990

On that particular Tuesday afternoon in July, it rained. Then it stopped. Then it rained again, making the streets wet, steamy and hot. The herbalist shop in one of the shabbier districts of south London was packed with customers. One stout, black, elderly woman in spectacles and a blue felt hat was leaning across the counter whispering in the assistant's ear:

"I want sometin' for me husband. 'E caan stop goin'. 'E runnin' to the toilet all the while." The pale assistant with the pale-rimmed glasses looked as though vegetable juice ran in her veins. She answered benignly:

"We have Cranesbill for incontinence."

"What?" The old woman screwed up her face.

"Cranesbill for urinary incontinence," the assistant said a little louder.

"What's that? I don' hear so good."

"Cranesbill for a weak bladder," shouted the assistant, causing a titter in the crowd.

"Yes. Gimme some o' dat. An' some tincture of cloves for me tooth."

The assistant made up the order briskly and neatly. Behind her on the wall hung one of the original, old-fashioned advertisements for "Balsam of Lungwort containing Horehound and Aniseed—A Boon to the Afflicted." The shop had been there since the beginning of the century. In the fifties it nearly closed through lack of trade. Then the black people started to arrive. Business picked up. As word spread, African and Caribbean people from all over London came seeking poke root for sore throats; senna pods for their bowels; fever grass for their colds; green camphor ointment; slippery elm; Irish moss; Jamaican sorrel; eucalyptus leaves; until Mr. Goodwin, the latest in a long line of Goodwins, far from shutting up shop, was obliged to take on two more assistants and one extra person to serve at the Sarsparilla counter.

Now, Mr. Goodwin stood patiently dispensing the order of two French hippies, the only white customers, who were taking an inordinately long time browsing through the list of potions and powders and gums and roots and barks, sniffing at herbs and examining tinctures of asafoetida and red capsicum with little crooning noises of surprise and delight. They were unaware of the jostling throng of some twenty people behind them. Wedged amongst these was a small, black boy of about ten, gazing about him in astonishment. He had thickly protruding lips and his head was closely shaven. In each ear sat a grey, plastic hearing-aid the shape Africa. The man at his side was restless and edgy. Jittery. His forehead kept wrinkling into a frown. His frizzy hair had something unkempt about it. His teeth were small and jagged. He wore a sweater, grey with a green diamond pattern on it, frayed at the neck and his trousers were old, brown and shapeless. Round his neck hung two silver chains, one carrying a small, gold box and the other a miniature pistol, which is why he was known as Pistol-Man. He looked vexed and was making small noises of dissatisfaction. When a young black woman pushed in from of him he could contain himself no longer:

"Hey! You pushin' in front of me. I don' come all the way from north London to wait at the back of the line. She pushin' in front of me," he complained. Then he rounded indignantly on two other people he had seen edging their way towards the front. "An' I see you pushin' in front of them." He started to wave his arms like the conductor of a large orchestra. "An' them people," he indicated a mother and child at the back, "was here before you," he tapped on the shoulder of a pompous-looking Trinidadian with a moustache. The man shrugged him off:

"Cool it, nuh. Cool it nuh, man. Everythin' cool till yuh open yuh big mouth. There ain' no lines."

The man with the pistol round his neck looked fit to explode:

"That's what I say. There ain' no lines." He threw up his hands in distress as if the disorder in the shop was somehow representative of all the disorder in the world; the chaos in Beirut; the turmoil in Sri-Lanka; the upheavals in the Philippines and to some extent the confusion in himself, and if only he could organise it properly, that and everything else in the world would be set to rights. Then, out of the corner of his eye, he spotted a gap in the crowd ahead of him and stepped quickly into it.

"Now you pushin' in front of me." The tall, light-skinned woman with red head-wrap smiled as she accused Pistol-Man. He looked abashed, mortified:

"I know," he said; looking round the room defensively, "but I was goin' to let you go before me. I'm fair." He spoke loud enough for everyone to hear. On the other side of the shop he saw someone he recognised:

"Hello! Hello Mrs. Ebanks. You still livin' in Stoke Newington? Long time I don' see you."

"Yes, we still there." The middle-aged woman stood stolidly beside her husband as if they were waiting for the millennium. Dismay crossed Pistol-Man's face as he watched someone push in front of them:

"You shouldn't let people push in front of you. You been waitin' long?"

"We fine, tank you." They stood stock still, both with their hands folded in front of them as though they were about to burst into hymns. Pistol-Man couldn't stop himself talking:

"Look," he said to nobody in particular, "I'm nearly there. Why it takin' so long? Some people have to get back to work. People got things to do," he said, righteously, although he himself fell into neither category. The main reason it was taking so long was because the French couple, oblivious to all that was going on behind them, were taking their time, fingering bottles with squeaks of pleasure and ordering remedy after remedy. Pistol-Man continued his beef:

"I got to get two buses to reach home and it nearly rushhour."

"You mekin' fuss?" boomed the surly Trinidadian with the moustache. Pistol-Man continued to grumble:

"Everybody look at you as if you mad but if I din' make fuss I never reach where I am now." He looked round for approval and smiled with relief when a wave of laughter swept through the assembled customers. An African girl turned round to him and said in her clipped accent:

"What you are saying is true. I know it is true because look how I push in front of you." She had a big smile and gold ear-rings.

"Yes," he replied, "but you laughin' so that's all right." Secretly, Pistol-Man was a bit wary of Africans. He believed that while the West Indians, like himself, came to the shop in search of cures, the Africans probably came to buy herbs that would make people ill.

Finally, triumphantly, he reached the counter. Then he remembered the cinnamon-skinned woman in the red head-wrap:

"Do you still want to come in front of me?" he asked, politely. Vera Mullins did indeed want to be served first. She had been on duty at the hospital since six in the morning and her feet were aching.

"Yes," she said, moving forward to address the woman behind the counter. "It's for my friend," she explained. "Her glands are all swollen in her neck and under her arms."

"We can't really treat that," said the assistant. "That is likely to be a symptom of something else and we would need to know . . ."

"Lavender oil," interrupted Pistol-Man loudly from behind Vera's shoulder. "Give she lavender oil."

Vera Mullins began to laugh. But she bought some lavender oil anyway. As she waited for it to be wrapped, the clean smell of peppermint floated into her nostrils from somewhere, reminding her of her grandmother in St. Vincent whose clothes always smelt of peppermint and bay rum. People in the shop were now laughing and talking noisily. That too reminded her of home and the market in Kingstown. Taking herself completely by surprise she found herself turning round to address the shoppers:

"All right," she said. "I driving back to Finsbury Park. Is who needs a lift in that direction—north London?" Pistol-Man was busy at the counter ordering the bitter aloes that settled his stomach after too many cans of McEwans Export Strong Lager. He cocked his ear, unable to believe his luck:

"I do," he said quickly.

"What about those other people from Stoke Newington?" Vera pointed towards Mr. and Mrs. Ebanks, who were standing, rooted to the same spot, having made no progress.

"The lady says do you want a lift home?" called Pistol-Man, in his cracked voice, gesticulating over the heads of waiting customers.

"No tanks," replied Mrs. Ebanks. "We fine. We jus' wait and take our time till it get less busy."

"Anyone else?" asked Vera, turning her head from side to side, expectantly. Brown, almond-shaped eyes looked enquiringly from a passive, oval face. Pistol-Man was staring at Vera with a mixture of pleasure and suspicious curiosity. He fingered the day's growth of stubble on his chin and wished he had shaved that morning. Alarmed to find that Pistol-Man was the only volunteer, Vera, for an instant, regretted her offer. She could feel something fractious and nervy about the man. London was full of dangerous strangers, unlike St. Vincent. No one else took up the offer. She managed a smile:

"My car's round the corner," she said.

Outside, rain speckled the pavement like a bird's egg. They walked past the drab shops, Pistol-Man talking fast and furious as a fire-cracker to disguise his self-consciousness. Somehow, the more he prattled, the more calm Vera Mullins became.

"Yes," he said. "Lavender oil is good, you know. Very good." His accent was cockney, grafted on to some now indistinguishable Caribbean base. "It helped get the swelling down when my tooth was bad. I was in terrible pain that time. Two dentists I went to and they couldn't see nothing wrong and then the third one found this tiny, tiny hole that was givin' all the trouble. He said it was the minutest hole he had ever come across," boasted Pistol-Man, pleased to have suffered from a condition that defied medical expertise. It made him feel different. Unique. It was for that same reason that when the council allocated him a basement flat in a house converted into Flats 1, 2 and 3, he had taken down the notice that said Flat 1, and written FLAT A on a piece of card and stuck it on the front door. It made him feel different. It was a matter of distinction.

As they rounded the corner, Vera realised that the little black boy with the deaf-aids was scurrying along behind them. Pistol-Man turned to see where she was looking:

"Oh yeah," said Pistol-Man. "That's my son. He's deaf and dumb from he was born. I raise him."

It was Vera's turn to feel curious. As she unlocked the door of the old, blue Ford with rusted streaks along its side, she caught the boy looking at her. His eyes were eager, full of merriment and intelligence, as if he were about to say something of great importance. If you could speak, she found herself thinking, you would say something beautiful. Suddenly, she felt safer about giving a lift to this talkative stranger who crackled with tension. Safer now that she knew the child would be with them:

"What's his name?" she asked.

"Avalon," replied Pistol-Man. "I named him that. I found it in a book of myths. I think it's Greek," he added.

Avalon. Avalon. Where wounded heroes go to rest. Where King Arthur went to heal his wounds. The boy scrambled into the back of the car.

"Sorry. This car is a tip," Vera apologised. Pistol-Man raised his head to the heavens and cackled incredulously. The woman saved him the fares, saved him a long tedious wait in bus queues. As if he would care about a little mess. He would have been grateful for a ride in a donkey cart. They set off through the wet street, full of litter from the market. Pistol-Man crowed with delight inside himself for having secured a ride, as if he had outwitted the Fates for once. But he talked non-stop, through a sort of shyness. He couldn't make the woman out. Because she said so little, he talked all the more. Because he did not often have the chance to talk, everything about his life and his son came out in a torrent:

"He's got five per cent hearing. He's all right. He can lip-read. He can do sign language. And he can lie as good as any normal boy," added the father proudly. "He's so convincing, you wouldn't believe it." Vera glanced over her shoulder at the child who could weave falsehoods with his hands. Avalon was sitting with his head twisted round trying to look at an old magazine on the floor of the car.

"Sometimes he's sad," continued Pistol-Man, "because no friends come to see us. I tell him friends will come some day. I quarrelled with my family, you see. I don't see them no more. It's just me and him now. It's a good thing to have a close family." He said it with regret, as if a family was something that had somehow passed him by, out of reach. The truth was that Pistol-Man quarrelled with every-body. He was a quarrelsome man, pig-headed, easily annoyed, impatient, fretful.

"He's at a Special School now. He's going to boarding school in September. Then I can get back to my music. I'm a musician you see. I want to form my own band. I've worked with other bands and it's no good. The people they make excuses. They don't turn up. There's too much hassle. Too much pressure. An' than I get vex, you see and I blow my top because the people them drive me mad. I can see it's goin' to happen but I can't stop it. I wish I could be six people at once, then I could be all the members of the band."

"Dad-dee." The hard-to-form words came from the back of the car. Pistol-Man turned to the boy. In the driving-mirror, Vera could see the boy's hands moving like butterflies. His father signed a reply.

"You can talk sign language?" asked Vera.

"I'm not very good at it, though," said Pistol-Man modestly. "I just told him "Lady give lift home.""

As edged through the rush-hour traffic, rain spotting the windscreen, Pistol-Man threw a sly, sidelong look at the woman sitting impassively at the wheel beside him:

"You could be giving a lift to a mad person," he said. "A killer person."

"I trusted you because of the child." As she spoke, Vera remembered she had offered the lift before knowing the child was with him. Pistol-Man had his face pressed to the window. She turned and smiled at Avalon who grinned with pleasure in return.

"He's all right." Pistol-Man looked over his shoulder at the boy. "He knows that whatever I have, he has too. We share everything. We're equal." His head jerked round as something in the street caught his attention. "D'you see that shop? They sell fluffy things in there that you can sit on and they roll out into sleeping bags. They're fluffy." He said it with relish. "I can't afford one. They're about eighty pounds." The quietness of the woman seeped into him, soothing him. Out of the blue, he said:

"Some people calm people down. They could get attacked but it goes the other way." He wished he had not been so loudmouthed in the herbalist's. "You mek fuss and people look at you as if you were mad, but if you don't mek fuss people walk all over you," he muttered, half to himself.

"Which road do you want?" asked Vera.

"Amhurst Road. Round to the left here. Do you know Hackney?"

"Yes."

"Did you know that this bit is Amhurst Road too?" He made it sound as though it was his special secret.

"Yes."

"Most people don't know that," he said with approval. "Most people think it ends further up. Here we are. Pull up by that tree." The man and the boy got out of the car:

"Bye . . . Bye." Avalon made the sounds a diver makes speaking under water.

"Just a minute. Just a minute. Would you like to come in for a drink?" Pistol-Man's forehead wrinkled into worried lines as he peered through the car window at her. She felt drawn to the man and the child. It can't do any harm, she thought.

To Pistol-Man's exasperation, the key stuck in the lock of the basement door. Avalon pulled a face at Vera that said clearly "Oh no, not again!" Finally the key turned and they stepped into a small, dark passage and then into the back room.

"Sit down. Sit down." He waved his guest towards an old settee with a crumpled, stone-coloured duvet on it that he pulled over himself at nights as he lay watching television.

"Wait there a minute," he said. "I've got to get him his tea." He felt awkward, unused to visitors. He disappeared into the kitchen, shutting the door behind him so that she would not see the washing-up piled in the sink. Vera looked round the room. The walls were painted yellow ochre. The furniture was cheap and ugly. On the floor was a grey carpet as thin as cardboard. On the mantel-piece rested a semi-circular mirror flanked on either side by two big, plastic Coca Cola bottles. Pistol-Man had cut the tops of these to use them as jars which held an assortment of rulers and pencils. Opposite her, under the low dresser, was a jumble of plimsolls and trainers belonging to the man and the boy. Piles of papers and folders were stashed untidily about the place. From the kitchen came the sound of something frizzling in the pan.

Avalon stood in the centre of the room with an expression of intense concentration on his face. Then he raised one hand, the finger pointed, as if to say, "I know what to do". He dived for his black school bag and showed Vera his pencil-case and some of his school books. He puzzled for a moment over what else he could do to entertain the guest. Then he ran to the sideboard and showed her the school photograph of himself smiling, framed in white card. He scratched his head, then remembered the snakes. Two yellow traffic lanterns that Pistol-Man had stolen from the street adorned the dresser. Looped around the handle of each was a wooden, jointed snake, one brightly painted in pink, the other in green. Avalon pointed to the pink one and pointed to himself. Then he pointed to the green one and said laboriously:

"My . . . dad."

Vera found the boy delightful. She pointed to a painting on a piece of paper, sellotaped to the wall. It was a picture of a boot with 'The Rogue Brogue' written underneath it with an exclamation mark.

"Did you do that?" she asked. He shook his head.

"My . . . dad," he said again.

Pistol-Man elbowed his way into the room carrying a plate with two hamburgers on it and some spaghetti from a tin. He put the food on the formica-topped table and turned to Avalon. He spoke and used sign language at the same time:

"Go and put your pyjamas on." He explained to Vera, "I have to tell him to do that because he gets his clothes dirty and it's me has to wash them. Do you want a drink? I've got McEwans Lager because that's what I drink."

"I don't drink alcohol. Have you got any juice?" She hoped this would not prove awkward for him but for a minute Pistol-Man looked flummoxed:

"Ribena," he said, "I've got some Ribena," He returned from the kitchen with a tumbler so brimful of the red liquid that he nearly spilled it.

"I hope that's not too sweet. Is it too sweet?" he enquired anxiously.

"It's fine," she said. Avalon bounced back into the room wearing a pair of white cotton pyjamas with navy-blue triangles on them. His presence relieved the sexual tension between the man and the woman. Pistol-Man straddled a chair by the table as Avalon sat down to eat his meal. He pulled the metal ring off his can of lager:

"Yeah. This is where I always am, every evening, with my cans of beer. I have to stay in, you see, because of him. He can't ever say to me 'You have more fun than me because you're grown-up,' because he sees that I stay in too. We both stay in. He knows that everything I have, I share with him. We're both the same. Both equal. Sometimes, he pretends to be worse than he is." Pistol-Man put his hand to his ear and pulled a sad face, mimicking the boy. "'I'm deaf,' he says, 'I'm deaf.' And I say, 'Yes, I know you're bloody deaf.' And we both laugh." He took a gulp of lager. "It's a sacrifice I make, you see. No. Not a sacrifice." He hunted for the right word. "No. It's a dedication." He looked over at the boy. "I growed him and raised him. It's like putting money in the bank. An investment. You watch it grow. Only it's love. I'm not really a materialist. I'm more a spiritual sort of man."

More or less the only trips Pistol-Man ever made were to the betting-shop round the corner which he visited as often as possible, optimism springing afresh in his breast on every occasion. He pulled his chair round to face the woman squarely.

"Now, I'm going to interrogate you," he said. "What do you do?"

"I'm a nurse," said Vera.

"Where do you come from?"

"St. Vincent—a long time ago."

"I'm from Buxton in Guyana," he said, "I don't remember that much either." He scrutinised his new friend. She sipped her Ribena. Usually, he would have said to a woman like that "You're looking nice and slim" or "That's a nice outfit you're wearing," but something about this woman prevented him from doing so. He took in her honey-coloured skin and slanting, serious, brown eyes. His own skin was dark.

"There's some Portuguese in my family somewhere," he said. "Portuguese are white people, you know." He rolled up the sleeve of his sweater and inspected his forearm as if expecting to see white patches appear magically on the brown.

"I like you," he said, looking directly at her. "Yes. I like you."

Vera thought that she should leave soon. Avalon was busy on the floor, drawing something with a ruler and pencil. Suddenly, Pistol-Man spotted the dirty plate on the table and leapt to his feet. Vera almost laughed at the tableau they made: the man pointing sternly at the plate and the boy with his eyes widening in dismay, his hand over his mouth. The deafness had made both of them expressive in face and gesture, like actors in a silent movie.

"Fair's fair," said Pistol-Man as Avalon went into the kitchen with the plate, giving Vera a broad grin as he went. "I cook for him, but he must wash up. That's only fair, isn't it? We both share the work."

"What happened to his mum?" Vera couldn't help asking. Pistol-Man gave an exasperated sort of sigh and shook his head:

"She left," he said, sitting back down in his chair. "She was a virgin when I met her, so I don't know why I went with her because I don't like virgins," he said candidly. "We lived in a little room in Stoke Newington. I was working as a cutter—you know—cloth—cutting cloth. Avalon was seventeen months old. She left on a Friday.

Well, you know how horrible Fridays are." He opened his arms wide as if to empha-sise the horribleness of Fridays. "You've been working all week and you're tired and you're looking forward to the weekend. Anyway, I came home and found a note stuck on the paraffin heater saying she'd gone. The baby was all pissed up in his cot. And that was that." He frowned as though it was still a puzzle to him. "Maybe I was a bit of a tyrant," he said regretfully. "But I didn't beat her or anything," he added hastily. "It was just that when I wanted something done, I wanted it done properly. I wanted it done the right way." Vera could see how the man could be bossy, cantan-kerous even. He continued with an expression of bewildered anguish on his face:

"It's because I want people to make progress. I want things to be better. Even with him," he gestured towards Avalon who had gone into the bathroom, "I want him to be somebody." He spoke with a burst of energy, enthusiasm and hope. "I want him to be something. He can't hear and he can't speak much but I want him to be the best he can. To be his own person." He got up and pointed out of the window. "That's why I've let the grass grow like that." Vera looked to where he was pointing. Outside, the grass had run wild, nearly waist-high, in the small garden. "The neigh-bours keep telling me I must cut it, but it's more interesting for him like that. There's lots of things he can discover in that grass: butterflies and worms, snails and cater-pillars and insects with long legs, lots of things. He can hide in it and imagine things. It's more of an adventure for him like that."

Avalon came in and took his father by both forearms, then he bared his teeth at him.

"Yes. That's all right," said Pistol-Man. He turned to Vera, a little shame-faced, to explain. "I make him do that because he didn't used to brush his teeth properly. I should stop him doing that really," he said. "He's too old for that now. Would you like to see his drawing? He's talented. Maybe he'll get trained one day."

He ushered Vera into the boy's bedroom. It was small and pokey. Two big ward-robes dwarfed the single bed. Over the head of the bed was a picture of Superman. On the other wall was Avalon's drawing of Elvis Presley. Vera smiled and nodded at Avalon in appreciation. Immediately, the boy jumped on the bed and tried to pull down a big folder from the top of the wardrobe, indicating that he wanted to give her all the drawings he had ever done.

"She don't want all those, silly," said Pistol-Man. He opened the wardrobe. Inside were half a drum-kit and a battered electric guitar. "Those are my instru-ments," he said proudly. "I'll show you my room."

The three of them peeked into his room. Vera was made shy by the sight of his double bed, neatly made up with a plain coverlet. She glanced quickly round. On a shelf was another photograph of Avalon with two schoolfriends. There was not much else in the room. She backed out. They returned to the living-room.

"I've got to go now," she said.

"You're shooting off then," said Pistol-Man. In his eagerness to do what she wanted he almost ran her out of the front door.

"Call in any time you want," he said. "We're always in from about six o'clock. Thanks again for the lift."

"Bye . . . Bye," said Avalon.

Vera waved goodbye. It had stopped raining. As she drove through the cramped streets an immense and irreparable sense of loss overwhelmed her for the island where she had once lived with its whispering seas and the sound of women's voices in the soft night air, dripping slowly and unevenly like molasses; for the people she had once known.

Back in his flat, Pistol-Man slapped himself on the forehead:

"Oh no! I forgot to ask her her name." Avalon pulled a face of commiseration. "Not that it matters." Pistol-Man no longer thought about women because of his dedication to the boy.

"Did you like her?" asked Pistol-Man. Avalon, his eyes shining, put his hands on his lips and then on his heart. He went back to his drawing on the floor. Pistol-Man sat on the settee and opened another can of lager. He felt good. He felt warm inside. Tomorrow, he decided, he would hoover the carpet and give the whole place a good clean-up. What luck, he thought, to get a lift home on a wet afternoon like that.

Suddenly, he leant forward and grasped his son by the arm to attract his attention. He spoke in sign language only:

"You see!" he said to the child who looked intently at him. "Good things do happen."

The Secret

Florence V. Mayberry
USA, 1992

Grandma said, "Time to get the milk, Sary."

I was glad it was time because then I could visit with Miss Abbie and the girls. This took a while. Sit in one of the cane-bottomed kitchen chairs, eat a cookie and watch the fluttering hands of Mable and Roxy, try to guess what they said before Miss Abbie translated for me. Mable and Roxy were deaf-and-dumb. Dumb of voice, not of mind, because Miss Abbie declared they were smart as tacks even if they hadn't had much school learning. She should know because she was their older sister and had been with them all their lives. Brightest little things you ever saw, she said, these twin baby girls, keeping an eye on everything from their crib, walked early, figured they'd talk early too. Only they didn't, beyond a queer baby gurgle deep in their throats. They could hear the loudest sounds, like a thunder clap, because they'd whirl their heads toward it. But any noise that didn't shake the house they'd pay no mind to. So you had to look right at them and move your lips slow, or use deaf-and-dumb talk with your hands like Miss Abbie did.

Grandma handed me the tin milk bucket and I walked barefooted down the grassy middle of the road to the house of Miss Abbie and the girls, avoiding the dusty ruts made by wagons and buggies. Nobody in our Missouri town had an automobile, danged things good for nothing but to scare horses. It was midsummer, hot but pleasant in early mornings and late afternoons because our town was in the Ozark Mountains in a high, rolling valley. On one side of the road, just beyond our house, was the woods where in spring I could find violets peeking through dead leaves packed by winter snows. Splitting the woods into two unequal parts, the larger part on the far side, ran the creek, arched over by joined tree branches. On the creek's near side was the pasture where Mable and Roxy let their two cows feed. On the creek's far side was a scrub pasture not fit for grazing. Gypsies and other folks traveling by covered wagon sometimes used it for a camping ground.

When I reached the yard of Miss Abbie and the girls, Roxy was walking to the house with her milk pail, leaning one-sided to balance its weight. She waved, her mouth spread in a laugh, and jabbed her finger excitedly toward the little barn where she and Mable did the milking. This meant she had won. Every night she and

Mable raced to see who could milk the fastest; they each did a cow, everything was twin with them.

"Evening, Roxy," I said, my lips making large and slow movements so she could read them.

"Yah-h-h-uh, gugh-gugh, yah-h-uh!" she said. She and Mable always tried to talk to me. I ached inside me when they did but I hated to ask Miss Abbie to have them stop, they were so pleased that I could hear their sounds. When they were together as they did that talking they would bob their heads at each other, grimace with laughter, turn and "Yah-h-h-uh, gugh-gugh, yah-h-uh!" at me again. It sent tingly chills down the back of my legs like when you hear that somebody cut their finger or broke a leg or something.

Mable came jog-trotting out of the barn, gargling and gurgling as she hurried, pointing at her milk pail to show it was fuller than Roxy's, then flying her free hand in deaf-and-dumb words at Roxy. Roxy's hand danced in answer and they both strangled out their laughter.

Miss Abbie came out on the back porch. "Evening, Sary . . . been expecting you. The girls thought you might be a little early so's you could watch them milk."

They were always wanting me to do that. Once, for manner's sake, I did, but afterwards I didn't drink milk for days; it was the first time I had really thought about how milk came out. So now I managed to come a little late.

The girls carried their milk pails down cellar beneath their house where big shallow pans were set out to hold the milk for cooling. "Come set a while," Miss Abbie said, taking my bucket. "The morning's milking is up here ready for you, nice and cool. Help yourself to a cookie from that crock on the table. The girls just baked them. They'll be up directly to visit with you. Your Grandma won't mind you waiting a bit, will she?"

I shook my head. Grandma never minded about me eating between meals, or waiting extra, or anything much I wanted to do. I was their orphaned baby girl, a skinny little kid she and Grandpa had had a time raising up to the age of seven. Or so they said. Actually I felt fine, just skinny.

I hurried to eat the cookie before Roxy got to the kitchen and did her trick. For reasons known only to herself, she thought letting her false teeth click together outside her mouth in a terrifying skeleton grin amused me. She did it at least once every time I came, followed by throwing back her head in a gargly laugh and gleefully patting her round stomach. She did it so often that finally the teeth loosened and sometimes dropped out when she didn't want them to. Like once in church when she was pretending to sing. Embarrassed her so, she ran out of church crying.

Except for their brown eyes, Mable and Roxy didn't look alike. Roxy was round, plump, and flouncy. A strong girl but always had poor teeth, Miss Abbie said. Probably from too much sucking on sugar lumps and eating sweets, young'un or grown, ruined her teeth and put weight on her. Mable was tall and slim with honey-blond hair. It really looked pretty with those brown eyes. Kept her own teeth, white as snow, too. Although the twins were in their thirties and should have seemed old to a child of seven, they didn't. Everybody called them the deaf-and-dumb girls and that's how I thought of them. As girls.

Roxy's cheeks were full and rosy, her dark brown hair kept in a knot on top of her head, her neck smooth and white. "It's a shame Roxy's deaf-and-dumb," Grandma sometimes said. "Strong, handy girl like that. Not exactly pretty, but right good-looking. And Mable, with a little fixing she'd be a beauty. I feel real bad those two girls have to end up old maids."

Grandpa would crinkle his brows, shake his head, and say, "Maybe won't need to, got to be men around would count it a blessing to have a deaf-and-dumb woman in the house." Then laugh when Grandma stomped her foot at him.

Mable for sure was the pretty one of the two. Wore her blonde hair in a braid like a crown around her head and looked like the Virgin Mary in the stained-glass window in our church. "Mable's a mite thin, though," decided Grandma, who was even plumper than Roxy. "And you watch it, Missy, or you'll end up the same way if you don't eat your vittles." Which did nothing to encourage my appetite. I wished I could end up looking like Mable.

When they had the milk in pans, the girls came up to the kitchen, Roxy's head peeking mischievously at me around the taller Mable. I stiffened as she opened her mouth, pushed out her teeth with her tongue, and clacked them at me. It made me afraid that next thing her eyes might pop from their sockets, her arms and legs fly off like a doll coming to pieces. I covered my eyes with my fingers, peeking through to see when she came together again. That was part of the game for Roxy. She popped her teeth inside and both girls laughed, gurgles bubbling in their barren throats.

Then Mable put her finger against her mouth in a hush gesture, a signal for me to stay put. "She has a surprise for you," Miss Abbie said. "Been working on it for days."

Mable left the kitchen and Roxy came and sat before me. The girls never sat beside me, always in front so they could watch what I said. Mable returned, one hand behind her back, the other fluttering at Miss Abbie. "She wants you to shut your eyes," Miss Abbie said. I did, felt Mable move close and a featherweight object fall on my lap. "Now look," Miss Abbie said.

I opened my eyes. On my lap was a tiny dress made of sprigged calico, a ribbon sash around its waist. I sprang up, holding the little dress before me, hopping in delight. It was the size of my china-headed doll, the one my mother had played with when she was a little girl. I ran to Mable and hugged my face against her flat stomach.

When I looked up she was crying, tears dripping down her cheeks. I turned to Miss Abbie, frightened. "What did I do?"

"Nothing but be happy like Mable hoped. She's crying because she's so glad you like it."

Mable's hands clenched and spread, making signs at her older sister. "She's saying, she wishes she had a little girl just like you."

"Why doesn't she get one then?"

Miss Abbie's hands moved, and the twins doubled over with soundless laughter. Along with Mable's tear-streaked cheeks and the doubling up, it looked peculiar, like they had stomachaches. It didn't seem to me I had said anything funny, but Roxy was so tickled she clacked out her teeth at me again. With her teeth grinning in front of her mouth, she handed me the cookie plate, motioning for me to take another. I didn't want to, but I did. Good manners make you never let on to a deaf-and-dumb girl you love that she makes you sick.

"Has the Gypsy tinkerman come to your place yet?" Miss Abbie asked. I shook my head. "Well, reckon he hasn't had time to get around, not been here either, even though he's camped right beside us. I got a kettle needs mending, maybe he'll come around tomorrow."

I almost choked on the cookie, I was so excited. "Oh, Miss Abbie, please let Roxy and Mable take me to see the Gypsies! Grandma won't ever let me go alone."

"Don't think that would be right. There's no women along with this Gypsy wagon, just two lone men," Miss Abbie said doubtfully. "Just an old man and a young one, maybe his son, look alike."

"Oh please, Miss Abbie! I've never ever visited a Gypsy camp. Roxy's big and strong, she can take care of Mable and me. Please!"

Miss Abbie looked uncertain, made deaf-and-dumb talk to the girls. They clapped their hands, excited as I was. Three pairs of hands danced in the air, and at last the girls motioned for me to follow them.

Miss Abbie trailed after us and we all passed through the cow lot, into the side pasture that led to the creek.

Across the creek a dark-skinned old man with white hair to his shoulders sat on a box beside the covered wagon watching a younger man stir something over a cookfire. Even though the second man was younger, to me he looked pretty old too, almost as old as Miss Abbie, who was forty-some. That man raised his face, saw us across the creek, and nodded his head in greeting. A big man, his arms heavy-muscled.

Miss Abbie nodded back, curt and quick, but Roxy and Mable were all smiles, nodding and waving. "Head for the house, Sary!" Miss Abbie ordered, soft but sharp. She yanked the girls around and shoved them toward the cow barn. "Never should've come, never should've come!" She kept muttering. "Run get your milk, Sary, and hike for home before your grandma gets anxious."

When we reached the back steps of their house, Mable turned fiercely on Miss Abbie, clenched her hands, stomped up and down, had a regular tantrum, her pretty face squeezed up and tears running down her cheeks. Roxy threw her arms around her twin and grunted at Miss Abbie like an angry little pig.

Miss Abbie looked flabbergasted. Her hands flashed before the girls, theirs answered back. "What on earth's got into these girls, wanting to hang around staring at that camp!" Miss Abbie wasn't really talking to me, just letting out her shock. "Waving, acting so tickled! Those men could take them wrong. I knew I shouldn'ta let you children go down there, it ain't ladylike."

That's how she felt about Roxy and Mable, like they were her children.

I scampered toward home, leaving Mable still snubbing Miss Abbie and Roxy sassing her with her hands.

As I sat on our front porch with Grandma that night, I saw the Gypsy campfire still burning. The sound of a mouth organ drifted to us, mingled with night sounds of a bird's sleepy twitter, frogs croaking, insects singing. Fireflies danced around our yard as the music switched from fast and bouncy to soft and sweet, dreamy and sad, back to bouncy. I got off Grandma's lap and whirled in the moonlight with the fireflies.

"Careful, or you'll be getting yourself with the moon madness," Grandma said, her voice easy and comfortable. It was just something to say because the night was so pretty.

After I went to bed I lay across its foot, my face by the window with the moonlight shining full on it. I wished I could catch the moon madness. Then I would be crazy enough to creep out of the house, run down the lane, cross the pasture, wade the creek, and sit beside the Gypsy fire and its music. When I fell asleep I dreamed I did.

Next afternoon when I went for the milk Roxy was still mad at Miss Abbie. Pouting, wouldn't make her fingers say anything. "I caught her down by the creek today after she let the cows into the pasture," Miss Abbie explained testily. "Just acting the fool, waving at that Gypsy man, so I sent her hiking home. So now she's stuffed up in a sulky fit."

Mable was acting strange too, broody, no fun at all. Quick as I could, I took my pail and started home.

But Roxy skittered between me and the back screen door, and clacked her teeth at me. A smile like that is pretty terrible, but I knew what she meant. She was sorry about being unfriendly. She took my milk pail, motioning she would carry it for me.

Once we were out of sight of the house she bent down with her finger to her lips, shaking her head back and forth. Sh-h-h-h, she meant. She pointed toward the pasture and the creek. Smoke from the Gypsy fire rose in a graceful frond, seeming to bear with it the lively sound of the mouth organ. Not that Roxy could hear the music, but she could see the younger man with the instrument at his mouth as he sat on a stack of firewood beside the fire. Maybe her skin felt the music.

She jabbed her finger toward the camp, pointed at herself, then at me, again at the camp.

I shook my head no, pointed toward my house, then toward where Miss Abbie was. Moved my mouth in a lip message, "Grandma— Miss Abbie—they won't let us go over there."

Her head bounced yes-yes-yes defiantly, and she pulled me behind the stable. Took a stub pencil and a piece of paper out of her apron pocket. "Tonight we go," she wrote. "Abbie sleep. Granma sleep. Mable sleep. Roxy Sary go jipsy have fun."

I shook my head.

Roxy stamped first one foot, then the other, hard. She wrote again: "I go my self alone."

Roxy was a grown woman and I was only seven. But she was deaf-and-dumb and everybody knew those girls had to be looked after, that's why Miss Abbie never married, gave her life to them. So what else could I do? A deaf-and-dumb girl shouldn't go traipsing out alone at night, maybe fall in the creek and drown, not being able to call for help.

Besides, I wanted to go.

"All right," I mouthed. "I go too."

Roxy whirled in a clumsy dance of pleasure. Then wrote with her stub pencil, "Tonight cum barn I here."

I nodded, ran for home as though the devil was after me. Quivered inside all through supper, knowing the devil would surely be waiting for me at the Gypsy camp, pitchfork and all, because of the sneakiness I was helping Roxy carry out.

"Think I'll set on the porch a while," Grandma said after supper. "Want me to sing to you?"

"Hunh-uh. I'm too sleepy."

"Mite sleepy myself," Grandma said. "I'll not set out long, just enough to settle the day. You run along to bed."

I lay in bed tight as a string in a hard knot, listening to the creak-creak of Grandma's cane rocker. Heard the far-off music of the mouth organ and Grandma begin to hum with it.

At last the creaking stopped and Grandma's solid steps crossed through the sitting room into the kitchen. The tin dipper clinked against the water bucket. She went into her bedroom and after a bit the bedsprings squeaked under her weight.

When her lighter snore joined Grandpa's I slipped off my nightgown, pulled on my dress, tiptoed away from the bed. Turned back, fluffed the quilt over my pillow so it looked like someone was in bed.

Out on the porch, Nervy, our big black tomcat, meowed and rubbed against my leg. I picked him up, stroked him to make him hush for fear Grandma would hear and get up to let him inside. I tiptoed into the shadows beside the porch, heart pounding, listening for Grandma's footsteps. When none came I ran from the yard, down the lane, toward the cow barn. Halfway there I realized I still had Nervy in my arms, dropped him, and ran on.

Roxy appeared so suddenly out of the barn that I had to stifle a squeal of fright. She began strangling with deaf-and-dumb sounds and I hushed her with my finger against her lips. Her head bobbed in agreement, she took my hand and led me to the pasture.

Both men were sitting beside their campfire but the old one looked asleep, his head drooped almost to his knees. As we hesitated, watching, he jerked and swayed, raised his head, dropped it again. Roxy pulled me forward until we stood opposite the campfire. The men, one nodding and the other busy with his mouth organ, didn't see us. Then the old one staggered to his feet, rubbed his back, went to the covered wagon, and climbed in.

The younger man put down his mouth organ to stir the fire, looked up, and saw us staring at him. He stood up and walked to the creek bank. Somehow, that close, he stopped looking like a foreign stranger but just a plain man, like he'd come in from just some other town. "Howdy!" he called. "Come on over and visit a while. Evening's nice."

Roxy stood there, grinning, too far away to read his lips. I said, "She's deaf-and dumb, she can't hear you."

He beckoned, smiling, pointing to the boxes set beside the fire. Roxy took a step forward, stopped bashfully. He beckoned again—another step, beckon, step, until she reached the water's edge. Then shook her head, pointed to her shoes, pointed at the water. I moved close to her, uncertain, ready to run back to the barn, felt the tremble in her body. The big man bent down, unlaced his shoes, kicked them off his unsocked feet, rolled up his pants legs. Then he waded calf-high across the creek, swung Roxy over his shoulder like a sack of potatoes, and carried her to the campfire. He turned and came back towards me.

I ran backwards toward the barn, tripped, fell, scrambled up like a terrified little animal. The man stood, hands on hips. "Don't be afeered, I'll carry you acrost."

I shook my head. He shrugged, waded back. I stood, watching to see that nothing happened to Roxy.

The firelight revealed a big happy grin on Roxy's face. She looked up at the man, pointed at her throat, shook her head; pointed at her ears, shook her head. Opened her mouth, went, "Aanh-aanh, aanh!" The man nodded, patted her back, urged her to sit down on a box, and sat on another beside her. He picked up his mouth organ, blew high piercing notes, dropped the organ, made signs meaning could she hear that. Roxy nodded, lying probably. Or maybe she did, the sound was so high pitched, because she kept nodding as he played. The man suddenly stood up, playing the organ with one hand, pulling Roxy to her feet with the other, swaying with the music, Roxy lumbering after him, hopping up and down, a look of unutterable joy on her face. She let go his hand, stomped her feet up and down in time with some awkward tune inside herself. It was like a show, the fire for footlights, the man and his music the orchestra, Roxy the dancer. I sat down to watch.

When I awoke, shivering on the damp rough pasture grass, the moon was still high. But the fire had burned to embers and the two figures were shadows leaning against each other.

I walked to the creek bank, motioned at Roxy. She jumped up, hurried to the creek, lifted her skirt like she was going to walk into the water with her shoes on. But the big man swung her to his shoulder and toted her across. When he set her beside me she was breathing hard and fast, gurgling in her throat. It maybe would have been a giggle if she hadn't been deaf-and-dumb.

Roxy walked me up to our gate and I skittered inside the house and into bed with my clothes still on. Listened for a sound from Grandma. Nothing but snores. Took off my clothes, found my nightgown, got into bed and fell down a tunnel of sleep.

Next afternoon I played like I had a stomachache and Grandpa went for the milk. I was afraid to face Roxy for fear one of us might let on to Miss Abbie we'd been up to something. Grandma gave me peppermint tea and sent me to bed early. I didn't mind, I was sleepy.

I stirred awake to the striking of our big old wall clock, counted ten. I crept out of bed, padded through a path of moonlight to the window that faced the pastures and the creek.

The tinkerman's campfire still burned, but I heard no music. This time I didn't bother to dress but slipped outdoors in my nightgown, ran barefooted through the damp grass growing between the wagon ruts, and across the cow paddock. I hid behind a clump of elderberry at the corner of the cow barn and watched what was happening across the creek.

I blinked my eyes, afraid I was still sleepy and not seeing right. But what I saw stayed the same. The tinkerman had his arms around Roxy and was kissing her right on the mouth. My cheeks burned with shame for her. Not even my Grandma and Grandpa did that and they had been married forty-two years.

I slipped back, close beside the barn, ran up the road to our house, got into bed, couldn't sleep. Next day I was really sick, no pretending about it, and had to take some of Grandma's patent medicine along with more peppermint tea.

It was two or three days before I felt like going for the milk again. I thought maybe Roxy would look sick too. She didn't. Her face was all shiny and her eyes sparkled like she might be watching a merry-go-round go round and round and she was fixing to get on it. It made me feel lots better. Maybe being kissed wasn't so bad after all.

Still, I wasn't sure I wanted to see any more of that kissing. For a whole week I didn't slip over to the pasture and creek in the nighttime. But I could hear the music from our front porch, see the dancing flames of the fire. It made me restless, and I argued with myself about it. Surely by this time Roxy and the tinkerman would be tired of kissing. So finally one night I crept out and hid again behind the elderberry bush.

Was I ever surprised! This time three figures sat beside the fire. Roxy, the big tinkerman. And Mable. The old man wasn't there. The three of them had their backs turned toward me and the creek, and the tinkerman was making shadow pictures against the white canvas top of the covered wagon with his hands and the firelight. He made a dog chase a rabbit, the dog's mouth snapping in fierce bites, the rabbit's ears going up and down. Then he made a man run, with a gun on his shoulder. The man vanished and a monkey climbed up and down the canvas.

The twins clapped their hands and Roxy jumped up to dance along with the shadow monkey, up and down, bouncy-bouncy. The tinkerman caught her hands and they danced around the fire while Mable clapped for them.

Then it happened. Not for fun, not to tease anybody. Caused by the bouncing, up and down, fast, fast. Roxy's teeth popped outside her mouth in a horrid skeleton grin at the tinkerman and he froze in his tracks. She shoved her teeth inside her mouth and ran to the creek, jumped into the water shoes and all, ran past me and the elderberry bush and around the barn.

With a detached smile, Mable watched the awkward, bulky figure of her sister vanish. Then she looked up at the tinkerman, her cheeks bright with reflected firelight. Her blond head ducked bashfully as the man sat beside her and took her hand in his. For a long time neither moved, so long that my eyes turned dry and scratchy like itchy marbles. I blinked to keep them open, started to edge backwards toward the road and home. Stopped, horrified. Because now the tinkerman was carrying on with Mable just like he had with Roxy. Kissing her.

Like I said, everything was twin with Roxy and Mable. So now, Mable was kissing him back.

I darted into the shadow of the barn, bent low, and took off. As I slipped past the paddock fence I saw Roxy leaning over its corner, oblivious of me, staring at the pair across the creek.

It gave me nightmares. All night I seemed to be running barely ahead of snapping teeth that were trying to kiss me.

Next day Grandma told Grandpa that those tinkermen seemed to be hanging around a mighty long time, who'd think there would be that much in town to mend, wonder if they were fixing to settle down here and stay.

Later in the day I asked Grandma, "Do deaf-and-dumb ladies get married?"

"Land's sake, what put that idea in your head?"

"Well, all grown-up ladies can get married, can't they, they don't have to end up old maids like you said the girls would, do they?"

"I wouldn't trouble myself over things like that at your age."

"Well, do they?"

She never answered me. Just said, "Now mind, when you go for the milk don't you be asking questions like that, those girls can read lips. Hurt their feelings."

When the girls came in from milking that evening I looked close at Mabel to see if she acted shiny like Roxy had after kissing the tinkerman. And she did, only dreamier, a smile slipping in and out on her face.

Roxy wasn't smiling. Her full lips were bit tight, her eyes flat and still. I sat at the kitchen table, a cookie in my hand, tensed for when she would play her game and drop her teeth at me. She didn't. For the very first time I wanted her to, and motioned at my mouth, pointing at hers. She shook her head.

"I think maybe Roxy's coming down with something," Miss Abbie fretted. "She's always so full of fun, but today she won't talk, even acts like she's mad at Mable. Deliberately shoved her so's Mable's pail slopped milk all down her apron. Mable smiling sweet as an angel, like she understood Roxy wasn't herself. I thought maybe Roxy had a warm weather fever, but her cheeks were cool."

Tinkerman's kisses, that's what. I might have been only seven but I could figure that out. Only I wasn't about to tell Miss Abbie and get us all in trouble. Roxy was mad because her teeth dropped out in front of the tinkerman, and afterwards he kissed Mable instead of her. I felt bad because it was the first time that everything wasn't twins with them. I felt so bad I told myself never to go near the tinkerman's camp anymore.

But in about a week curiosity got the best of me.

That night Grandma felt like singing all her old songs to me. Usually I loved her mournful singing of "The Drunkard's Lone Child," "The Little Brown Church in the Vale," and the sad ballad about the girl who hanged herself because a man married somebody else. But not on this night with the tinkerman's fire flickering down in the pasture and maybe both the girls already sneaking over to it. Which would he kiss tonight? Maybe both.

I played like I fell asleep against the porch post. And then I did. Grandma shook me awake, led me inside, and helped me undress. But the nap had taken the sleep out of me and now I was wide awake, tensed up to hear Grandma settle in bed and start her snoring.

The moon had changed and the night was dark when I left our yard. Instead of going to the barn I cut across the back end of the pasture, headed for a lone fence post which speared through a tangle of wild grape near the creek bank, the rest of the fence rotted and vanished long ago. I crept behind the tangle.

Down by the cow barn I saw first one shadow, then a second slip past its dark outlines. The first shadow reached the creek's bank. The second hung back, its stocky outlines telling me it was Roxy. The big tinkerman left the fire, walked to his side of the creek, beckoned. Mable quickly knelt, took off her shoes, raised her skirt, dipped her bare feet in the water. She waded quickly across and stood beside the fire, skirt still held high, her white legs gleaming in the firelight.

Roxy waited, hesitant, staring at them.

In the flickering light and shadow of the fire, the tinkerman moved close to Mable, bent his head, put his hands on her shoulders. This galvanized Roxy into action. She bent over, began unlacing her shoes. The tinkerman looked over at her, suddenly lifted Mable in his arms, took long, fast steps with her toward the dark clump of woods that bordered the pasture.

Roxy, with her head bent down, fooling with her shoes, hadn't seen them leave. Her head still bent, she picked a careful way through the water. When she reached the fire, she stamped her feet, tossed up her head. And saw she was alone. Swung around, her head twisting and turning, fighting the darkness. At the last moment she saw the shadow-blurred figure of the tinkerman with Mable in his arms vanish into the impenetrable darkness of the woods.

Her enraged gargle rose up and down as she plunged after them, across the pasture, toward the woods. Then was absorbed into its blackness.

Roxy had been so loud that I feared Miss Abbie would hear and come running. Then the heavy thrashing and grunting sounds that came out of the stand of oak and black walnut trees took my mind clean off Miss Abbie or anything but those girls alone with the tinkerman. Was he killing them? Should I scream for Grandpa? Get my bottom blistered?

I ran along the creek to the woods, splashed knee-high through the water to the opposite bank. As I clambered up its slippery side the tinkerman bumped into me, backing out of the trees. He stared down at me, turned, and ran to his camp.

The violent thrashing inside the woods continued, twigs snapping, a heavy object falling, a pounding on the earth.

I hurried toward the sounds, bushes scratching and snagging me. Two flailing shadows, more sensed than seen, rolled and tumbled, in company with the crackling of snapping twigs and enraged grunting, at the foot of a big tree. I grabbed at one of the shadows. Felt the cloth of its dress yank free and the brush of its kicking feet. Desperately I felt around for a broken-off branch, found it, switched at the shadows. Hopeless. I tossed the little stick into the tangled bodies, turned, and ran for help.

I beat on Miss Abbie's back screen, yelling, "Hurry, hurry! The girls are killing each other!"

It seemed forever before she appeared on the back porch, stumbling with sleep. "Hurry, Miss Abbie! Roxy 'n Mable—they're out in the woods killing each other!"

She ran from the house, through the cow lot and the pasture, her white night-gown flapping, me at her heels. I took a quick look at the tinker camp. The old man was up, hurrying with the tinkerman to hitch up their horses.

As Miss Abbie and I neared the woods I could hear that the heavy thrashing had become a heavy thud, measured and steady. Miss Abbie plunged into the dark, following the sound. I could feel her body pull, slap, and at last fling the broader, chunkier shadow aside from the slimmer one lying on the ground. That broader shadow fell against me, tumbled to the ground. A grey film of light that sifted through the tree branches revealed Roxy's teeth dangling palely across her mouth.

Miss Abbie shook the shadow still on the ground, half crying, half moaning, "Mable baby, wake up, dear God, oh, Mable! It's Abbie, wake up!"

No sound came from Mable. Miss Abbie stopped shaking her, sobbed, "She's killed her! Roxy's killed her own sister!"

In the distance wagon wheels creaked as they bumped unevenly across the pasture and onto the road.

Miss Abbie stood up, grabbed Roxy, yanked her over to Mable. Together they lifted the sagging body and staggered with it across the creek, me behind them. At the house they laid Mable on the porch until Miss Abbie could light the oil lamp, then carried her to her cot.

Mable's forehead was gashed, her face blood-streaked. Beneath that red rivulet she was still and white, eyes closed. Miss Abbie's hands waggled furiously in deaf-and-dumb talk and Roxy, her eyes large and frightened, ran to the kitchen, returned with a pan of water. She looked awful. Her teeth had fallen out somewhere in the woods or creek and her face had collapsed, as though she were swallowing herself to escape the terrible thing she had done.

"Run for your grandpa, Sary, have him fetch the doctor," Miss Abbie ordered. I ran.

You can imagine that our town did a lot of talking about what happened that night. Trying to figure out why Roxy had half killed Mable, pounding her head with a rock. Everybody kept at me, asking did I know what started such a ruckus and what on earth had made me get up in the night to catch those girls at it. And why ever were they out in the woods anyway.

Even at seven years old, maybe even especially at seven, you know when things ought to be a secret. So I said I'd heard our cat meowing, got up to let him in, and then heard the racket in the woods.

"Mighty odd those tinkermen packed up and left that same night," Grandma mused. "What in the name of sense would those girls be fighting over? Sure you don't know anything more about it, Sary?"

I shook my head.

When Mable got well she and Roxy didn't act like twins anymore, wouldn't even talk to each other except indirectly through Miss Abbie. Roxy never dropped her teeth at me either, because she never could find them even though she scrounged through the leaves in the woods and waded up and down the creek bed days on end looking for them. A heavy rain had fallen after that fight and the creek was running full, no telling where the teeth traveled.

Actually the only time those girls ever seemed happy anymore was when they played with the baby. Loved that baby together like they always had loved every-thing together before the fight. Certainly was lucky Miss Abbie had found that baby on their front doorstep one early morning and they decided to keep it. I don't see why whoever gave that baby away couldn't have just walked up the road a piece and left it at Grandma and Grandpa's house so it could be orphans with me; I needed somebody to play with. So cute, too, big black eyes, dark curly hair, a little boy kicking and gurgling if you tickled his stomach. "Brightest little thing, watches every move any of us make," Miss Abbie bragged. "And already spoiled rotten from all the attention he gets. I have to time those girls so's one don't hold him a minute more'n the other. I'll not stand any more squabbling around here."

"Whose baby is it?" I asked Miss Abbie one day when the girls had the baby outside in the yard for a breath of fresh air.

"The Lord's," she said.

"Well, why'd He pick your house to leave it? He could've sent it to our house just as well, couldn't He?"

She thought for a minute, then said, "I reckon not. You see, the Lord's ways are His, real special, and we never figure out exactly where they're headed, or why. It's kind of a secret, the Lord's secret."

"I love secrets," I said. "They're fun. Especially when they're about presents. Do you suppose that's why the Lord sent the baby here, giving you him as a present so Roxy and Mable would make up?"

Miss Abbie took kind of a deep breath, turned to look out the window at the girls sitting on a blanket in the yard, the baby between them. "Maybe so," she agreed. "Anyway, it's working."

Of Silence and Slow Time

Karawynn Long
USA, 1995

Thou still unravished bride of quietness,
Thou foster-child of silence and slow time . . .
—*John Keats, "Ode on a Grecian Urn"*

The restaurant door was a heavy brass-and-glass affair that opened outward in the old style instead of sliding. Marina's cheeks prickled in the rush of warm air and the smell of cooking food made her stomach rumble. Her hair whipped around and clung to her face as she unwound the wool scarf from her neck.

The restaurant was crowded and presumably quite noisy. People stood in bright-coated clumps near the entrance, waiting for tables; a lucky few were squeezed onto one of the two benches. Beyond the silhouetted heads clustered around the bar, two white-shirted bartenders shook and poured drinks with practiced speed. Marina gripped her shoulder bag, afraid of jarring its contents in the press of people. The coolpack was padded, but it didn't hurt to be safe.

The host appeared and said something. Marina smiled at him but shook her head. "I'm meeting someone," she said loudly. He gave her an odd look, and Marina wondered if maybe it wasn't as noisy as she'd assumed. She pushed her way into the dining room.

Jeff was at a window table, facing in her direction but looking outside at the bundled people hurrying up and down Michigan Avenue. Marina threaded between the white-draped tables until she was only a few feet away, then stopped. Jeff had been a jeans-and-sweatshirt man in their college days, never very concerned with style. Now he wore a deep maroon shirt with black paisleys and a classy onyx pin at the throat. He glanced up and saw her.

There was a pause while he stared at her, and then he smiled and stood up. "Marina," he said, holding out a hand. She took it, warm and rough against her own. Familiar, after all this time.

"Hi Jeff," she said.

Then their hands dropped, and she busied herself with unbuttoning her long coat and draping it and the scarf over the chair before she sat down. The shoulder bag she placed carefully at her feet where it wouldn't get jostled by a passing waiter. "How have you been?" she asked when she was seated.

"Oh, good, I guess," Jeff replied, and something else that she missed. He shrugged, seeming uncomfortable. The next part was indecipherable, but she caught the word "surprise" and then "after the way things ended."

She blinked once, hard, trying to concentrate, shuffling phonemes around in her head. A long "e," an "f" or a "v," an "m" . . . "surprised to hear from you." That seemed to fit.

For a moment she considered explaining right then, but decided it was too dangerous. She needed time to feel him out, first. "Oh, curiosity, mostly," she answered. "It's been more than four years." She shrugged, smiling a little. "Don't you ever wonder what happened to people you used to know?"

He stared at her. Marina gripped her hands together under the table but returned his stare calmly, still smiling. "Yeah, I guess I do," he said. He leaned back and began unrolling his linen napkin and arranging the silverware in a precise row on the white tablecloth.

Marina realized the first move was up to her. "So, are you—" She broke off as a waiter appeared beside their table and looked at her expectantly. Flustered, she glanced down at her menu and ordered the first thing she saw, an enchilada platter. The waiter punched their orders into his pocket computer. His hands were thin and delicate, the nails short. The computer spat out a printed ticket; he placed it on the table and was gone.

Marina took a deep breath. "Are you still at GeneSys? Susan Li told me you'd hired on there, but that was a while ago." She sipped at her water, trying to downplay the importance of the answer.

"Yeah." He nodded. "In fact,"—something—"promoted in October. Senior Research Director, if you can believe that," Jeff said, shrugging a little. "Pissed off a lot of people who thought I'd been promoted over their heads. They all want the pick"—he'd moved his hands apart, no, it must be "big." Or "bigger." Celery? That didn't make any sense. Oh, "salary." Then "nobody" with a shake of the head, and a garbled string. Marina blinked rapidly, trying to make sense of it, to keep up, barely catching the next part: "—seventy-eight-hour work weeks." Or maybe it was "seventy- and eighty-hour work weeks." Marina suppressed a flare of irritation. It would be easier with the interpreter, except she was afraid it would alienate her from Jeff even further.

Jeff paused. "And you? Are you still painting?" With one hand he rotated his water glass, sunlight reflecting sharply off the ice cubes.

Marina was concentrating so closely on his lips that it took her a moment to realize his eyebrows were raised. He'd asked her a question. Painting. "No," she answered quickly. "No. I haven't painted since . . . right after college."

Jeff looked genuinely disappointed; he said something that ended with her name, then cocked his head. "So what are you doing now?" he asked.

"Oh, I'm still an artist. Limited-edition holographic jewelry." She touched her pendant, then held it out for him. It was a hologram of a huge spreading apple tree, her first really successful piece and a sentimental favorite.

Jeff leaned closer, squinting a little. Her name again, and she caught nothing else except the last word: "real." He glanced up, looking astonished. She studied his expression and decided he hadn't seen all of it.

"Have you ever read the Bible? Genesis?" she asked.

He frowned. "Yeah." There was more, but once she had the affirmative Marina didn't try to figure out the rest. He peered at the pendant again, jaw dropping when he saw it, and she couldn't help grinning. She'd camouflaged a serpent among the tree branches; it was hard to see, yet once found it seemed obvious.

Jeff blinked and shook his head. "That is really rare." He mouthed the words slowly—the first thing he'd said so far she didn't have to struggle to decipher. Suddenly he jumped a little and turned to the left, glancing over his shoulder. "Sorry," he said. "Somebody broke a glass or something back there. Startled me."

She nodded, dropping the pendant back to her chest. After twenty-seven years, she was used to having people react oddly to sounds she couldn't hear.

Jeff watched her with narrowed eyes. "You never got an implant, did you." His expression was disapproving. "You spoke so well, I thought maybe you had . . ." He waved a hand vaguely around his ear.

"No," she said. "Just speech therapy." This was too close to the reason for their breakup four years ago, and she didn't want to talk about it now. She pulled her interpreter from the bag at her feet and thumbed it on. She had thought Jeff would feel more comfortable if she could look at his face rather than down at a screen, but she'd forgotten how much *work* it was to lipread, and how easy it was to miss things.

"Anyway," she continued, "Iridium Gallery just down Michigan here started carrying my pieces last summer, and they've done real well. Better than I'd hoped." She had fought long and hard with the owner, who had wanted to feature the fact that she was deaf in the little plaque of information about each artist. Marina had adamantly refused. She wanted people to appreciate her art for itself, not out of misplaced pity for the "disadvantaged" artist.

Just then their dinners arrived, and when Marina saw Jeff's grilled swordfish she wished she'd taken more time with the menu. Jeff noticed her gazing at it and insisted they trade.

"Grant—my roommate—is a vegetarian, so I don't get to eat a lot of fish," she explained. "We trade off cooking, three nights apiece per week. Although he owes me a week or two at least," she added, rolling her eyes. "Somehow he's always on call at the hospital when it's his turn, never mine."

"He's a doctor?"

Marina chewed and swallowed, shaking her head. "An ob-gyn. Serving his residency at UIC, and they just work him to death up there."

"Ah," Jeff said noncommittally. "I—" usually? generally? Marina wasn't sure. "—eat out. I hate cooking for just myself."

She tried to appear casual. "You could cook for your girlfriend."

"I used to, but she left me two years ago. I think she ate my Jill."

Marina glanced down at the interpreter, startled. The last line read, [I think she hated my chili.]

She suppressed a giggle. "Oh, that's a shame. You did make excellent chili."

"Aha. Then you had no excuse for leaving." He smiled easily, and the look in his eyes was indecipherable.

Marina glanced away; suddenly sober. A single red carnation rested in a glass bud vase behind the array of condiments. The outer petals had begun to shrivel and turn dark. "We just lived in different worlds, you know?" She looked back at him. "Hearing and Deaf. It was too much for me. I didn't mean to hurt you, I . . .I was just too young to end it with any grace."

"It's okay, really." He seemed uncomfortable again, and changed the subject by telling her a joke about the Bears, who had had a particularly dismal season. She had to read it off the screen, but it was still funny, and Jeff seemed pleased when she laughed at the punch line.

They talked about inconsequentials for a while. Marina found herself watching his face, the line of his eyebrows, the way one side of his mouth smiled before the other. She remembered him sitting on her bed, laughing up at her; hunched over the Scrabble board, frowning and chewing on his lip; the way he used to gaze at her so intently just before he kissed her. . . . Her heart turned over a little. She realized, all unexpectedly, that she'd missed him.

"I miss hearing your laugh," he said, breaking into her thoughts. "You have a beautiful voice."

That sobered her up. He had told her that so often while they were together that the phrase had taken on overtones of reproach. As a compliment, it was meaningless to her. Why should she care what her voice sounded like? It was her mother who had forced her through years of speech therapy, and while it was occasionally useful to be able to speak directly to hearing people, it wasn't how she *communicated*.

Jeff took a long drink, draining the glass, then set it down heavily. She felt the thump through the table and tensed. "So," he said. "Is Grant your lover?"

Marina breathed out, relieved. "Oh, no. No, he's gay. We slept together once, mostly out of curiosity, but I don't think his heart was truly in it. He tried not to let on, though, so not to hurt my feelings."

Jeff nodded, his expression betraying nothing.

"I'm going to get pregnant," she blurted, then cringed at the way it must have sounded. She hurried to explain. "I've wanted a baby for years, but couldn't afford it. Now my jewelry is selling well enough, and Grant will be around to help out at first. So I'm going to get pregnant." She took a drink of water, more to keep herself from saying anything else than because she was thirsty.

Jeff looked only slightly puzzled at the change of subject. "Mother" was all she caught. Marina glanced down at the screen. [Wonderful. I'm sure you'll make a terrific mother.]

"Perhaps." Marina picked up her spoon, began playing with it. Now. She had to say it now.

"Jeff," she said, and waited until he looked up at her. "I want to have a Deaf baby." She mouthed the words precisely, barely voicing.

He stared at her, turning incredulous as it sank in. "Marina!" He paused and looked around, and then began again—more quietly, she supposed. [Marina, you can't be serious! They located those sequences—god, twenty-five years ago at least.]

She caught her breath for a moment, hurt. "No. Only twenty-four." The reason for everything, for her own existence.

He grimaced ruefully and leaned back, avoiding her gaze. "Of course." There was an awkward pause.

She had been not quite three when the last sequence of genes responsible for hearing impairment was located on human DNA, and hereditary deafness was added, with fanfare, to the list of afflictions no child would ever have to suffer again. She remembered the day: her mother had been crying, her face red and frightening, and she had pushed Marina away when she tried to crawl in her lap for comfort. As she grew up, they hit her with it again and again, her mother in resentment, others in pity. "Three more years," her mother would say when Marina did something clumsy, as if her mind and fingers were as useless as her ears. "Just three more years and I could have had a normal child."

Marina shook off the memory. "I want to have a Deaf baby, Jeff. And I need you to help me."

He stared at her, eyes widening as the implications sank in. She spoke before he could begin voicing objections. "Look, it's not as bad as you think. I'll get you the fertilized eggs; there ought to be examples of all the necessary gene sequences there already. All you have to do is run a virus through and splice them together, right?"

Jeff was shaking his head, spitting out words she couldn't understand. Her gaze flickered back and forth between his face and the interpreter screen. [You have absolutely no concept—] He broke off suddenly and looked around them. "Shit." [These tables are too close together.] He handed a card to a passing waiter, who ran it through a reader on his belt and returned it. Jeff rose, grabbing his coat from the chair.

"Come on," he said. "Let's go walk by the lake."

"It's freezing," she protested.

"It's private," he replied, and started for the door.

Awkwardly she grabbed her things and hurried to catch up.

They walked along a winding path in the park, not speaking. A squirrel ran across in front of them and skittered up a tree trunk, tail flickering in agitation. Snow was piled in drifts around the benches and shrubs, and two and three inches high on the thicker tree branches. An occasional gust of wind scattered the flakes like dust. Eventually they reached the lakeshore. Jeff brushed snow off one of the rock steps and sat down, and Marina did the same. He turned to face her.

"Your deafness puts you in a—" Marina couldn't make it out. She held the interpreter up where she could see it. [—puts you in a high-risk group for genetic defects.] Marina started to protest, but he shook his head and kept talking. [As soon as—I'm sorry, but most people *will* see it as a defect. As soon as your ob-gyn confirms you're pregnant—and legally, you know, you have to see a doctor within five weeks of a possible or suspected pregnancy—she'll take an embryonic sample and have a full workup done. Furthermore, again because you're in that high-risk group, they're going to want to know who the father is, or at the very least a short list of possible fathers, and they're not going to take "I don't remember" as an answer. And if you tell them a name that doesn't match with the gene typing, you're in big trouble.]

Marina looked up again when the words stopped scrolling. "I'll tell them the truth. Grant has agreed to be the natural father."

He digested this for a moment "Does Grant know about all of this? That his baby will be deaf? And he approves of it?"

She shrugged. "He knows. He supports my choice."

"He's deaf too?"

"No, he's hearing. His parents are Deaf, though, and his older sister." For a moment she thought of Nancy with envy. How much easier it would have been to grow up Deaf-of-Deaf.

"Huh." Jeff stared at her, then shook his head dismissively. "Okay, so you name Grant as the father. But there's no way those gene markers are going to get past whoever does the typing. As soon as the test results come back, they'll perform replacement therapy on the fetus, and you'll have a hearing child anyway."

Marina nodded. Grant had raised the same objection—and then, to her immense relief, had provided a solution. "Besides research, GeneSys also does standard lab work, right, gene-testing embryo cell samples and so on?"

Jeff shook his head, which made her heart drop for a moment, until he began to speak. [They have to. Part of the government contract. But that doesn't mean—]

She didn't wait for him to finish. "Okay. So I go to a gynecologist for a checkup. She sends the sample to GeneSys for testing. Then all you have to do is make sure it comes up clear. Change the label or something. I know it's not your department, but it shouldn't be that hard."

"Whoa, Marina. Slow down." He took a deep breath, and began ticking items off on his fingers. [First of all, there are a half-dozen other biotech companies in the metro area. What are the odds that your doctor even sends her stuff to GeneSys?]

"So I go to a different doctor. One that we know uses GeneSys."

"Second, that's not just 'not my department.' It's not even close. It's—" Marina couldn't make out the rest. Annoyed, she looked down at the interpreter again. [It's on the other side of the building.]

She felt everything slipping away from her. "And the 'Senior Research Director' doesn't have a passkey?" She smiled at him sidelong, making it a challenge.

Reluctantly, Jeff chuckled. She waited a moment, then sneaked a look at the screen to see what he'd said. [Well—yes, actually. My card would open those labs. But I don't have any reason to be over there, and if someone came in . . .] He shook his head, sober again. [I'm afraid there would be a lot more involved than changing a label. I'd have to *find* it first,] he said, gesturing with both hands. [They'll have the doctor's name on them, but not the patients'—just an identifying number . . .] He trailed off, thinking.

Marina smiled to herself. He was seeing it as a puzzle now, an exercise in logistics. She remembered the brilliant premed student who read mystery novels through an entire semester of biology, and broke the curve on the final anyway.

"Wait a minute." He shook his head, frowning. "There's something I don't understand. [How are you going to get the fertilized ova to begin with? No, wait—] He grimaced and held up a hand. [I can imagine how you can get them fertilized, that's not what I meant. But you'd have to have them extracted later, and you need to see a doctor for that.]

"Oh. That's the easy part." She pulled her shoulder bag around, found the coolpack and handed it to Jeff. "Already been done. Grant fertilized them. He'll reimplant the altered embryo, too."

"This?" He pulled at the Velcro and peered inside. "These are your ova?"

"Not just ova. Embryos." She made a face at him, trying to lighten the mood. "It wasn't nearly as steamy as you seem to think. Grant opted for the old petri dish. He said it would be easier that way, but *I* think he just didn't want to embarrass us both by trying to screw me again." Jeff just stared down at the rows of vials nestled in the coolpack. She couldn't see his lips from that angle, but the cursor moved across the screen. [How many are there?]

"Twelve. Grant thought that would be plenty, but we can get more if you need them."

[Uh, no. This should be more than enough.] Then he caught himself. [*If* I were to try to do this. But I don't think you truly understand what is involved here, what you are risking.] Carefully he closed the Velcro strip. [The government takes its Child Protection Acts very seriously.]

"No. Believe me, I know exactly what is at stake here."

[Then why? Why do you want this so badly?]

She looked at him, surprised and a little angry. "I'm Deaf," she said. "You *never* really understood what that means. I have not, as everyone seems to assume, lived my whole life wishing to be a part of the hearing world. I wouldn't even be the same person, if I could hear. Deaf is my identity, my culture. It is a whole community, with its own customs and a language that is graceful and unique and expressive of ideas your English can never contain. And the government," she twisted the word bitterly, "has decided that we are 'defective' and must be exterminated."

She looked away from him then, out at the water rushing up in foamy waves, and blinked back the tears that threatened. "It's is a horrible thing, Jeffrey, to watch your culture dying all around you, because no children are born to carry it forward. You can't imagine it."

He was silent, the cursor still. She turned back, searching for something that would make an impact, make him understand how important this was to her. "Telling me that my child must be hearing is like—like telling a black woman that she is only allowed to bear white babies. It's wrong, Jeff. You always believed in freedom of choice, in abolishing discrimination—well, that's exactly what this is. Jeff, please . . ." She trailed off.

He sighed. "Marina, even if I could manage it somehow," he said gently, "and you gave birth to a deaf baby—" Awkwardly he tried to sign to her, touching a finger to lips and ear for "deaf," making a cradling gesture for "baby." Marina swallowed around a sudden lump in her throat, loving him for that effort. But she'd lost track, and had to read the rest off the screen. Her head was beginning to hurt. [—you know they'll never let you keep it. You might have six months before someone noticed, and then they would put the child in a foster home—with hearing people, you can be sure—and you would go to jail. They'd never let you see your son or daughter again, and your culture, as you put it, would still be lost.]

Marina shook her head emphatically. "They'd only do that if they can prove it was done on purpose. And we'll make sure they don't even *suspect*. The only people who know—the only ones who *will* know—are me, Grant, and you. As long as *you* don't say anything, we'll be fine.

"Furthermore, a DNA test won't reveal anything unusual," she continued, "because there won't be any engineered genes involved. Nothing that doesn't come directly from either me or Grant. Besides—what hearing person," she spat the words, "is going to believe I actually *wanted* a deaf child? I'll be appropriately sorrowful and outraged when my baby is diagnosed 'defective.' The whole thing will be put down to a lab mix-up."

He shook his head. [Extremely risky. The media will be climbing all over this, you can be sure—the first child born deaf in America in twenty-five years!]

"Jeff." She looked at him calmly. "You're not going to change my mind. I want this more than anything, and if you won't help me I will find some other way." She paused, hands balling into fists on her thighs. "It *can* be done, I know it can. I just need to know if you're willing to help me." She held his gaze challengingly.

"God, Marina. Do you have any idea of what you're really asking me to do here? What kind of risks are involved? Any idea at all?" His eyes flicked back and forth between hers, his expression open and pleading.

Marina glanced down, ashamed. [Any idea at all?] The cursor blinked on the interpreter, waiting. Of course, he was in just as much danger from this as she was. A long jail term; his career destroyed. And with nothing but an abstract principle urging him forward. In that moment she realized, with cold certainty, that he would turn her down . . . and more, that she couldn't blame him. "I know—I know it's a lot to ask. You don't owe me this, Jeff, okay? You don't owe me anything." Marina stuffed the interpreter back into her shoulder bag and jumped down to the step below. She put a hand lightly on his leg. It was the only time they had touched since the handshake in the restaurant. "Thanks for buying lunch. I'll return the favor sometime." She reached up to retrieve the coolpack from his lap.

He held tight to the strap and didn't let her have it, just stared at her, studying her face. Then he looked off over her left shoulder, eyes unfocused. Tiny lines between his eyebrows came and went and came again. Finally he took a deep breath and closed his eyes. "I'll do it," he said, and she thought she must have read it wrong, but he met her eyes then and said it again. "I'll do it."

She let go and leaned up against the rock step. He looked off to the right again, out at the water.

[We'll need to stay away from each other as much as possible. It's bad enough that the child's father is a gynecologist, though I'll admit it makes for a tighter conspiracy. It wouldn't do for you to suddenly start spending a lot of time with a biogeneticist, too. I'll have to see you once more, though, to give you the embryos. I think I can get the recomb done this weekend— I'll do several, in case the first one doesn't implant. Just hang on to the extra ones. I'll call you and we can meet for lunch again next week; that shouldn't be too unusual.]

[Okay, that ought to do it for now. Oh, and a list of ob-gyns that use GeneSys's labs. Shit.] She glanced up to see him rubbing a hand across his forehead. [I have no idea how I'm going to manage that. There should be a file somewhere—well, I'll figure something out. I guess I'll need you to let me know which doctor, and when she takes the cell sample. In fact, get a Friday appointment. That way it'll be at the lab all weekend, and I'll have more time. God, I don't believe I'm doing this.] He got up and dusted the snow off his pants. "Let's go."

Marina followed, afraid that anything she said might change his mind. Because of course what she had told him wasn't true at all. Anyone else she went to would be a complete stranger, and might turn her in before she even got her chance. She shivered a little in the rising wind.

They walked out of the park together, and back up Michigan Avenue past the restaurant. The windows were tinted, making it impossible to see more than vague shadows inside. When they got to the corner where she would turn toward the train station, Marina stopped.

"Well, I'll call you." Jeff's hand went up along his jaw in a Y shape. Call. Pointing at her. You. "We'll do lunch, right?" An L at the lips. Lunch. He started away without waiting for her answer, stopped, then turned around and walked back. Reaching out, he gently pried the interpreter from her cold-numbed hand, faced away from her and spoke into it for a moment. Then, with a lopsided, ironic sort of grin, he handed it back to her, turned a second time and walked down the street.

[I think you should know—I'm not really doing this for the principle of it. I'm not sure what to believe about that part right now. I'm doing it because a woman I once loved—maybe still do love—has asked me to, and I can't seem to bring myself to tell her no.]

Marina stood still and watched him go, trying to think of something to say to that, and finding nothing that would not have made things worse. In less than two blocks she had lost him in the crowd.

As it turned out, she didn't have lunch with Jeff again after all.

Leaving the apartment for a grocery-store run Tuesday afternoon, she nearly ran into a dark-haired woman whom she had not, of course, heard approaching.

They apologized to each other and the woman began to walk on, then took a second look at the apartment number on the door.

"Would you be Marina"—something. Not her last name, which would have been logical.

Marina blinked. "Yes?"

"Oh, good. I'm a friend of Jeff Langford's, we work together, and he asked me to come by and give this to you." She handed Marina the gift-wrapped package she was carrying in one hand.

Marina stared down at the bright blue bow, realizing what this must be, and missed the woman's next few words.

"—sorry he couldn't come himself," she was saying when Marina looked up again, "he's been really"—something—"at work, you know, it's terrible what they"— something else, ending in "oo." Marina picked it up again with " . . . tell you to have a really happy birthday, and he'll call you later."

"Uh, thanks." The woman was beginning to look concerned. It was her birthday, Marina realized; she was supposed to be enthusiastic, not confused. "This is great," she tried. "I can't wait to see what it is! Tell Jeff I said thanks. And thank you for bringing it over."

The woman smiled cheerfully. "Oh, no problem, it was practically on my way home. You have a good birthday, okay?" She walked back down the hall, waving just before she turned the corner.

Marina hit the door lock and stepped back inside, tearing paper as she went. Inside the box was an insulated coolpack, about fist-sized. Inside the coolpack, were six tiny padded vials.

Six embryos. She wondered what happened that had made Jeff nervous enough to forgo a second lunch.

It had been thirteen days since her last period. Grant implanted the first embryo that very evening. They had agreed to try only one at a time, despite the possible delay, because the birth of deaf fraternal twins would be suspicious. Even with modern methods and medications, the chance that a given embryo would implant and survive was only forty percent.

Ten days later, a home blood test confirmed that she was, indeed, pregnant.

The following Wednesday, Marina was at her room terminal accessing a graphics file when the lights began flashing in the short-short-long pattern that meant someone was inquiring at the door. A message appeared across the bottom of her screen: [Visitor for Marina Carmichael: Jivval from Market Gardens . . . Floral Delivery . . . ID CONFIRMED]

Marina stared at this a moment, then rose to answer the door. She tried to think of who might be sending her flowers, and why, and came up blank. No one except Grant knew yet that she was pregnant. Maybe it was a mistake.

She pressed the door panel. A dark-skinned teenage boy stood outside, holding a long white box. He grinned at her, offering a slate for her to sign. She did so, and maneuvered the box through the doorway. The door slid shut behind her.

She took the box into the dining room and laid it on the table. Grant was sitting, eating a sandwich; he looked over with interest.

Marina lifted the lid, revealing blue roses, a dozen long-stemmed ones. A small white envelope lay nestled among the stems. She picked it up, avoiding the thorns, broke the seal with a fingernail, and pulled out the card.

It contained a handwritten list of eight doctors' names, and the word "Friday," underlined twice. The card was unsigned. She handed it to Grant. "Jeff," she told him. Then she shook her head. "Why flowers?" she signed, pointing. "Blue expensive, wow! Why-not E-mail? Why-not phone?"

Grant shrugged. "Maybe he think need careful. Now no," he spelled, "e-l-e-c-t-r-o-n-i-c record of message, if later person authority look-closely. Maybe he think card with flowers not easy notice they, not make suspicious they." He handed the card back to her, and she took it absentmindedly, staring at the blue roses, and hoping, despite herself, that they were more than camouflage.

Since the blood test Marina had asked several of her female friends for ob-gyn recommendations. Three of the eight names on Jeff's list were also on her own.

She began calling, and was able to make a 10:00 A.M. appointment with the third doctor for the following Friday.

She printed out the address, and then checked to be sure none of the other doctors' offices were in the same area. Then she E-mailed Jeff.

> Enjoyed our lunch the other day. Could we do it again? I have an appointment Friday morning the 24th, near Clark and Division—perhaps we could meet at the Wallflower around noon? Let me know. Love, Marina

Saturday's mail list, when it scrolled up, contained a letter from her friend Jenny in Seattle, several notices she didn't recognize—probably advertisements—and a note from Jeff, which she displayed immediately.

> Marina—sorry, but I can't make the lunch date. I've got a big project coming together at work; will probably have to work all next weekend. Some other time, okay? Jeff.

He was avoiding her, she realized. He didn't ever intend to see her again. Well, that was just *fine*, then. She hit the table explosively. She wouldn't chase after him. It would never work with a hearing man anyway. And she'd gotten what she needed. Her hand dropped to her still-flat belly, caressing it gently.

"You sure not-want come party you?" Marina signed with one hand, the other paused just over the door panel.

Grant sighed, running his fingers through his short hair. "Yes, I sure. Very-exhausted. And I promise Paul two-of-us watch movie tonight. Say hello to mother-father, please? I call them next-week."

Marina shrugged and nodded. "C-U-L," she spelled, dropping the "L" forward in the shorthand for "See you later."

She walked the three blocks to the el station deep in thought, not noticing the familiar surroundings at all. She was six weeks' pregnant now, which meant she had only two weeks left in which to change her mind. After that, the pregnancy would be too far along for mifepristone to stop, and the only way out would be to have an illegal surgical abortion, a prospect which frightened her more than going to jail for fetal abuse.

As she climbed the stairs to the platform the old wooden framework began to vibrate. She hurried up the last steps and found a seat on the waiting train.

The party was at Bill and Lianna's house, in Evanston. It was an older house, remodeled but not in a modern style. When Marina pressed the door button she could see the lights begin to flash through the little circular window in the wooden door.

Then Lianna opened the door. "Marina!" she signed, smiling and pulling her in. The short hallway opened to the right into a large room where about fifteen or sixteen people her age and older sat or stood in small circles. Heads turned to see who had arrived, and several people smiled and waved. Marina could feel a rapid thump through the floor and guessed that someone had music on with the bass turned up high. "I-take your coat," Lianna offered, and Marina shrugged out of it and handed it to her.

She joined the nearest group of people, which consisted of Bill, Stephan, Nancy, Elsabeth, and Grant's mother Joanna. "Grant where?" Joanna signed, raising her eyebrows, and Marina relayed Grant's message. Joanna shook her head. "That boy he say-say-say he call, but none." Next to her, Bill appeared to be having a political argument with Elsabeth and Stephan, on Marina's right.

"Busy," Marina agreed. "Hospital work very-long hours he. I help he remember he." Elsabeth signed "no-no-no" at Bill. Stephan signed "president," fingerspelled something quickly—the angle was wrong for Marina—and finished up with an emphatic "plan bullshit."

Nancy caught her eye. "Discuss-continue same for hour," she signed, rolling her eyes. "Boring they. You want two-of-us go-away?"

Marina shrugged and followed her across the room. They sat down next to Susan, Julio, and a black man she didn't know. "Marina, good see-you!" Susan said. Julio waved a hand.

Susan pointed at the stranger. "This L-a-r-r-y, last-name T-u-r-n-e-r." He smiled at her, signing his name-sign, which was the word "turn" initialized with an L. Marina grinned at the pun. Susan was spelling Marina's name for Larry.

"Larry live Seattle Washington," Susan said, turning back to Marina and Nancy.

Marina waved for Larry's attention. "You know J-e-n-n-y last-name H-a-v-e-l-o-c-k?" she asked.

Larry raised his eyebrows. "Yes, she good-friend me. You know her?"

"We go school together finish. She good-friend."

Larry nodded. "Deaf small world."

"Becoming-smaller," Julio interjected, a sour expression on his face. His hands came together until there was almost no space between them at all. He directed this toward Susan, obviously resuming a conversation interrupted by their arrival. "Soon none Deaf remaining. Genocide."

Susan shrugged. "Know-that," she signed, her posture expressing condescension. "Everyone know-that." Her gesture indicated the whole room. "Doesn't-matter. Can't change."

Larry had turned to Nancy and begun to talk. Marina concentrated until she felt her awareness split, so that she could keep up with both conversations at once. "Film all sign—drama, conversation, party same this," he was explaining. "Try save all sign for future deaf." Marina was fascinated by the contrast between his pink palms and his dark skin as his large hands turned.

"But *none* future deaf!" Marina signed at him. "All children born hearing!"

"No change because you—" Julio made a sharp sign, like a turtle pulling its head into its shell. "If we organize group l-o-b-b-y Congress, argue laws culture protect . . ."

Marina stood up abruptly. She'd had this conversation a hundred times before, and she suddenly didn't want to participate in it again. No one ever did anything about it. Except her. And she wanted to tell them, and couldn't. "Toilet?" she signed when Nancy glanced up at her.

Nancy pointed toward the kitchen. "Turn right."

As she passed the refrigerator, Marina noticed a child's drawing clipped to the front with a magnet. She stopped to look closer. It was a brown animal—a dog or a rabbit, Marina guessed from the ears—sitting in tall grass surrounded by four-petaled flowers. Her own mother had never put anything of Marina's on the refrigerator, she thought bitterly. Her mother had never encouraged her in art at all, had even forbidden Marina to draw for years. Which didn't mean that she'd stopped, only that she'd had to hide it. Everything worthwhile she'd ever accomplished had been in direct defiance of her mother.

Lianna came in from the living room carrying two empty glasses, which she set down on the counter.

"Pretty," Marina signed. "Picture it your daughter draw herself?"

Lianna smiled, flipping her long dark hair behind her shoulder. "Yes, she school draw. She old-eight now."

"Where she now?"

Lianna pointed upstairs. "She put-in-suitcase clothes she. Go all-night party girl-friend house she."

As if on cue, Lianna's daughter ran in from the living room then. "I ready go," she signed to her mother. Marina was startled, and then felt foolish. She knew Lianna couldn't speechread very well, and couldn't vocalize at all, so of course her daughter would have to sign.

"You pack-suitcase finish you?" asked Lianna. "Feed cat finish you?"

The girl nodded vigorously, ponytail bouncing. "I finish, finish." She signed a name initialized with a C. "Her father drive us."

"OK," signed Lianna. "You know number phone?" The girl rolled her eyes and signed the seven-digit number in a blur. "Okay, Mom?" she asked aloud.

Lianna nodded and held out her arms. Her daughter grinned and gave her a hug, then ran out again. Marina watched, caught in a wave of longing. She couldn't remember her own mother ever hugging her like that.

"Lianna," she said impulsively, "you think difficult have hearing child?"

Lianna looked thoughtful. "I-don't-know if hearing child difficult more than Deaf child. Maybe different. All kids difficult. Worry worry worry." She sighed, staring at the picture. "Long-time-ago I want Deaf baby. But my daughter I-love-her." She turned back to Marina, looking at her closely. "You pregnant you?" she asked. "For-for you-ask-me g-y-n doctor name, yes?"

Marina hesitated, then nodded.

Lianna smiled and gave her a big hug. When she pulled back, she signed, "Not worry. You will fine. You see."

For a moment Marina considered telling her the whole story, but she realized that would be foolish, and would only endanger Lianna if something went wrong. So Marina smiled as if reassured, and walked back to the living room with her.

Larry broke away from his conversation with Nancy and came up to admire her earrings. She smiled when he instantly discovered the hidden aspect; it tended to elude hearing people, but Deaf people invariably got it right away. Each earring was a dangling cylinder containing a holographic hand; as the cylinders rotated, the hand changed positions, spelling out a word. The left one spelled d-e-a-f, the right one l-o-v-e. "Appropriate," signed Larry, his other hand caressing her jaw lightly as he released the earring.

He drew her into talking about her work, and slowly she began to relax and enjoy the party. It was such a relief to be able to communicate without the constant struggle. She missed this feeling of camaraderie and sharing that made even Larry seem like an old friend instead of someone she'd just met. She found herself flirting with him, and realized how long it had been since she'd felt even that comfortable with a man.

She pushed all other thoughts aside. Time to worry about that decision later.

Two weeks went by in an agonizing crawl, and Marina did nothing. Then it was as if a weight had been lifted off of her chest. Somehow, knowing she couldn't change her mind made her situation easier to deal with. She felt calm and secure and competent.

As far as she knew, no one had ever been accused of deliberately *engineering* a defective child. She didn't know what the consequences of that would be, and was grimly determined that she would never find out. She had to make it obvious that she was expecting a hearing child.

Marina went shopping. She bought baby clothes, and toys, and a crib—and a little minidisc player to go in her room, which the baby would share until they moved into a larger apartment, and a dozen different albums of children's songs and lullabies.

Seven months later, Marina gave birth to a baby boy. The doctors checked him over and pronounced him perfectly healthy, and let them both go home the next day.

Marina walked to her bedroom and collapsed gratefully onto the bed. She had foolishly thought that once she'd had the baby, the hard part was over. She hadn't realized she would be so *exhausted* afterward. And so sore in every muscle she could barely move.

Grant came in behind her with the bassinet, which he placed on the stand beside the bed. He touched her leg to get her attention, but she was too tired to even look at him.

Marina dozed for about half an hour before her wristwatch began to vibrate in response to the baby's cries. Grant came in to make sure she was awake. "Sorry, sweetheart," he signed. "I-know exhausted you. If I can feed baby from"—he pointed to his chest, grinning a little—"I change-places-with-you."

"I wish," Marina signed, yawning. She sat up and rearranged her clothes to expose a breast.

Grant grimaced ironically. "But you lucky. You not must hear sweet baby scream he." He picked the baby up and handed him to Marina, who smiled and settled him in the crook of her arm. He hunted for the nipple and she positioned it for him, pressing the breast back so he could breathe.

The truth was, she almost regretted not being able to hear him. She was completely in love. He fit so perfectly into her arm. She loved the weight of him there against her chest, the baby-smell of him. He was beautiful, he was perfect. The pull she felt as he nursed satisfied something deep inside her. With a start, she realized she was humming to him. She could feel the thrumming deep in her chest.

She glanced up, and discovered that Grant had left the room. Almost guiltily, she began humming again. The baby closed his eyes and suckled sweetly.

The next afternoon brought an unexpected visitor. Marina happened to be up getting a glass of orange juice when the lights began flashing, short-short-long. She walked to the front door and pushed a button on the panel. Red LED words appeared on the tiny screen: [Visitor for Marina Carmichael: Jeffrey Langford . . . ID CONFIRMED]

She blinked, surprised, then opened the door. Jeff smiled awkwardly. "Hi! Come on in," she said. Grant came up as he did so. "Grant, this is Jeff Langford."

"Hi," Grant said aloud. He extended a hand, and the two men shook. Marina tugged at Jeff's other arm. "Come on," she urged, "come see the baby." She led him back to her room, where the baby was nestled in the wicker bassinet next to her bed. She pulled the interpreter out of the bag she'd brought from the hospital and thumbed it on.

[He's beautiful,] Jeff said. He looked concerned, though, and Marina touched his arm.

"He's fine," she said. "We're both fine."

He nodded, but the worried look didn't dissipate. "What's his name?" he asked.

"I don't know, yet." She smiled. "We wanted to get to know him first, before we picked out a permanent name."

Jeff nodded. Marina gazed down at the baby. She touched one tiny curled hand, marveling at its softness.

Jeff touched her arm to get her attention. [You should talk to him, you know. Babies respond to the sound of their mothers' voices.] She looked up in time to catch his wistful smile. "And I always told you you had a beautiful voice."

She gave a small laugh, even though she didn't think the joke was very funny. Jeff didn't smile at all, and suddenly the expression on his face registered. It was more than just concern, it was . . . guilt. He wouldn't meet her eyes. Dread settled in the pit of her stomach.

"What," she said. When he didn't reply, she said it again, loud enough that she could feel the rumble in her chest. "Jeff, what!"

He looked away, then back, defiantly. "He's not deaf, Marina. I didn't do it."

Marina thought she must have misunderstood, but the words were there on her screen, in stark and terrible confirmation. She turned and stared at the sleeping baby. Hearing. My child is hearing. It didn't mean anything to her yet.

"Why." It was all she could think of to say. But before he could answer, the rest exploded from her in a rush. "I thought you understood, how important it was, you said— Oh! You never told me! Nine-months pregnant I, you-tell-me nothing, all-time baby hearing!" She began to cry. "Why? Why you do this? Why not you-tell-me beginning 'no, can't help-you I'?"

He was staring at her, confused, and she realized that she had stopped vocalizing and was only signing, hands jerking with grief and anger. She forced herself to slow down and speak.

"You had no right to make that decision for me. You tricked me into bearing a child I did not want. This was *my* baby, *my* choice, and if you didn't want to take the risk, you could have just told me. You offered to help me and then you chose to back out and save your own skin, and didn't even have the guts to tell me. Or did you *want* to see me suffer? Acting out some little revenge fantasy because I dumped you five years ago? How could you be so hateful?"

He shook his head, pleading. "I didn't do it to save my own skin, whatever you might think. And I don't want to see you hurt." He reached out toward her arm and she jerked it away. His hand dropped awkwardly. [I *wanted* to help you, Marina. I tried, but I just couldn't. You weren't only making a choice for yourself, don't you understand—you were making one for that baby, too, one that he would have to live with all his life!]

"Oh, so you think you're playing the great hero," she sneered, "rescuing this little innocent child from the terrible handicap his mother wished to impose upon him?" Her wristband began to vibrate, but she ignored it.

[No, I *don't* think that deafness has to be a handicap. But it was different for you, Marina. You had the chance to make friends with people like yourself, your own age. But the last deaf child was born twenty-five years ago! You know how conformist kids are; they all want to wear the same brand of jeans, for god's sake. Do you really think he wouldn't resent being the only one who couldn't hear? Did you ever think, what's to stop him from getting a cochlear implant the moment he's old enough to understand he has that choice?]

That shook her, and she didn't say anything. She hadn't thought of that at all, that her son might rebel and *choose* to be hearing. The same way, as a teenager, she'd finally stopped trying to please her mother and embraced the Deaf world. Suddenly she thought of Lianna's daughter, who had gone off to a hearing friend's house rather than stay with the adults at the Deaf party. And Lianna had let her. And the girl had signed to her mother, and hugged her before she went.

"Marina, please try to understand." He gestured toward the bassinet. "He would have been so terribly, terribly alone."

"He would have had me." And behind that, the other thought, the she didn't say: and I would have him. The way she'd never really had anyone—not Jeff, not even dear Grant, or any of her other friends or lovers down the years, even the Deaf ones. Not her own mother.

She stared down at the child, his face mottled red and his mouth open in a scream. He would grow up part of the hearing world, and she would never understand him. They would be separate forever. All the dreams she had, all the things she had wanted to share with her child, all of them crumbled into dust. He would be ashamed of her, his deaf mother, the way her mother had been ashamed of her deaf daughter.

Jeff made a small motion. She had forgotten he was there, but now she looked up, hatefully. "Get out. Get the fuck out and don't ever come near me again." She threw the interpreter at the bed.

He stared sorrowfully at her for a moment, and then started for the door. In the doorway he turned around again, and waited until she gave in and glared up at him. He spoke slowly and carefully, making sure she had time to speechread. "If you love him, Marina, it won't matter that he can hear. He will learn your language and your culture because it is yours and he loves you." Then he was gone, and she collapsed onto the bed, curled up, and began to sob. Her watch was still vibrating, and she pulled it off and flung it across the room.

Sometime later, Grant came in. He didn't ask why she had been crying, so she assumed Jeff must have told him. She was grateful not to have to explain. He didn't say anything, just sat on the side of the bed and stroked her hair off her forehead.

"You know," he said after a while, speaking and signing together, "when scientists prove gay g-e-n-e-t-i-c finish, gay almost become class" —he paused, "d-e-f-e-c-t," he spelled, "same deaf. Only because many many of us . . ." He looked off for a moment, then spoke in English only. "And still the political climate could reverse again at any time." He turned back to her, taking her hands in his. "I understand what you are losing, Marina, what you fear. And the battle you must fight.

"But do it yourself, love. Not through your child. Your son doesn't deserve your love any less just because he is different from you." He leaned forward and kissed her gently on the cheek. "You think about," he signed. "Now, I believe you need chocolate milk s-h-a-k-e. Good?"

Marina wiped tears off her cheek and nodded. Grant smiled. "B-right-B," he signed.

After he left, she leaned over and looked at her son, sleeping now on his stomach in the bassinet. Because he is different from me, she thought.

She thought about her own mother, who must have wanted so much for her daughter to be like herself. How frustrating my deafness must have been for her, Marina realized suddenly. A fundamental difference that permeated every aspect of her life, completely alien and . . . frightening. Abruptly her perspective shifted, and Marina could see her mother's actions as born, not of resentment or hatred, but of confusion and fear. It didn't make them any better, but at least she understood, a little.

She brushed the baby's thin down of hair with her fingertips. In a moment of brutal self-honesty, Marina acknowledged that above anything else, her son had been an act of defiance toward her mother, who had shamed her every day of her life for not being a "normal" child. And if she resented her own son for not being Deaf, what was the difference?

She reached into the bassinet and picked up the baby. He stirred and yawned, his tiny mouth open wide, and nuzzled sweetly against her neck. She thought of Lianna and her daughter, holding each other. Marina rested her cheek on the top of the baby's soft head and made him a silent promise.

I will not make the mistake my mother did, she told him. *I will not try to mold you selfishly in my own image. No matter how hard it is. I will let you grow to be your own person, and take joy in that.* She squeezed her eyes shut against the pain expanding in her chest, and tears tracked across her nose, dampening the baby's fine hair. *Even if it means you grow away from me.*

When she looked up again her gaze fell on the disc player, dusty on its table in the corner by the crib. She walked over to it and flipped through the rack of minidiscs, pulling one out. It was still in its ricepaper wrapper, and she tore at it one-handed, holding the baby against her chest, reluctant to put him down even for a minute. Afraid that this tenuous bond might break. She put the disc in the tray and pushed the play button.

The quality of the silence in the room did not change at all. The afternoon sunlight streamed gold through the thin ivory curtains as Marina held her son in both arms and danced to her own internal rhythm.

Stone Deaf

Morris Smith
USA, 1997

Sometimes I hated to play with Gwen, our cousin, not because of her hearing problem, either.

"Tell Gwen to turn around, come back this way," our fat aunt Ethel hollered from the bench beside the lake. "She's getting out too far."

We were playing Blind Gator, kind of like Blindman's Bluff in the water. We stopped our game in its wet tracks. "Gw-en," my older sister Elizabeth sang out. She splashed water to draw attention, but Gwen didn't turn. Gwen was watching our other cousin, Kenneth, who was "it" and out a ways, even with the end of the little dock.

"You try, Maggie," Aunt Ethel yelled at me.

Gwen was only to her shoulders in the brown lake water, which, I thought, made it silly to call her in. Gwen was young, almost seven, an only child, and deaf. (Not quite stone deaf, Mother reminded us, although she seemed that way to me.) Mother said all this was why Aunt Ethel hollered so. Aunt Ethel also had a big chest with plenty of lungs.

I scooted water hard and screamed as loud as Aunt Ethel, "Look here!" Gwen turned, her yellow hair slicked back from her round face.

"Out too far," I mouthed for her to lip-read, and rolled my eyes toward her mother. Gwen minded her mother, too much.

"Aw-right," said Gwen, leaning forward and pushing herself toward the shore.

Kenneth, who was nine, my age, went on thrashing his skinny arms through the water, trying to tag us, his eyes squeezed closed. On the bench, Aunt Ethel fanned the August gnats with a white untanned hand. She had driven us to the lake, but she never went in herself. We'd have snickered if big Aunt Ethel had ever put on a bathing suit, but never to her face. I'd as soon snicker aloud at a tiger.

Kenneth tagged me, then I tagged Gwen. When she was "it," we usually let her peep a little since she couldn't hear us splashing. Eyes slit, Gwen lunged at us and missed. Elizabeth, who was twelve, came in close to let herself get caught. Suddenly I could see every bit of grayish pupils, the water standing on her pale lashes. "She's looking all the way," I cried.

Kenneth said, "She's cheating!" We splashed her.

"No chee," Gwen claimed, sinking to her shoulders in the water. Gwen talked from the back of her mouth and you had to get used to the way she said things. "I not cheeing."

"Yes, you were," we all cried, splashing her again.

Aunt Ethel hopped up, pumping her arms so that rolls of fat wiggled. "Stop that! You know she can't hear."

"Gwen knows she's not supposed to just look," Kenneth called bravely, then ducked.

"Give her another turn," Aunt Ethel at the edge of the tea-colored lake, "or you'll *all* have to get out."

Gwen stood up, knee-deep in water, and gave a smug little smile. She had on a new white latex bathing suit, one I would have liked myself and that made her smirky smile harder to take. Kenneth, Elizabeth, and I froze, thigh-deep in the lake. Then Gwen blinked her eyes sheepishly, and said, "I won't loo' next time, but I no wan to be 'it.'"

Aunt Ethel sat back down, but the game was over. We switched to diving off the dock. Climbing up the rickety ladder, I ripped the skirt of my faded cotton suit on a nail so that it hung down and dripped water on my leg like a trickling faucet. It made me feel crabby and tacky. I was glad when we changed into our clothes.

Later, riding into town in Aunt Ethel's sedan, Gwen twisted in the front seat and said, "Need a new bath suit, Ma-bie." Gwen couldn't say Maggie, my name, very well.

"I'll get one," I sang out, although I felt embarrassed, trapped between Elizabeth and Kenneth in the back seat with nowhere to go. It would be next summer before Mother thought about a new suit for me; then I doubted it would be latex. Aunt Ethel glanced over her shoulder, hands on the wheel, and told us about the deaf school in St. Augustine where Gwen was going for a session. Gwen was wearing a cute seersucker sunsuit I had never seen before. I figured Aunt Ethel would buy her more clothes just to go to that stupid school.

"I'm getting sick of Gwen," I whispered to Elizabeth. "I'm going to get her one of these days when Aunt Ethel's not around."

"Un-huh!" Kenneth grinned as though he hoped I would.

"Oh, Gwen doesn't mean anything," Elizabeth said, her wet brown hair plastered to her small head. Elizabeth thought her head was pointy looking, and that it showed particularly when her hair was wet. It wasn't, but I said anyway, "Your head looks awfully pointy right now."

⌐

After Labor Day, school started. We lived four miles from town and every morning Papa drove Elizabeth and me and our older brother, Gil, to our separate brick buildings. Elizabeth and I loved school, and Gil tolerated it without much complaining. Gwen was off in St. Augustine, doing whatever they do at deaf schools. On Sunday afternoons, Kenneth or some friends would come out and we played under the shady oaks in our big back yard. Gil pushed us in the tire swing.

Then, at breakfast one November morning, the day before Gwen was to come home, the tree nearest our back steps with the tire swing—the widest-branched oak of all—fell. It just keeled over, like a soldier at attention fainting from the sun. It wasn't even windy. We heard a great whoosh, then *ka-bang*.

Papa stopped eating his curd; his face went funny. "What was that?" Gil asked, his brown eyes wide. Mother's spoon stopped in mid-air. Elizabeth groaned, "Something big just hit the ground."

We all ran to the backyard. "Tree fell, tree-fell!" we hollered, amazed at the change. The bushy oak lay stretched toward the smokehouse, taking up all the yard, branches everywhere, leaves right up to the back steps.

Gil and Elizabeth and I hopped all over the small limbs and climbed onto the big ones. "Gwen's coming out on Sunday. Where'll we play with these branches everywhere?" Elizabeth asked, but Papa didn't hear. It was as though the tree had filled his mind as well as the yard. He had deep furrows in his forehead and several times he said, "I'm sure glad it didn't fall toward the house." He usually worried that a fire would burn us out. Sometimes at night, driving home from church, he'd check the sky for an orange glow out our way. Other times he talked about lightning strikes. I doubt he ever worried about a tree crashing into the roof. Now one had just missed.

We left for school, Mother driving for a change. Papa hired two men to spend all day cleaning, carrying off limbs.

By the next day, Saturday, all the leaves and small branches were gone. The thick trunk sat, upended, its snaky roots caked with dirt. During the morning, the men sawed the thickest limbs into sections so we could burn them in the fireplace come winter. On some nights, we were already building fires.

Elizabeth and I watched the men haul the logs to the woodpile, their dark muscles straining, and we rolled the patched-up tire that used to be a swing back and forth in the cleared places. No more swings from that tree, I realized. Papa said the oak fell because it had rotted inside; wind had nothing to do with it. I couldn't get over how easily it had happened. "I didn't know big trees just fell," I kept saying. It left a gaping space overhead. Where there used to be branches, now was only bare sky, a hole in the universe. Our back yard looked naked.

Elizabeth didn't seem to mind that the tree had collapsed and would never again hold a swing. "This is fun!" she yelled, standing on a log. It was early afternoon and the men were gone for the day, leaving some of the thickest sections scattered across the yard. Elizabeth took some shuffling steps and made the log move. "Look, Maggie, I'm log rolling, just like in the picture show."

"I can too," I yelled, taking a giant step to the top of one. We'd seen a western at the Palace where men rolled logs in a river.

At first we inched along, hopping off when we lost our balance. Once or twice we fell. After practicing, we could guide our logs some, "I'm good!" said Elizabeth, rolling past me. She'd picked a log with smooth bark and it moved pretty fast. "We can do it again tomorrow after church."

My log had a bump on it. I rolled a foot and was jarred off. "Not for long," I said. "Gwen's back from St. Augustine, remember? She won't be able to do this."

Elizabeth stopped and frowned. "Can't she try?"

"Aunt Ethel will be on the porch," I said, making a face. "If Gwen falls, you know what." We both groaned. We kept rolling and before we stopped, I'd changed my mind. "Gwen ought to learn how to roll," I said. "We'll do it where Aunt Ethel can't see."

⌒

In church Gwen sat at her usual place in the pew in front of us, sandwiched between thin Uncle Charlie on the end and Aunt Ethel. Gwen's blond hair was pulled back with a barrette so that her fair-skinned cheeks showed. She was kind of pretty, I grudgingly admitted.

Aunt Ethel had the fox fur neckpiece she wore on cool days around her full shoulders, and a furry tail dribbled down her back when we stood for a hymn. "Sweet hour of pray-er, sweet hour of prayer", we sang. Aunt Ethel's rich alto blended with my mother's clear soprano, their voices wrapping all around us. The singing made me feel good. Gwen glanced my way. I wiggled my fingers, and she smiled.

Mother saw and gave me a little pat. She liked Gwen. Sometimes she compared us, unfairly I thought. "Gwen may have a ninety percent hearing loss," Mother often said, "but she tries to mind. And you, Maggie, with perfect hearing, don't listen to a thing."

During the prayer, I did something that Elizabeth and I had done before—pretended to bow my head but really leaned forward to get a good look at the brown tails and tiny feet hanging from Aunt Ethel's shoulders. The neckpiece was fancy-looking but weird. It had lots of dangling parts. Elizabeth and I had never been able to decide if it was one fox, split up, or two. One, I thought, getting close. A small pointed head sat on Aunt Ethel's shoulder, its teeth snapping down on its own tail. The hard little glass eyes stared up. I was about to touch the fox's nose, just to prove I could, when the prayer ended.

Gwen turned in her seat. Her plain dress had an embroidered collar that made it almost a party dress. "This afternoon, I come play," she said too loud to Elizabeth, sitting behind her.

"Shuss," Aunt Ethel hissed over her shoulder, aiming her warning at us instead of Gwen.

Elizabeth and I exchanged looks, rolled our eyes. "Grr," I said low. Then I pointed at Aunt Ethel's neckpiece and whispered, "One fox." Elizabeth smiled, shook her head, and mouthed, "Two."

$$\backsim$$

That afternoon, Elizabeth and I grinned when Aunt Ethel and Uncle Charlie, standing in the hall, said they'd just leave Gwen and come back later. They were going to a reception where children weren't allowed. Aunt Ethel talked on while Uncle Charlie gazed out at the remaining logs and the stump in the back yard. "Used to climb that tree when I was a boy," he mused. "It was old then. Guess it had to go." Aunt Ethel gave us a sweet and threatening look. Her eyes made me think of the fox. "You girls be careful now," she said. "You can play paper dolls."

"Bye, Mauwa," Gwen said, stepping quickly away from Aunt Ethel as though eager for her parents to leave. Gwen still had a little baby fat around her waist and she wore a fuzzy red sweater that made her look even chubbier. The sweater was darling, with a yarn picture of a black poodle on the front, the very same sweater I'd seen at Churchwell's. I'd begged my mother to charge it. "No, Maggie," she had said, looking at me hard. "Seven dollars is far too much. Anyway, for someone so young, you think too much about clothes. Remember: 'Pretty is as pretty does.'"

In the hall, I touched the poodle on Gwen's sweater. "Doggie-doggie. Too nice to play in," I said. Elizabeth gave me a "watch-it" look—almost an Aunt Ethel look.

"Let's pway in the yard," said Gwen, not paying attention to what I'd said. She actually liked Elizabeth and me, even when we teased her.

Mother led us to the back porch and told us to be careful. Then she headed for the garden, never mentioning the logs. When no aunts and uncles were visiting, she gave herself permission to work in the flower beds even though it was Sunday. No one was supposed to work on Sunday since it was God's day. The men in our family didn't even go fishing. Mother did lots at church—taught Sunday School, started a Bible class at the colored church on Grady Street; still she allowed herself to pull weeds on Sunday if she wanted to. I liked the way my mother was, except for not buying sweaters.

Walking down the steps, I was struck again by the big hole in the sky where the branches had been. There was blue, blue, everywhere—too much. The hole seemed to leave us open to the very eye of God. To push away the scary feeling, I said, "We'll show you how to log roll, Gwen." A perfect time for it, I thought. Mother was in the garden, Papa was off somewhere, and even Bird, our cook, had left.

"*I'll* show her after while," said Elizabeth, skipping ahead on her thin legs as if she owned the yard. "Let's do something easy first. Hop-scotch."

"She can't do that very good either," I said pretty loud. "Let's go ahead and roll."

"We'll have to be careful. She can't hear us tell her how."

"Can't hear? That's news to me!" I squinched up my face. Elizabeth was acting like Aunt Ethel. "She can *see*, can't she?" I hopped on a thick log and did a pushing step so that it inched along. "See, Gwen?" I screamed as though I could make her hear. "LOG ROLLLNG." I shuffled the log toward Elizabeth who stood by the stump, arms folded, a put-out expression on her face.

"Look, nobody's here but us," I said softly to Elizabeth. "Big trees don't fall every day. Get a log." I forgot about God looking down through the hole.

Elizabeth let go a smile. Aunt Ethel wasn't around, so Gwen wouldn't do any smirking this afternoon. And we could actually help her learn something new.

"Watch," hollered Elizabeth, hopping on a log. She shuffled, and it scooted in a semi-circle. "It's eas-y."

"Can't," said Gwen on the steps. She had on black patent Mary Jane shoes, and, with the sweater bunching at her waist, she looked like a chubby doll.

"Whee!" we hollered, rolling around, waving our arms for balance. When we fell off, we climbed back on.

Gwen laughed, seeing it was fun, and came down the steps into the yard. "I'll twry," she said, putting one foot up on a small log. About six more were scattered around the yard. Gwen brought up the other foot and stood on the log, arms out, a weak smile on her face.

"Good. Let's get going," I shouted.

Elizabeth stopped her log and jumped off by Gwen who was still balancing on hers, legs shaking. "Now shuffle your feet," Elizabeth said, pursing her mouth like a teacher. I'd seen her do that before—act superior. Made me sick.

Gwen did a funny sliding step, then flailed in the air. Elizabeth grabbed her. Wobbling, Gwen regained her balance. "Ooh, I nearly fwall," she said.

"If you start to fall, just hop off," I said, looking right at her so she could read my lips. "Silly!"

Gwen tried a step, then quivered again.

"She's wearing the wrong kind of shoes," stated Elizabeth. "They're slippery."

I said, "Gwen, do it again." Gwen tried, lost her balance, and toppled down to her knees. Standing up, she rubbed her hands on the poodle part of her sweater.

"Doggie, doggie! Getting dirty!" I cried. "Get up."

"That's OK, Gwen. We fall too," said Elizabeth, and she turned to me. "I'm going in and get her some tennis shoes. Don't let her roll yet." She ran toward the house.

"See, Gwen." I hopped off my log and faced her. "Just jump off when you start to fall. Easier than getting off a bike. Change to that big log there."

"Aw-right." Gwen took a breath and stepped up on a log with rough dark bark, the thickest in the yard. She took a forward step, quivered, then tried another. The log wiggled, but Gwen couldn't get her feet going right.

"Shuffle!" I screamed. "Do something!"

Gwen pushed with a foot. The log moved.

"You're rolling! We'll show Elizabeth," I yelled. "Now push hard. Go in a circle. Do figure eights!" Of course I hadn't done any eights myself.

"I roll," cried Gwen, sticking out her arms and shuffling. The log bumped forward.

"Faster, faster," I urged.

She pushed, poised on top, but her feet couldn't keep up with the turn. "Yee-ah!" Gwen hollered and beat the air. She pitched forward.

As she hit the ground, the moving log caught her on the back of the leg, and I heard a snap, like a twig breaking. Gwen screamed, her chin in the dirt, arms thrown out. One leg was hooked under the log.

Quickly I shoved the log back and pulled at her arm, trying to raise her. I didn't even have time to feel sorry. In my mind Aunt Ethel's voice thundered, "Maggie! What have you done?"

"Stop," said Gwen, twisting so her light hair swept the dirt. "Ooh," she moaned.

"You're not hurt bad," I said, my insides like Jell-O.

Elizabeth slammed out the back door, holding the tennis shoes. "Maggie!" she yelled, running down the steps. "I told you to wait!"

We managed to lift Gwen from the ground. She cried and groaned and wouldn't put any weight on her left leg, so we held her on either side. "It's not hurt bad," I said again.

"Only a little," put in Elizabeth, giving me a mean look. Then she rolled her eyes, and I knew she was hearing Aunt Ethel in her head, too. We lugged Gwen up the steps. "Ooh," she cried, tears streaming. But at least she was holding onto me and Elizabeth, and not acting mad.

In the living room, we stretched Gwen out on the brown wicker sofa, and Elizabeth ran to get the bottle of Vicks. That's what Mother rubbed on everything.

"Hurts," Gwen wailed and pointed to a pinkish knot rising on her shin.

We smeared on the greenish goo, me gently rubbing it just above her white sock and Elizabeth outlining the knot. "This'll fix it," we kept saying. Gwen whimpered, stretched out on her back, her sweater all hiked up, and her slip showing at her stomach. Elizabeth gave me a frightened stare. I shivered. Elizabeth wouldn't tell, I thought, but Aunt Ethel might guess I was the one who had egged Gwen on. My eyes watered. The thought of Aunt Ethel's voice battering me down seemed much worse than any broken leg. At least Gwen herself hadn't heard the leg snap.

I smoothed down the poodle sweater, no longer wishing it were mine, and spread the Vicks thick. "Mother rubs this on us when we feel sick," I said weakly, but I knew it wasn't going to mend a bone.

The back door slammed. Mother must have heard Gwen's moans, and she rushed into the living room.

I let the Vicks bottle fall from my hand. "Gwen's leg may be broken," I said hopelessly. "I heard a snap. Aunt Ethel is going to kill me."

A minute later Mother was on the hall phone. "Ethel, I have warned them about those logs," she said. "It's my fault." I looked up from the loveseat where I had wilted down. Mother held the black receiver out from her ear, her knuckles smudged with dirt from the garden, and I could hear the thunder in Aunt Ethel's voice. With her free hand, Mother pushed her glasses up the bridge of her nose, shot me a frown—but not too bad a frown, just worried—and hung on. She was wonderful.

Later, hearing Aunt Ethel plowing up the front steps, I ducked behind the big rocker. Elizabeth had vanished.

"Gwen!" Aunt Ethel charged down our hall ahead of Uncle Charlie and flung herself into the living room. "Oh, my ba-by," she cried. Mother said, "She needs a doctor." There were scraping and grunting noises, and I knew Uncle Charlie was lifting Gwen.

I moved and stood by the front door. I had to say something, I guessed, but my mouth felt full of glue.

"Get out of the way," Aunt Ethel bellowed, as though I were an inconvenient piece of furniture, one she could talk to. "Gwen's hurt. Clear the way!"

"Aunt Ethel, I'm sorry about Gwen."

"Maggie, you can't play with Gwen again!" She pushed me aside, her rings scraping my shoulder. "You're the one that led her on, I bet, and then you spread that mess all over my child's poor leg. Elizabeth was always sweeter to Gwen than you. You can't play with her anymore. You hear?"

I felt shoved underwater. I did slow somersaults, going down, down.

As Uncle Charlie turned sideways to get Gwen's legs through the front door, she looked at me, not too mean, nothing like a smirk. "Ma-bie," she said, and raised a hand so I could see the poodle on the dirt-smeared sweater. "I fell, didn't I?" Right then, I would have bought her a new sweater myself, if I'd had the money.

⌒

The next Sunday Gwen thumped down the church aisle on crutches. Below her plaid skirt was a bone-white plaster cast. Uncle Charlie was at her elbow, and behind sailed Aunt Ethel, a full-blown dirigible, her posture erect, the fur neckpiece making her shoulders look grand. Uncle Charlie guided Gwen into the pew in front of us, and the crutches clanked against the wood of the seat like oak limbs knocking together.

At home, the logs were gone from our yard, and where the tree trunk had been was a chewed-up place in the ground. Overhead, instead of leafy branches, was the hole God could spy through when He wanted to, I guessed. I think He'd forgotten to look on the day Gwen fell, or maybe He was just waiting to glare down on me when I was alone. I still wasn't used to all that blank sky.

I hadn't seen Gwen since she was carried out of our house. The times Mother had talked to Aunt Ethel on the phone, her voice was tense when they spoke about Gwen's "greenstick" fracture. More wood, it seemed, but anything called "greenstick" couldn't be all that bad,

In the pew in front of me, Aunt Ethel settled back. The fox head on her shoulder pointed in my direction. The little eyes stared meanly, as if they were saying I was bad and could never again play with Gwen. Still, before the first song, I leaned close. Elizabeth sat further down, next to Papa, her feet in new flat-heeled pumps planted on the floor and she shot me a look that said, "Back away!" But I didn't. Those eyes dared me, and I lightly touched the fox's nose.

Aunt Ethel must have felt it. She glanced sideways, her fat neck wrinkling. "Gwen," she whispered, bending toward her daughter. "There's Ma-bie." She said it just like Gwen did. And she didn't say it like I was an outcast forever.

I raised one finger and wiggled it. Gwen looked pleased. I decided that next summer, if Aunt Ethel let me play with Gwen, when she opened her eyes during Blind Gator I would carefully explain the rules, even though she already knew them. She could put her fingers on my chin, as she'd learned to do, so she could feel the words. We'd figure out a way she could catch somebody without cheating.

Craning my neck, I saw a second fox head on Aunt Ethel's chest. Its teeth gripped another tail, and it looked like a complete head, not a split-down-the-middle one. This head had eyes that were looking the other way, but they seemed nicer, smoother, and darker than the first fox. I poked Elizabeth, who was flipping through the song book. "Two foxes," I whispered.

She stared at the neckpiece. Grinning, she nodded and held up two fingers. "I told you."

We all stood to sing. "We've reached the land of corn and wine and sweet de-liv-erance there is mine, . . . Oh, Beu-lah land, sweet Beu-lah land." Mother's high soprano and Aunt Ethel's full alto wrapped all around us. Even Gwen's monotone and Uncle Charlie's braying bass.

⌣

Months later, I had a dream about Gwen.

In the dream, she held out a little tree branch with ordinary oval leaves. "Maggie, what kind of plant is this?" she asked, speaking plainly. She didn't say 'Ma-bie.'

I laughed. In spite of her improved speech she looked the same, the Gwen I could boss around—broad-faced, blond hair growing too low on her forehead, forming in the middle a fuzzy little peak. Actually her hair was thick with all kinds of nice, wiggly waves—prettier hair than mine. "What kind of plant?" I wrinkled my nose and spoke carefully, as though reminding her that she had to read lips. "Silly, that's just part of a regular tree."

"A big tree?" she asked, her eyes trusting me.

A pin shaped like a dog sparkled on her white Peter Pan collar. I wished I had a cute shiny pin.

"Yeah. A huge one." Quick as a flash I yanked off her doggy pin.

"Stop!" She grabbed at her collar. "My pin!"

"Can't hear you," I hollered, and I ran and ran and ran.

Into Silence

Marlin Barton
USA, 2009

From where she sat at the end of the porch she noticed a tall man walking toward her house. The sight of a stranger in Riverfield always raised curiosity, and strangers did come through with some regularity these days, looking for work they knew they wouldn't find or for food they hoped they'd be offered. They were lost men, lost from family and friends, and the closest they could come to home was someone else's doorstep.

This man, though, wasn't walking alone, and to see her mother walking beside him struck her as a little odd. She'd never been one to offer help to those passing through. The faces that held hunger and want didn't seem to move her beyond a concern for herself and her daughter, two women alone.

As they neared the house, she saw how small her mother looked beside him. And yet it wasn't just his height that rendered her mother so small. There was some other dimension to him. Maybe it was his carriage or something in his demeanor that she'd see or feel more clearly when they were closer.

Soon they stood at the steps, and she saw the angular lines of his face and his sharp eyes examining, shifting from one point to another, taking in the house, and her. Then her mother was talking, out loud, not with her hands. "Janey, this is Mr. Clark. I met him up at Anderson's store. He's going to take a look at the room under the stairs."

Her mother spoke too slowly and carefully, so that Janey could he sure to read each word as it was said. She had told her mother many times that she didn't have to do this, but her mother almost always did. When they were in front of people Janey didn't have to hear how it must have sounded to be embarrassed.

Mr. Clark looked at her and nodded but didn't speak. She saw one thing clearly about him now. He wasn't one of those lost men that traveled through. His clothes were clean and fit him well, and his hat, which he removed to reveal a mixture of dark and graying hair cut close, looked almost new. The shirt he wore was neatly pressed, the sleeves rolled up just high enough to show muscular forearms. He'd come here for some purpose. She saw that. She wondered if her mother knew what.

He kept looking at Janey, intently, but not staring. His eyes were a dark brown, like creek water that ran through rich soil. She grew uncomfortable after a moment.

Maybe, because of the way her mother had spoken, he suspected she was deaf. It would be like her mother not to have mentioned it. Perhaps he was waiting to see if she'd speak so that he could confirm his suspicion. She simply left her silence open to interpretation.

"Will you show him the room?" her mother said.

She nodded again, stood, and then turned so that he would follow her. The front door opened into a small entrance hall. To the left, narrow stairs wound their way up to the second story, which they didn't use, and to the right was the door that opened into the living room and the rest of the house. Directly ahead and beneath a portion of the stairs was a single bedroom that didn't connect to any other room. Her mother had rented it off and on the last few years when money had become too tight. She hadn't wanted to do it. Janey knew she'd felt embarrassed at such a public announcement that money was short.

She opened the door and a close musty smell came to her. He walked past and went to the one window and raised it. She felt a sudden cross breeze that cleansed the air and ruffled her clothing. Then she smelled the sharp masculine scent of gasoline or motor oil and knew it must have come from his hands. He turned and looked at her, and she grew uncomfortable again under his gaze, though she didn't feel as if he were looking at her as a woman, the way a woman might want if it was the right man. She felt she'd gone past the age for that and into a settled middle age. It was a passing she'd mourned, then gotten over.

He lifted his hand slowly and held it in front of his chest. His palm was stained with what looked like motor oil. She couldn't have been more surprised at the sight of his fingers moving. "I like the room," he spelled out. "I'll take it."

That was all. No conversation, no explanation about when or why he'd learned to speak, or how he'd known for certain that she was deaf. But his large fingers had moved quickly and easily.

He walked past her again, and this time she followed him. He spoke briefly to her mother, then went down the porch steps and away, his movements purposeful, businesslike.

"He's going to get his car from where he left it at the store," her mother said.

She started to tell her mother how he had spoken, then decided not to, at least for now. It would be some small thing she could keep to herself, or maybe for herself.

Only two other people in Riverfield had ever known how to speak to her, an Episcopal minister who'd finally moved to a larger church in Selma, and Louise Anderson, whose son owned the store where the man was now headed. Louise had learned as an offer of friendship, and when she visited, the two of them sitting out on the porch, their hands flying with words and sometimes a little gossip, her mother would stand in the dark of the doorway, watching, and would finally emerge and tell Janey that she needed her for some chore, usually one that had either already been done or didn't need doing. She'd always been this way, continually calling Janey to her; but, after Janey's father had died, it had grown worse.

Janey signed a question for her mother now.

"He works for the W.P.A.," she said, again speaking too slowly. "Travels around the state taking pictures."

"Of what?"

"Buildings. Old houses and slave quarters, plantation homes. Says there are people like him doing this all over the South."

"Our house?" Janey said.

Her mother nodded and looked down. She knew why. The house wasn't what it had been. The roof needed replacing. The steps were warped. Her grandfather, Jason Teclaw, had built the house with slave labor, and made a large comfortable home, the one oddity in its design the columns across the front and side of the house. The branch stubs at the tops of the tree trunks they'd used had never been completely cut away, so each column looked as though it grew up out of the ground. There were knotholes, too, visible in the sides of each column; and, now that the paint on the house was completely gone, the columns looked even more like trees that had reached a certain height and had their growth stunted or stopped. Bricks around the cellar walls had come loose, leaving holes into the darkness that had once been, for a brief period, the saloon that had gotten her grandfather kicked out of the Methodist congregation. He'd then bought the Episcopal church that stood in the next county, had it dismantled and shipped across the Tennahpush River, and finally erected where it stood now, just down the road, from where Janey had heard her last sound.

Music was her entry into silence. She'd been only ten years old, sitting on the end of the porch above the steps, listening to the Episcopal choir rehearse "Our God to Whom We Turn" not fifty yards down the road. Their voices had carried easily through the open church doors and on the light breeze, and that breeze had felt like music itself against her skin. Then her head began to reel and spin, and she fell backward into sound and air and finally nothing as all her senses went dark.

She woke into darkness nights later, there in her room, in her bed. She'd called out from her confusion as any child would, and her mother was there instantly, always her mother. But something sounded wrong, or had not sounded, except inside her where illness and confusion grew. She hadn't heard herself, hadn't heard the call she'd made—Mama. And though her mother was already gripping her tightly, she'd called out again, but only into silence, which is where she lived now, had been living for so many years that she didn't feel uncomfortable inside its invisibility. Sometimes she thought it saved her, gave her a separate place to retreat into as far as she might need at any given moment—and there were moments.

After he had unloaded his car and carried in his suitcase and camera and other equipment, Mr. Clark asked her about meals. "He wants room and board," she told her mother, who was pleased at the chance to bring in a little more money.

He ate a supper of soup and cornbread with them that night, at the table in the middle of the kitchen. They'd had plenty of soup left from the day before, and Janey had made the cornbread herself, though it was never as good as her mother's, which her mother always found ways to point out.

"Nice to have good cooking," Mr. Clark said, but he wouldn't respond to the protests pointed at him by her mother about how poor the soup tasted. He appeared indifferent at the hints for another compliment. He mostly remained silent, nodding when he had to, and watching first her mother, then her, studying them, it seemed, from some far removed place, where quiet held value.

But the quiet soon became more than her mother could bear. "Are you married, Mr. Clark?" she said. She spoke quickly, abruptly. Janey wondered if her mother hadn't wanted her to read the question, but she'd seen the shape of the words. She'd also noticed earlier that he didn't wear a wedding ring, just as her mother must have noticed.

He nodded yes, but offered nothing else, not even his wife's name.

Then her mother must have asked another question, but her face had been turned away.

"She's staying with her folks now, in Calera, while I travel," he said.

"Children?" she spoke quickly again, but Janey had seen.

"No," he said and looked down, as though children had been something denied him.

Her mother's expression turned suddenly sad. "I don't know what I'd do without my daughter beside me," she said, and Janey looked then at Mr. Clark, and his eyes shifted back and forth between them. Finally he looked away, as though he'd taken some partial measure of them, or perhaps she'd only imagined it.

In the morning he loaded his camera and tripod into his car. He'd told her mother at breakfast, when she asked, that he would begin with some of the buildings clustered around the post office and the store. It was a short walk, but he couldn't have carried everything he needed, so loading the car was a necessity.

He had hardly acknowledged Janey at breakfast, but now, after closing the car door, he walked toward where she sat. She tensed at his approach, perhaps because of his own tense expression. He looked tired, irritated. Maybe her mother had said something to him, or asked one too many questions.

"You might be able to help me," he signed.

She'd half expected him to say he'd be leaving by the end of the day, and felt more relief at his asking her for help than she have anticipated. Afraid of him or not, she liked what his presence made her feel. "If I can," she spelled with her fingers.

"I'll need to know something about the buildings, the ones I take pictures of, for my notes. Maybe tonight you can tell me some history about them, who built them."

"I'd be glad to try. I can certainly tell you about this house."

She watched him back out of the drive, and felt glad to be needed, in some small way. When she stood to go inside, she caught her mother watching from the door.

"You didn't tell me," her mother said.

"What?"

"You know."

"That he knows how to speak to me?"

"Yes, that."

"No, I didn't tell you." she said, suddenly bold, thrusting her hand as she formed the letters and made her irritation clear.

Her mother turned and walked into the house. Janey felt her footsteps in the boards of the porch. The floor had always carried her mother's anger. She'd learned this first as a little girl when her mother and father argued. Their words might not have existed as sound for her, but anger always caused its own vibration.

She hadn't been exactly sure why they argued all those years ago, but sensed, the way a child will, that it was usually about her. And when she grew older she decided that it must have been about what she could and couldn't do, about what would be allowed and what wouldn't, and finally about what would be done with her, or for her, though she couldn't have put all of this into words as a child, words thought or spoken in any form.

After their arguments her mother would come to her, take her into the kitchen while she worked, keeping her close, the stove's heat encircling her, pressing against her, taking her breath almost with its expansion through the room. Then her father might come in later, pick her up or take her by the hand, and quickly they would go out of the house and up to the store or maybe to the depot to watch the afternoon train arrive and depart northward. He would sit with her, hold her hand, smoke his cigar, the smell and smoke surrounding them in a masculine world of men loading and unloading, of coal and iron rails and more smoke and dreams of departure, the two of them headed away.

And then they did head away, but not before more silences and anger that she felt kept her parents from listening to each other, each made deaf in his or her own way. But the day arrived when, her suitcases packed, she and her father boarded the train for Talladega. After three days, he left her there, settled, as best she could be at the age of twelve, in her dorm room and in a school for the deaf and blind.

She'd loved it there, had learned the alphabet on her fingers and how to sign, and how to read lips. She'd continued, finally, with her regular schooling too, and taken art and began to paint with oils. The other children there were like her, lived in her world of silence that was no longer quiet but filled with the voices of fingers and hands flying—thin fingers, long fingers, the beautiful hands of boys. It was wonderful to be able to give shape to words. She knew that her speaking voice was something she'd had less and less control over, and so seldom used it. Now words came through her fingers, the muscles there growing stronger and more sure, giving her a voice again, a voice that wanted to shout, or even sing.

Her mother wouldn't visit, but wrote desperate letters about home, about missing her and wanting her there, those cursive words on the page like pieces of string tying and knotting her emotions. During her trips home she taught her father to speak to her, but her mother could not, or would not, learn. "You read lips," she would say. "That's enough for me."

"What about me?" she'd sign, and, of course, no answer came, and wouldn't have even if she'd forced herself to ask it aloud, from out of her throat and off her tongue. But her mother did learn to read it . . .

Her mother wouldn't want her to go places with her father, would become silent and withdrawn when they returned. She didn't want Janey going to the store by herself, even for a quick errand. One day her mother found her playing in the woods behind their house, and when she wouldn't follow her mother home, her mother grabbed her by the arm and yanked her through the trees. She finally yanked back and shouted at her, not in words but in her old voice that expressed all she felt in one great vibration. Her mother spoke with a hand then. She slapped her hard across her face.

When she left for school a week later, her mother wouldn't go with them to the depot but held her at the door. She felt her mother shaking and knew her mother loved her, but love was sometimes like silence, beautiful but hard to bear. At the train station her father told her, "She can't help herself. I don't why. I never have."

Late that morning, from her place on the porch, she watched Mr. Clark work around the buildings in town. He moved his camera from one position to another, then disappeared beneath the black cloth before moving again. At intervals he'd go inside the store or speak to people passing. She'd thought he would come home for lunch, but he must have eaten at the store, perhaps asking questions for his notes. Maybe he wouldn't need her after all.

That afternoon she saw him load his car and expected him to soon pull into their drive, but watched with surprise, and disappointment, as he drove directly past, picking up speed and raising dust behind him. She spotted Uncle Silas, the old black man who'd worked for her father's side of the family, in the back seat and knew then where they were headed, several miles away to the old home of her father's people, her cousins, some of them several times removed. The house stood three stories with a cupola and had white columns and a grand porch, with slave quarters behind. He'd want pictures of all that, of course. Her mother wouldn't have wanted her to go up there with them. There was a distance between her mother and her father's people. It had always been there.

Her mother was bathing when he finally drove in. She'd been put out that he hadn't come at the time she'd told him supper would be ready. "Tardiness is rude," she had said.

Janey waited, gave him time to put his things away, then went and tapped on his door, and as her knuckles hit against the wood, she felt that the door was closed on some secret, something private and obscure that she shouldn't approach.

The door opened suddenly, and he stood there with a small towel in one hand. She'd filled the washbasin on his dresser with fresh water earlier. He looked tired, but not angry or irritated. "Supper's ready for you," she signed.

He nodded and followed her.

Once they reached the kitchen she fixed his plate and set it before him. He looked at her and motioned to the chair across the table. She hadn't known if she should sit with him or not and felt relief at his invitation.

He only ate at first and didn't try to speak, his hands being occupied. She sat and waited, watched him bent over his plate. Each movement he made was so deliberate and sure. His masculine demeanor seemed to make the whole house feel different, as if the house had a slightly altered design. He stopped eating finally and put his knife and fork down.

"People at the store told me what I needed for my notes. Others too. Everyone was curious and wanted to talk. It's like that everywhere."

She was certain that he saw her disappointment, no matter how hard she tried to hide it. He apologized then for being late, and it was as though he felt a need to say something considerate to assuage her feelings. He went on and told her, too, after taking a few bites, about driving out to the antebellum home of her father's side of the family, being polite enough not to mention the disrepair it was in. "Someone in town told me about the house," he was saying, and she saw that he'd begun to speak aloud as he signed—his lips were forming words—and she felt confused, couldn't understand why he would do this. She couldn't read his lips and watch him sign at the same time. He must have known that. He paused and studied her, watched her expression more closely. "I could have asked you to ride out there with me, couldn't I? You might have wanted to go. You might have enjoyed that. Some time away from here." He motioned around the room.

She looked toward the kitchen door, not aware at first why she turned that way. Perhaps she'd simply turned away from him out of embarrassment, or perhaps she understood, on some unconscious level, what she hadn't a moment before. Her mother was standing there. She'd been listening to him. He had wanted her to hear.

When she turned back to him she read his lips. "Why don't you go with me tomorrow?"

She felt the quick vibration of her mother's approach but wouldn't turn to face her. "Yes, ma'am," he was saying, looking past Janey. "I know, but she could help me. Be a guide. I could even pay her a little. Why don't we ask her?"

Janey saw his hard gaze still focused on her mother, maybe even gathered strength from it, and she stood then, turned to her mother, and saw her mother's anger and fear, the way she'd always seen them after her father had explained her mother as best he could. She drew in her breath and forced the two breath-filled words out in a hoarse whisper that might have sounded, for all she knew, like a sick child or someone dying. "I'll go," she said.

Her mother stared at her in surprise, and Janey wasn't sure if her mother was more shocked that she had used what was left of her voice, or at what she'd said. Mr. Clark showed no reaction at all but took another bite of food and drank from his glass.

"You can't. You just can't." her mother said. "I need you to help me with some things around the house tomorrow."

"No," she signed, then shook her head. "You don't."

"You know good and well I do. There's cleaning to be done."

"It will wait," she said and walked out before her mother could say more.

She went to her room and imagined the two of them at the table still, imagined what they might be saying, and her father came to mind suddenly. It was as if Mr. Clark had become, for the moment, the man her father had been, the two of them in there now acting out the old ritual of her parents, except this time she had spoken, and they both had heard her wishes.

She could still hear her father's voice, the memory of it clear in a way that her mother's wasn't. It had been deep, but not extraordinarily so, and gentle, though when he scolded her there was a sharpness to it that crushed her and made her want forgiveness, which always came quickly, and he would hold her and wipe her tears and smile.

It was the telegram that took him away from her, the one her mother sent and that she received at school. "Come home," it said. "Your father has died of fever." She was fifteen, and even then after the first shock, she realized that the demand to come home had come first, as if coming home were more important than the death of her father. So she went, and saw her father buried, suffered the quiet of the funeral that she could not hear but only feel. A few days later she walked to the grave alone and left her handprints in the mound of dirt over his casket and body.

She stayed then, not quite strong enough without him to get back on the train, though she planned to and spoke as if she would, her mother ignoring her.

Two months later the school shipped her belongings home. The first she knew of it was when they were delivered from the depot in the back of a wagon. She saw the boxes and felt somehow that her life had been returned to her mother. Each box bore her mother's name.

Janey didn't see her the next morning, and she didn't look in her room to check on her, which is what she knew her mother wanted. Instead she bathed and dressed early, then fixed breakfast and packed a lunch for herself and Mr. Clark, putting everything away afterward, leaving no plate of food covered with a cloth.

She planned to take him up the road to Oakhill, show him the old house at the top of the hill, and introduce him to the people there. If she'd given him directions he could have found it on his own, but that didn't matter. He'd asked her to go with him, and he'd known what he'd really been asking. She'd entered into the conspiracy with him and needed to see it through. Not to would have been a kind of failure.

After he loaded the car she climbed into the passenger seat. When he stopped and filled up with gas at the store she saw people looking at her in the car and enjoyed their curiosity. He drove too fast, and she felt an exhilaration at their increasing speed and at the plume of dust they raised that blocked her view of everything behind them. Neither tried to speak, and she had the feeling that even if his hands hadn't been busy, he would have remained quiet. The look on his face in profile was hard set, concentrated on something beyond driving it seemed.

The road rose toward Oakhill, and at the top before they turned into the long drive that led to the house she saw the open pastures and fields spread out before her like a patchwork quilt and suddenly felt like a child wanting to run across them, as if they lay there waiting for her. A silly notion, but it made her smile.

The house stood beyond the oak grove and came into full view after they rounded a final curve. It was two-story with small white columns. No mansion, but clearly built by a land-owning family.

They got out of the car and walked up the steps to the porch. Janey knocked on the screen door and waited for Mrs. Spence to come, but instead an older black woman Janey knew as Aunt Minnie appeared in the hall and opened the door. She nodded at Janey and said, "How you, Miss Janey?" Then looked at the strange man beside her. "I bet you that picture man. I done heard about you."

Mr. Clark spoke, but Janey didn't catch any of his words.

"The mister and missus, they done gone into town, up to Valhia. Is you come to take pictures?"

Janey watched him speak this time. He asked if he could at least take pictures of the outside of the house since the owners weren't home.

She nodded. "They won't mind that, I don't reckon. What about my house, out back? You gon' take a picture of it? You can go inside. It's mine. Least I calls it mine." She smiled. "I'd like a picture took of it."

"I was going to ask you if I could," he said. "Inside too."

Janey wondered if he was speaking the truth or humoring her.

"Come on around," the woman said. "You can do the big house later."

They followed. Clark carried only a small camera around his neck. The large camera with the tripod and black cloth he left in the car for now.

Several outbuildings stood directly behind the house. One of them, Janey imagined, had been a kitchen back when they were built separately so heat wouldn't overtake the house in summer and, in case of fire, wouldn't burn down the entire home. Farther on stood a small unpainted shack, one window to the right of the door. It had already occurred to her that she had never been in a black person's house, or in the house of someone so poor. She knew her mother hadn't either, just as her mother had never let those lost men traveling through come to the back door and eat a meal. Janey realized that if her mother had been with them that she would never have set foot inside where they were headed, would be appalled at the idea, and wouldn't let Janey inside, not without protest and argument.

"My grandmother was born a slave in this house," the woman said now. "We always worked for the Spences. Far back as I know of."

Mr. Clark stopped and took several pictures of the front of the house. "You don't mind if we go on in?" he said when he finished.

"I keeps my house clean always. Not ashamed of anything I got either."

They walked onto the small porch and boards gave under their feet. Aunt Minnie went in first, then Mr. Clark. Janey held hack a moment, imagined again what her mother would say if she knew, then stepped through the doorway into the cramped slave house and felt, in some place within herself, as if she'd walked into one of those open fields she had seen from the car, was straying like some child running just ahead of her mother.

The house was clean, neat, the bed made with a colorful quilt across it. Newspaper pages that had not yet yellowed covered the walls, cut and pasted as carefully as any new store-bought wallpaper. A calendar from Anderson's store with May 23rd circled hung by the door. There was a back window, and she noticed how clean the panes were, how the light broke through them and opened the room, made it somehow larger, as if it brought the whole of outdoors inside. The small black stove was wiped down, and the few pots and pans hung in order on the wall behind it. Aunt Minnie had been right. There was nothing here to be ashamed of, nothing to look down upon. Janey wished this were a place she could stay and felt a sense of envy. Then she decided no—she felt a kind of admiration for Minnie.

Mr. Clark took pictures, including one of Minnie in a chair beside the bed. She wasn't smiling but seemed at ease with herself and everything around her.

Once they were back outside, Mr. Clark got his large camera and set it up for pictures of the main house. He moved every few minutes, capturing the house at different angles. When he finished he told Minnie that he would come again and see about taking some pictures inside, if the people didn't mind.

"Come on. They be glad to see you," she said. Then she asked if she might have a copy of the picture he'd taken of her.

"I'll see to it," he said. "It'll be a while, but I'll send it."

In the car Janey asked if he'd ever taken pictures inside a house like Minnie's.

"No," he said, and didn't elaborate. "I need those people home when I go back," he added after a moment.

His whole demeanor had changed, and Janey felt that she'd been chastised, that it was somehow her fault that the Spences hadn't been home.

A question came to her, one that she had to ask, though she feared the answer. "Do people often ask for copies of the photographs you take?"

"All the time," he signed, then put the car into gear.

"Do you send them?"

He looked away, kept his eyes on the narrow drive, and both hands on the wheel.

They drove to several churches spread around the countryside, their conversation minimal. He took pictures both inside and out, working quickly and methodically, clearly knowing exactly what he wanted as soon as he saw each structure. They ate a late lunch that she had packed at a table on the grounds of a small A.M.E. church, and she didn't try to speak. He seemed even further removed, already traveling on his own. She wondered where he was in his mind, wondered if she had done something to make him more distant.

Late that afternoon he told her he wanted to head back, but had one more stop in mind, the Episcopal church near her house. When they parked in front of it she began to tell him how the church had been brought across the river and why. "Later," he signed. "Tell me later." Then he got out of the car.

She stood well away from him while he worked, wandered into the graveyard behind the church, and finally to her father's grave. The grass grew thick and neat over it, but she recalled the mound of bare dirt, the way it had felt against her hands when she placed them there, the way their prints looked so perfectly made, but so empty.

He appeared then, setting up his camera, and waited for her to move, without asking, so he could take a picture of the back of the church with the gravestones in the foreground.

She obliged him, went around the building and sat on the steps at the double side doors. In a little while he walked around from the front and approached her without his camera. He was clearly ready to go. She didn't move but looked up at him, then began to speak. He didn't turn away now but watched, though impatiently, it seemed. She didn't care.

"The last sound I ever heard came from here, through these open doors. Choir voices, all joined together. They were beautiful. A final gift to me."

She placed her hands in her lap and remained still, not really looking to see if he reacted to what she'd said. He turned slowly and walked away, but she didn't follow. She could easily walk home by herself, decided she would like to do just that, but not quite yet. She wanted to be alone.

He came back though carrying the small camera around his neck. She looked up at him but kept still. He raised the camera slowly, peered through it, then lowered it after a moment and stepped toward her. He reached out with his right hand and touched her just under her chin. The warmth of his fingers made a dampness on her skin. He gently turned her face at a more downward angle, then backed away and adjusted the camera. She watched the shutter close and open and imagined the sound it made, imagined what part of her the camera might capture.

Her mother had been up while they were gone. Janey saw a book left open on the sofa, and there was a single dish left in the kitchen sink. She wondered if her mother had heard them pull into the drive and gone quickly to her room, not expecting them back quite so early. She was probably in bed, pretending to be asleep. Of course it was possible that she was sick. She did tire more easily these last few years. Still Janey wouldn't go to her; and, if she didn't, she knew that her mother would finally show herself.

She did, before good dark came. Janey was sitting in a chair on the porch, by herself, considering what she might do about supper. Her mother walked out of her bedroom door, the one that opened directly onto the porch and that she seldom used. She sat down in the chair next to Janey.

"Have you not been feeling well today?" Janey knew what the answer would be. Her mother shook her head, then looked away for a moment.

"Do you feel like you can eat something?"

"Whatever you can fix," she said, then turned away again. It was something she did often, the turning away, a way of ignoring Janey, of not listening, because it took sight for her to be listened to. Sometimes it amused Janey, her mother's turning, but not now. She had been ignored enough today. She thought about telling her mother where they'd gone, about going inside Aunt Minnie's house and taking pictures—just to see her reaction, for spite, she guessed. But she stayed quiet. Upsetting her mother would have been too easy, and maybe pointless.

She watched the evening come on, remembered the glissando of locusts at this time of year from when she was a little girl, and wondered if they were out there now, appearing from their yearslong silence and making their one sound.

Her mother looked toward the front door and Janey saw Mr. Clark had walked out of his room. He'd changed into a fresh shirt and was rolling the sleeves up. He greeted her mother, then stood before them as if he had something important to say. This time Janey turned, perhaps afraid of what he might announce. He wouldn't be staying with them for months, or even weeks. How many more days would it be?

When she looked back at them she saw the words *colored churches* form on Mr. Clark's lips. Her mother's eyes widened. "You went inside them?"

"A few," he said, studying her, measuring her reaction. He looked at Janey then, as though he were waiting on her to speak and when she didn't he continued, his eyes lingering on her, perhaps taking some measure of her this time. "We went in one of the shacks up at Oakhill. Aunt Minnie's house. An old slave quarters."

Her mother looked down at her feet, closed her eyes, and slowly shook her head, as if she'd received news that someone was ill. "You shouldn't be going into colored people's houses, Janey," she said. "At least the Spences weren't home to see you."

Mr. Clark seemed to be waiting on Janey again, and something inside her didn't want to disappoint him.

"Why not?" she said. "Why not go into a colored person's house?"

"You know why. Because it doesn't look good." She stood, seemed to have regained her strength, and walked back into her bedroom, clearly unwilling to respond to any more such absurd questions.

Mr. Clark nodded at Janey, which she understood as a kind of approval, but something about it bothered her, made her feel presided over, and the way he stood there, above her, made her uncomfortable, as she had felt with him at the outset. Before she realized what he was doing, he walked to the end of the porch, down the steps, and kept going, past his parked car – headed to the store, she imagined. She realized she would be eating alone that night.

Her mother remained secluded in the morning, which Janey had expected. What she hadn't been sure of was whether or not Mr. Clark wanted her to go along with him again, but at breakfast he made clear that he did. She told him about some of the larger houses down toward the Tennahpush River that he might want to look at. He seemed more open to listening to her today, his mood changed from the day before.

She made a lunch for them while he loaded his car. When she walked out the front door and pulled it to behind her, she suddenly expected to see her mother's door open, and it did. Her mother stood there in her bedclothes and without a robe, motioning to Janey, the door angled between herself and Mr. Clark at his car.

"What, Mother?" she signed.

"I don't feel well."

"I know that."

"I mean I'm worse today."

Janey took a few steps toward her and then looked past the oddly made columns surrounding the porch. Mr. Clark stood against the front of his car, his arms folded, watching her, waiting.

"My chest hurts," her mother said, "and my breath doesn't come easy. You know I don't have a normal heartbeat."

Janey knew about the irregular heart, and had heard all these complaints before, too many times to take them seriously.

"Come here," her mother said, and held out a piece of paper. "Please, I've got to get back in bed."

Janey walked to her and took the paper. It was a note to Dr. Hannah asking him to come see her.

"There's nothing wrong with you," she said. "We both know that."

"You can't go with that man today. I need you here," she said aloud. "I need you to bring the doctor here."

For once she wasn't speaking slowly.

Janey looked and saw Mr. Clark at the bottom of the steps now, waiting, impatient, wanting what he wanted from her. Her mother pulled the door closer to her but didn't retreat back into the room, though she seemed to sense Mr. Clark's nearness.

She wanted to retreat, to surrender into the most silent of places within herself, where her own thoughts couldn't find voice.

"All right," she said finally. "I'll stay and get him just to prove to you there's nothing wrong, and that's the only reason. I'll go with him tomorrow."

Her mother nodded, clearly relieved, and slowly shut the door.

Janey walked down to Mr. Clark. He hadn't moved. His expression said nothing.

"I can't go today," she signed. "I've got to get the doctor. Tomorrow I'll go."

"There's nothing wrong with her." He signed the words.

"I know."

"Then get in the car. Now."

"I can't."

He focused his eyes on her the way he might when he looked through a camera, capturing her, exposing her weakness for her to see. His face showed neither pity nor disgust. Whatever was there she couldn't read the way she could spoken words, and he didn't give her any further opportunity. He turned, climbed inside his car, and drove away, leaving her standing alone in the middle of the drive. She pulled her mother's note from her pocket, held it in her hand, and felt for a moment as if it were meant for her, like one of her mother's letters that came for her when she'd been at school.

Doctor Hannah walked out of her mother's room, his black bag in his hand. He looked tired already, even at mid-morning. He began to speak carefully, and quietly, she knew, so that her mother couldn't overhear. "There's nothing wrong, other than maybe nerves."

"Her heart?" Janey wrote on a small notepad.

"She's had an arrhythmia since I first came here and saw her as a patient, but there's been no deterioration. I'm certain of that. My only mistake was telling her about it."

"So she's fine?"

He nodded. "I gave her a shot, a mild sedative, to calm her nerves. That's all."

"Thank you," she wrote.

He smiled slightly and touched her shoulder for a moment, the way her father might have. She imagined that going into people's homes and seeing to the ill had taught him a lot about what people needed, both the sick and the well.

She checked on her mother after lunch and found her sitting up in bed.

"I'm feeling better now. I knew seeing Dr. Hannah would help."

Janey didn't respond, didn't move past the door's threshold.

"I'm going to bathe and dress," her mother said. "Could you fix me something to eat? I'll take it in my room so I won't tire myself out."

She slowly signed yes, glad for the moment that she no longer used speech, because she knew how angry her tone would have sounded. But what would that have mattered? Except for the fact that she was most angry at herself. For staying. She should have been in the car with Mr. Clark. He wouldn't be here much longer, and after he was gone nothing would be changed. Perhaps that was what made her angriest. His presence had shown her something that she'd kept her eyes closed to—a willful blindness on her part, another killing of the senses.

She finally carried a tray to her mother and saw that she'd dressed and put on makeup.

"This is so nice. Thank you," her mother said slowly.

Janey only nodded.

She wasn't aware that Mr. Clark had returned until she looked out a front window and happened to see his camera set up in the yard. She didn't see him, though, and then there he was, back at the camera, about to pull the dark cloth over his head. She tried to picture what he saw—the rusted roof, the unpainted boards, the strange columns with branches cut short, all of it upside down, and she felt as though every-thing inside herself had fallen out of place, all of it turned by his hand.

He moved the camera from one place to another, and she watched from various windows, careful to stand far enough away so that her image wasn't captured behind a pane.

When she saw him photographing the back of the house she walked onto the porch and waited for him to come back around front. She wondered if he would take pictures inside too. Sometimes he did, sometimes not.

It surprised her when she saw him at his car in the drive, bent over beside it, but there he was, loading his equipment again. He was going back out. She could go with him now that she had seen to her mother. Perhaps that was why he'd come, not just to take the pictures but to give her another opportunity. She stood when he finished loading, ready to leave without a word to her mother, and he turned and saw her. She expected him to motion to her, or to speak with his hands, but after the briefest glance her way he opened the driver's side door and climbed in, his face shadowed by the brim of his hat, and then all of him disappeared behind the glare of the sun on the windshield.

His coming in the middle of the afternoon must have been only one more stop for him, one more house to photograph and move away from. But he had to have come when he did for a reason. It would have made so much more sense for him to take pictures of her house as his last stop of the day. Maybe he had been taunting her, or speaking his anger at her as loudly as he knew how—treating her as no more important than a stranger at yet another stop.

He backed all the way to the road, and though there were no cars coming from either direction, he sat idling. Moments passed. She was puzzled, and couldn't see if he was looking her way or not. She remained still, waiting, for what she didn't know. Maybe he was waiting too, giving her one more chance to come down the steps on her own. Then he was gone.

It was well past dark, late, in fact, after eleven o'clock, when he returned. She felt his steps through the house, felt his door closing. She looked out her front window to see if he would make the trips to unload his car, which was something he never failed to do, but he didn't come back out. Maybe he'd driven all the way to town, to Demandile, for a meal at the hotel, and then found a drink somewhere. Or maybe he'd found a drink here and had never gone into town at all or bothered with supper.

She didn't sleep. At eleven-thirty she sat up in bed and pulled on her robe. She stood then, telling herself she was going into the kitchen, but when she found it empty, as she knew she would, she walked slowly and softly to the front door, opened it, and stepped into the house's entryway. The distance he had shown her the last two days drew her to his door; and, emboldened now in the way she should have been earlier in the day, she knocked twice.

He opened the door after a moment. A lamp was burning, and she saw he was still dressed in shirt and pants. She also smelled liquor, strongly, but he appeared in control of himself, though he looked disheveled, his shirttail out, his sleeves rolled up loosely, not into his usual neat cuffs, though revealing again his strong forearms. He motioned for her to sit in the one chair, and he sat on a chest at the foot of the bed. He didn't seem surprised to see her, which she found unsettling.

She started to tell him that she'd wanted to leave with him after he'd taken pictures of her house, but she decided he already knew that. There was no need to say it.

"If you'd just waited another minute," she signed, knowing he'd understand.

Except for a barely perceptible nod, if only to let her know that he was reading her, he didn't respond.

His silence was as frustrating as before. She needed him to talk. He already knew what she had to say. Did he have anything at all to say to her?

He looked at her through squinted, shadowed eyes. "I knew about you before I came," he signed.

"How?" she said. "What did you know?"

"That a deaf woman and her mother lived here, that they sometimes rented a room. In one town I ask about the next, or what might be the next. So I heard that, and came."

"Why?" she asked, uncertain if he would say more.

He remained still at first, his hands at rest. Then he looked at her, studied her. "I was told there were places here I ought to take pictures of. This place too, the columns with the limbs on them. I wanted to see that, to make a record of it."

She waited again, for what he hadn't said yet. She saw that she would have to push him. "The deaf woman you heard about—I'm part of why you came."

He nodded, but that was all.

"Why?"

"My mother," he said, as though she could follow.

The lamp grew dimmer, and the shift in light seemed to carry him further away from her.

"My mother lost her hearing when I was very young. She was still young too, but I didn't know how young, not then. I learned sign as she learned." He paused, then his hands seemed to find the words in the air. "My father didn't."

"What?"

"Didn't learn. Didn't treat her well. He never had."

She became bold again, understanding through some instinct she didn't know she had, then spelling it out. "He hit her."

He nodded again, slowly, even further away from her now, carried away by memory, and perhaps more alcohol than she'd realized.

"She suffered. It was terrible. There were awful beatings, and more and more of them."

She saw the anger in him still, in his face and clenched fists. It had been there all along, when he'd first walked to the porch with her mother, but it had taken this long to recognize it, and words from him to understand it.

"What happened?" She asked the question with a building fear, not of him but of what the answer might be.

"She took me. We left in the night."

She sighed with relief, but another question came to her. "She's dead now?" She felt she knew the answer.

"Yes." His hands stopped a moment, hung in the air. "It didn't take him long. He found her."

She took the words from his hands, felt the weight of them within her. "And you?" she managed to ask.

He shrugged his shoulders. He was through – or almost.

"Your wife?" she said then, trying to imagine the life he might have made for himself, already fearing the answer.

"There's no wife. There never has been."

She simply nodded.

"My mother tried. She did what she could, for me and for herself. I owe her a debt for that, and have to find someone to pay."

Even in the dim room she saw the brightness in his eyes, their focus directly on her, and she became afraid, of him this time, and of what she caught glimpses of behind the reflection of light in his eyes. She felt she saw ghosts within him, his mother's and his own ghost, small and lost.

She awoke knowing that he was gone. When she rose and checked his room, she found the door open, the bed made, and none of his belongings. He'd left the window open too for some reason. She felt the cross breeze.

Within an hour she'd dressed and tried to occupy herself with cleaning, but her work was careless, and she knew it. She finally put the dusting cloth away and gave in to a sense of mourning for something lost.

Her mother hadn't gotten up by noon. Perhaps this was her way of making Janey check on her. It wouldn't work, not this time. But after an hour passed, she entered the room and saw her mother was awake but still in bed and wouldn't rise from her pillow. Janey walked closer and started to sign, but she saw the stare then and knew, saw the lack of any movement, not even the gentle lifting and falling of the sheet across her body.

She felt a greater loss to mourn now, and it fell upon her heavily, in a way she might not have expected. She sat at the foot of the bed, looked again at her mother's stare, and wondered if she had known death was coming. Had it come from inside her, out of the irregular beat of her heart, or had she seen it walk into the room and bend over her, its hands reaching for the pillow on which she now lay? She felt she knew that answer, but knew she would not speak it, would say only that her mother had been up after Mr. Clark left, if anyone wanted to ask. If no one did, her silence would speak for her, as it always had.

The Limner

Julian Barnes
England, 2009

Mr. Tuttle had been argumentative from the beginning: about the fee—twelve dollars—the size of the canvas, and the prospect to be shown through the window. Fortunately, there had been swift accord about the pose and the costume. Over these, Wadsworth was happy to oblige the customs collector; happy also to give him the appearance, as far as it was within his skill, of a gentleman. That was, after all, his business. He was a limner but also an artisan, and paid at an artisan's rate to produce what suited the client. In thirty years, few would remember what the collector of customs had looked like; the only relic of his physical presence after he had met his Maker would be this portrait. And, in Wadsworth's experience, clients held it more important to be pictured as sober, God-fearing men and women than they did to be a true likeness. This was not a matter that perturbed him.

From the edge of his eye, Wadsworth became aware that his client had spoken, but he did not divert his gaze from the tip of his brush. Instead he pointed to the bound notebook in which so many sitters had written comments, expressed their praise and blame, wisdom and fatuity. He might as well have opened the book at any page and asked his client to select the appropriate remark left by a predecessor five or ten years before. The opinions of this customs collector so far had been as predictable as his waistcoat buttons, if less interesting. Fortunately, Wadsworth was paid to represent waistcoats, not opinions. Of course, it was more complicated than that: to represent the waistcoat, and the wig, and the breeches, *was* to represent an opinion—indeed, a whole corpus of them. The waistcoat and breeches showed the body beneath, as the wig and hat showed the brain beneath—though, in some cases, it was a pictorial exaggeration to suggest that any brains lay beneath.

He would be happy to leave this town, to pack his brushes and canvases, his pigments and palette, into the small cart, to saddle his mare, and then take the forest trails that, in three days, would lead him home. There he would rest, and reflect, and perhaps decide to live differently, without this constant travail of the itinerant. A peddler's life; also a supplicant's. As always, he had come to this town, taken lodgings by the night, and placed an advertisement in the newspaper, indicating his competence, his prices, and his availability. "If no application is made within six days," the advertisement ended, "Mr. Wadsworth will quit the town."

He had already painted the small daughter of the drygoods salesman, and Deacon Zebediah Harries, who had given him Christian hospitality in his house, and recommended him to the collector of customs.

Mr. Tuttle had not offered lodging, but the limner willingly slept in the stable with his mare for company, and ate in the kitchen. And then there had been that incident on the third evening, against which he had failed—or felt unable—to protest. It had made him sleep uneasily. It had wounded him, too, if the truth were known. He ought to have written the collector down for an oaf and a bully—he had painted enough in his years—and forgotten the matter. Perhaps he should indeed consider his retirement, let his mare grow fat, and live from what crops he could grow and what farm stock he could raise. He could always paint windows and doors for a trade, instead of people; he would not judge this an indignity.

Late on the first morning, Wadsworth had been obliged to introduce the collector of customs to the notebook. The fellow, like many another, had imagined that merely opening his mouth wider might be enough to effect communication. Wadsworth had watched the pen travel across the page, and then the fore-finger tap impatiently. "If God is merciful," the man had written, "perhaps in Heaven you will hear." In reply, he had half smiled, and given a brief nod, from which surprise and gratitude might be inferred. He had read the thought many times before. Often it was a true expression of Christian feeling and sympathetic hope; occasionally, it represented, as now, a scarcely concealed dismay that the world contained those with such frustrating defects. Mr. Tuttle was among the masters who preferred their servants to be mute, deaf, and blind—except when his convenience required the matter otherwise. Of course, masters and servants had become citizens and hired help once the juster republic had declared itself. But masters and servants did not die out; nor did the essential inclinations of man.

Wadsworth did not think that he was judging the collector in an un-Christian fashion. His opinion had been forged on first contact, and confirmed on that third evening. The incident had been the crueller in that it had involved a child, a garden boy who had scarcely entered the years of understanding. The limner always felt tenderly toward children: for themselves, for the grateful fact that they overlooked his defect, and also because he had no issue himself. He had never known the company of a wife. Perhaps he might yet do so, though he would have to insure that she was beyond childbearing years. He could not inflict his defect on others. Some had tried explaining that his fears were unfounded, since the affliction had arrived not at birth but after an attack of the spotted fever when he was a boy of five. Further, they pressed, had he not made his way in the world, and might not a son of his, howsoever constructed, do likewise? Perhaps that would be the case, but what of a daughter? The notion of a girl living as an outcast was too much for him. True, she might stay at home, and there would be a shared sympathy between them. But what would happen to such a child after his death?

No, he would go home and paint his mare. This had always been his intention, and perhaps now he would execute it. She had been his companion for twelve years, understood him easily, and took no heed of the noises that issued from his mouth when they were alone in the forest. His plan had been this: to paint her, on the same size of canvas used for Mr. Tuttle, though turned on its horizontal axis, and, afterward, to cast a blanket over the picture and uncover it only on the mare's death. It was presumptuous to compare the daily reality of God's living creation with a human simulacrum formed by an inadequate hand—even if this was the very purpose for which his clients employed him.

He did not expect it would be easy to paint the mare. She would lack the patience, and the vanity, to stand immobile for him, one hoof proudly advanced. But, then, neither would his mare have the vanity to come around and examine the canvas even as he worked on it. The collector of customs was now doing so, leaning over his shoulder, peering and pointing. There was something he did not approve. Wadsworth glanced upward, from the immobile face to the mobile one. Even though he had a distant memory of speaking and hearing, he had never learned the facility of reading words upon the tongue. Wadsworth raised the narrowest of his brushes from the waistcoat button's boss and transferred his eye to the notebook as the collector dipped his pen. "More dignity," the man wrote, and then underlined the words.

Wadsworth felt that he had already given Mr. Tuttle dignity enough. He had increased his height, reduced his belly, ignored the hairy moles on the fellow's neck, and generally attempted to represent surliness as diligence, irascibility as moral principle. And now he wanted more of it! This was an un-Christian demand, and it would be an un-Christian act on Wadsworth's part to accede to it. It would do the man no service in God's eyes if the limner allowed him to appear puffed up with all the dignity he demanded.

⌒

He had painted infants, children, men, and women, and even corpses. Three times he had urged his mare to a deathbed where he was asked to perform resuscitation—to represent as living someone he had just met as dead. If he could do that, surely he should be able to render the quickness of his mare as she shook her tail against the flies, or impatiently raised her neck while he prepared the little painting cart, or pricked her ears as he made noises to the forest.

At one time he had tried to make his meaning plain to his fellow-mortals by gesture and by sound. It was true that a few simple actions could be easily imitated: he could indicate, for example, how a client might wish to stand. But other gestures often resulted in humiliating games of guessing, while the sounds he was able to utter failed to establish either his requirements or his shared nature as a human being—part of the Almighty's work, if differently made. Women judged the noises he made embarrassing, children found them a source of amusement, men a proof of imbecility. He had tried to advance in this way, but had not succeeded, and so he had retreated into the muteness they expected, and perhaps preferred. It was at this point that he had purchased his calfskin logbook, in which all human statement and opinion recurred. *Do you think, sir, there will be painting in Heaven? Do you think, sir, there will be hearing in Heaven?*

But his understanding of men, such as it had developed, came less from what they wrote down, more from his mute observation. Men—and women, too—imagined that they could alter their voice and meaning without its showing in their face. In this they were much deceived. His own face, as he observed the human carnival, was as inexpressive as his tongue, but his eye told him more than they could guess. Formerly, he had carried, inside his logbook, a set of handwritten cards, bearing useful responses, necessary suggestions, and civil corrections to what was being proposed. He even had one special card, for when he was being condescended to by his interlocutor beyond what he found proper. It read, "Sir, the understanding does not cease to function when the portals of the mind are blocked." This was sometimes accepted as a just rebuke, sometimes held to be an impertinence from a mere artisan who slept in the stable. Wadsworth had abandoned its use, not because of either response but because it admitted too much knowledge. Those in the world of tongue held the advantage: they were his paymasters, they exercised authority, they entered society, they exchanged thoughts and opinions naturally. Though, for all this, Wadsworth did not see that speaking was in itself a promoter of virtue. His own advantages were only two: that he could represent on canvas those who spoke, and could silently perceive their meaning. It would have been foolish to give away this second advantage.

The business with the piano, for instance. Wadsworth had first inquired, by pointing to his fee scale, if the collector of customs wished for a portrait of the entire family, matching portraits of himself and his wife, or a joint portrait, with perhaps miniatures of the children. Mr. Tuttle, without looking at his wife, had pointed to his own breast and written on the fee sheet, "Myself alone." Then he had glanced at his wife, put one hand to his chin, and added, "Beside the piano." Wadsworth had noticed the handsome, claw-footed rosewood instrument, and asked with a gesture if he might go across to it. Whereupon he had demonstrated several poses: from sitting informally beside the open keyboard with a favorite song on display to standing more formally beside the instrument. Tuttle had taken Wadsworth's place, arranged himself, advanced one foot, and then, after consideration, closed the piano lid. Wadsworth deduced from this that only Mrs. Tuttle played the piano; further, that Tuttle's desire to include it was an indirect way of including her in the portrait. Indirect, and also less expensive.

The limner had shown the customs collector some miniatures of children, hoping to change his mind, but Tuttle merely shook his head. Wadsworth was disappointed, partly for reasons of money but more because his delight in painting children had increased as that in painting their progenitors had declined. Children were more mobile than adults, more deliquescent of shape, it was true. But they also looked him in the eye, and when you were deaf you heard with your eyes. Children held his gaze, and he thereby perceived their nature. Adults often looked away, whether from modesty or a desire for concealment, while some, like the collector, held his gaze challengingly, with a false honesty, as if to say, Yes, of course my eyes are concealing things, but you lack the discernment to realize it. Such clients judged Wadsworth's affinity with children proof that he was as deficient in understanding as the children were. Whereas Wadsworth believed children's affinity with him proof that they saw as clearly as he did.

When he had first taken up his trade, he had carried his brushes and pigments on his back, and walked the forest trails like a peddler. He found himself on his own, reliant upon recommendation and advertisement. But he was industrious and, being possessed of a companionable nature, grateful that his skill allowed him access to the lives of others. He would enter a household, and, whether placed in the stable, quartered with the help, or, very occasionally, and only in the most Christian of dwellings, treated like a guest, he had, for those few days, a function and a recognition. This did not mean that he was treated with any less condescension than other artisans, but at least he was being judged a normal human being; that is to say, one who merited condescension. He was happy, perhaps for the first time in his life.

And then, without any help beyond his own perceptions, he began to understand that he had more than just a function; he had strength of his own. This was not something that those who employed him would admit, but his eyes told him that it was the case. Slowly, he realized the truth of his craft: that the client was the master, except when he, James Wadsworth, was the client's master. For a start, he was the client's master when his eye discerned what the client would prefer him not to know. A husband's contempt. A wife's dissatisfaction. A deacon's hypocrisy. A child's suffering. A man's pleasure at having his wife's money to spend. A husband's eye for the hired girl. Large matters in small kingdoms.

And, beyond this, he realized that when he rose in the stable and brushed the horsehair from his clothes, then crossed to the house and took up a brush made from the hair of another animal, he became more than he was taken for. Those who sat for him and paid him did not truly know what their money would buy. They knew what they had agreed on—the size of the canvas, the pose and the decorative elements (the bowl of strawberries, the bird on a string, the piano, the view from the window)—and from this agreement they inferred mastery. But this was the very moment at which mastery passed to the other side of the canvas. Hitherto in their lives they had seen themselves in looking glasses and hand mirrors, in the backs of spoons, and, dimly, in clear still water. It was even said that lovers were able to see their reflections in each other's eyes, but the limner had no experience of this. Yet all such images depended upon the person in front of the glass, the spoon, the water, the eye. When Wadsworth provided his clients with their portraits, it was habitually the first time that they had seen themselves as someone else saw them. Sometimes, when the picture was presented, the limner would detect a sudden chill passing over the subject's skin, as if he were thinking, So this is how I truly am? It was a moment of unaccountable seriousness: this image was how he would be remembered when he was dead. And there was a seriousness beyond even this. Wadsworth did not think himself presumptuous when his eye told him that often the subject's next reflection was "And is this perhaps how the Almighty sees me, too?"

Those who did not have the modesty to be struck by such doubts tended to comport themselves as the collector now did: to ask for adjustments and to tell the limner that his hand and eye were faulty. Would they have the vanity to complain to God in His turn? "More dignity, more dignity." An instruction all the more repugnant given Mr. Tuttle's behavior in the kitchen two nights ago.

Wadsworth had been taking his supper, content with his day's labor. He had just finished the piano. The instrument's narrow leg, which ran parallel to Tuttle's more massive limb, ended in a gilt claw, which Wadsworth had had some trouble representing. But now he was able to refresh himself, to stretch by the fire, to feed, and to observe the society of the help. There were more of these than expected. A collector of customs might earn fifteen dollars a week, enough to keep a hired girl. Yet Tuttle also kept a cook and a boy to work the garden. Since the collector did not appear to be a man lavish with his own money, Wadsworth deduced that it was Mrs. Tuttle's portion that permitted such luxury of attention.

Once they became accustomed to his defect, the help treated him easily, as if his deafness rendered him their equal. It was an equality that Wadsworth was happy to concede. The garden boy, an elf with eyes of burnt umber, had taken to entertaining him with tricks. It was as if he imagined that the limner, being shorn of words, thereby lacked amusement. This was not the case, but Wadsworth indulged this indulgence of him and smiled as the boy turned cartwheels, stole up behind the cook while she bent to the bake oven, or played a guessing game with acorns hidden in his fists.

The limner had finished his broth and was warming himself before the fire— an element that Tuttle was not generous with elsewhere in the house—when an idea came to him. He drew a charred stick from the edge of the ashes, touched the garden boy on the shoulder to make him stay as he was, then pulled a drawing book from his pocket. The cook and the hired girl tried to watch what he was doing, but he held them away with a hand, as if to say that this particular trick, one he was offering in thanks for the boy's own tricks, would not work if observed. It was a rough sketch—it could only be so, given the crudeness of the instrument—but it contained some part of a likeness. He tore the page from the book and handed it to the boy. The child looked up at him, with astonishment and gratitude, placed the sketch on the table, took Wadsworth's drawing hand, and kissed it. I should always paint children, the limner thought, looking the boy in the eye.

He was almost unaware of the laughing tumult that broke out when the other two examined the drawing, and then of the silence that fell when the collector of customs, drawn by the sudden noise, entered the kitchen.

The limner watched as Tuttle stood there, one foot advanced, as in his portrait, his mouth opening and closing in a manner that did not suggest dignity. He watched as the cook and the girl rearranged themselves in more decorous attitudes. He watched as the boy, alert to his master's gaze, picked up the drawing and modestly, proudly, handed it over. He watched as Tuttle took the paper calmly, examined it, looked at the boy, glanced at Wadsworth, nodded, then deliberately tore the sketch in four, placed it in the fire, waited until it blazed, said something further when in quarter-profile to the limner, and made his exit. He watched as the boy wept.

The portrait was finished: both rosewood piano and collector of customs gleamed. A small white customs house filled the window at Mr. Tuttle's elbow—not that there was any real window there, or, if there had been, any customs house visible through it. Yet everyone understood this modest transcendence of reality. And perhaps the collector, in his own mind, was only asking for a similar transcendence of reality when he demanded more dignity. He was still leaning over Wadsworth, gesturing at the representation of his face, chest, leg. It did not matter in the least that the limner could not hear what he was saying. He knew exactly what was meant, and also how little it signified. Indeed, it was an advantage not to hear, for the particularities would doubtless have raised him to an even greater anger than that which he presently felt.

He reached for his notebook. "Sir," he wrote, "We agreed upon five days for my labor. I must leave tomorrow morning by daybreak. We agreed that you would pay me tonight. Pay me, give me three candles, and by the morning I shall work such improvement as you require."

It was rare for him to treat a client with so little deference. It would be bad for his reputation in the county, but he no longer cared. He offered the pen in the direction of Mr. Tuttle, who did not deign to receive it. Instead, he left the room. While waiting, the limner examined his work. It was well done: the proportions were pleasing, the colors harmonious, and the likeness within the bounds of honesty. The collector ought to be satisfied, posterity impressed, and his Maker—always assuming he was vouchsafed Heaven—not too rebuking.

Tuttle returned and handed over six dollars—half the fee—and two candles. Doubtless the cost of them would be deducted from the second half of the fee when it came to be paid. If it came to be paid. Wadsworth looked long at the portrait, which, over the last days, had come to assume for him equal reality with its fleshly subject, and then he made several decisions.

He took his supper as usual in the kitchen. His companions had been subdued these last two nights. He did not think they blamed him for the incident with the garden boy; at most, they thought his presence had led to their own misjudgment, and so they were chastened. This, at any rate, was how Wadsworth saw matters, and he did not think that their meaning would be clearer if he could hear speech or read lips; indeed, perhaps the opposite. If his notebook of men's thoughts and observations was anything to judge by, the world's knowledge of itself, when spoken and written down, did not amount to much.

This time, he selected a piece of charcoal more carefully and, with his pocket-knife, scraped its end to a semblance of sharpness. Then, as the boy sat opposite him, immobile more through apprehension than through a sitter's sense of duty, the limner drew him again. When he had finished, he tore out the sheet and, with the boy's eyes upon him, folded it, mimed the act of concealing it beneath his shirt, and handed it across the table. The boy immediately did as he had seen, and smiled for the first time that evening. Then, sharpening his piece of charcoal before each task, Wadsworth drew the cook and the hired girl. Each took the folded sheet and concealed it without looking. Then he rose, shook their hands, embraced the garden boy, and returned to his night's work.

"More dignity," he repeated to himself as he lit the candles and took up his brush. Well, then, a dignified man is one whose appearance implies a lifetime of thought, one whose brow expresses it. Yes, there was an improvement to be made there. He measured the distance between the eyebrow and the hairline, and at the midpoint, in line with the right eyeball, he developed the brow: an enlargement, a small mound, almost as if something were beginning to grow. Then he did the same above the left eye. Yes, that was better. But dignity was also to be inferred from the state of a man's chin. Not that there was anything patently insufficient about Tuttle's jawline. But perhaps the discernible beginnings of a beard might help—a few touches on each point of the chin. Nothing to cause immediate remark, let alone offense, merely an indication.

And perhaps another indication was required. He followed the collector's sturdily dignified leg down its stockinged calf to the buckled shoe. Then he followed the parallel leg of the piano down from the closed keyboard lid to the gilt claw that had so delayed him. Perhaps that trouble could have been avoided? The collector had not specified that the piano be rendered exactly. If a little transcendence had been applied to the window and the customs house, why not to the piano as well? The more so since the spectacle of a claw beside a customs man might suggest a grasping and rapacious nature, which no client would wish implied, whether there was evidence for it or not. Wadsworth therefore painted out the feline paw and replaced it with a quieter hoof, gray in color and lightly bifurcated.

Habit and prudence urged him to snuff out the two candles he had been awarded, but the limner decided to leave them burning. They were his now—or, at least, he would have paid for them soon. He washed his brushes in the kitchen, packed his painting box, saddled his mare, and harnessed the little cart to her. She seemed as happy to leave as he. As they walked from the stable, he saw windows outlined by candlelight. He hauled himself into the saddle, the mare moved beneath him, and he began to feel cold air on his face. At daybreak, an hour from now, his penultimate portrait would be examined by the hired girl pinching out the wasteful candles. He hoped that there would be painting in Heaven, but more than this he hoped that there would be deafness in Heaven. The mare, soon to be the subject of his final portrait, found her own way to the trail. After a while, with Mr. Tuttle's house far behind them, Wadsworth shouted into the silence of the forest.

Reading Deaf Characters

Having read and taught scores of stories and novels with deaf characters in the course of my career teaching literature to postsecondary Deaf (and some deaf) students, I suspect that most writers have no idea how much research is required to create a believable deaf character. Some seem to have assumed that their readership would not include any deaf people: deaf readers can easily pick out these authors. Some perhaps presumed that deaf people are simple—intellectually unsophisticated and psychologically uncomplex—and that there could be nothing to know or understand about their lives. I have not included any stories in this volume that seem to come from authors who made these assumptions. Perhaps Carson McCullers has best said what many authors think: when her husband suggested, while she was working on *The Heart Is a Lonely Hunter*, that she might want to observe a "convention of deaf mutes in a town near-by, . . . I told him that it was the last thing I wanted to do because I already had made my conception of deaf mutes and didn't want it to be disturbed."[1]

The deaf characters that ring most true are almost always created by authors who either know deaf people firsthand or who have done their homework, so to speak. To take an easy example, Carole Glickfeld had deaf parents and grew up intimately familiar with the signing deaf community in Manhattan, as readers could easily surmise by the depth, detail, and pitch-perfect tone of conversations she creates among deaf people at the Union League. Arnold Payne, the author of the novel *King Silence*, excerpted in Batson and Bergman's *Angels and Outcasts*, was the son of B. H. Payne, the deaf headmaster of the Cambrian Institution, a now-defunct residential school for deaf children in Wales, and a noted advocate of British Sign Language (BSL) in the nineteenth century. The younger Payne grew up at the school, matriculated at the Gallaudet College Normal School, and, as an ordained Anglican minister, worked in the British deaf community for the acceptance of BSL until incapacitated by illness. His novel is autobiographical, with the characters Mr. and Mrs. Gordon based on his parents, and it is heavily didactic, arguing for sign language at every turn.[2]

Other writers for whom firsthand experience with deaf people and deaf communities is obvious include William Henry Bishop, who was born in 1847 in Hartford, Connecticut, then the mecca of the American deaf world, where the first school for the deaf in North America was just thirty years old. Bishop plainly had some substantial inside contact with that school and its pupils before he wrote "Jerry and Clarinda" when he was twenty-one. He later taught at the New York

School for the Deaf and wrote two articles for the *American Annals of the Deaf* on deaf education in Europe. Joanne Greenberg's association with deaf people came from contact with more poorly educated adults. As she told me in an e-mail conversation, she had extensive interaction with her husband's deaf clients in the 1960s. In those days before the compact and affordable TTY, let alone relay services, deaf people had to go in person to see anyone they needed to consult, and Greenberg learned American Sign Language (ASL) so that she could converse with them when they appeared at her door. That she also made close friends in the deaf community is evident. Karawynn Long's history of interaction with deaf people, she told me, began with an ASL course she took in high school and continued with a stint of substitute teaching at the Texas School for the Deaf. She must also have attended more than one deaf party because her dialogue is spot on. Warren Kliewer's widow did not recall her husband talking about any deaf people in his hometown, Mountain Lake, Minnesota, on which he based the fictional town where his deaf character, Maria Becker, lives, but a search of the Minnesota School for the Deaf *Annual Reports* shows that there were two students from Mountain Lake during the years Kliewer was growing up. In a town with no more than two thousand residents, the existence of two deaf children, even if they were away at a residential school through the school year, makes it all but conclusive that he knew them personally—and knew that they would startle, as Maria does, when a heavy object was dropped on the wooden church pew on which they were sitting. The same may be said about Weldon Kees: during the years he was growing up in Beatrice, Nebraska, a larger town than Mountain Lake but still with a population not much more than ten thousand (small enough to have only one high school), four deaf children from that town attended the Nebraska School for the Deaf. Julian Barnes is an example of an author who does not know any deaf people personally but whose visit to an exhibit of portraits by the deaf artist John Brewster (1766–1854) at the Fenimore Art Museum in Cooperstown, New York, in 2006, made him wonder, as he explained to me, about "how, as a deaf painter, coming into someone's household for a few days and looking at them seated in front of you in a formal pose, do you understand, let alone convey, their character?" That exhibit was mounted with the input of Harlan Lane, a prominent expert in Deaf history, whose book on Brewster was for sale at the exhibit. Barnes apparently bought the book because he told me on a jocular note that he must have "pillaged" something from Lane as well as from what he saw at the exhibit—which, of course, is how writers get their characters right.

Because many writers do not do even the most basic research, however, their portrayals of deaf characters, created *ex nihilo*, are excellent cultural artifacts of the uninformed notions held by the societies in which they and their intended readers lived. The aim of this essay is to identify and isolate specific features of these characters both to spot commonalities and to provide a basis for comparison among stories. When I began my investigation into narrative uses and treatments of deaf characters, and authorial attitudes toward them, I soon discovered that these were not nearly as firm as I had imagined. In fact, most were quite fluid and the characters were seemingly wide open to whatever significance the author wished to develop. This phenomenon can be seen clearly by comparing the deaf character with, for example, the figure of the Jew, who, as Stanley Fish has written, is so "oversaturated" with stereotypes that when one thinks of a Jew today one might automatically think "Holocaust victim" or "shyster lawyer," and it is even possible to entertain both stereotypes at the same time.[3] Deaf figures also carry some of this self-contradictory baggage, being seen at times as preternaturally spiritual beings and at others as brutishly subhuman. But they are not perceived as both at the same time, and, most importantly, not to the exclusion of any other meaning the author cares to bestow on her deaf character. We find outcasts, we find angels, and we also find just about everything else.

The following discussion is based on the stories in this volume as well as on other narrative literature not anthologized here but listed in the Works Cited. As I mentioned, a few of the stories I cite here are too disturbing in their inexplicably uninformed and thoughtlessly callous portrayals of deaf characters for me to willingly reprint them, whatever their literary merit. Most of the stories I mention in this essay, however, I would gladly have included if I could. The same is true for most of the novels cited and two or three of the crime fictions—I wish I had been able to print excerpts from many of them. Since many readers will not (yet) have read these other stories and novels, I have indicated the context for the motif I am discussing so that readers can follow the discussion and, I hope, be enticed to continue reading beyond this volume's back cover. All of these other works are available through most libraries and bookstores. The few films I mention are all widely available for home viewing.

Lipreading

How are deaf characters depicted as communicating? Supernatural lipreading skill is a favorite old joke of many deaf people today, so let's look at lipreading first. It is no surprise that lipreading (with speech) is the most common means of communication, since, until the last decades of the twentieth century, few writers—or readers—could conceive that signing was in fact the use of language. A writer who needed to put a deaf character in communication with a hearing character will have used lipreading without further thought. The fact that lipreading is not nearly as easy or foolproof as these writers make it seem does not make this literary device any more absurd than what we see in film when hearing people who speak different languages communicate with ease because of some highly unlikely, even bizarre, happenstance. Many a classic Hollywood Nazi and Colombian drug lord, for example, happen to speak fluent English and do so, preposterously, even in dialogue with other Germans or Colombians. Nowadays, we find slightly less ham-handed contrivances. In *Dances with Wolves*, for example, the tribe into which Lt. Dunbar assimilates happens to include the white woman Stands With A Fist, who is able to speak and understand a language she hasn't heard since she was a toddler. Without the implausible memory skills of Stands With A Fist, there would be no movie because there would be no way for Lt. Dunbar to go native, so to speak. Movie audiences are used to the provision of such contrivances, and we willingly suspend our disbelief because we accept the limitations of the art form and keep our interest focused on character, theme, and style while ignoring scaffolding like improbable interpreters. My view is that lipreading serves the same function in narratives that feature a deaf character. It is not supposed to be any more realistic.

Some instances, however, are easier to swallow than others. Hortense Calisher's David Mannix, in her 1966 novel *The New Yorkers*, is clearly the product of a very pricey oral education, while Stephen King's Nick, in *The Stand* (1978), owes his skills to the one-on-one tutoring he had as an adolescent. At the other end of the believability scale, we have the 1948 film version of *Johnny Belinda*, in which Belinda learns to lipread virtually overnight and without even a passing acquaintance with the language she is supposed to be piecing together off the face. (She has been keeping her father's mill records in a code of invented symbols.) Considering that this was the first Hollywood film to use sign language, its overly rosy depiction of lipreading is striking.[4] Among the stories collected here, Gordon Woodward's deaf ten-year-old also lipreads both English and Italian without any way to have learned either language, while Auguste Villiers de L'Isle-Adam's unknown woman can lipread in the dark. Crime novels are notorious for supernatural lipreading skills: Jack Livingston's deaf detective Joe Binney can lipread a Latin American speaking accented English while torturing him, and T. J. Waters's Heath Rasco can lipread well enough to be a field agent in the Secret Service. Instructively, however, other incredible lipreaders are deaf author Douglas Bullard's Lyson Sulla (though Lyson is not lipreading in the excerpt given here) and the deaf heroine of deaf author Philip Zazove's 2009 novel *Four Days in Michigan*, who can lipread from a face not only in the dark but actually in profile, though admittedly missing "half of what he said."[5]

Again, my view is that faultless, effortless lipreading is just one of those devices for which readers must willingly suspend disbelief—even if they know better from personal experience—if the plot is to develop by means of dialogue with the hearing characters. A wise writer who does not want to put too much strain on readers' ability to swallow extraordinary lipreading can simply jettison his deaf character when the going gets tough, as Stephen King does when he kills off Nick just as the group sets off on foot from Colorado for Las Vegas, a trek over the Rocky Mountains being about as nonconducive to lipreading as a moonless night. Each work of fiction must be approached *sui generis*: as John Lee Clark pointed out to me, Bullard himself, while an ardent advocate for ASL, was also an expert lipreader with an elite oral education, so his view of Lyson's skills as he was creating this character would have been different from that of most of the book's deaf readers. In addition, the novel is a dream in which natural laws are routinely suspended. Again, I believe that, with exceptions, the mechanics of storytelling are what is usually behind these lipreading wonders.

A few writers more realistically describe the difficulties of lipreading. Karawynn Long's Marina struggles to lipread an old boyfriend because she is asking him for a favor and is afraid he will be "alienated" by her electronic interpreter. This science fiction story set in 2020 describes a portable, practical voice-to-print interpreter that in 2012 is still some years in the future, but the hearing character's unease in the face of any kind of interpreter is old-fashioned realism. In her 2003 novel *Deafening* set during World War I, Frances Itani accurately depicts the kind of intensive, years-long, one-on-one tutoring required for even minimal facility in lipreading. In the following passage, her deaf protagonist, Grania, describes her frustrations:

> When there are more than two people in a room, if hearing people are talking and change the subject, the deaf person in the room doesn't know. We are back in the old conversation, left behind. . . . We don't hear the asides, the sudden shifts. We can only watch one pair of lips at a time. If someone speaks when we're not looking, well. . . .[6]

Later, the narrator depicts Grania's difficulties even under the optimal condition of a group seated in a circle: "In the sewing circle, eyes looked down as the women followed their stitches. Grania watched conversation ripple from one pair of lips to another. As always, in a group, words jumped the circle quickly and could not be read."[7] Yet Grania's mother believes that her daughter simply chooses not to understand, a sentiment that is not often stated in the literature but that surely underlies the attitudes of many hearing characters, as it does in real life.

A particularly poignant example of a good lipreader getting hopelessly lost in conversation is seen in T. C. Boyle's 2006 *Talk Talk*, where the deaf heroine, Dana, accompanies her hearing boyfriend, Bridger, to dinner with some hearing friends of his whom she has just met.

> Matt Kralik said something and Bridger said something back and Patricia joined in, the conversation wheeling off in unforeseen directions even as the food came and Bridger's hands got busy with his shish kebab and Dana lost track of what they were saying. Eventually, she just lowered her eyes and concentrated on the plate before her.

When the foursome moves on to a club,

> after half an hour of watching everybody's mouths chew air, [Dana] told [Bridger] she wanted to go back to the motel and he gave her a look she didn't like and she walked the six blocks alone and let herself into the sterile little box of a room, got under the covers and turned on the TV.[8]

Sad? Many deaf readers will admire Dana for having the backbone to get up and walk out.

Nicholas Quinn, the eponymous deaf protagonist of deaf British crime writer Colin Dexter, admits that his lipreading ability is a gift, a "most sophisticated skill," and yet he still must take great pains to maximize his view of others' faces, as, for example, with careful seating at a table. The plot turns on the fact that Quinn mistakes "Dr. Bartlett" as "Donald Martin"—try that in a mirror to see that the names are identical by sight alone. Dexter even takes readers inside a lipreading class to demonstrate its limits. While Inspector Morse is interviewing the teacher about Quinn,

> A bell sounded throughout the building. It was 9 P.M. and time for everyone to leave the premises.
> "Would he have been able to hear that?" asked Morse.
> But the teacher had temporarily turned away to mark the register. The bell was still ringing. "Would Quinn have been able to hear that?" repeated Morse.
> But she still didn't hear him and, belatedly, Morse guessed the truth. When finally she looked up again, he repeated his question once more. "Could Quinn hear the bell?"
> "Could Quinn hear them all, did you say? I'm sorry, I didn't quite catch—"
> "H-ear th-e b-e-ll," mouthed Morse, with ridiculous exaggeration.
> "Oh, the bell. Is it ringing?"[9]

Deaf readers will smile over Inspector Morse's "ridiculous exaggeration" as soon as he realizes the teacher is deaf, even though she had been understanding him perfectly as long as she could see his face.

Aldous Huxley, writing in 1921 oralist England ten years before he began his masterwork, *Brave New World*, shows similar results for the best lipreading training that money can buy when he writes this scene for Jenny, a wealthy deaf woman, in his early novel *Crome Yellow*:

> "I hope you slept well," he said.
> "Yes, isn't it lovely?" Jenny replied. "But we had such awful thunderstorms last week."[10]

Such scenes are rare in the literature, though, leaving most readers just as ignorant of the challenges and limitations of lipreading as they were when they picked up the novel.

Speech

Speech is the tandem skill that makes a lipreading deaf character fully integrated into a story. Characters with mystifyingly clear speech appear regularly. Three upper-class spinsters—Huxley's Jenny (whom we have just seen misunderstanding a conventional remark), Elizabeth Bowen's Queenie in the 1941 story "Summer Night," and Viola Meynell's Bertha—all apparently speak just like hearing people, since there is no narrative comment about the quality of their voices, while Auguste Villiers de l'Isle-Adam refers to the "purity" of voice of the unknown woman, a fourth such character. More common, however, is the narrative that seems to be obsessed with a deaf character's unnatural speech. In Boyle's novel *Talk Talk*, for example, the author cannot seem to remind readers often enough that Dana sounds deaf: her boyfriend makes mental notes on her tone and volume nearly every time she opens her mouth, at one point thinking it was "so caustic and inhuman it could set off all the alarms up and down the block."[11] Strangers are forever looking at her askance, and, what is worse, Dana herself is depicted as obsessed with how she sounds to hearing people, so fearful that she becomes dysfunctional when she knows she has to speak to a Mail Box clerk.

Examples from other literary works, however, show a concurrent tendency toward more neutral descriptions: Philip Roth's Joey Cucuzza, in *The Plot Against America*, has a "hollow, honking voice," Sharon Oard Warner's Libby in the 1992 story "Learning to Dance" has speech that is "flat, guttural," Daphne du Maurier's Maud Stoll in the 1971 story "Not after Midnight" has a voice "without any expression," Alice Blanchard's Willa in her 1996 "Puddle Tongue"—the story's title comes from a nickname that made Willa cry as a child—has a "syrupy lisp . . . soft and damp-sounding, muted as notes blown from an old clarinet whose pads had never been changed," and Christopher Davis's sexy deaf linotype operators in his 1963 *Saturday Evening Post* story have speech that is "thick and grating."[12] Among the stories collected here, Greenberg's four deaf boys in "And Sarah Laughed" have "robot voices," in the view of their hearing mother, but this is said not unkindly; and in Umans's story "Uncle Leo's voice would soar and whoop," which the narrator finds attractive. But only Umans, Itani in *Deafening*, and Greenberg in "And Sarah Laughed" depict the most realistic situation: that the deaf person's speech cannot be understood by anyone outside his own family.

Two instances of upper-class deaf characters provide an interesting contrast in how an author can make use of the tonal and enunciation anomalies in deaf speech and are examined here at some length to demonstrate how important it is to consider the deaf character in the context of the entire work. Both come from novels: Boris Pasternak's 1957 *Doctor Zhivago* and Tom McCarthy's 2010 novel *C*. Both scenes concern a physician trying to diagnose a medical condition from his perception of deaf speech, yet the functions of these scenes differ widely.

In McCarthy's novel, Dr. Learmont, assisting Mrs. Carrefax in childbirth, thinks "her voice is soft and grainy. There's something slightly unusual about it, something beyond fatigue, that Learmont can't quite place: it's not a foreign voice, but not quite native either."[13] Mrs. Carrefax is a carefully and believably sketched oral deaf woman who is the wife of the hearing headmaster of an oral deaf school. This school employs a deaf gardener, Bodner, who communicates only in sign, which the Carrefax children surreptitiously mimic. This is a promising scenario for an interesting story. But readers soon realize that the setting's premise is wholly preposterous, the school being dedicated to teaching deaf pupils to recite lengthy passages of Ovid's *Metamorphoses* while the Carrefaxes conduct telegraphy experiments and run a silkworm farm on campus. By page 84, the story is off to a different set of outlandish events related in some way to the protagonist's fascination with communication technology, leaving the deaf gardener, the deaf pupils, and the deaf Mrs. Carrefax behind. Readers may well suspect that these characters are intended merely as the first of a long series of freaky people with weird communication behavior. *C* is an experimental, postmodern novel, not a venue in which we would expect deaf life to be treated seriously.

In contrast, Pasternak writes a similar scene into a complex web of the novel's back story of the Russian Revolution, in which readers get a clear view of attitudes toward deaf people and of the life of an oral deaf man. Here is Doctor Zhivago trying to figure out what is wrong with the young man sharing his train compartment:

> The young man turned out to have an unpleasantly high voice, at its highest verging on a metallic falsetto. Another oddity: by all tokens a Russian, he pronounced one vowel, namely the *u*, in a most peculiar way. He softened it like the French *u* or the German *ü*. Moreover, this defective *u* was very hard for him to get out; he articulated its sound more loudly than all the others, straining terribly, with a slight shriek. [. . .]
>
> "What is this?" Zhivago wondered. "I'm sure I've read about it, as a doctor I ought to know, but I can't think what it is. It must be some brain trouble, that causes defective speech."[14]

It is important to understand, first, that much of the novel and many of its important scenes are set on various trains, and that these train scenes provide not only atmosphere but also the theme of the antiquest since Zhivago never seems to be seeking or finding anything on all these trains that keep breaking down and being misrouted.[15] This particular scene, which was omitted from the film script (as were all but one of the train trips), takes place in the summer of 1917, when Russia is both in the midst of fighting World War I and in a period of unsettled government after the February Revolution and the abdication of the czar in March of that year (and before the October Revolution when the Bolsheviks seize power). Zhivago has been working in a military hospital in the Urals, where he has fallen in love with Lara, a nurse at the same hospital, and he is now on his way back to his wife in Moscow. A village near that military hospital had "seceded" from Russia under the leadership of a local miller, said to have been assisted by his sidekick, a mysterious "talking deaf mute." This story seems rank superstition until Zhivago discovers that the strange young man on the train is deaf, comes from a well-to-do family, has had an excellent oral education as "a phenomenally gifted pupil of either Hartmann's or Ostrogradsky's school," regards himself as a revolutionary, and is in fact the "talking deaf mute" of the rumors Zhivago had been hearing. Not only that, but the uprising led by the miller was actually instigated by this deaf man as a "pretext . . . for applying his own ideas."[16] Here, Pasternak has given us an authentic deaf man with an elite education, comparable to Hortense Calisher's David Mannix but more fully characterized, and has situated his story in such a way as to make some astringent comments on the Russian Revolution, for the scene implies that it was rich young men's experiments on an ignorant and superstitious peasantry, rather than spontaneous peasant uprisings, that enabled the Bolshevik Revolution and the formation of the Soviet Union.

Sometimes we see a character who has stopped using his speech out of embarrassment. Carson McCullers's *The Heart Is a Lonely Hunter* tells us that John Singer stopped speaking for this reason: "From the blank expression on people's faces to whom he talked in this way he felt that his voice must be like the sound of some animal." Barnes's Wadsworth stopped speaking because "women judged the noises he made embarrassing, children found them a source of amusement, men a proof of imbecility." Usually, however, deaf characters who do not speak are depicted as never having spoken at all, though often with the implication that they could if they would. In Flora Thompson's *Lark Rise to Candleford* (1945), a semi-autobiographical account of English country life at the turn of the past century, the villagers believe that deaf people "could talk if they'd a mind to, but they think if they did we'd set 'em to work." Grania's mother in *Deafening* expresses a similar notion when she says that Grania could lipread if she wanted to. This idea must underlie many of the attitudes we see in these narratives as hearing characters cannot rid themselves of the belief that the deaf are malingerers or, more recently, ideologues when they state a preference for communicating in sign. A particularly sad example is found in a 1994 Renée Manfredi story, "Ice Music," in which a hearing woman forces her deaf father to speak at her wedding, making him practice until he can say his line to her satisfaction and then expecting him to stand through the ceremony without an interpreter. "All these years I have been using your language. Now all I ask is that you use two words of mine. Just for once think of someone besides yourself," she tells him. The young woman has not grasped that, for deaf people, learning to speak is in no way equivalent to hearing people learning to sign. What is sad about this shabby treatment of a deaf man by his daughter is that the narrative suggests that we readers are to side with the daughter.[17]

In all these examples of speech and lipreading as the "default setting," however, it is surprisingly difficult to come up with any examples of stories that straightforwardly endorse oralism. Elizabeth Bowen's *Eva Trout*, with its characters who think an oral education will "cure" Jeremy, is not realistic fiction, and we know from an earlier short story that Bowen knew enough about the human limits of oral communication to have depicted how exasperating the hearing characters find it to interact with the realistic oral success, Queenie. In George Elliott's "Miss Cudahy of Stowes Landing," Bingham plans to take Phoebe away from her foster mother and put her in school where she will be taught to speak and so be "saved," but Bingham is a pathetic character who cannot even manage his own life and thus is clearly not speaking for the author or for the world Elliott creates in this story, which features Phoebe happily teaching ASL to Bingham.

While we do not find any outright endorsements of oralism, we do see what looks like morbid obsession with the vocalizations of "mute" deaf characters. There are the (barely) neutral descriptions: "incomprehensible sounds," "grunting and waving her hand," "odd, grunting tone," and "a short moaning sound." Elsewhere we find "loud inarticulate cries" and "rapid whimpering."[18] Most, however, are derogatory, ranging from "rattling, eerie," through "pathetic, ugly," "ugly, just ugly," "hideous," and "demented," to "inarticulate and indescribable cries—something between the chattering of an ape and the gobbling of a turkey—a startling, soulless, unholy sound, the language of the devil."[19]

Few authors seem to realize, because they have neither spent time around a deaf person nor are they attempting to take the deaf character's view, that most deaf people and any hearing friends and family they may have, simply are not obsessed with how their speech or vocalizations sound. Quite the contrary: while deaf people don't want to put off hearing strangers, worrying about it is just not a constant preoccupation—and we trust the same is true of our hearing parents and children.

Signing

Unlike lipreading and speech, signing appears only rarely. In fact, it seems never to have occurred to some authors, even those Batson calls "serious, intelligent authors," although, since at least the middle of the nineteenth century, it has been "the central issue of life for deaf readers"—those deaf people who sign, at any rate.[20] In a 1968 David Helwig story called "Something for Olivia's Scrapbook I Guess," Toronto hippies try everything they can think of to communicate with a runaway deaf girl, but the one thing they—and the author, presumably—never think of is sign language, or even fingerspelling. Coincidentally, we see the same ignorance in the same year with another group of hippies in the movie *Psych-Out*, where the Jack Nicholson character Stoney and his fellow stoners try everything they can think of—sex and drugs and rock and roll—to communicate with a deaf girl: everything but signs or even gestures, that is.

What is worse, in many of the stories portraying characters who do sign, the author clearly knows next to nothing about sign language. In a Diane Benedict story published in the *Atlantic Monthly* in 1982, the author posits two deaf people in a small town who, for reasons unimaginable to any deaf reader, cannot understand one another's signing, and then depicts one of them inadvertently sending the other over a ledge to her death when he signs in his sleep! Perhaps most galling to many deaf readers is a story's assumption that a deaf child's home signs have been invented by his parents or that deaf children need to be taught to sign by a hearing teacher, both implausible notions, to put it most kindly. Isabel Allende's deaf boy, in a 1991 story in *The Stories of Eva Luna*, uses "the sign language his great-grandfather had invented for him," while Flora Thompson says of the deaf youth "Luney Joe" and his mother, who lived in an English market town at the turn of the last century, "at home the two of them used a rough language of signs which his mother had invented," and although this may be a case of Thompson simply relaying what is believed in the village, she presents it as fact.[21] In the 1948 film version of *Johnny Belinda*, Belinda does not make even the most natural gestures to her father until a hearing physician teaches her to sign ASL, which he says was "devised by a Frenchman"—the scriptwriter or playwright evidently believed ASL was invented by the Abbé de l'Epée, who in actuality was merely the first hearing person to adapt the indigenous Parisian sign language for classroom use. Charlotte Elizabeth is the only author reprinted here who gets it right when she says that it was the deaf child who taught signs to the teacher: "our signs were all of his own contriving." A good example of this process can be glimpsed in Itani's *Deafening*, where Grania and her hearing sister develop a private sign language.

In the case of Pete Fromm's 1994 story "Grayfish" about two brothers on a fishing trip, it is unavoidable to conclude that it is the author, not the hearing protagonist Marty, who is ignorant of sign language. Marty has extreme difficulty communicating with his deaf brother, John, seeming to find it tedious even to make eye contact let alone to gesture. He does use home signs on three occasions: "the Careful Sign," "the Last-Cast Sign," and pointing to his wrist and nodding his head to indicate that there is still enough time. But let's look at this scene:

> Then Marty started to laugh, pointing, and finally pulling on John's beard, the tip of which was curled and shortened from the heat of the fire. "You burned your beard!" he said, laughing.

John did not understand him, and Marty tugged harder on his beard, trying to pull it around for John to see. John winced and slapped Marty's arm away. Marty went through the necessary pantomime then . . .[22]

The story leaves us thinking that the best that can be done with a deaf brother is to pull on his beard and laugh at him, since nothing in the story suggests otherwise to the reader.

When a deaf character is depicted as signing realistically, it is often seen through or mediated by a more or less informed hearing character, presumably to help the hearing reader stay with the story. For example, Bishop's "Jerry and Clarinda" is narrated by a well-informed hearing person, while the story of Elliott's "Miss Cudahy," in contrast, is told from the perspective of the timid and asexual Bingham, who remains clueless about what Phoebe really wants. More recently, however, we find writers dispensing with such mediators; for example, Karawynn Long, Marlin Barton, and Julian Barnes tell their stories through the eyes of their deaf protagonists, a device perhaps pioneered by Joanne Greenberg in her 1970 novel *In This Sign* but still found very rarely. This trend, if trend it is, is important for the opportunities it provides readers to identify with a deaf character.

Descriptions of deaf people signing extended narratives, beyond the back and forth of a dialogue aimed at exchanging simple information with hearing characters, are surprisingly rare at any date, though we do see Richard Dehan's Lord Polkstone "prattling away" in fingerspelling with the hearing woman he will marry. In her memoir, Charlotte Elizabeth, who apparently did not sign at all herself, includes quite a bit of Jack Britt's signed monologues, not only stories but actual theological discourse, as when Jack explains that God made trees but men make the wooden crucifixes used by Roman Catholics, or when, in a passage not included here, he comforts her on her brother's death by explaining how he prays for Jesus to make wings for the dead man.[23] Jack, like deaf signers today, is an expert at metaphor, but it is difficult to come up with other literary examples.

More recent writing sometimes includes descriptions of signs, a literary technique we wish had been thought of earlier so that we would have some descriptions of nineteenth-century signing preserved. Of course, when an author unfamiliar with the language is describing a sign for a hearing readership, the descriptions can be semantically so far afield as to quite inadvertently trivialize or make a mockery of the utterance. This example comes from the opening of the Alice Blanchard's 1994 story, where Willa is the deaf character:

"I don't want to talk about it," Willa insisted, signing *no, no, no* in Dori's face, her hand forming the head of a duck, her fingers making its bill go quack, quack, quack.[24]

Willa and her hearing cousin Dori are discussing Willa's abandoned plans to attend Gallaudet University, their topic very far indeed from ducks, the image of which inadvertently trivializes their conversation. Here is a second example from a 2008 Maureen Jennings murder mystery: "Jessica clenched her fist and made a gesture as if knocking on a table."[25] Here, the signer, Jessica, is a grief-stricken friend of a murdered woman and is helping the policewoman through whose eyes we see her sign "yes." The only function this fist-clenching, table-knocking description can possibly have for readers who do not know ASL is to make both Jessica and the language she is using look weird and foreign. For readers who do know ASL, the description unintentionally suggests that the policewoman's mind is wandering, which is not an idea the narrative is intending to convey. In some of these stories, one gets the distinct feeling that the author is presenting descriptions of sign articulations as part of his "deaf issues" program, as the critic Adam Gopnik calls it, the pedantic digressions on deaf life that have no natural function in the story.

This same technique, the insertion of a sign description, can be used for real literary punch, as we see in J. D. Salinger's 1955 novella *Raise High the Roof Beam, Carpenters*. The main character, Buddy, has found himself uncomfortably stuck in a car with his brother's tiresome would-be in-laws, after the groom failed to appear at his own wedding. One of these wedding guests is a mysterious little man in a top hat. As Buddy narrates it, "with an enormous grin at all of us collectively, he raised his cigar hand and, with one finger, significantly tapped first his mouth, then his ear. The gesture, as *he* made it, seemed related to a perfectly first-class joke of some kind."[26] Of course, the author and (one hopes) his readers recognize this "gesture" as ASL for "I'm deaf," and the joke is on Buddy, Salinger's narrator, who reveals himself as less sophisticated than he thinks he is.

What about that *rara avis*, the hearing character who signs fluently? Outside of Greenberg's Rose, who signs "like a native," and the smattering of ASL interpreters, it is difficult to come up with examples. In T. C. Boyle's *Talk Talk*, the deaf protagonist is a teacher in a deaf school where the hearing principal's "signing would have been as proficient as a native speaker's if he hadn't lacked expression,"[27] which, as deaf readers will recognize, makes him extremely difficult to understand—very much like most of the hearing signers such readers know.

How to represent ASL dialogue in written English is always a challenge. An author can render an ASL utterance by glossing its signs one by one, as Doug Bullard does throughout *Islay*, for example, "*My friend, you know Emil, himself carpenter, expert.*"[28] But because ASL syntax is different from English syntax, the author risks portraying deaf characters as uneducated. He also faces difficulties in getting the meaning across when there is no lexical equivalent in English. In the example just given, Bullard had to deviate from his practice of word-for-sign gloss to add the word *you* in "*you know Emil,*" which, in an ASL sentence such as this, is indicated with eye gaze concurrent with the sign glossed *know*, not with a discrete sign for *you*. Bullard has in fact been criticized by deaf readers for his rendering of ASL dialogue—for example, his use of the gloss *thrill* to translate the sign that means "What's up?" At least deaf readers are able to understand that the English word *thrill* glosses an ASL sign that, with appropriate eyebrow action, can mean "What's up?" How readers with no knowledge of ASL would manage that reading is anyone's guess. A similar complaint was made about the title of Leah Hager Cohen's first book, *Train Go Sorry*, a fascinating portrait of the Lexington School for the Deaf and its pupils in the late twentieth century. "Train go sorry" is a gloss of an ASL expression meaning something like "you missed the boat" or, more specifically, "you missed any opportunities you may have had, and you won't get any more." Did the title give readers who do not know ASL the impression that the language is just "broken English?" It would be unfortunate if it did because the ASL expression perfectly suits Cohen's theme: that for the minority and immigrant deaf students at Lexington today, "train go sorry" sums up their lives of missed opportunity. Carole Glickfeld and Karawynn Long take similar glossing tacks and run into similar challenges. Glickfeld's perfectly glossed ASL sentence "You devil, t-o-o many nosey" ("You're a scamp; you're too nosey") and Long's "You pack-suitcase finish you?" ("Have you packed your suitcase?") will be nothing more than local color at best, or broken English at worst, for most readers. The playwright Willy Conley has written at greater length about these choices, while G. Thomas Couser discusses some of these issues, as well the issue of transcribing deaf speech.[29]

Joanne Greenberg, in contrast, translates her signed dialogue into English, but her English translations retain hints of ASL to remind readers that the characters are not really using English: "There were other Deaf there" or "I'm not tricking" are examples from "Like a Native." Similar sentences in her novel *In This Sign* succeed miraculously both in recreating the signed dialogue on the page without word-for-word glossing and in being comprehensible to the English monolingual, for example, "They have a Scientific Man, so much, it took him three different colleges."[30]

Only one story in this volume openly advocates for signing, and this is Greenberg's "And Sarah Laughed." It is interesting that among all the writers who simply assume that lipreading is the way to communicate, not one of them advocates for oralism the way Greenberg, like Arnold Payne before her in his 1918 novel *King Silence*, advocates for ASL. One can spot, however, in stories not included here, an unfortunate trend to demonize signers as crazy ideologues. Renée Manfredi, in the story cited previously, seems to side with the hearing bride who forces her deaf father to speak at her wedding, and she would have us believe that when Emery's late wife "insisted that [their daughter] Sidney use only sign language," this is evidence that she "had never forgiven her daughter for being able to hear."[31] Simply being deaf, though, is ample reason for insisting that one's children sign, and there is no call for putting this deaf mother on the couch. In the Jennings murder mystery, mentioned previously for its trouble describing the ASL sign for "yes," the deaf characters who sign are crazed militants, while those who have enough hearing to have useful speech are good citizens who help the police.

Depictions of hearing parents who will not sign to deaf offspring are unfortunately all too true to life. In Itani's *Deafening*, Grania learns to sign when she is sent to the Ontario School for the Deaf at Belleville, but her mother will not learn to sign. Neither will Dana Halter's mother in Boyle's *Talk Talk*, nor Jerry's father in Bishop's story, who claims, "I don't understand his lingo; he's learned the devil's own crinklum-crunklums that nobody but themselves knows anything about." The only story known to me to feature a hearing protagonist who wishes she could sign (and undertakes to learn) is Greenberg's "And Sarah Laughed," though Dehan's "Under the Electrics" gives us a hearing narrator who realizes she missed her chance to marry the heir to a large fortune because she didn't know the "deaf and dumb alphabet." As deaf signers still say today, "Train go sorry."

One method of communication between deaf and hearing people that does not appear often in literature is writing. Julian Barnes's Wadsworth keeps a notebook in which his clients are asked to write, though Mr. Tuttle is as reluctant to use it as hearing people often are in real life. Carson McCullers's John Singer keeps handy a pad and his trademark gold pen. Kees's narrator writes to his sister Betty Lou, but she ignores his note. Pete Fromm's Marty, who feels no responsibility for making himself understood to his deaf brother, communicates with John by writing in the sand with a stick. But written communication is seen in the literature only rarely, perhaps because a deaf character who does not speak is presumed to be illiterate, a point readers can decide for themselves on a story-by-story basis.

Facial Expressivity

Readers who are deaf themselves or who have spent quality time with deaf people know that facial expressions are an integral part of ASL. They might even say that they could pick a deaf person out of a queue or a waiting room by the way she keeps her eyes on the alert. Sometimes we do indeed find such explanations in literature. Unsurprisingly, the one author who states this outright is deaf herself: discussing this feature in deaf children, Charlotte Elizabeth attributes "the life and animation that generally characterize" the deaf to their use of "looks and gestures as a substitute for words." Pauline Melville accurately captures the expressive faces of "Pistol-Man" and his deaf son, Avalon, but these characters are purposefully depicted as unassimilated immigrants from Guyana in contrast with a protagonist who has adopted English manners, and this may account for their animation more than their use of BSL. Isak Dinesen, on the other hand, seems to be attributing Karomenya's facial expression to his being deaf, not black, when she writes, "If he realized you were addressing him, his face at once lightened up . . . in a prompt resolute alacrity." Some deaf characters are shown as animated for the sole purpose of getting someone to communicate with them or to give the impression that they are following a conversation: Meynell's Bertha has "an alert air of willingness to respond to any form of social overture that might be made to her"; Manzini's deaf Italian husband adopted a fixed smile "anxious as he was to convey the impression that he understood everything even when no one spoke to him." One example of an author using alertness as a clue that the person is deaf is Sharon Oard Warner in "Learning to Dance," when her hearing narrator, who is in the process of renting out a bedroom to a stranger she does not yet know is deaf, thinks, "Suddenly, I recognize it all: the alertness of her eyes, the way her head tilts slightly forward."[32]

Many animated deaf characters are depicted as being entertained by their own thoughts, which are unknowable to the hearing characters and can make them uncomfortable: Slosson's Clavis has a "mysterious, all-knowing smile," and Elliott's Phoebe smiles "as though she were suppressing some private amusement." In a Raymond Carver story from 1977, "The Third Thing That Killed My Father Off," Dummy has a "crafty expression"; Elizabeth Bowen's Queenie in "Summer Night" is said to have a "mysterious" and "secretive" smile and to give "plumbing looks"; Salinger's wedding guest seems to be making "a perfectly first-class joke . . . that he fully meant to share with all of us."[33] Aldous Huxley's Jenny creates the same unease in the hearing Denis:

> In the secret tower of her deafness she sat apart, looking down at the world through sharply piercing eyes. . . . In her enigmatic remoteness Jenny was a little disquieting. Even now some interior joke seemed to be amusing her, for she was smiling to herself.[34]

Even Flannery O'Connor's simpleton, Lucynell, has a "cautious, sly look."

Just as in the real world where a deaf woman's natural alertness is sometimes mistaken for and reduced to a signal of sexual availability, so too in literary worlds do we find deaf body language spelling nothing more nuanced than a sexual come-on: Betty Lou, in Kees's "I Should Worry," smiles and crosses her legs to attract a man's attention and then practically drags him off to bed (while her hearing brother pockets the fee); Elliott's Phoebe is not quite that forward but her eyes light up when she flirts with the narrator; Richard Dehan's deaf viscount, Lord Polkstone, makes calf eyes at a showgirl that cannot be misunderstood.

Sometimes we find writers describing deaf characters as being, on the contrary, expressionless. For example, in a 1976 story by Annabel Thomas, the "other one," as the deaf character is called, has "no expression on her face," and her sister calls her a "block of wood." Perhaps the explanation for this rather common but erroneous conceit is, as Itani's Grania explains to her hearing fiancé when he asks her whether it feels good to come home and relax her attention from lipreading, "Most of the time, I *am* turned off. Only when I want to make the effort, that's when I turn on—that's when I'm most alert."[35] Unfortunately, too many writers seem to be assuming that the "turned off" mode that deaf people sometimes go into when they are hopelessly surrounded by spoken conversation is normal deaf deportment. It is not, and one does not see deaf people turned off like that in all-deaf groups.

Perhaps this is the place to mention the handful of "deaf rage" scenes, an imaginary phenomenon that has somehow caught the fancy of a few of our authors. The usually mousy Simon Datnow overturns his work table in Nadine Gordimer's "Charmed Lives." Gregory Dene, the deaf character in Vita Sackville-West's little-known 1921 novel *The Dragon in Shallow Waters,* tears his home apart, smashing dishes and ripping up curtains, when he realizes his wife loves a hearing man. Even mild-mannered Matthew Ryder in Greenberg's "And Sarah Laughed" knocks a stack of dishes out of his wife's hands and cries out, "Ah ahm dehf! Ah ahm dehf!" Perhaps we should see John Singer's suicide in McCullers's *The Heart Is a Lonely Hunter* in the same light.

Artists

Visual arts seem like a natural vocation or hobby for deaf people, but I do not think statistics from the real world would bear out the suggestion we get from the literature that a deaf person is more likely to sketch or paint than a hearing person. Huxley's Jenny, an idle member of the upper class, turns out to be an astute carica-turist. Long's Marina is a professional artist. Barnes's Wadsworth is a professional portraitist who sees what no one else can: "A husband's contempt. A wife's dissatis-faction." Wadsworth must conceal his superior perception in order to earn a living, but it also seems to be a game with him, experimenting in how far he can get away with exposing his patrons, in their portraits, for what they are. Among artistically talented deaf children, Kim Tongni's Nangi draws pictures while her father tells stories to their hosts, and she leaves behind her portrait of a shaman. Pauline Melville's deaf boy, Avalon, draws while a visitor is having tea with his father and then tries to give her all the drawings he ever made; Elizabeth Bowen's Jeremy (in *Eva Trout*) finds his métier in art lessons; Alonzo Lennox, the uneducated deaf boy in Mary E. Wilkins's 1927 story "A New England Prophet," has "inborn artistic skill," but the fantastic pictures he draws for his own amusement are taken by the Millerite community in which he lives to convey impending eschatological events.[36]

Gregory Dene, the deaf man who has a meltdown in Sackville-West's *The Dragon in Shallow Waters,* is a factory worker obsessed with redesigning the fac-tory's industrial machinery, and he spends all his free time drafting his ideas, since he cannot otherwise express them: "He was lost in his silent world of smooth-sliding precision and perfection."[37] He fantasizes about the day he will unveil his plans to the factory owner and be hailed as a genius. Gregory Dene's drawings, however, seem more like the skills attributed to deaf craftsmen such as Gordimer's watchmaker Simon Datnow, McCullers's engraver John Singer, or even Lyson Sulla as he builds a replica of the Merry Bandstand in Bullard's *Islay.* In contrast, the talent exhibited by Huxley's Jenny, Barnes's Wadsworth, Kim's Nangi, Wilkins's Alonzo Lennox, and perhaps by Eva Trout's son Jeremy seems instead more closely connected with superior perception, whether supported by the narrative or merely attributed to the deaf artist by the hearing characters.

In some stories, the connection between artistic talent and superior perception takes a turn toward clairvoyance. We can see the difference between superior perception and clairvoyance in a pair of stories by Warren Kliewer. In "Uncle Wilhelm's Love Affair," not reprinted here but from the same story collection in which "Sybil" was published, Maria Becker is the first in the village to notice that Uncle Wilhelm is meeting the strange girl every morning, and it seems only natural that Maria is the first to put together what is in front of everyone's eyes. In "Sybil," however, when Maria is waiting for the train that she thinks will bring her brother home, she draws a picture of what will happen to him if he gets off the train, and we soon learn that a stranger waiting for the train has exactly the plan that Maria draws. The motif as it appears in "Sybil," however, is undercut by its placement in the story cycle *The Violators*, which comprises stories with a shared setting, shared characters, and a heavy aura of what I would call Mennonite Gothic. Kliewer was a multitalented artist—a poet, fiction writer, playwright, editor, producer, director, actor, and theater founder—who grappled with his Minnesota Mennonite upbringing in much of his work. In *The Violators*, Kliewer's fictionalized hometown becomes an isolated and darkly foreboding village where many strange things occur, most of them a good deal stranger than Maria Becker's moment of clairvoyance. The Mary E. Wilkins story "New England Prophet" takes a more direct route to similarly undercut the supernatural element, disproving the prophetic quality of the deaf boy's drawings when readers learn that they were simply copied out of an illustrated Bible his mother had been showing him.

Clairvoyants

Kliewer's and Wilkins's stories aside, there are some outright seers among deaf characters, as well as characters with highly developed or supernatural perception. We can see the usual use made of this motif in the film version of *Johnny Belinda*, when Belinda senses that something has happened to her father the moment he is killed on a remote path. Villiers de l'Isle-Adam's unknown woman spells out how being deaf has given her supernatural perception, making

> my mind sensitive to the vibrations of eternal things, whereof the creatures of my sex usually know nothing but a parody. To those marvelous echoes, to those glorious reverberations, their ears are sealed! And so, to the sharpness of their hearing they are indebted for nothing beyond the faculty of perceiving only the external and the instinctive in the most delicate and pure of voluptuous delights.

Two stories about deaf children go even further, positing that these kids actually know the meaning of life. We have seen Slosson's Clavis (a name that means "key"), who dies before she can remind the narrator of the meaning. The other story appeared in *Harper's Magazine* in 1920: Edwina Stanton Babcock's "Gargoyle." The title character is a deaf boy, John Berber, nicknamed Gargoyle by his hearing foster parents, who knows the meaning of life when he is a happy deaf child but cannot say what it is when he grows up and is not deaf anymore. Gargoyle's foster parents believe that because, as a deaf child, he was never trained in what to notice or how to see, he has "unconscious knowledge," while a doctor calls him a "psychic freak." Once he can hear and speak, however, he cannot convey what he knows because language is only "empty words."[38] Naturally, this theme is ready-made for science fiction stories, such as Margaret St. Clair's "The Listening Child," in which a deaf boy can hear deaths taking place in the future.

Daniel Defoe's Duncan Campbell is the only deaf character I know who makes his living as a seer, turning to profit a gift he claims to have had from childhood. In a passage earlier in the book than what is reprinted here, Defoe provides an explanation of how young Campbell receives the prophecies he makes—by fingerspelled messages.

> I shall see my pretty youth and my lamb by and by, in the fields, near a little coppice or grove, where I go often to play with them, and I would not lose their company for the whole world; for they and I are mighty familiar together and the boy tells me everything that gets me my reputation. . . .
>
> [The boy] writes sometimes, but oftener he speaks with his fingers, and mighty swift; no man can do it so quick, or write half so soon.[39]

All these characters—Clavis, Gargoyle, and Duncan Campbell—are examples of a motif common in world mythology as well as in the popular imagination today: the compensation motif. Blind men, for example, are often clairvoyants in myths, and blind people are assumed in the popular mind to have some sort of sixth sense that sighted people do not have. In the real world, there is no compensation, just fuller exploitation of whatever sensory perception one has. Deaf people do not have any wider a field of vision than hearing people, as the hearing sometimes suppose (and, conversely, hearing people do not really have tunnel vision, as it often seems to the deaf)—the deaf have just learned how to use the "tails of their eyes" (as Bullard likes to say in *Islay*) and to pay attention to the periphery of their field of vision. The motif lives on in literature, however, and here, specifically, with all these clairvoyant deaf characters.

This anthology does not treat myths, but one story, Kim's "Portrait of a Shaman," deals directly with the conflict between the mythological motif of compensation and the New Testament view that illness, deafness, or what have you, is the result of an evil spirit taking up residence in one's body. As we have seen, Nangi is thought by her mother to be the incarnation of the dragon god's twelfth daughter, Flower. Because Flower was impatient to marry, she was punished by the dragon god with deafness. Now incarnated as Nangi, she is compensated with artistic talent. Nangi's Christian brother, Ugi, however, believes that she is deaf because of a "deaf spirit." This story juxtaposes animist and Christian views: in the animist view, the deaf girl must be cared for and cherished, whereas in the Christian view, she must be cured by exorcism. When the villagers begin to believe that her mother, an animist shaman, will "drive the dumb spirit out of the body of Nangi," we see just how far the Christian worldview has penetrated the popular view.

In *Angels and Outcasts*, Batson and Bergman discuss a tendency for stories to make their deaf characters out to be "good, better than their hearing counterparts,"[40] but I see this tendency in the motif of superior perception much more than in that of superior morality. Examples of superior morality might include Nadine Gordimer's Simon Datnow (who was the only family member to repay Mr. Shand for his passage), Nick in Stephen King's *The Stand*, and the deaf woman Dosifeya in Dmitry Mamin-Sibiryak's 1883 novel *The Privalov Fortune*, whom we see realistically signing with her family, by the way, and, perhaps less realistically, as endlessly empathetic. Dosifeya's empathy and her simple religious faith are present in this novel as a sharp contrast to the shallow and cruel pretensions of her hearing sister. Perhaps this case could be made for Madonna in Wilkie Collins's *Hide and Seek*, or Sophie in Charles Dickens's "Doctor Marigold," although most of the children in Dickens and Collins are morally superior to adult characters, and, in any case, these two Victorian novelists habitually catapult characters with disabilities from the subhuman category in which they were actually placed by society at the time, to a superhuman category that, as Leslie Fiedler points out, does not make them any more human. Carson McCullers planned for John Singer to exhibit "a certain mystic superiority,"[41] and we would not be far wrong if we saw in Singer a deaf version of the "magical negro," the patient and wise black man who appears out of nowhere to advise or otherwise assist a story's white protagonist. There is certainly a tendency for deaf murderers to be motivated by nothing but the purest of motives: in one of William Faulkner's Gavin Stevens stories, "Hand upon the Waters," a nearly feral deaf boy named Joe murders out of revenge for the wanton killing of his protector, and in David Helwig's 1968 story, mentioned earlier as an example of what looks like complete ignorance of sign language, the unnamed deaf girl has murdered her mother (with an ice pick!) but only after years of abuse. Daphne du Maurier's deaf murderer, Maud Stoll, is a counterexample in that regardless of how much the reader is led to despise her husband, Mrs. Stoll kills him not because he is loathsome but rather because she fears that he, like her other victim, will interfere with her criminal removal of priceless artifacts from Crete. In any case, the literature leaves the definite impression that if the deaf character is superior, it is likely in his ability to divine what the hearing characters cannot.

Social Isolation

Perhaps the single most important point we can make about deaf characters in literature is that, until the 1970s, they are almost invariably solitary figures, isolated in the hearing world. This fact may correlate with writers' habits of reaching for a deaf character only when there is a need to embody a motif of isolation or alienation. It almost certainly has something to do with the fact that few writers of literature until very recent times had any idea that deaf people in the real world—signing deaf people, at least—have historically demonstrated a very marked tendency to congregate. Bishop's "Jerry and Clarinda" provided a model of that tendency in 1868, had other authors wished to follow suit. When Bishop's Jerry runs away from his drunken father and cruel stepmother, the first thing that happens when he gets off the train in a strange town is that he meets a deaf man, a "local celebrity." Later the same day, he bumps into a deaf girl he knew in school. Deaf readers will see these kinds of meetings as normal and expected—not at all unlikely coincidences—and wonder why such things do not happen to deaf characters in other stories. Bishop also takes some care in having his hearing narrator describe "a ball and reunion of deaf-mutes . . . to honor the birthday of some celebrity in the annals of deaf-mute education" a tradition that was common by the year he was writing. (The "celebrity" is, unbeknownst to the story's hearing narrator but certainly known to the author, Thomas Hopkins Gallaudet.)

The difficulty for earlier writers, other than Bishop, to develop much of a plot when a deaf community is the setting is underscored by recent stories that must acknowledge the existence of deaf communities—because readers now know they exist—but make careful efforts to remove a deaf character from her community so that the hearing characters can interact with her *on their own terms*. Morris Smith's Gwen is on summer vacation with her hearing family before heading off to the Florida School for the Deaf and Blind in the fall, and what is more, Smith's narrator and main character, Maggie, is wholly uninterested in "whatever they do at deaf schools," so we learn no more about Gwen's life there and never see her in the company of school friends. Similarly, Alice Blanchard's story, mentioned earlier for its description of the ASL sign for "no" as a quacking duck, has Willa refusing to enroll at Gallaudet University and, instead, living with her hearing cousin, the protagonist, while she looks for a job. Sharon Oard Warner's story "Learning to Dance," mentioned previously for having a hearing narrator who notes Libby's alert expression as evidence that she is deaf, has Libby attending a summer course out of town, where she must lodge with the hearing protagonist. T. C. Boyle's protagonist in *Talk Talk*, Dana Halter, is a deaf woman with a PhD who is fired from her job teaching English at a deaf school in California right at the beginning of the book and is hired onto the Gallaudet University English faculty at the end, but all the action in between is cast entirely among the hearing characters. Trent Batson may be right when he says that "the life patterns of deaf people [that is, that they are gregarious] do not generally suit the artistic purposes of writers,"[42] but the same phenomenon can be explained by either simple ignorance or a wise caution to avoid, in one's writing, a society that would require too much time and trouble to get right.

Keep in mind, however, before criticizing these authors' decisions to decline the challenges of setting a story in a deaf community or even between a pair of deaf friends or siblings, that while creating a deaf character today amounts to a commitment to probing the edges of the possible in fiction writing, that was not the case in the past. A deaf character conceived before the 1970s, when we first began to believe it possible that a signed language actually could convey hopes and dreams, poetry and instructions to build a rocket, is therefore almost inevitably going to be one of two things: (1) a well-assimilated lipreading and speaking marvel, of which we have seen many, or (2) an isolated "dummy," a scarcely human two-dimensional character who functions more as a circumstance in which the hearing characters find themselves or with which they must deal. Flannery O'Connor's "The Life You Save May Be Your Own" provides an especially flagrant example of the "dummy" in its languageless simpleton Lucynell Crater, who is bartered and abandoned so that readers can judge the depravity of the two main characters: her mother and the one-armed bum who marries her for a car. "The Life You Save" arguably contains the most negative description of a deaf person ever written, but in O'Connor's Gothic oeuvre, it is pretty mild, as negative descriptions go. The fact that O'Connor did not violate standards of realism in her fiction tells us that among rural Georgians of Great Depression times, it was within the realm of the possible to raise a deaf child to middle age without any means of communication.

A rare example of a literary glimpse of a deaf community written before recent times is found in Saul Bellow's 1949 *The Adventures of Augie March*. This early work of an American author who was later to receive the Nobel Prize for Literature is a picaresque story in which Augie, in the course of growing to manhood, seems to have everything but the kitchen sink thrown at him as he bounces from situation to ever-dicier situation, providing readers with a panoramic view of mid-century America. In this scene, which Augie narrates, he is overhearing a police officer report to his sergeant about three deaf people he has just arrested. Augie gives readers the gist of the policeman's report:

> This guy attacked the other with a hammer, was what he said; he said that the woman was a lousy bitch and didn't care for whom she spread, and the bastard was the biggest cause of trouble in the deaf-mute community even if she did look like a schoolteacher. I report what the cop told the sergeant.

"What's my idea," he said, "is that this poor jerk thought he was engaged to her and then he caught her with this other joker."

"What doin'?"

"I wouldn't know. It depends on how much of a sorehead he is. But with the pants off, I wouldn't be surprised."

"I wonder what makes 'em so randy. They fight more about love than the dagoes,' said the sergeant.[43]

While this would not be a flattering picture of deaf people in the view of many readers, this short passage shows us a vibrant deaf community in which people have friends, enemies, lovers, reputations, libidos, and jealousies, just as in hearing communities. The woman may look prim ("like a schoolteacher"), but she sleeps around ("didn't care for whom she spread") and her fiancé has attacked the other man with a hammer when he found the two together "with the pants off." What is so wonderful about this glimpse into a 1940s deaf community is that Bellow's police sergeant seems to see the deaf as an ethnic group like any other, here the Italians ("dagoes"). Surprisingly, for 1949, the scene closes with the sergeant deciding to get a sign language interpreter and sort it all out in the morning.

Authors writing closer to the present time who have attempted deaf communities can be counted on the fingers of one hand. Long shows Marina at a party with deaf friends. Glickfeld's Ruthie has deaf parents and connections in the Manhattan deaf community. In the various short stories that constitute her book, Glickfeld includes vivid scenes at the Union League and at deaf picnics on Coney Island. Doug Bullard begins *Islay* by depicting Lyson Sulla as a member of an active deaf community, in which he is annoyed with his (deaf) wife's (deaf) friends. Joanne Greenberg's novel *In This Sign* depicts an isolated deaf couple behind whom a deaf community is implied and can be glimpsed: Abel and Janice Ryder are so poorly educated and ashamed of themselves that they live apart from other deaf people in town, whom we readers see briefly at a deaf church and a print shop. In Greenberg's "Like a Native," Rose, whose experiences with deaf patients in a psychiatric hospital Greenberg told me were based on her own, interacts directly with a deaf church group and we see her very authentically shut out when they realize she is hearing. In a mass market novel, *My Sister's Voice*, Mary Carter shows Lacey Gears in the bosom of a deaf artists' community and hanging with her best friend, a deaf gay actor. In many other cases, however, any implied deaf community remains so far in the background as to be invisible. The film version of *Children of a Lesser God* is an example of this phenomenon: it is set at a deaf school where the two principal characters are employed, and we do see deaf children in classroom situations, but where are all the other deaf adults? We see one deaf get-together, but the deaf protagonist Sarah sulks on the sidelines. It is incredible that she has no friends among what must be a sizable community of deaf teachers, dorm counselors, and other employees. The same can be said for T. C. Boyle's deaf protagonist, Dana Halter—where are her deaf friends and colleagues when she discovers she has been the victim of identity theft?

Applying the Bechdel test to stories with deaf characters shows how shockingly missing the deaf community is. This test, first proposed in 1985 by Alison Bechdel in her comic strip *Dykes to Watch Out For*, was designed for evaluating film treatment of women characters, but it works perfectly for deaf characters in literature as well. A nonexploitative, respectful treatment of a deaf character would mean that

1. There are at least two deaf characters in the story.
2. These deaf characters converse with one another.
3. Their topic of conversation is something other than being deaf, the deaf community, etc.

Some users of the Bechdel test would strengthen criterion 1 as follows: There are at least two deaf characters *who have names*. (Can we agree that "Dummy" does not count as a name?)

In addition to deaf authors Charlotte Elizabeth and Doug Bullard, only six of the hearing authors discussed here pass this test: William Henry Bishop, Carole Glickfeld, Joanne Greenberg, Florence V. Mayberry, Mary Carter, and Christopher Davis. If the test is stretched a bit, we could add two more: Diane Benedict, whose two deaf characters in her 1982 *Atlantic Monthly* story use mutually incomprehensible sign languages but do interact on a topic other than being deaf, and Karawynn Long, who depicts an authentic deaf party, although partygoers discuss little else but the future of the deaf community and the trials of having a hearing child.

It is the solitary deaf figure, therefore, that is as common in literature as it is uncommon in life in the present-day West. As Batson and Bergman point out in *Angels and Outcasts*, the isolated deaf character can be seen as uncorrupted by society, a natural man so to speak, and therefore superior to the hearing characters. Perhaps that notion can be glimpsed in Bishop's "Jerry and Clarinda," where Jerry is "decidedly superior in aspect" to his father, who is a drunk, and to his cruel stepmother, but I do not find this a major motif in the literature in general. An author's decision to isolate his deaf character is probably most often dictated by his ignorance of deaf communities and concomitant belief that deaf people are "lonely, isolated, 'strange,'" as Batson and Bergman say,[44] or—and this is important—by the needs of the plot, which must advance by bringing the deaf character on stage to interact with the hearing characters.

Some writers have defensible reasons for depicting a deaf character isolated among the hearing, and their stories provide highly successful sketches of such solitary deaf figures. Barnes's deaf portrait painter Wadsworth in "The Limner" is based on John Brewster (1766–1854), who pursued the lonely life of an itinerant portraitist between 1795 and 1834. Although Brewster attended the newly founded American Asylum in Hartford, Connecticut, between 1817 and 1820 (when he was in his fifties), there is no evidence that he sought out deaf friends or contacts after he left the school.[45] Kees depicts a deaf woman who lives with her brother above the family auto-parts store in a small town in the Depression-Era Midwest, presumably modeled on Kees's hometown, Beatrice, Nebraska, where she is entirely isolated by the siblings' inability to communicate. But such isolated deaf people were surely the usual sorry product of the Nebraska School for the Deaf (NSD) after it established one of the strictest oralist policies in the country. We know, from a brief mention in his only novel, that Kees knew about at least one of the oralist teachers at NSD. (Kees's last book, oddly, was *Nonverbal Communication*, 1956, which mentions sign language only in passing.)

Other deaf characters who are quite realistically isolated are the very rich and the very poor. Hortense Calisher's David Mannix is too rich ever to have been mingled with other deaf children, all of whom necessarily would be from less privileged backgrounds, and the same must be true of Richard Dehan's Lord Polkstone. J. D. Salinger's wedding guest is perhaps explained the same way, although it is hardly unusual for lone deaf family members of every social class to be stranded among the hearing guests in such circumstances. Pasternak's deaf youth who shares a train compartment with Doctor Zhivago is clearly from the tiny land-owning class of prerevolutionary Russia. Huxley's Jenny and Bowen's Queenie are both independently wealthy and can hobnob with hearing people of their social class, who are kind to and tolerant of them because of their social positions.

Among the characters too poor to have had any chance to meet other deaf people are the serf Gerasim in Ivan Turgenev's "Mumu" (1854), Maupassant's peasant Gargan in the "The Deaf Mute" (1886), and Kim Tongni's Nangi, who is the daughter of a Korean sorceress living in a small hamlet in premodern times. The poor black girl in Julia Peterkin's 1924 story "Over the River" has no family and picks cotton for a living. Faulkner's Joe, mentioned previously, is an orphan who has found a home, of sorts, in the woods with a mentally retarded man. Eudora Welty's Joel Mayes, who also is an orphan, lives on the western frontier, far beyond the reach of deaf communities. Isabel Allende's deaf boy, Juan, is born to a single mother in an isolated Latin American village. All these authors—Kim, Peterkin, Faulkner, Welty, and Allende—are known for setting their stories in their signature cultural backwaters. And Kim Tongni (the pseudonym of Korean writer Kim Sijong) is best known for stories that, like "Portrait of a Shaman," draw on Korean myth.

There are other rationales for depicting a deaf character as born into such a small or isolated community that deaf schools and other deaf people would not likely be present. Albert Camus's deaf character, Étienne (sometimes called Ernest), in the autobiographical, unfinished novel *The First Man*, was born into a working-class colonial family in Algiers during the Great Depression and works as a cooper. Because we know that this character was based on Camus's uncle, we can surmise that his isolation among the hearing was due to the size and economic condition of the francophone community in Algiers at this time and the consequent lack of any schools for this community's deaf children. However, none of this enters into the story, in which Étienne and his lonely, hard of hearing sister, based on Camus's mother, appear as completely isolated figures for whom no explanation is necessary. Deaf author Howard T. Hofsteater similarly isolates Dummy in a farming community that appears to be unaware of schools for deaf children. Hofsteater's parents both came from such communities, and his story can be read as making the case for deaf education. The Mary E. Wilkins story, "A New England Prophet," is set in a rural New England Millerite community of the 1830s or 1840s, where her deaf character, young Alonzo Lennox, is growing up without any education or even socialization even though the American School for the Deaf enrolled children from all over New England at this time. Perhaps we are to understand that his parents are so intent on the second coming of Christ, which they believe to be imminent, that they have not bothered to send him to school. Warren Kliewer's story "The Sybil" is part of a cycle of stories set in a town that is itself so isolated, both geographically and by the self-imposed isolation of the religion practiced there, that the train does not even stop, so Maria Becker is quite plausibly the only deaf person in town.

That these characters, if they were real people, would naturally live their entire lives in isolation is historically accurate. More puzzling is why other writers depict middle-class or working-class deaf characters as isolated without any explanation for how this unlikely circumstance has come about. Why is Phoebe in "Miss Cudahy of Stowes Landing" living with Miss Cudahy in an isolated mansion on the California coast, although her use of good ASL shows that she has attended a signing school? Why is the husband in Gianna Manzini's "The Deaf Man's Wife" reduced to "discussing" the newspaper with his hearing wife by "exchanging glances" and raising an eyebrow instead of stepping out to whichever cafe is patronized by the deaf residents of Florence, where the story is set, so that he can discuss the news of the day with deaf friends in sign language? In stories not collected here, why are both Stella, the deaf high diver in George Garrett's 1961 "An Evening Performance," and the unnamed deaf escape artist in Truman Capote's 1945 "A Tree of Night," married to and traveling with hearing spouses who appear to be exploiting them? Why does Raymond Carver's Dummy have no deaf friends or associates? Why does John, the deaf brother in Pete Fromm's "Grayfish," enjoy going fishing with his hearing brother, Marty, who can barely tolerate him, rather than hooking up with some other deaf guys for a fishing weekend? In these cases, it seems the answer can only be that the authors in question have no idea that deaf people, signing deaf people at least, have deaf friends whenever and wherever possible.

Problematic Sex and Marriage

We have seen that deaf characters are taken out of any plausible deaf community for the purposes of a story; we now turn to how they are taken out of any probable family network, examining first the motifs of failure to marry and of marriages that are childless and fraught with distaste, infidelity, or even horror.

It was common in the past for deaf people of all social classes except, perhaps, those of the very lowest class to remain single, so this common characteristic of fictional deaf adults is partly explained by history. Martha Stoddard Holmes, a disability studies scholar, has made a tightly reasoned argument with a great many examples (and some counterexamples) about how and why Victorian authors usually contrived to mark their deaf, blind, or crippled women characters with excessive passion or sexuality, making them unfit for marriage as it was conceived in that era. For our purposes, however, it is sufficient to say that when a reason is given for a fictional deaf person not to have married, it is either the wish to avoid deaf children or, in the case of deaf women, that her family has kept her at home as a companion or even servant. In many cases no reason is given, and readers are left with the feeling that the author just could not conceive of a marriage scenario.

Barnes's Wadsworth never married because he feared deaf children, even though he knows that adventitious deafness cannot be passed on, but Barton's middle-aged Janey still lives with her mother who has apparently kept her from marriage so that Janey can be her caregiver in her old age. Is the same true of Elliott's Phoebe, whose foster mother, Miss Cudahy, treats her like a servant? Or is Phoebe in the same position as O'Connor's Lucynell Crater, whose mother is trying to marry her off as a bargaining chip to get a man around the house? In the novel *Deafening*, Grania O'Neill, whom author Frances Itani modeled on her own deaf grandmother, is assumed by neighbors and to some extent by her own parents to be unmarriageable, a permanent burden on her mother. When Grania finally introduces Jim, her parents are "cautious." In Bowen's "Summer Night," in contrast, forty-something Queenie did have a suitor at one time, but we never learn what became of him beyond what her brother says: "There was some fellow once, but I never heard more of him. You'd have to be very oncoming, I daresay, to make any way with a deaf girl."[46] Bowen thus leaves it up to readers to decide just how marriageable Queenie was in her youth.

Other barriers to marriage are various. Dehan's Lord Polkstone cannot get the rather dense chorus girl who is the object of his affections to respond to his overtures and is finally engaged only when he finds a woman who can fingerspell and thus understands his intentions. The wealthy unknown woman in the story by Villiers de l'Isle-Adam rejects a suitor by claiming that "it would be criminal" for her to marry because any husband would soon learn to resent her.

Hofsteater's Dummy, the son of poor farmers, is so childlike and naive that he pesters a friend of his own age to go nutting with him, not comprehending that it is her wedding day. As John Lee Clark pointed out in a personal communication, the Hofsteater story ends with telling imagery as Dummy sits on a dead log with the empty sacks that were to have held the nuts he hoped to collect—and this is from a deaf author. Camus states explicitly that Étienne is not marriageable: "despite his handicap he had several adventures with women, which could not lead to marriage." Instead, he and his hard of hearing sister live together like an old married couple. Dwight Steward's forty-four-year-old deaf detective Sampson Trehune is happily single but, when he wins the affections of the lawyer Belinda Shaw at the end of the book and plans to spend the night at her place, his hearing friend and interpreter calls him a dirty old man, as though there is something unnatural about deaf men enjoying sex.[47] Simon Datnow's bachelorhood is unquestioned in Gordimer's "Charmed Lives," as is John Singer's in McCullers's *The Heart Is a Lonely Hunter,* and both interact with young girls without a shred of sexual tension, as though they were completely asexual. (Present-day college students tend to assume, and to argue, that Singer is gay, but that is an indefensible, anachronistic reading.) Meynell's story offers a unique explanation for spinsterhood, as thirty-five-year-old Bertha is kept from marriage by her family because her hearing father died when her deaf mother failed to hear his cries for help.

On the other hand, there are actually a number of deaf sex objects in the literature. Villiers de l'Isle-Adam's unknown woman maddens the hearing protagonist, who calls her a "temptress" and is bent on marrying her. Phoebe, in Elliott's story, seems to be begging for sexual relations, although Bingham is too repressed to respond. Kees's Betty Lou is a prostitute in a skin-tight dress whom men cannot stop ogling. Elsewhere, crime writer Ed McBain's deaf character Teddy certainly qualifies as an enchantress, and what makes her so enchanting has everything to do with the fact that she neither hears nor speaks—her miming drives Detective Steve Carella wild. Some readers find Wilkie Collins's Madonna to be "an object of desire" and believe that the author "eroticizes deafness."[48] In a 1978 story by Lloyd Rose about the untimely emergence of a bride's lesbian desire, a newlywed couple, direct from the church and on the first day of their honeymoon, pick up a deaf woman hitchhiker who is so attractive to the bride that she refuses to consummate her marriage. Of all these sexually attractive characters, however, only Teddy is headed for family life, in her case, married to a police detective. It is interesting to note that deaf men who are depicted as desirable mates are desirable for reasons other than the fact that they are deaf: Dehan's Lord Polkstone is a good-looking heir to a fortune and is seen wearing a diamond stud in his shirt front, and deaf detectives Sampson Trehune (Steward) and Joe Binney (Livingston) display superior intelligence and fearlessness in the face of danger that prove irresistible to women.

Deaf characters are sometimes shown as married to hearing people, but when this occurs, the marriages are portrayed as total disasters—usually childless, and the hearing spouse an adulterer, or something close to that. The marriage of Drops and Gargan in Maupassant's "The Deaf Mute" is a prime example. In another example of the same motif, Raymond Carver's Dummy, in the 1977 "The Third Thing That Killed My Father Off," is married to a woman who cheats on him with "Mexicans," which is the subject of gossip. The Maupassant story tells us that Drops engages in sexual promiscuity to pay for her alcohol habit, while the Carver story is silent about the motivations of Dummy's wife.

Other stories are quite explicit about the aversion the hearing spouse feels for the deaf spouse. In Vita Sackville-West's 1921 novel *The Dragon in Shallow Waters*, which she completed only a year before she met her most famous lover, Virginia Woolf, Nan finds her deaf husband, Gregory Dene, repulsive: "She winced—oh yes! she winced. She turned away from him, said he bothered her, kept herself unnecessarily busy." Here is a scene in which Gregory is looking for a quickie from his sleeping wife before he leaves on a business trip:

> She woke with a cry, to find Gregory's face near hers as he knelt on the floor. It was very fortunate that he could not hear the cry, which, at first merely startled, changed to horror as she recognised him. . . . She pushed with both hands against his chest, struggling silently; only half awake, she had not the wisdom not to struggle; now, she knew only his distastefulness. He held her, hardened to a cold fury by her resistance. . . . She could not plead with him, as she could have with another man; their strife must be soundless; she pushed, and twisted herself within his grasp, both quite in vain, then, relaxing, she lay quiet, with his arm still beneath her. . . . She tried to escape from the opposite side of her bed, but he seized her again, holding her down, determined, revengeful, and unshaken by pity. She sought wildly in her mind for some means of release.[49]

Not coincidentally, Nan is in love with a nice hearing boy. Yet it is hard to understand what motivates this scene, and readers wonder why Nan married Gregory in the first place. Manzini's "The Deaf Man's Wife" begins in the mind of the wife while she is in her lover's bed, running over in her mind her claustrophobic life with a deaf husband. He speaks in a monotone, keeps his eyes open during sex, and pauses in front of closed doors before pushing them open. There is nothing in the story to put these deafisms in perspective, so one can only assume that the author intended her readers to sympathize with poor, hearing Giulia, who has to put up with them. This wife does not even have to make up an excuse for being gone overnight because "it is sufficient for her to be aware that she is the only one who knows how to speak with him"!

Charlotte Elizabeth, elsewhere in her autobiography, describes herself as having been married to a hearing man but as living apart from him while she plays mother to Jack, having no children of her own. Umans's Leo Murray is married and has children but leaves that life behind when he comes out of the closet. Greenberg's Sarah is bored and resentful living with her deaf family, and jealous of a daughter-in-law who can sign with her husband and sons. Years before, when she contemplated marriage with Matthew, Sarah's fears had been practical (for example, Matthew's inability to be summoned in case of a fire), but she later sees that it is the silence she should have feared. Even the poor deaf woodcutter Adomas in the Juozas Grušas story is taunted because, having married a widow with children, he is "feeding someone else's children." And let us not forget the embedded backstory in Meynell, in which a husband dies locked in the cellar because his deaf wife cannot hear him trying to get out.

In the nineteenth century, both Charles Dickens and Alfred de Musset wrote stories about deaf girls who grew up to marry deaf gentlemen, and William Henry Bishop wrote of a deaf boy who grew up to marry a deaf girl. However, all three stories skip from the wedding to the birth of a hearing child (which is, in their time, the requisite happy ending), making no effort to portray the marriage itself. A 1957 Hollywood film, *Man of a Thousand Faces*, authentically portrayed a historical deaf couple, the parents of actor Lon Chaney, but I know of no literary treatment of deaf marriage between Bishop's in 1868 and Greenberg's *In This Sign* in 1970.

It was Greenberg, then, who exposed twentieth-century readers to a marriage in which a deaf man and a deaf woman—Abel and Janice Ryder—form a household and raise (hearing) children—but what we see is not pretty. Greenberg's novel tells how the oldest child, Margaret, is put under tremendous pressure to act as her parents' ears and interpreter, actually a common and practically inescapable fact of life for hearing children of deaf parents before modern technology produced telecommunications equipment and baby monitors. The Ryders' second child, Bradley, dies from a fall down a flight of stairs when their attention is distracted, and their parenting skills are in general so deficient that Margaret grows up scarred by her childhood experiences.

Glickfeld's Hannah and Albert Zimmer are another deaf couple. Although Hannah is a better mother than Janice Ryder, perhaps chiefly because the family is not so mired in poverty and Hannah can be a full-time homemaker, Albert is depicted as so psychotic that, as we learn later in the story sequence *Useful Gifts*, one of his children commits suicide and the other two remain estranged from him as adults. In an extreme example of bad parenting by deaf characters, Peterkin's unnamed deaf woman, the farm worker who is mocked by the father of her child, kills her baby when the child's father denies knowing her. Lyson and Mary Sulla in Bullard's *Islay* have been married for twelve years and have formed a kind of mother/son partnership. When asked if he has children, Lyson is "shamefaced," and the reader is left to conclude that Lyson and Mary do not have sexual relations at all.[50]

It seems that deaf characters either remain single or they enter into marriages that are sterile or produce badly damaged children. And yet, that is certainly not the message of any one of these narratives taken singly. On its own terms, each is best read as a circumstance particular to its characters, not a statement about how deaf people live. Lyson Sulla is a big baby; Janice Ryder is so ill-educated as to be functionally illiterate; Albert Zimmer's psychotic behavior has nothing to do with the fact that he is a deaf man. Taken as a whole, however, these narratives paint a gloomy picture of deaf adults' sexuality.

Orphans

Just as deaf characters are often denied normal parenthood in fiction, they are also frequently bereft of their own parents. The number of orphans is astonishing: Defoe's Duncan Campbell, Bishop's Clarinda, Slosson's Clavis, Kees's Betty Lou, presumably Elliott's Phoebe (since she appears to have been adopted, perhaps not legally, by Miss Cudahy), and, in stories not included in this volume, Collins's Madonna, Mamin-Sibiryak's Dosifeya, Faulkner's Joe, Bowen's Jeremy (in *Eva Trout*), Welty's Joel Mayes (in "First Love"), Dianne Benedict's Angel, Blanchard's Willa, and the list goes on. In some cases, the story makes it explicit that the parents abandoned the child (Welty's "First Love") or committed suicide (Kees). Bishops's Jerry, Bierce's unnamed deaf boy, and Barton's Janey are orphaned in the course of their stories.

If the deaf child is not outright parentless, the family web has been broken in some other way—Kim's Nangi has an absent father before the death of her mother; Pauline Melville's Avalon lives with his father but all further family ties are broken; Barton's Janey lost her father as a teenager and was taken from her school by an unsympathetic mother; Allende's Juan is raised by his great-grandfather; and Thompson's Luney Joe has a single mother. This motif is popular in film, too. In *Children of a Lesser God*, Sarah's mother blames her deaf child for her husband's abandonment of the family, and Sarah ends up estranged from her mother as well as her father. In *Johnny Belinda*, Belinda's father claims that she "killed her mother," by which he means that Belinda's mother died in childbirth.

Among deaf children snatched from their parents, Edwina Stanton Babcock's Gargoyle, in her 1920 story of the same name, and Charlotte Elizabeth's Jack are both taken from their working-class parents by members of the middle or idle-rich classes, although both boys are shown to have loving families. John "Gargoyle" Berber, the son of the Stangs' gardener, is made into a garden pet, while Jack is picked up off the street to serve as Mrs. Phelan's experiment in deaf education.

Even in the best of circumstances—an intact, two-parent family—a parent (the mother, usually) detaches herself from culturally normative caring. This theme is probably too complex to make much of an appearance in a short story, but it is a strong thread in both Boyle's *Talk Talk* and Itani's *Deafening*. In *Talk Talk*, Dana's mother talks to her daughter's hearing boyfriend, seeking his sympathy for having a daughter so stubborn that she declined to get a cochlear implant. In *Deafening*, Grania's mother throws herself into her work so that she is "too busy" to learn sign language, neglecting her deaf daughter in all respects except to drag her around the province and across Lake Ontario for yet another hearing test or miracle cure. Three years after she finished school, Grania still "felt the hard wall that was Mother's will, Mother's intent."[51]

In real life, it is not uncommon for hearing parents to take a hearing son- or daughter-in-law or a grandchild into their confidence to complain about a deaf son or daughter. Yet, literary depictions of this are rare, perhaps because such episodes, which send shivers of recognition through many deaf readers, can easily be misinterpreted by readers who have no real experience with deaf people. In rural western New York at a meeting of a library book club that had read *Talk Talk* at my suggestion, the other (hearing) members were initially in agreement that Dana was remarkably willful and self-centered for a woman with a "hearing deficit," and they pitied her mother—much to my surprise and, I have to admit, chagrin.

What all these orphaned characters have to say about perceptions of deaf people is not what one might expect, however. In Western storytelling traditions, orphaned or abandoned heroes are remarkably common, from Moses, Oedipus, and King Arthur of Camelot all the way through to Oliver Twist, Jane Eyre, and Harry Potter, but in stories with hearing orphans, the point is that the orphans overcome tremendous odds to succeed in life. Deaf orphans, in contrast, remain isolated and unhappy, the deaf characters of Dickens, Musset, and Bishop notwithstanding.

Hearing siblings also fall short of conventional moral expectations. Kees's narrator in "I Should Worry" sells his deaf sister for a drink. Fromm's Marty, in "Grayfish," as we have seen, is not even civil to his deaf brother, speaking to Marty when his face cannot be seen and pulling on his beard before he finally goes through what he regards as "the necessary pantomime." Queenie's brother Justin, in Bowen's "Summer Night," finds it oppressive to be around her, although he can sign, or perhaps simply mime, and they have no problem communicating. Annabel Thomas's Wileem, in "The Other One," tells her deaf sister, "I purely hate you!"[52] Exceptions to this apparent rule have appeared in more recent literature: in Itani's *Deafening*, Grania and her hearing sister are very close, while in Mary Carter's romance *My Sister's Voice*, the story centers on the hearing sister's need to reunite with her deaf sister Lacey, who is not all that interested.

Nature

While deaf characters are thus removed both from deaf communities and from families for the purposes of the narrative, they are frequently placed in contexts or described metaphorically as associated with nature. Babcock's deaf boy in "Gargoyle" is introduced in the first paragraph of the story with his arms "full of field flowers" and then disappears behind "masses of rhododendron." He is the son of a gardener and does little else in childhood but play with flowers. In fact, the wealthy family who fosters him does so because the husband wants his estate kept in the condition of "untrammeled nature . . . tolerant of lichens, mushrooms, and vagabond vines," and, in line with these preferences, gives his gardener's deaf son the run of the place.[53] Slosson's Clavis likewise is brought up "far away from the busy world, in the very heart of nature, among trees and hills and streams, with birds and flowers and wild free things."

Babcock's and Slosson's stories are quite explicit about the connection between deaf people and the natural world, but this is an idea one sees with some frequency across two centuries of writing, although it is not often so clearly articulated. In Tom McCarthy's 2010 novel *C*, Bodner, a deaf (and mute) gardener at the oral deaf school, is seen with a "bucketfull of crimsonberries" or "half-lost among the swollen, bulbous heads" of poppies.[54] Dehan's Lord Polkstone woos the showgirl with many (unaddressed) bouquets of flowers. Woodward's Ronnie is in trouble for picking a neighbor's flowers. Kim's Nangi lives with her mother in a house that is reverting to untamed nature.

> On the roof tiles mushrooms sprouted dark green, yielding a sickening smell of decay. . . . The rainwater stood stagnant, . . . the pool of water was covered all year around with dark green moss, and above it, standing entangled, was a mass of bulrushes, goosefoots, foxtails, and many other weeds, all taller than a man of average stature. Underneath this growth long serpentine earthworms wriggled, and aged frogs, as loathsome as toads, budged once in a while, awaiting the approach of night. The house was like a haunted den, long deserted by human inhabitants.

In Grušas's "Fairer Than the Sun," the woodcutter lies dead in the forest "covered as if with a green wreath" by the fir trees he felled. Hofsteater's Dummy is obsessed with collecting nuts in the forest. Elliott's Phoebe lives in a house completely blocked from sight by tall hedges and surrounded by a garden so extensive as to require a full-time gardener, who is the only servant in the household. Sheila Kohler's Isabelle is discovered to be deaf when she is on the beach toddling toward the sea.

Other examples include Carver's 1977 story, in which Dummy is so obsessed with his fish pond that he surrounds it with barbed wire to keep people out; Wilkie Collins's depiction of Madonna in a garden with a garland of flowers around her neck, offering a bunch of posies to a dog as her history is related to Valentine Blyth and to readers; and Helwig's 1968 story about a runaway deaf girl who has murdered her mother with an ice pick and who is bedecked with flowers by the hippies who pick her up. Faulkner's Joe actually lives in the woods, as do the deaf couple in a 1982 story by Canadian author Eric Cameron entitled "One Summer." Cameron's couple live so far from civilization that a surveying crew travels more than a week without seeing any signs of human habitation before they stumble on the house. Fromm's John is seen by his hearing brother Marty only on fishing trips, not in social settings. In *Doctor Zhivago,* Pasternak's deaf youth is coming home from a hunting trip and has his dog—and a bag full of dead birds—on the train. As with Camus's Étienne, the dog is prominent.

Christopher Krentz and other scholars frequently remark that deaf characters are commonly compared to animals,[55] but the literature suggests that when this is done, it is often with a light touch. However, figurative language comparing people with animals is extremely common in general and hardly limited to deaf characters. Literary characters, like people in real life, give bear hugs, take cat naps, are lone wolves, or show dog-like devotion. What is different, of course, are instances of deaf vocalizations being likened to animal sounds, like Bierce's description of "something between the chattering of an ape and the gobbling of a turkey."

Aside from vocalizations, animal imagery appears from time to time. In Wilkins's "New England Prophet," the deaf boy is shown sleeping at all hours in front of the hearth and behaving "like a distressed animal." Camus's description of Étienne ascribes to him "animal-like devotion" to his mother and sister, Faulkner's Joe is a "creature" with dog-like devotion to his friend Lonnie (67), and Sackville-West's Gregory Dene is "like a baboon"—recall his wife's repugnance for him.[56] In the stories collected here, such remarks are often put into the mouth of a none-too-admirable character, as in Rasheed Gbadamosi's "The Sexton's Deaf Son," when Joshua's Aunt Roda, an obnoxious old woman, asks him, "Do you know deaf boys are animals? They don't talk and they can't hear; just like animals. They have strength like wild animals." At the end of the story, Joshua concludes that it is his hearing playmates who are the animals. Greenberg's Sarah in "And Sarah Laughed," before her enlightenment on the topic of signing, says, "I don't like people waving their hands around like monkeys in a zoo!" and readers are to understand that this statement is an expression of her terrible error. This technique is similar to that used by Kliewer—when Maria Becker's mother says she does not know how she will get home in a snowstorm because her "deaf and dumb" twenty-year-old daughter is with her, readers get the idea that the woman is not very smart. We should also note that when such comments come from a narrator, they are qualified by context: Camus's Étienne, for example, is a wholly admirable character in *The First Man,* in fact the only admirable adult in the young protagonist's life, and his "animal-like devotion" is far more human than the grandmother's coldness.

Infantilization

Deaf people today often remark among themselves that deaf characters in literature and film are usually women or children, rarely men. Some critics share this belief. For example, Elizabeth Gitter has written about how, in the eighteenth and early nineteenth centuries, the best-known deaf people were men and how that focus changed to deaf women after the 1820s, and Christopher Krentz finds deaf females to be the rule for nineteenth-century American literature. However, the literature in English and available in English translation up through the present day suggests that this is not as true of the larger corpus. Outstanding depictions of fictional deaf men include Barnes's intelligent and self-reliant Wadsworth, Gordimer's abject watchmaker Simon Datnow, and Glickfeld's horrifying domestic tyrant Albert Zimmer, as well as Carver's paranoid Dummy, Greenberg's hard-working Abel Ryder (*In This Sign*), Steward's astute book collector (and amateur sleuth) Sampson Trehune, and Itani's sweet and courageous Colin who tries three times to enlist in the Canadian army by pretending to be hearing—the list could go on.

Perhaps the reason for our impression of the predominance of women and children is the tendency of writers to infantilize deaf people of either sex.[57] O'Connor's Lucynell "looks like a baby doll" according to her mother, and acts like a four-year-old; her mother passes her off as a teenager when she is actually "nearly thirty." Grušas's deaf woodcutter is "tiny" and a "doll." Elliott's Phoebe sits through tea "like a little girl" and lies on a bed "like a child." In Greenberg's story "Like a Native," the hearing protagonist Rose grows up while her deaf playmates continue their childhood games: "their world was slower to widen." In other works, Blanchard's Willa, a recent high-school graduate, is easy to deceive, carries an old stuffed zebra in her suitcase, and ends the story shivering in her hearing cousin's arms. Faulkner's Joe is "an adult, yet with something childlike about him." Camus's Étienne looks like a young man at age fifty. Mary E. Wilkins's Alonzo Lennox, at age fourteen, looks no older than ten. Sharon Oard Warner's Libby wears an outfit "you'd expect to see on a little girl." Truman Capote's deaf man wears a Mickey Mouse watch and is spoken to by his hearing wife "as if she were talking to an inattentive child." Huxley's Jenny is regarded by the main character, Denis, as "curiously childish," though this judgment is proved wrong when he sees the caricature of himself that Jenny has drawn. Even the otherwise very adult Sampson Trehune of Steward's *Acupuncture Murders* sees himself as Eeyore, a character in the Winnie-the-Pooh stories by A. A. Milne, while Itani's Grania, as a young married woman, repeats to herself captions from the children's picture book her grandmother used for speech practice: "Tell Dulcie to run for help," and so on. There seems to have been a caption for every situation in which the adult Grania finds herself.[58]

Curiously, deaf author Howard T. Hofsteater's Dummy, at age twenty-three, never realizes he is an adult: "that they [he and Miriam] were now grown-up people never occurred to him." Another deaf author, Bullard, portrays his deaf protagonist Lyson Sulla as a big baby who attracts women by triggering their mothering instincts. Lyson's wife, Mary, who sees him as a "huge baby" craving contact with her bosom, speaks to him with "the tenderness of a mother toward a child" and has to pull him out from where he is hiding and cringing behind her to face a stranger at the door. It is interesting to see that even when an author does not overtly describe a deaf character as childlike, readers may supply that interpretation themselves. For example, in McCullers's *The Heart Is a Lonely Hunter*, John Singer's deaf friend Antonapoulos is lazy, reads the comics page of the newspaper, and likes candy, liverwurst, and, most of all, "drinking and a certain solitary secret pleasure."[59] In the 1968 film version, this hard-drinking, masturbating character is shown playing hopscotch and sleeping with a teddy bear!

Then there are the stories about deaf children that end before the child grows up. Perhaps the most harrowing stories for us to read today are those in which a child is kept at home, uneducated and languageless, isolated among the hearing until disaster strikes suddenly at the story's end. Horrified readers will want to know whether (a) the author is simply ignorant of deaf schools and believes that this is a deaf child's fate, (b) the story is showing that the hearing characters are ignorant (or cruel) in keeping the child from school, (c) such opportunities truly did not exist in the time and place in which the story is set, or (d) we are reading some sort of nonrealistic story. The answers are various and sometimes uncertain. For example, in "The Edge of Sound," first published in 1955, Gordon Woodward tells what is in many ways a compelling and realistic story set in his own time and place, British Columbia, 1955, which, as some readers will know, had a publicly supported residential deaf school, Jericho Hill, that was later infamous for sexual abuse of its pupils. Yet, the story presumes a deaf ten-year-old living in a two-parent family in an apartment building in an urban setting with other adults who know him, who is not only entirely unschooled but whose father "was always saying they should have put him away somewhere because he was deaf and dumb." Could it be that not only the author but also his first editors were entirely ignorant of deaf education and therefore thought the premise possible? Or is this a parable of some sort? Without knowing more of Woodward's work, we cannot say.

A contrasting example is Elizabeth Bowen's 1968 novel, *Eva Trout*. We can be sure that Bowen knew something about orally educated deaf people because in her 1941 story "Summer Night," she created an authentic deaf character, Queenie, who speaks and lipreads perfectly but otherwise behaves like a normal deaf person. (It is interesting that in this story several of the hearing characters seem to experience anxiety over telephone calls, which were certainly a novelty in 1940 rural Ireland where the story is set, and the telephone-anxiety motif lends calmly deaf Queenie an additional bit of cachet.) Yet in Bowen's later novel *Eva Trout*, the main character, Eva, a fabulously wealthy and weirdly eccentric woman, travels to America to adopt—or, as the narrative seems to suggest, buy—a deaf child, whom she takes with her on her travels around Europe. After a series of oddly unreal and unmotivated events and a great deal of emphasis on unsent letters, the visual arts, and cinematic similes that give the impression of a "wordless universe," Eva finally agrees to send Jeremy to doctors who "worked by a method they had themselves evolved—its success depended on certain factors, in the main psychic." When these doctors next allow Jeremy, whom they have been guarding jealously and who now has attained some language skills, a brief reunion with Eva for her wedding, he shoots her dead. Bowen thus makes it perfectly clear to readers that, with this novel, she is breaking out of the "classical realism and its customary methods" in which the bulk of her work was created.[60] What the novel seems to be about is not Eva and Jeremy but rather the necessary role of language in our inner lives. The unhappy Eva, more Bowen's thought experiment than a literary character, thinks wholly in pictures and must die when her son breaks into language. That Bowen depicts language as spoken language is an accident of her time and place, mid-twentieth-century Britain, and should not be understood as her view on deaf education.

One explanation for the pervasive infantilization of deaf people in literary representation has been articulated by Leslie Fiedler, whose work seeks to discover the re-emergence of myth in literature and popular culture. Speaking of disabled rather than of deaf people, Fiedler believes we simultaneously pity and fear them and have split this conflicting response into two figures: the innocent child, whom we pity (for example, Tiny Tim or the old Easter Seals poster child, whom Fiedler calls the "cripple of the year") and the evil old man, whom we fear (Long John Silver, Richard III, Captain Ahab). This would certainly explain why, when authors want to evoke a positive response in readers, the deaf character is portrayed as childlike. Martha Stoddard Holmes, following Fiedler here, expatiates on the Victorian association of children with innocent suffering and adults with suffering that is, in contrast, only too well deserved, so that even though, for example, most blind people in Victorian times were adults, it is blind children we meet in novels because these could not have been the authors of their own misfortunes. Fiedler speculates that pity, rather than an organic response to disability and, by extension, deaf people, "is only a disguised form of our aboriginal terror; and in any case it leads us to evade rather than confront the problem of our relationship to the disabled by tempting us into weepy voyeurism and self-congratulatory smugness."[61] In other words, in Fiedler's view, no matter how warmly readers may respond to a deaf character who is portrayed as childlike, this experience will never help them cope with an encounter with a real deaf adult they may chance to meet. But then, that is hardly literature's job.

Miriam Nathan Lerner, writing about deaf characters in film, astutely points out that we never see the foundational experiences of the deaf person, that is, a childhood spent without natural communication. The same is true, unfortunately, for literature. Of course, until Freud, it was not commonly understood how important childhood is in shaping the adult, so it is no surprise that writers before this time were either uninterested in childhood experiences or failed to connect them realistically to adults' psychological characteristics. For example, Babcock's John Berber, the little deaf boy nicknamed Gargoyle who was snatched from his family and set to roam in the garden of the local gentry as a household pet, later appears, after his off-stage schooling, as a hearing, speaking, well-educated adult. In a counterexample, Daniel Defoe expends considerable effort in describing Duncan Campbell's education by means of fingerspelling. In the early pages of the book dealing with Campbell's childhood, Defoe reprints an excerpt from John Wallis on a method for educating the deaf. Like the boy called Gargoyle, Duncan Campbell grows up to have native-like fluency in written English, although, unlike Babcock's fanciful hero, he is still deaf and does not speak. Perhaps Defoe was persuaded by Wallis, who was his brother-in-law, that deaf children taught by this method really did grow up to be as erudite as Campbell.

Charlotte Elizabeth is a second author who provides detailed descriptions of deaf education—via fingerspelling and alphabet blocks—but unlike Duncan Campbell, her Jack's adult English more credibly shows the limits of an education begun too late: "All bads, all bads go fire . . . One Jesus Christ, one" is a representative sample of his English.[62] Among more recent writers, we find neither such gross implausibilities as Duncan Campbell and Babcock's John Berber nor much serious effort to face the stunted childhoods that produce some of these stunted deaf adults. The only two narratives I have seen that attempt the realities of the deaf childhood and then see that child through to an adult character are Joanne Greenberg's *In This Sign* and Frances Itani's *Deafening*. Greenberg's depiction of Abel Ryder's early schooling, which is spent sitting in a hearing classroom, rings true:

> Time-time. Years. The air got filled, got empty. Children were up
> and down, went and came back, some with books and some with
> papers, mouth-mouth, important-too-fast, nothing to follow, so
> he sat until the things were done for him, or until his seatmate . . .
> jabbed him in the ribs.[63]

But this is only a brief segment in her novel. The same is true for Itani's description of Grania in a public school before her mother becomes resigned to sending her to the Ontario School for the Deaf.

Itani expends a good deal of narrative space on Grania's years at the deaf school, and, while Grania is not a typical student, having been deafened after she acquired spoken English and privately tutored in speech and lipreading by her grandmother, Itani paints an accurate picture of the difficulties Grania's classmates have with standard English. Bishop's "Jerry and Clarinda" is remarkable for its close approximation of Deaf English in the letters the lovers write to each other, although Bishop was wrong in describing it as "a quaint dialect constructed upon analogy with their language of signs." Perhaps the Sheila Kohler story should be considered here as well. Kohler depicts the parents of a toddler they do not yet know to be deaf as in denial, taking the first step in depriving a deaf child of a normal, linguistically rich childhood.

Blunders and Insights

As we read and reread the stories discussed here, it is easy to pick out mistakes made by authors who have not done sufficient, or any, research on deaf life. Some authors make basic, superficial mistakes in terminology, such as referring to finger-spelling as "hand-spelling." Other stories contain mistakes on matters that most people would probably not even think to check: Allende's deaf infant "would lie awake for hours, not fussing," whereas deaf infants howl as much as hearing babies;[64] Benedict's deaf immigrant knows only a German sign language, not ASL, although he came to America young enough to have learned to write idiomatic English, which presumably could only have been learned in a school for the deaf where he would also have picked up ASL. In Barton's story, Mr. Clark's mother learned to sign when she lost her hearing as a young married woman and mother of an infant. In reality, around 1900, when this would have taken place, no one would have thought that a deafened, married adult would want to acquire sign language and there were no classes available to such people as there are today—ASL could be acquired only informally, by living in a dormitory with deaf signers.

Other errors seem to be the result of either carelessness or a complete disregard of easily determined facts. Edwina Stanton Babcock states that little Gargoyle was known to be deaf before he could walk, an unlikely premise since, as all parents know, children typically walk before they speak or are observed to fail to speak, the only sure sign until recently that a baby was deaf. Renée Manfredi, in "Ice Story," asks us to accept that the father "as a young man, believed his inability to speak caused his deafness."[65] As a child, perhaps, but no deaf young man thinks he has been deafened by his failure to speak. Rick Rofihe's story about a deaf violinist is built on more thorough-going errors: it is simply impossible for a deaf person to learn to play an unfretted string instrument, where articulation of notes is totally dependent upon the ear. Further, when she plays her instrument medium loud, she claims it sounds quiet to her, whereas a real deaf person with any residual hearing might hear some notes accurately while others would be distorted or inaudible—being deaf, or hard of hearing, is not like living with cotton in your ears that muffles all sounds equally. T. J. Waters's 2010 crime novel is structured on the erroneous premise that videophone relay operators do not identify themselves as such to the hearing call recipients, making it possible for a hearing male con man to dupe a victim into believing that the voice of the female relay interpreter is that of the caller. In fact, relay interpreters are scrupulous in identifying themselves as such and providing their identification numbers, and they will not omit to do so at a caller's request, as happens here. Eric Cameron's 1982 story featuring a deaf couple living deep in a Canadian forest is entirely premised on the impossible circumstance of their hearing daughter being unable to vocalize at all, even to save her life, on account of having grown up with deaf parents. In Edwina Stanton Babcock's "Gargoyle," speech therapy results in a "cure" of the deaf boy, actually making him able to hear. Whether errors such as these ruin the story will depend upon the reader.

Some types of mistakes, however, are more annoying, and a deaf character's obsession with hearing is one of these. Manzini's deaf husband, who is also obsessed with guessing the exact moment when church bells will toll, wants to hear music "most of all"— an odd thing for a deaf man to say, especially in 1929, before electronic technology made listening to music such a large—and taken-for-granted—part of daily life. Defoe's Duncan Campbell also wishes he could hear, and in a scene that better reflects the hearing author's interest in what it is like to be deaf than a typical deaf person's interest in what it is like to be hearing, he speculates at length about what hearing must feel like. In contrast, a deaf character's statement that being deaf is "a fearful affliction," silence is "horrible," and she is "dying of shame" (Villiers de l'Isle-Adam), while annoying to read today, may be historically valid—even Laurent Clerc, the Frenchman who cofounded deaf education in the United States, considered it a blessing that all his children and grandchildren were hearing.[66] The notion that lipreading is easy and foolproof is, of course, the most common mistake in the literature, but is usually attributable, as I have argued, to the mechanics of the plot. Sometimes, however, an author will make another type of mistake about lipreading, as Gordon Woodward does when he gives a child perfect lipreading skills in a story whose premise has given the boy no opportunity to have learned English.

Equally grating is a story's implication that the deaf character is monumentally stupid. For example, Ambrose Bierce's deaf six-year-old cannot see that a man with his jaw ripped off is in fact a horribly wounded man, not a clown. (Bierce's penchant for trick endings, however, means that readers do not yet know that the boy is deaf when he grotesquely construes the wounded men as horsing around for his amusement.) Bishop's otherwise thoroughly authentic 1868 story of a deaf courtship gives us to understand that the adult Jerry is so naive that he does not realize his father is a drunk.

Then there are the patronizing attitudes, but these are almost always attributed to another character and are not endorsed in the world of the story. In Elliott's "Miss Cudahy," the neurotic Bingham is proud of his patronizing behavior to the "afflicted" Phoebe as he projects pity into his smile at her, while in Alice Blanchard's 1994 story about a young mother, Dori, having her deaf cousin Willa as a houseguest, the protagonist tells Willa that "Gallaudet will help you learn to live in the real world better." Both Bingham and Dori are flawed characters: Dori learns and grows during the course of the story but Bingham does not. The only example known to me of a story that really seems to endorse pity for a deaf character as the only available stance is Pete Fromm's "Grayfish," in which Marty lets a record-breaking grayling get away in order not to outdo his deaf brother, John, who is "whooping" over the length of *his* grayling: Marty had "broken the fish off purposely, out of pity, and Marty hated himself for that. John had never pitied himself a day in his life." [67] Even if we accept that the hearing brother hates himself, the story leaves us with no sense of what Marty might have done instead. The author might be quite surprised to learn what many deaf readers would say: he needs to learn to sign.

Another old chestnut is that deaf people's lives are lived in silence, a mistake easily seen in the titles of stories, even those by authors who know better—"Into Silence," "Silence," *The Silent World of Nicholas Quinn*, "A Cry of Silence," and "Of Silence and Slow Time," this last an allusion to Keats's apostrophe to a Grecian urn, but still, the story is about a deaf woman. Bertha Coombs lives in a "cavern of silence" (Meynell), the "unknown woman" refers to "this horrible silence" (Villiers de L'Isle-Adam), Simon Datnow "apprehended the world from a remove . . . look-ing through glass into an aquarium where silent mouthing fish swam up to him incomprehensibly and swam away" (Gordimer), and so on. Few deaf people have absolutely no residual hearing, but even those few do not think of their lives as "silent." A century ago, when deaf people commonly used the word *silent* in the names of their organizations and publications, for example, the Goodyear Silents football team, *The Silent Worker*, and *The Silent News*, the reference was to them-selves as signers rather than speakers, as is the title of the Bragg essay "Telling Silence," which is about muteness in myth. The Bateman Cannon essay "Silent Stereotypes," the work of an ASL interpreter, is an example of a title intended to denigrate the belief that silence dominates deaf lives. In short, the notion that deaf people live in silence is current only among the uninformed hearing. While under-standable, it has unfortunately led to the view that being deaf means leading an empty life. [68]

So much for the irritating errors. Amusing errors include the deployment of what I call the "OMG" aspects of deaf life: the details of daily living that strike some authors and readers who are new to deaf people as amazing, even shock-ingly so. Even when these outbursts are given to a character in the story rather than the narrator, it is usually clear that the story expects its readers to share the astonishment. A prominent critic in feminist and disability studies, Sandra Gilbert, has claimed that the "wonder" we feel when we meet a blind person in real life or in a D. H. Lawrence short story is "magic," "a pure surprise or awe untouched by pity or fear." [69] Some deaf readers will snigger at such notions, but it is well to keep in mind that this one seems to be widely held. The "wonder" that is apparently felt upon meeting a deaf person who can dance, for example, seems to be widely regarded as a normal reaction. As long ago as 1868, Bishop inserted a deaf dance scene in "Jerry and Clarinda," presumably only for the sensationalist value since it rather slows down the story. In the film version of *Children of a Lesser God*, we see Sarah doing a sensuous dance that amazes the speech teacher, James, and provides viewers so inclined with a bit of sexual titillation in an otherwise rather prudish film.

Then there is the assistive technology, the junk, increasingly electronic, that deaf people need to live in a world designed by the hearing majority. Elliott's main character Bingham is fascinated by a 1960s home signaling system that summons Phoebe to a particular room by color-coded flags. Philip Roth's young narrator in *The Plot Against America* is obsessed with his neighbor Joey's hearing aid—as the story is set in the 1930s, it is a big box aid worn on the chest—finding it "nearly as intriguing" as a night watchman's pistol, handcuffs, and blackjack but "more gruesome."[70] Crime writer Ed McBain's Teddy is alerted that someone is at her door by the twisting of the door knob, a detail so fascinatingly odd to both the author and his hearing characters that it becomes the lynchpin of the book's climax. Hortense Calisher's David Mannix has a silent alarm clock equipped with the latest 1950s technology for awakening the deaf, described in enthusiastic detail, while a hearing housemate in Maureen Jennings's murder mystery exclaims, "We've got so many flashing lights to signal the door, the phone, fire, the kid, you name it. It's freaky at times."[71] Presumably, these lights are much more "freaky" than the beeps, buzzes, and ringtones amid which hearing people live. These instances can be compared with the matter-of-fact manner in which assistive technology is handled by deaf author Doug Bullard. In the excerpt from *Islay* reprinted here, Lyson calls home from a hotel room on a "teletypewriter," or TTY, that he had brought with him in his suitcase. Bullard incorporates only the briefest of explanations about how this technology works, so the scene may be mystifying to readers who were not members or friends of the Deaf community in the 1980s and 1990s when this technology was cutting edge. Far from playing the scene for the "OMG" effect it would have on uninitiated hearing readers, Bullard instead turns it into an inside joke when, later in the chapter, the police who have tapped Lyson's phone think that the TTY clicking is a code and Lyson a spy!

On a more serious topic, Karawynn Long provides her readers with perhaps the biggest OMG reaction to normal deaf life: the fact that, given a choice, many deaf people would prefer to have deaf children. Members of the deaf community should try reading her insightful story about Marina's hopes and fears as many hearing readers would have read it back in the mid-1990s to get the full impact. Maureen Jennings also takes on this topic, her murder victim being the single mother of a planned deaf child, but since the woman is dead at the start of the novel, there is no vehicle for airing her views, and Jennings can give us only the tsk-tsking of the hearing characters over her decision. When, in future publications, we find this topic treated in fiction by deaf authors, we can expect to see the tables turned on the naive hearing characters much as Bullard did by satirizing the police response to TTY technology.

All this said, it is amazing how many of the authors here have an occasionally excellent insight into real deaf life with all its warts. Crime writer Dwight Steward depicts Sampson Trehune as perpetually sarcastic about hearing people, an attitude he expresses in sign language right in front of their faces. Something of this trait is evident in Philip Roth's Joey Cucuzza, who regards an audiological examination as "the bullshit test" and mocks his audiologist (and rightly so) for telling his father, "Your boy is going to hear the grass growing." Mocking hearing people is a not infrequent deaf indulgence, albeit not a very nice one, which I would wager few hearing people have ever suspected. Steward also shows Trehune exploiting his deafness to avoid a boring situation; again, something few hearing people suspect is commonly done. Jack Livingston's deaf detective, Joe Binney, has a marvelously astute insight when he explains why policemen get so flustered by deaf people: "they often count on impressing people, and it is hard to impress a guy who's reading your lips." [72] When I read that sentence, I suddenly realized why hearing academics get so flustered talking to me! T. C. Boyle and Joanne Greenberg (in *In This Sign*) both depict an aberrant interpreter who holds a grudge against, and judges, deaf clients, an occasional and unfortunate problem few hearing people know about or could suspect. Greenberg is also the only author to my knowledge who tackles the class issue: the fact that most deaf people have historically ended up in the working class and that this has everything to do with an early childhood spent deprived of language, as happened to Abel and Janice Ryder. Defoe makes hay of the scrapes Duncan Campbell gets into because he cannot hear the bailiffs who have come to arrest him or the sound of the curfew bell, but few people outside the deaf community will realize that this plot motif is the basis for many comic ASL stories, and we see it in Bullard's bubble bath scene, which comes straight from the ASL storytelling tradition.

Concluding Remarks

Deaf characters in literature are certainly a mixed bag. As we have seen, they are definitely not "oversaturated" as Fish defines it—not conceived by either author or reader as prepackaged with stereotyped cultural significance—but instead can pick up both individualizing traits and any of a variety of stereotypes the author has at hand. In other words, any menu of deaf character types we may come up with—the dummy, the clairvoyant, the artist, the orphan, and so on—will leave out many of our actual deaf characters, from Jack Britt (Charlotte Elizabeth) and Isabelle (Kohler) to Uncle Leo (Umans) and Albert Zimmer

(Glickfeld). Four little boys in this volume, Karomenya (Dinesen), the sexton's son (Gbadamosi), Avalon (P. Melville), and Jack Britt (Charlotte Elizabeth), all seem to have been drawn from life and all sparkle on the pages as real little individuals. The deaf people in Greenberg's "Like a Native" will be seen as stereotypical by *deaf* readers, but these characters are hardly literary stereotypes. We find nothing at all like the off-the-shelf identification often remarked in disability studies by which a one-handed man, in stories from *Peter Pan* to *The Fugitive*, automatically signals evil; in fact, our one example of a no-handed deaf man (in the Bishop story) is wholly positive. And our deaf Jewish characters are refreshingly neither Holocaust victims nor shyster lawyers, as Stanley Fish complained. As we learn from reading Glickfeld's entire story sequence, Albert Zimmer keeps his money in a safe deposit box like any good Calvinist instead of putting it out for interest as the Jewish stereotype would have him do.

Of course we do see a few deaf stereotypes—but what is wrong with stereotypes? Every writer uses stereotypes and stock characters when he creates *hearing* characters. In the stories in this volume, we find the dim-witted chorus girl who narrates the Dehan story; the malicious old gossips Mrs. Meryon (Meynell), Mrs. Shand (Gordimer), and Aunt Roda (Gbadamosi); and the stuffed shirts Mr. Tuttle (Barnes), Mr. Shand (Gordimer), and Ronnie's father (Woodward). Jerry has a stereotypically wicked stepmother (Bishop) right out of the tale of Cinderella, and Ronnie's mother (Woodward) is a *Madonna dolorosa* who might have stepped right out of a Renaissance pietà. It could well be that the most stereotyped characters in these stories are not the deaf but the hearing who interact with them.

My favorite deaf character, Wadsworth, in fact comprises a large number of stereotypes, as Julian Barnes scoops up and exploits many of those we have uncovered. Wadsworth is an artist, he is preternaturally perspicacious, his behavior is braver and more ethical than that of the hearing characters, he is both a life-long bachelor and socially isolated, and he is associated with an animal—the being he cares most about in the world is his horse. On a mythological level, he is a trickster figure, "The Limner" being a story "in which the lowly and apparently weak play[s] pranks and outwit[s] the high and mighty,"[73] a very common story type in ASL literature. At this level, we are talking about archetypes, not stereotypes, which perhaps explains why I am so fond of Wadsworth. He lives with the daily insults and frustrations created by the condescending, annoyed, or disgusted attitudes of the hearing, but, unlike real-life deaf people, he is capable of sticking it to them in the end, providing readers with a great deal of vicarious pleasure. There is a bit of the trickster, too, in this collection's two loveable rogues, Duncan Campbell (Defoe) and Lyson Sulla (Bullard), two more characters who prevail in the end.

A few other characters end well but seemingly only by accident, as when Lord Polkstone (Dehan) finds a bride who knows the finger alphabet, Mable and Roxy (Mayberry) get the sexual experience they crave—and a baby!—from a chance gypsy, and the runaway Jerry (Bishop) finds not only Clarinda but a hearing protector. The other deaf characters collected here end their stories in a kind of stasis, if not outright defeat. Jack Britt (Charlotte Elizabeth), Clavis (Slosson), Adomas (Grušas), Ronnie (Woodward), and Gwen (in "Fardels," near the end of Smith's story sequence) are dead at the end of their stories. Bierce's deaf boy, Karomenya (Dinesen), Lucynell Crater (O'Connor), the four Ryder boys (Greenberg's "And Sarah Laughed"), the sexton's son (Gbadamosi), Isabelle (Kohler), and Avalon (P. Melville) face uncertain futures in which truly good outcomes are unlikely. The rest are left to face another dreary day, whether they have tried and failed like Marina (Long), missed their chance like Phoebe (Elliott), or never even envisioned a life with dignity like Bertha (Meynell). For me, this downward story trajectory, not stereotyping, is the real disservice that literary depictions of deaf people do to real-life deaf people. When stories so consistently suggest to readers that there is no imaginable path to autonomy, dignity, or even simple contentment, it stands to reason that the general public is persuaded that this is so.

This brings us back to a question raised in the introduction: if it is not the job of literature "to persuade and reform us by showing us the error of our ways and moving us to right action," as Fiedler says, but nevertheless true that "every representation of [a deaf person] has the potential to shape the way [being deaf] is understood in the general culture, and some of those representations can in fact do extraordinarily powerful—or harmful—cultural and political work," as Bérubé asserts, what ought deaf readers and our friends and allies to do? Well, we can speak up. When John S. Schuchman was writing his study of deaf film characters and deaf actors nearly twenty-five years ago, he described himself as "puzzled by the comparative absence of complaints" from the deaf community about its often outrageous treatment by filmmakers. His guess was that deaf movie and television audiences had little idea of how they were being depicted because films and TV dramas were not captioned—then. But what about now? And what about literature? Why are we so, well, silent?[74]

Most public libraries now sponsor book clubs; what about getting involved and proposing a book with a deaf character? Just be prepared for some surprises. Or bring your friends to the book club for a panel presentation. With publication no longer a barrier now that we have digital and web resources, we can review stories, novels, films, and television shows to provide thoughtful, reasoned evaluations of deaf characters and then get those reviews posted where they will be read by hearing people. This means that ASL essays must be captioned or voiced over and posted on sites where hearing people will find them. A considered review posted on an online bookstore or movie rental site, for example, has the capacity to engage an interested readership or audience in the ideas they will take away from the book or movie and gives them a chance to reconsider the extent to which they can accept the deaf character as depicted.

There was a lot of grumbling among educated deaf readers when Boyle's *Talk Talk* first came out, but a search of the web for complaints from deaf readers turns up little of any substance that would be seen or could be understood by a typical hearing reader. For example, on AllDeaf.com, a deaf would-be reader asks about the "deaf expression" that Boyle refers to as "talk talk," and two other deaf posters say that they do not know of it either. Actually, it is Boyle's error: the "expression," a sign lexeme that I have always glossed in my head as "chat, chat" because of the set of the mouth that accompanies the sign, is not formed the way he says it is, but none of the three posters suggests that, and the discussion fizzles out. At Amazon.com, however, a deaf reviewer identified as Al Lecks of Indiana states that Boyle makes "a very telling error" with his description of the sign he says means "talk talk" and then goes on to say, "I am insulted by Boyle's appropriation of my experience . . . If he wasn't prepared to truly learn about Deafhood and the language, then he should have left it alone." When another reader, taking what we have seen as Leslie Fiedler's position, posts a comment asking, "It's a novel not a treatise on ASL or deaf culture, no?" Al Lecks answers, "You have no understanding of Deaf issues or ASL," and goes on to restate what we have seen as Bérubé's position that "misconceptions [about deaf people] are created by so-called 'harmless' novels or television shows or movies, etc. Art is powerful. It should be practiced responsibly." That is the end of that thread.[75]

I have a lot of sympathy for the position taken by Al Lecks and often feel just the same, but I would make two points in response. One is a question: do you have a hobby or area of interest about which you know a whole lot and which you really love? Mine is historical hand-knitting techniques; yours might be vintage Italian motor scooters. Have you ever noticed the way every book or movie that shows someone knitting or riding a Vespa makes some kind of mistake with it? Examples include knitting needles of a gauge or material that did not exist at that time and place, and a red Vespa that was not available in that shade in the period when the film is set. It does not automatically mean the writer or filmmaker did not try to get it right, though that does seem to be the case occasionally. It means that you know more about the topic than he does. It is natural that you would want to correct that error for others. As I said in the first paragraph of this essay, most writers seem to have no idea how much research it would take to get a deaf character right, but that does not mean they did not make any attempt at all, and their errors should be corrected in the same spirit as setting the record straight on that red Vespa. We have seen how Boyle, as much as he has fallen short, has learned enough about deaf people to get several tricky aspects of his deaf heroine's life spot on. But there is something about Deaf life that makes people unusually angry about any mistake, and this anger is a challenge to get under control.

The second point is that when it comes to the Deaf World, what one reader judges a misrepresentation is another reader's *déjà vu* moment, and indeed, the

Amazon.com reviews of *Talk Talk* provide us with an example of another deaf reader with a completely different view. Identified as Larry from Capitol Heights, Maryland, he tells Amazon shoppers how much he liked the book, saying "I found myself laughing and groaning with some of the situations that Dana found herself in."[76]

For me, a corner was finally turned when I read Donna McDonald's doctoral dissertation and discovered that another deaf woman with an education similar to mine—her doctoral work is in creative writing, mine in literature—held views nearly diametrically opposite mine about every book with deaf characters we had ever read. She commends a novel that I found unreadable and pans another novel that I liked so much that I have not only discussed it extensively here but have even taught it in one of my Deaf Literature classes. This was a humbling experience, and I have tried to keep in mind, as I've written this essay, just how diverse the Deaf World really is. The same is true of the deaf character in literature. As uninformed as many stories are about how deaf people experience and interact with the world, a deaf character, in the hands of a reasonably skilled and serious writer, can still tell us something true about what it means for someone, somewhere, at some time to be deaf. Assembling this book has granted me many such moments of insight and has been a great adventure. It is wonderful to think that one of my readers will someday edit a new and improved anthology of the next generation of deaf characters in literature.

Notes

Editor's Note: Stories and excerpts that appear in this volume are not referenced in the notes.

1. McCullers, *The Mortgaged Heart*, 275–76.
2. See Sayers, "B. H. and Arnold H. Payne," for discussion.
3. Fish, "What's Up With the Jews?" n.p.
4. Schuchman, *Hollywood Speaks*, 7.
5. Zazove, *Four Days in Michigan*, 12.
6. Itani, *Deafening*, 138.
7. Ibid., 244.
8. Boyle, *Talk Talk*, 203, 204.
9. Dexter, *Silent World of Nicholas Quinn*, 235.
10. Huxley, *Crome Yellow*, 31.
11. Boyle, *Talk Talk*, 149.
12. Roth, *The Plot Against America*, 344; Warner, "Learning to Dance," 158; du Maurier, "Not after Midnight," 133; Blanchard, "Puddle Tongue," 137; Davis, "Silence," 51.
13. McCarthy, *C*, 8.
14. Pasternak, *Doctor Zhivago*, 140.
15. Clowes, "Introduction," 28, 37.

16. Pasternak, *Doctor Zhivago*, 144.

17. McCullers, *The Heart Is a Lonely Hunter*, 8; Thompson, *Lark Rise to Candleford*, 440; Manfredi, "Ice Music," 77.

18. Gbadamosi, Kliewer, Greenberg ("And Sarah Laughed"), and Woodward, this volume; Thompson, *Lark Rise to Candleford*, 441; Faulkner, "Hand upon the Waters," 64.

19. Babcock, "Gargoyle," 16; Elliott, this volume; Boyle, *Talk Talk*, 278; Wilkins, "A New England Prophet," 124; Fromm, "Grayfish," 39; Bierce, this volume.

20. Batson, "The Deaf Person in Fiction," 18.

21. Allende, "The Road North," 208; Thompson, *Lark Rise to Candleford*, 440.

22. Fromm, "Grayfish," 42, 45, 40.

23. Charlotte Elizabeth, "Letter VIII," 116.

24. Blanchard, "Puddle Tongue," 137.

25. Jennings, *The K Handshape*, 101.

26. Salinger, *Raise High the Roof Beam, Carpenters and Seymour*, 55.

27. Boyle, *Talk Talk*, 58.

28. Bullard, *Islay*, 9. Bullard uses italics to indicate signed dialogue.

29. See W. Conley, "In Search of the Perfect Sign Language Script"; Couser, *Recovering Bodies*, 275–81.

30. Greenberg, *In This Sign*, 225.

31. Manfredi, "Ice Music," 70.

32. Warner, "Learning to Dance," 156.

33. Carver, "The Third Thing That Killed My Father Off," 90; Bowen, "Summer Night," 294–96; Salinger, *Raise High the Roof Beam, Carpenters and Seymour*," 55.

34. Huxley, *Crome Yellow*, 20.

35. Thomas, "The Other One," 27, 31; Itani, *Deafening*, 137.

36. Wilkins, "A New England Prophet," 125.

37. Sackville-West, *The Dragon in Shallow Waters*, 24.

38. Babcock, "Gargoyle," 15, 21, 31.

39. Defoe, *The Life and Adventures of Mr. Duncan Campbell*, 55.

40. Batson and Bergman, *Angels and Outcasts*, 3.

41. Fiedler, "Pity and Fear," n.p.; McCullers, *The Mortgaged* Heart, 125.

42. Batson, "The Deaf Person in Fiction," 16.

43. Bellow, *The Adventures of Augie March*, 172.

44. Batson and Bergman, *Angels and Outcasts*, xiii.

45. See Lane, *A Deaf Artist in Early America*, on Brewster's life.

46. Itani, *Deafening*, 113; Bowen, "Summer Night," 303.

47. Camus, *The First Man*, 102nb; Steward, *The Acupuncture Murders*, 173.

48. Holmes, *Fictions of Affliction*, 77, 76.

49. Sackville-West, *The Dragon in Shallow Waters*, 207–8.

50. Bullard, *Islay*, 189.

51. Itani, *Deafening*, 98, 124.

52. Fromm, "Grayfish," 40; Bowen, "Summer Night," 295; Thomas, "The Other One," 31.

53. Babcock, "Gargoyle," 12, 13.

54. McCarthy, *C*, 31, 40.

55. Krentz, *Writing Deafness*, 127.

56. Wilkins, "A New England Prophet," 146; Camus, *The First Man*, 123; Faulkner, "Hand upon the Waters," 79, 67; Sackville-West, *The Dragon in Shallow Waters*, 219.

57. See, for example, Krentz, *Writing Deafness*, 118–19.

58. Blanchard, "Puddle Tongue"; Faulkner, "Hand upon the Waters," 64; Camus, *The First Man*, 55; Wilkins, "A New England Prophet"; Warner, "Learning to Dance," 154; Capote, "A Tree of Night," 80; Huxley, *Crome Yellow*, 256; Itani, *Deafening*, 281.

59. Bullard, *Islay*, 313, 317, 289; McCullers, *The Heart Is a Lonely Hunter*, 4.

60. Ellmann, *Elizabeth Bowen: The Shadow across the Page*, 221; Bowen, *Eva Trout*, 238; Corcoran, *Elizabeth Bowen: The Enforced Return*, 4.

61. Holmes, *Fictions of Affliction*, 102; Fiedler, "Pity and Fear," n.p.

62. Charlotte Elizabeth, *Personal Recollections*, 132.

63. Greenberg, *In This Sign*, 40–41.

64. Rofihe, "Quiet," 74; Allende, "The Road North," 203.

65. Manfredi, "Ice Story," 68.

66. Clerc, "Autobiography," 9.

67. Blanchard, "Puddle Tongue," 137; Fromm, "Grayfish," 47.

68. Bateman-Cannon, "Silent Stereotypes."

69. Gilbert, "Responses to Leslie Fiedler, III," n.p.

70. Roth, *The Plot Against America*, 282–84.

71. Jennings, *The K Handshape*, 32.

72. Roth, *The Plot Against America*, 346; Livingston, *A Piece of the Silence*, 4.

73. Erdoes and Ortiz, *American Indian Trickster Tales*, xiii.

74. Fiedler, "Pity and Fear," n.p.; Bérubé, "The Cultural Representation of People with Disabilities," B4; Schuchman, *Hollywood Speaks*, 105.

75. Al Leeks, Customer review of *Talk Talk* and comments, posted December 14, 2010, and August 9, 2011, at http://www.amazon.com.

76. Larry, Customer review of *Talk Talk*, posted August, 31, 2006, at http://www.amazon.com

Works Cited

Primary Sources

Allende, Isabel. "The Road North." In *The Stories of Eva Luna*, translated by Margaret Sayers Peden, 197–210. New York: Atheneum, 1991.

Babcock, Edwina Stanton. "Gargoyle." In *Best American Short Stories of 1920*, 12–35. Boston: Small, Maynard, 1921. First published 1920.

Barnes, Julian. "The Limner." *New Yorker*, January 5, 2009. Reprinted in *Pulse*, New York: Knopf, 2011.

Barton, Marlin. "Into Silence." *Sewanee Review* 117, no. 3 (Summer 2009): 335–59.

Bellow, Saul. *The Adventures of Augie March*. New York: Modern Library, 1965. First published 1949.

Benedict, Diane. "Where the Water Is Wide." *Atlantic Monthly*, May 1982, 76–82.

Bierce, Ambrose. "Chickamauga." Retrieved from http://en.wikisource.org/wiki/Chickamauga. First published in *Tales of Soldiers and Civilians*. New York: United States Book Co., 1891.

Bishop, William Henry. "Jerry and Clarinda." In *The Brown Stone Boy and Other Queer People*, 79–125. New York: Cassell, 1868. Reprinted in *Harper's Magazine*, May 1887, and *The Silent Worker*, January, February, March, and April 1897.

Blanchard, Alice. "Puddle Tongue." In *The Stuntman's Daughter*, 137–54. Denton: University of North Texas Press, 1996. First published in *Iowa Woman Annual Literary Competition* 14, no. 2 (1994).

Bowen, Elizabeth. *Eva Trout, or Changing Scenes*. New York: Knopf, 1968.

———. "Summer Night." In *Look at All Those Roses*, 288–329. New York: Knopf, 1941.

Boyle, T. Coraghessan. *Talk Talk*. New York: Viking, 2006.

Bullard, Douglas. *Islay*. Silver Spring, MD: TJ Publishers, 1986.

Calisher, Hortense. *The New Yorkers*. Boston: Little, Brown, 1966.

Cameron, Eric. "One Summer." *Short Story International* 34 (1982): 23–32.

Camus, Albert. *The First Man*. Translated by David Hapgood. New York: Vintage, 1995.

Capote, Truman. "A Tree of Night." In *The Complete Stories of Truman Capote*, 77–90. New York: Random House, 2004. First published 1945.

Carter, Mary. *My Sister's Voice*. New York: Kensington Books, 2010.

Carver, Raymond. "The Third Thing That Killed My Father Off." In *What We Talk About When We Talk About Love*, 89–103. New York: Knopf, 1981. First published as "Dummy" in 1977.

Charlotte Elizabeth. "Letter VIII: The Dumb Boy. In *Personal Recollections,* Abridged. Gloucester, England: Dodo Press, 2006. First published London: Seeley and Burnside, 1841.

Clerc, Laurent. "Autobiography." In *Deaf World: A Historical Reader and Primary Sourcebook*, edited by Lois Bragg, 1–9. New York: New York University Press, 2001.

Collins, Wilkie. *Hide and Seek*. Oxford: Oxford University Press, 1993. First published 1854.

Crompton, Richmal [Richmal C. Lamburn]. "The Christmas Present." In *Best British Short Stories, 1922*, edited by Edward Joseph Harrington O'Brien and John Cournos, 86–90. Boston: Small, Maynard, 1922.

Darío, Rubén. "The Deaf Satyr." In *Great Short Stories of the World: A Collection of Complete Short Stories Chosen from the Literatures of All Periods and Countries*, edited by Barrett H. Clark and Maxim Lieber, 923–26. New York: A. & C. Boni, 1931. First published in *Azul: Prose Tales and Poems*, 1888.

Davis, Christopher. "Silence." *Saturday Evening Post*, November 9, 1963, 48–55.

Defoe, Daniel. *The Life and Adventures of Mr. Duncan Campbell*. In *The Novels and Miscellaneous Works of Daniel Defoe*, Vol. 19, 1–244. Oxford: Talboys, 1841. First published 1729.

Dehan, Richard [Clotilde Inez Mary Graves]. "Under the Electrics: A Show-Lady Is Eloquent." In *Off Sandy Hook*, 59–66. London: William Heinemann, 1915.

Dexter, Colin. *The Silent World of Nicholas Quinn*. New York: Ivy Books, 1997. First published 1977.

Dickens, Charles. "Doctor Marigold." In *Angels and Outcasts: An Anthology of Deaf Characters in Literature*, edited by Trent Batson and Eugene Bergman, 58–83. Washington, DC: Gallaudet University Press, 1985. First published 1865.

Dinesen, Isak. *Out of Africa*. New York: Random House, 1938.

du Maurier, Daphne. "Not after Midnight." In *Don't Look Now*, 107–158. Garden City, NY: Doubleday, 1971.

Elliott, George P. "Miss Cudahy of Stowes Landing." In *Prize Stories 1955: The O. Henry Awards*, edited by Paul Engle and Hansford Martin, 117–40. Garden City, NY: Doubleday, 1955. First published in *Hudson Review* 7, no. 1 (Spring 1954): 58–82.

Faulkner, William. "Hand upon the Waters." In *Knight's Gambit*, 63–81. New York: Random House, 1949. First published in *The Saturday Evening Post*, November 4, 1939.

Fromm, Pete. "Grayfish." In *King of the Mountain: Sporting Stories*, 37–48. Mechanicsburg, PA: Stackpole Books, 1994.

Garrett, George. "An Evening Performance." In *In the Briar Patch*, 163–74. Austin: University of Texas Press, 1961. Reprinted in *An Evening Performance*, Garden City, NY: Doubleday, 1985.

Gbadamosi, Rasheed A. "The Sexton's Deaf Son." In *African Writing Today*, edited by Charles Angoff and John Povey, 121–24. New York: Manyland Books, 1969.

Glickfeld, Carole. "My Father's Darling." In *Useful Gifts*, 102–17. Athens: University of Georgia Press, 1989.

Gordimer, Nadine. "Charmed Lives." In *Six Feet of the Country: Fifteen Short Stories*, 169–83. New York: Simon and Schuster, 1956.

Greenberg, Joanne. "And Sarah Laughed." In *Rites of Passage*, 119–32. New York: Holt, Rinehart and Winston, 1972. First published as "A Cry of Silence" in 1967.

———. *In This Sign*. New York: Holt, Rinehart and Winston, 1970.

———. "Like a Native." In *With the Snow Queen*, 172–86. New York: Arcade, 1991. First published 1985.

Grušas, Juozas. "Fairer Than the Sun." In *Selected Lithuanian Short Stories,* 2nd ed., edited by Stepas Zobarskas, translated by Kestutis Skrupskelis and Clark Mills, 141–50. New York: Voyages Press, 1960. First published 1937.

Helwig, David. "Something for Olivia's Scrapbook I Guess." In *Toronto Short Stories*, edited by Morris Wolfe and Douglas Daymond, 215–30. Toronto: Doubleday Canada, 1977. First published 1968.

Hofsteater, Howard T. "Dummy." *Clerc Scar* 20, no. 9 (January 7, 2010). http://www.clercscar.com. First published in *The Buff and Blue*, 1930.

Huxley, Aldous. *Crome Yellow*. London: Chatto & Windus, 1921.

Itani, Frances. *Deafening*. New York: Atlantic Monthly Press, 2003.

Jennings, Maureen. *The K Handshape*. Toronto: Dundurn, 2008.

Kees, Weldon. "I Should Worry." In *The Ceremony and Other Stories*, edited by Dana Gioia, 9–17. Port Townsend, WA: Graywolf Press, 1984. First published in *New Directions Annual #4*, 1939.

Kim Tongni. "Portrait of a Shaman." In *Flowers of Fire: Twentieth-Century Korean Stories*, edited by Peter H. Lee, translated by Kim Yongch'ŏl, 58–90. Honolulu: University of Hawai'i Press, 1974. First published in Korean, 1936.

King, Stephen. *The Stand*. New York: Doubleday, 1979.

Kitto, John. *The Lost Senses*. Edinburgh: Oliphant, n.d. Autobiographical passages reprinted in *Angels and Outcasts: An Anthology of Deaf Characters in Literature*, edited by Trent Batson and Eugene Berman, 209–60. Washington, DC: Gallaudet University Press, 1985.

Kliewer, Warren. "The Sybil." In *The Violators: Short Stories*, 70–78. Francestown, NH: Marshall Jones, 1964.

———. "Uncle Wilhelm's Love Affair." In *The Violators: Short Stories*, 122–37. Francestown, NH: Marshall Jones, 1964.

Kohler, Sheila. "Miracles in America." In *Miracles in America*, 31–47. New York: Knopf, 1990.

Livingston, Jack. *A Piece of the Silence*. New York: St. Martin's, 1982.

Long, Karawynn. "Of Silence and Slow Time." In *Full Spectrum V*, edited by Jennifer Hershey, Tom Dupree, and Janna Silverstein, 132–50. New York: Bantam, 1995.

Mamin-Sibiriak, Dmitri Narkisovich. *The Privalov Fortune*, translated by V. Shneerson. Moscow: Foreign Languages Publishing House, 1950. First published in Russian, 1883.

Manfredi, Renée. "Ice Music." In *Where Love Leaves Us*, 68–80. Iowa City: University of Iowa Press, 1994.

Manzini, Gianna. "The Wife of the Deaf Man," translated by Corinna del Greco Lobner. *James Joyce Quarterly* 40, no. 3 (2003): 555–63. First published in Italian as "La moglie del sordo," Milan: Mondadori, 1929.

Maupassant, Guy de. "The Deaf Mute." In *Angels and Outcasts: An Anthology of Deaf Characters in Literature*, edited by Trent Batson and Eugene Bergman, 125–34. Washington, DC: Gallaudet University Press, 1985. First published in French as "Les bécasses," 1886.

Mayberry, Florence V. "The Secret." In *Death on the Verandah: Mystery Stories of the South*, edited by Cynthia Manson, 215–31. New York: Carroll and Graf, 1994. First published in *Ellery Queen's Mystery Magazine,* 1992.

McBain, Ed [Evan Hunter]. *Cop Hater*. New York: Pocket Books, 1999. First published 1956.

McCarthy, Tom. *C.* New York: Knopf, 2010.

McCullers, Carson. *The Heart Is a Lonely Hunter.* Boston: Houghton Mifflin, 2000. First published 1940.

Melville, Herman. *The Confidence Man: His Masquerade*, 2nd ed., edited by Hershel Parker and Mark Niemeyer. New York: Norton, 2006. First published 1857.

———. "Fragments from the Writing Desk, No. 2." *Democratic Press and Lansingburgh Advertiser*, May 18, 1839. Also available in *Tales, Poems, and Other Writings*, edited by John Bryant, 5–13. New York: Modern Library, 2001.

Melville, Pauline. "A Quarrelsome Man." In *Shape-Shifter*, 61–73. London: Women's Press, 1990.

Meynell, Viola. "We Were Just Saying." In *Best British Short Stories of 1924*, edited by Edward J. O'Brien and John Cournos, 159–67. Boston: Small, Maynard, 1924.

Musset, Alfred de. "Pierre and Camille." In *Angels and Outcasts: An Anthology of Deaf Characters in Literature*, edited by Trent Batson and Eugene Bergman, 8–56. Washington, DC: Gallaudet University Press, 1985. From *The Complete Writings of Alfred de Musset*, Vol. 7, translated by R. Pellisier. First published in French, 1844.

O'Connor, Flannery. "The Life You Save May Be Your Own." In *The Complete Stories of Flannery O'Connor*, 145–56. New York: Farrar, Straus and Giroux, 1971. First published in *A Good Man Is Hard to Find*. New York: Harcourt, Brace, 1955.

Pasternak, Boris. *Doctor Zhivago.* Translated by Richard Pevear and Larissa Volokhonsky. New York: Pantheon, 2010. First published in Italian, 1957.

Payne, Arnold. *King Silence.* Excerpted in *Angels and Outcasts: An Anthology of Deaf Characters in Literature*, edited by Trent Batson and Eugene Bergman, 154–57. Washington, DC: Gallaudet University Press, 1985. First published 1918.

Peterkin, Julia. "Over the River." In *Collected Short Stories of Julia Peterkin*, edited by Frank Durham, 99–112. Columbia: University of South Carolina Press, 1970. First published in *Reviewer* IV, January 1924.

Rofihe, Rick. "Quiet." In *A Father Must: Stories*, 69–79. New York: Farrar, Straus and Giroux, 1991.

Rose, Lloyd. "The Wedding Trip." In *Love Stories by New Women*, edited by Charleen Swansea and Barbara Campbell, 111–17. Charlotte, NC: Red Clay, 1978.

Roth, Philip. *The Plot Against America.* New York: Houghton Mifflin, 2004.

Sackville-West, Vita. *The Dragon in Shallow Waters.* London: W. Collins Sons, 1921.

Salinger, J. D. *Raise High the Roof Beam, Carpenters and Seymour: An Introduction.* Boston: Little, Brown, 1955.

Slosson, Annie Trumball. "Clavis." In *Representative Short Stories 1923*, edited by Alexander Jessup, 700–706. Boston: Allyn and Bacon, 1923. First published in *Harper's Magazine*, 1896.

Smith, Morris. "Fardels." In *Spencer Road: A Short Story Sequence*, 111–27. Knoxville: University of Tennessee Press, 1997.

———. "Stone Deaf." In *Spencer Road: A Short Story Sequence*, 54–65. Knoxville: University of Tennessee Press, 1997.

St. Clair, Margaret. "The Listening Child." In *The Best of Margaret St. Clair*, edited by Martin H. Greenberg, 98–108. Chicago: Academy Chicago Publishers, 1985. First published under the pseudonym Idris Seabright, 1950.

Steward, Dwight. *The Acupuncture Murders.* New York: Warner Paperback Library, 1974. First published 1973.

Thomas, Annabel. "The Other One." In *The Phototropic Woman*, 24–31. Iowa City: University of Iowa Press, 1981. First published in *Kansas Quarterly* 8, 1976.

Thompson, Flora. *Lark Rise to Candleford.* London: Oxford University Press, 1945.

Turgenev, Ivan. "Mumu." In *Angels and Outcasts: An Anthology of Deaf Characters in Literature*, edited by Trent Batson and Eugene Bergman, 85–121. Washington, DC: Gallaudet University Press, 1985. From *The Novels and Stories of Ivan Turgenieff: Vol. 11*, translated by I. F. Hapgood New York: Charles Scribner's Sons, 1904. First published in Russian, 1852.

———. "The Watch." In *Three Novellas*, translated by Marion Mainwaring. New York: Farrar, Straus and Giroux, 1968.

Umans, Richard. "Speech." In *Men on Men*, edited by George Stambolian, 13–18. New York: New American Library, 1986.

Villiers de L'Isle-Adam, Auguste. "The Unknown." In *Sardonic Tales,* translated by Hamish Miles, 212–26. New York: Knopf, 1927. First published in French in *Contes Cruels*, 1883.

Warner, Sharon Oard. "Learning to Dance." In *Learning to Dance and Other Stories*, 153–70. Minneapolis, MN: New Rivers Press, 1992.

Waters, T. J. *Secret Signs.* Washington, DC: Gallaudet University Press, 2010.

Welsh, Irvine. "The House of John Deaf." In *The Acid House*, 99–102. New York: Norton, 1995.

Welty, Eudora. "First Love." In *The Wide Net and Other Stories*, 3–33. New York: Harcourt, 1943. First published in *Harper's Bazaar*, February 1942.

Wilkins, Mary E. [Mary Wilkins Freeman]. "A New England Prophet." In *Best Stories of Mary E. Wilkins*, edited by Henry Wysham Lanier, 120–49. New York: Harper, 1927. First published in *Harper's New Monthly*, September 1894.

Woodward, Gordon. "The Edge of Sound." In *New Voices 2: American Writing Today*, edited by Don M. Wolfe, 211–26. New York: Hendricks House, 1955.

Zazove, Philip. *Four Days in Michigan.* Dallas, TX: Durban House, 2009.

Secondary Sources

Bateman Cannon, McCall. "Silent Stereotypes: The Representation of Deafness in Film." *Deaf Studies Today* 2 (2006): 247–62.

Batson, Trent. "The Deaf Person in Fiction: From Sainthood to Rorschach Blot." *Interracial Books for Children Bulletin* 11, no. 1–2 (1980): 16–18.

Batson, Trent, and Eugene Bergman, eds. *Angels and Outcasts: An Anthology of Deaf Characters in Literature.* 3rd edition. Washington, DC: Gallaudet University Press, 1985.

Bérubé, Michael. "On the Cultural Representation of People with Disabilities." *Chronicle of Higher Education*, May 30, 1997: B4–B5.

Bragg, Lois. "Telling Silence: Alingualism in Old Icelandic Myth, Legend, and Saga." *Journal of Indo-European Studies* 32, no. 3–4 (2004): 267–95.

Clowes, Edith. "Introduction." In *Doctor Zhivago: A Critical Companion*, edited by Edith Clowes. Chicago: Northwestern University Press, 1995.

Cohen, Leah Hager. *Train Go Sorry: Inside a Deaf World.* Boston: Houghton Mifflin, 1994.

Conley, Pamela. "An Analysis of Two Stories with Deaf Characters in Nineteenth-Century American Periodicals." *Deaf Studies Today* 2 (2006): 203–14.

Conley, Willy. "In Search of the Perfect Sign Language Script." In *Deaf World: A Historical Reader and Primary Sourcebook*, edited by Lois Bragg, 147–61. New York: New York University Press, 2001.

Corcoran, Neil. *Elizabeth Bowen: The Enforced Return.* Oxford: Clarenden Press, 2004.

Couser, G. Thomas. *Recovering Bodies: Illness, Disability, and Life-writing.* Madison: University of Wisconsin Press, 1997.

Ellmann, Maud. *Elizabeth Bowen: The Shadow across the Page.* Edinburgh: Edinburgh University Press, 2003.

Erdoes, Richard, and Alfonso Ortiz, eds. *American Indian Trickster Tales.* New York: Viking, 1998.

Fiedler, Leslie. "Pity and Fear: Images of the Disabled in Literature and the Popular Arts." In *Pity and Fear: Myths and Images of the Disabled in Literature Old and New.* New York: International Center for the Disabled, 1981. Unpaginated.

Fish, Stanley. "What's Up with the Jews?" *New York Times*, May 23, 2011. http://opinionator.blogs.nytimes.com/2011/05/23.

Gilbert, Sandra. "Responses to Leslie Fiedler, III." In *Pity and Fear: Myths and Images of the Disabled in Literature Old and New.* New York: International Center for the Disabled, 1981. Unpaginated.

Gitter, Elizabeth. "Deaf-Mutes and Heroines in the Victorian Era." *Victorian Literature and Culture* 20 (1992): 179–96.

Gopnik, Adam. "Reimagined." Review of *Wonderstruck*, by Brian Selznick. In *New York Times Book Review*, September 18, 2011, 18.

Grant, Brian, ed. *The Quiet Ear: Deafness in Literature.* Boston: Faber and Faber, 1987.

Guire, Oscar. "Deaf Characters in Literature." *Silent Worker*, August 1961, 3–5.

———. "Deaf Characters in Literature." *Silent Worker*, July–August 1963, 10–12.

———. "Deaf-mutes in Russian Literature." *Silent Worker*, July 1959, 4.

Holmes, Martha Stoddard. *Fictions of Affliction: Physical Disability in Victorian Culture.* Ann Arbor: University of Michigan Press, 2004.

I. V. J. "The Deaf in Literature." *Silent Worker* 6, no. 4, December 1893, 3.

Krentz, Christopher. *Writing Deafness: The Hearing Line in Nineteenth-Century American Literature.* Chapel Hill: University of North Carolina Press, 2007.

Lane, Harlan. *A Deaf Artist in Early America: The Worlds of John Brewster, Jr.* Boston: Beacon Press, 2004.

Lang, Andrew. "Mr. Wilkie Collins's Novels." *Contemporary Review* 57 (January 1890): 20–28.

Lerner, Miriam Nathan. "Narrative Function of Deafness and Deaf Characters in Film." *M/C Journal* 13, no. 3 (2010). http://journal.media-culture.org.au/index.php/mcjournal / article/view/260.

McCullers, Carson. *The Mortgaged Heart*, edited by Margarita G. Smith. Boston: Houghton Mifflin, 1971.

McDonald, Donna. "Hearsay: How Stories about Deafness and Deaf People Are Told." PhD diss., University of Queensland, 2010.

————. "Not Silent, Invisible: Literature's Chance Encounters with Deaf Heroes and Heroines." *American Annals of the Deaf* 154, no. 5 (2010): 463–70.

Miller, Jonathan. "The Rustle of a Star: An Annotated Bibliography of Deaf Characters in Fiction." *Library Trends* 41, no.1 (Summer 1992): 42–60.

Pajka-West, Sharon. "Representations of Deafness and Deaf People in Young Adult Fiction." *M/C Journal* 13, no. 3 (2010). http://journal.media-culture.org.au/index.php / mcjournal/article/view/260.

Panara, Robert F. "Deaf Characters in Fiction and Drama." *Deaf American* 24, no. 9 (May 1972): 3–9.

————. "Deaf Studies in the English Curriculum." *Deaf American* 26, no. 5 (January 1974): 15–17.

Robinson, Paul. "Responses to Leslie Fiedler, II." In *Pity and Fear: Myths and Images of the Disabled in Literature Old and New*. New York: International Center for the Disabled, 1981. Unpaginated.

Sayers, Edna Edith. "B. H. and Arnold H. Payne: Early Champions of Sign Language in the United Kingdom." *Deaf History Review* 5 (2007): 22–30.

Schuchman, John S. *Hollywood Speaks: Deafness and the Film Entertainment Industry*. Urbana: University of Illinois Press, 1988.

Taylor, Gladys M. "Deaf Characters in Short Stories: A Selective Bibliography." *Deaf American* 26, no.9 (May 1974): 6–8.

Veditz, George. *Proceedings of the Ninth Convention of the National Association of the Deaf and the Third World's Congress of the Deaf, 1910*, 30. Los Angeles: Philocophus Press, 1912.

Permissions and Credits

Julian Barnes: "The Limner," originally published in *The New Yorker* (January 5, 2009). Copyright 2009 by Julian Barnes. Reprinted by permission.

Marlin Barton: "Into Silence," first published in the *Sewanee Review*, vol. 117, no. 3 (Summer 2009). Copyright 2009 by the University of the South. Reprinted by permission of the author.

Douglas Bullard: From Chapter 3 of *Islay* (Silver Spring, MD: TJ Publishers, 1986). Copyright 1986 by Douglas Bullard. Reprinted by permission.

Isak Dinesen: "Karomenya" in *Out of Africa* (New York: Random House, 1938), 307–310. Copyright 1938 by Random House. Reprinted by permission.

George P. Elliott: "Miss Cudahy of Stowes Landing" originally published in *The Hudson Review*, vol. 7, no. 1 (Spring 1954), pp. 58–82.

Rasheed A. Gbadamosi: "The Sexton's Deaf Son" in *African Writing Today: Ethiopia, Ghana, Kenya, Nigeria, Sierra Leone, Uganda, Zambia*, edited by Charles Angoff and John Povey (New York: Manyland Books), 121–124. All attempts to contact the copyright holder were unsuccessful.

Carole L. Glickfeld: "My Father's Darling" in *Useful Gifts* (Athens: University of Georgia Press, 1989), 102–117. Copyright 1989 by Carole L. Glickfeld. Reprinted by permission of the University of Georgia Press.

Nadine Gordimer: "Charmed Lives" in *Six Feet of the Country and Other Stories* (London: Penguin Books). Copyright 1956 by Nadine Gordimer, renewed 1982 by Nadine Gordimer. Reprinted by permission of Russell & Volkening as agents for the author.

Joanne Greenberg: "And Sarah Laughed," copyright 1967 by Joanne Greenberg; "Like a Native," copyright 1985 by Joanne Greenberg. Reprinted by permission of the Wallace Literary Agency, Inc.

Juozas Grušas: "Fairer Than the Sun," originally published as "Už Saulę Gražesnis" in *Sunki Ranka* (*The Heavy Hand*) (Kaunas: Falcon, 1937). English translation by Kestutis Skrupskelis and Clark Mills, published in *Selected Lithuanian Short Stories*, 2nd ed., edited by Stepas Zobarskas (New York: Voyages Press, 1960), 141–150.

Howard T. Hofsteater: "Dummy," reprinted in *Clerc Scar* 20, no. 9 (January 7, 2010). Originally published in *The Buff and Blue*, Gallaudet University, 1930.